The Unborn Child, Article 40.3.3° and Abortion in Ireland

Dedication:

In Memory of Anne Schweppe

The Unborn Child, Article 40.3.3° and Abortion in Ireland

Twenty-Five Years of Protection?

Edited by
Jennifer Schweppe

The Liffey Press

Published by
The Liffey Press
Ashbrook House, 10 Main Street
Raheny, Dublin 5, Ireland
www.theliffeypress.com

A catalogue record of this book is
available from the British Library.

ISBN 978-1-905785-51-3

Printed in the Republic of Ireland by Colour Books.

CONTENTS

Part Two
The Maternal–Foetal Conflict

Part Three
Article 40.3.3° and the Law

Part Four
Reproduction, Medicine, Health and Ethics

FOREWORD

"Twenty-five years after the introduction of Article 40.3.3°, the legal position in relation to termination of pregnancy and the right to life of the unborn has never been so unclear." This is the conclusion of this book's editor in her own contribution to the present collection of essays. It is hard to disagree with her.

This book is welcome in presenting a serious and informative discussion of the differing aspects of a subject which unfortunately, over the years since 1983, has more frequently given rise to sterile wrangling or vitriolic abuse. In this collection of essays the editor has aimed at addressing Article 40.3.3° "in a broader manner that has heretofore been done" and this aim has indeed been achieved. The editor correctly points out that despite the fact that virtually all discussion of the Article proceeds on the assumption that it refers solely to abortion – and indeed that seems to have been the aim of its advocates from the beginning – the Article itself does not mention the term "abortion" at all. It is also, of course, true that the word "child" does not occur in the Article, and here one might have a slight quibble with the chosen title of this book. Proceeding from a wider reading of the Article, a number of the essays included here draw attention to other ways in which right to life of the unborn child may require respect, vindication and defence by the State, as mandated in the wording of 40.3.3°.

In his essay Liam Curran writes from the point of view of an experienced social worker of the lasting damage that may be done to the child before birth through maternal consumption of drugs and excessive alcohol, and other difficulties such as poverty and deprivation, during pregnancy. Recent statistics released at the time of writing of this foreword underline the reality of his warnings and his criticisms of the general weakness of services to deal with these problems. Dr Gerard Casey, from a legal background, also refers to this area. He describes the levels of criminalisation of pregnant women accused of damaging their unborn children in the various State jurisdictions in the United States, and contrasts this with the non-interventionist stance of the courts in England and Canada. Dr Casey very fairly admits to being undecided ("a prey to conflicting intuitions") on the proper course for the law to take. For myself, I cannot but feel that before even considering such a drastic step as the criminalisation of pregnant mothers the State should at the very least provide the preventive and protective health and social services advocated by Mr Curran. One must agree with him that "It is somewhat of a contradiction within Irish social and legal policy that, given our constitutional status of the unborn in Article 40.3.3°, we do not offer any form of interventionist practice (outside of the abortion decision) to secure and vindicate the life of the unborn". Personally I find it saddening that his description of the lack of communication and trust that still exists between the relevant services so closely parallels the situation as I found it fifteen years ago at the time of the Kilkenny Incest Inquiry.

A fuller discussion of the many thought-provoking insights and analyses contained in these essays would, unfortunately, go far beyond the limits of a Foreword. I can but mention a few. The book is divided into four sections, dealing with the politics of Article 40.3.3°, the maternal-foetal conflict, the legal impact of the Article, and reproduction, medicine, health and ethics. In the politics section I found Morgan Healey's account of her (unattributed) interviews with women politicians struck a familiar chord, having myself been an involved politician in 1983. Ms Healey speaks of the "vitriolic historic legacy of the abortion debate in Ireland" which persists in the memory of women politicians who are dependent on electoral support and who are still most reluctant to discuss the topic. Having been a recipient of some of that vitriol I cannot but feel a degree of sympathy for Ms Healey's interviewees.

In the second section Dr Neville Cox's innovative analysis of the significance of foetal personhood is particularly interesting and we have much to learn from the approach of the German constitutional court. On the medical side Dr Deirdre Madden's account of the effect of Article

40.3.3° on assisted human reproduction in this country and Dr Patricia Casey's survey of literature on the psychological effects of abortion are both useful. It would, perhaps have been good to hear also from a doctor practising in the area of obstetrics and gynaecology – perhaps a former Master of one of the main maternity hospitals – who could give a view from the front line where the hard decisions fall to be made.

In the more purely legal section Dr Karen Brennan gives a comprehensive account of the (also somewhat ill-defined) state of abortion law in Northern Ireland, a subject of which many in this jurisdiction are largely ignorant. Anyone familiar with the politics of Northern Ireland, however, will not be entirely surprised by her description of the debate on proposed guidelines on abortion law in the Northern Ireland Assembly, or by her conclusion that "only a few members expressed any genuine and considered interest in the current law on abortion, including the fact that it is legal in certain circumstances and is an issue that requires urgent clarification". In the same section Professor William Binchy writes with moving sincerity on the "deep structure", prophetic nature, and integrity of the Irish Constitution and the existential significance of human life. In the light of these views he also provides a detailed and carefully argued criticism of the judgments of the Supreme Court in *Attorney General v X* [1992] IR 1 and of the High Court in *MR v TR* [2006] IEHC 359. It has to be pointed out, however, that the courts are faced with "the facts of the case", with the tragic human dilemmas that defy the perfections of theory, and with the necessity to make a real life decision on the actual issues put before them.

All in all, this book is most welcome. Readers will find much more of interest in it than I have had space to mention, and I hope that it will lead to a more rational and charitable debate of the issues involved than we have experienced in the main hitherto.

Catherine McGuinness

PREFACE

When staring my own legal career in 1995, the *X* case (1992) was still very fresh in the minds of students, and it was not hard to imagine the polarising effect the 1983 referendum had on Irish society. When teaching my students about Article 40.3.3° and the *X* case in 2007, it occurred to me that their perspective on the "abortion issue" was very different to that of students ten years before. I realised that many of the students in my class hadn't even started primary school when the *X* case came before the Irish courts. Not only that, but they could not relate to the stories I told about violent protests outside the Four Courts of Ireland during the *X* case, and the schism it caused in Irish society. It occurred to me that in the 15 years since the *X* case and the 24 years since the Eighth Amendment to the Constitution, Ireland had changed dramatically in a way which was indescribable to these twenty-first century students.

This book, and the preceding conference held at the University of Limerick on 8 March 2008, is intended to assess the impact Article 40.3.3° has had on Irish law, society, medicine and politics in the last twenty-five years. It looks at the issue from a multi-disciplinary perspective, with experts from the fields of medicine, sociology, politics and law addressing issues not only relating to abortion in Ireland, but looking at the broader impact of Article 40.3.3°. Recurring themes throughout the book include the problems faced by the medical profession when dealing with pregnant women wishing to terminate their pregnancy, whether suicidal or not; the relevance of international principles in relation to reproductive rights in an Irish context; and the problems caused by the paucity of legislation in the area. The book is broken into four sections, each of which shines a unique light on the impact Article 40.3.3° has had on Irish society.

Part 1 The Politics of Article 40.3.3°

Sandra McAvoy presents an analysis of abortion rights activism over the last twenty-five years. She traces aspects of the development of this activism, from anti-amendment to pro-choice and reproductive justice, in Ireland taking account of changing social, cultural and political contexts and philosophical perspectives in the period 1983 to 2008.

Lisa Smyth analyses the dynamics of contemporary debate on women's reproductive choices and rights in the context of a changing Ireland. She assesses the continuities and discontinuities in the dynamics of contemporary abortion politics in the society, with a focus on the shifting moral grammar framing the debate.

Morgan Healey presents the findings of her interviews with a number of female Irish politicians, which asks how these women make sense of the discourse surrounding abortion and construct their own position on it. She examines the "internal battles" of the women, when they try to make sense of the issue while also not wanting to alienate an electorate, discussing how the women speak about the "abortion issue".

Part 2 The Maternal-Foetal Conflict

Neville Cox analyses what it means to give constitutional protection to the foetus, drawing comparison with the United States and Germany. He proposes a new way of thinking about Article 40.3.3° to inform discussion on the reality and breadth of the constitutional provision.

Liam Curran's chapter assesses how healthcare workers view their responsibility to protect the right to life of the unborn in the context of pregnant women seeking pre-natal care. Ultimately, he shows the need for increased services to protect and promote the welfare and post-birth outcome of children born to illicit drug and alcohol users.

Eimear Spain addresses the situation where harm is incurred by a foetus at the hands of a third party acting against the express or implied wishes of the pregnant woman. Having assessed the international law on the issue she argues that, rather than posing the issue in the context of foetal rights, the question should be framed from the rights of the woman, and her right to carry her child to term.

Gerard Casey looks at the legal issues raised by a pregnant woman's use of illegal drugs or alcohol or tobacco, or a refusal to accept medical treatment. Having looked at the approaches adopted in England, Canada and the USA to these questions, he then addresses the possible approach that might be adopted in Ireland on whether the State can intervene to protect the unborn.

Part 3 Article 40.3.3° and the Law

William Binchy assesses Article 40.3.3° from the broader and deeper context of the Constitution generally. Arguing that the Constitution has a consistent regard for a philosophy of the equality of value of every human being, he questions the interpretation of Article 40.3.3° by the Courts in this context.

Siobhán Mullally examines the struggle for reproductive autonomy within the context of the abortion debate in Ireland. Analysing case law, she assesses the clash between religious and nationalist principles and the struggle for reproductive autonomy in Ireland.

Karen Brennan provides an examination of the recent case law and resulting debates and issues surrounding abortion in Northern Ireland. She assesses the possibilities and problems of legislating for more liberal abortion laws in the political and religious climate that exists there.

Peter Morriss examines the law relating to abortion pre-1983 by providing a historical analysis of sections 58 and 59 of the Offences Against the Person Act 1861. He assesses the scope of the sections, by asking what protection is offered to the pre-implantation embryo and what constitutes an unlawful termination under the Act.

Part 4 Reproduction, Medicine, Health and Ethics

Deirdre Madden examines the development of assisted human reproduction services in Ireland and the extent to which these developments have been influenced by the Constitutional provision. She looks at the extent to which this uncertainty regarding this whole area has been exacerbated by the different legal interpretations that may be put on the meaning of the word “unborn”.

Ruth Fletcher identifies the obstacles and potential for developing reproductive justice in the context of abortion law in Ireland. In particular, she argues for the contextualisation of a negative right to be free from an abortion prohibition, within a positive right to reproductive self-determination.

Jennifer Schweppe examines the Miss D case (2007) and the role of the HSE in assisting those wishing to travel abroad to terminate their pregnancies. She then assesses the broader implications of the 2007 judgment in the context of young people consenting to medical treatment.

Finally, Patricia Casey assesses the notion of informed consent in the context of the psychological aspects of abortion. In particular, the question concerning whether abortion has adverse psychological consequences and whether there are psychological indications for abortion is examined.

Acknowledgements

I would like to thank all the authors of essays in this book for the enormous amount of work they put into their essays, and for contributing to the conference held in the University of Limerick on 8 March 2008. The quality of scholarship in this collection is outstanding, and every essay contributes significantly to the debate on Article 40.3.3° in Ireland today.

I would also like to extend the warmest of thanks to the Honourable Mrs Justice Catherine McGuinness for kindly agreeing to write the foreword to this book.

David Givens of The Liffey Press managed to get this book published in a truly unfeasibly short period of time, and put an enormous of amount of work into it. His consistent hard work and good cheer made the process of producing this book an infinitely easier task for me.

My thanks also go to my colleagues at the School of Law in the University of Limerick for their support of this project. In particular, I would like to thank Professor Paul McCutcheon and Raymond Friel, former and current Heads of the Law School. Carol Noonan provided an enormous amount of administrative help. I would also like to extend a personal thanks to Sinead Eaton and Una Woods.

My personal thanks also go to my friends and family, including Brian Schweppe, Máire NíAodha and Gerard Corless. A final word of thanks goes to James Mayo, for his unwavering love and support.

Jennifer Schweppe
Limerick, September 2008

About the Contributors

Professor William Binchy

William Binchy is Regius Professor of Laws at Trinity College Dublin. He was formerly a special legal adviser on family law reform to the Irish Department of Justice and Research Counsellor to the Law Reform Commission. He is a member of the Irish Human Rights Commission. He was Visiting Fellow at Corpus Christi College, Cambridge (Michaelmas Term 2002). He has authored and co-authored books on private international law, torts and family law and organises the Annual Workshop on Constitutionalism for African Chief Justices and Senior Judiciary, held at the Law School, now in its tenth year. He has represented Ireland at the Hague Conference on Private International Law on the themes of marriage and inter-country adoption. He was a member of the Committee on the Offences Against the State Acts, Chaired by the Hon Mr Justice Anthony Hederman. He has acted as consultant to the Irish Department of Foreign Affairs in relation to the Timor-Leste judicial system, making a field visit in August 2005. He has organised visits of the members of the Tanzanian Judiciary to Trinity College Dublin in March 2005 and of members of the Irish Judiciary to the University of Dar-es-Salaam in June 2006.

Dr Karen Brennan

Karen Brennan lectures in law in Queen's University Belfast. She graduated with a PhD in law from University College Dublin in 2006. Her doctoral research, which was funded by a Government of Ireland Research Scholarship for the Humanities and Social Sciences, examined the phenomenon of infanticide from the perspectives of law, history and culture, with particular focus on the historical development of infanticide laws in Britain and Ireland. Karen continues research on the subject of infanticide. She is also interested in studying other aspects of the criminal law and is currently engaged in research in the area of sexual offences. Karen has presented papers on infanticide and other topics at national and international conferences, and has published articles on infanticide in national law journals. In 2006, she was appointed as Researcher to the Criminal Law Rapporteur on the Legal Protection of Children in the Republic of Ireland. Karen joined Queen's University Belfast in October 2006, where she teaches in the areas of criminal law, criminal process, sentencing and evidence.

Dr Gerard Casey

Gerard Casey is currently a member of the School of Philosophy at University College Dublin and Adjunct Professor at the Maryvale Institute. He was Head of School from 2000 to 2006. He previously taught at the University of Notre Dame, 1980-1981 and was a Professor at the School of Philosophy, the Catholic University of America in Washington. He is a member of UCD's Governing Authority and NUI Consultor to the State Examination Commission in Religious Education. His *Born Alive: The Legal Status of the Unborn Child in England and the USA,* Barry Rose Law Publishers, was published in 2005. This work explores the philosophical underpinnings of the law of homicide via a historical, thematic, logical and philosophical analysis of the anomalous legal status of the unborn child in the two major common-law jurisdictions – England and Wales and the USA.

Professor Patricia Casey

Professor Casey is Professor of Psychiatry at the Department of Psychiatry, UCD and the Mater Misericordiae University Hospital. She is the author of five books, including *Psychiatry and the Law*, and her research interests include personality disorder and suicide. She is one of the five principle investigators in the ODIN (Outcome of Depression International Network) Group, an international group investigating depressive disorders in Europe. This has lead to over forty publications in peer reviewed journals such as the *British Medical Journal*, the *British Journal of Psychiatry*, etc. She is editor of the *Psychiatric Bulletin* (published by the Royal College of Psychiatrists, London). She chaired the Fitness to Practice Medical Council Committee from 1994 to 1999. She is a regular contributor to the Irish media and currently has a weekly column in the *Irish Independent* newspaper.

Dr Neville Cox

Dr Neville Cox FTCD is a practising barrister and a senior lecturer in Law in Trinity College Dublin. He is the author of, amongst others, *Blasphemy and the Law* (2000), *Sport and the Law* (2004) and *Defamation Law* (2007).

Liam Curran

Liam Curran MSc is a NQSWB Registered Social Worker with over 22 years of experience within the field of social care and social work. He has extensive experience of front line practice within child protection systems of both Ireland and the UK. He is member of the Irish Association of Social Workers and currently operates as a Principal Social Worker within the voluntary sector.

Dr Ruth Fletcher

Ruth Fletcher LLB MA LLM DJur is a Senior Lecturer in Law at Keele University and Associate Director of the AHRC Research Centre for Law, Gender and Sexuality, a research partnership between Keele, Kent and Westminster universities. She has published widely on reproductive law and socio-legal theory and was recently a contributing co-editor (with Professor Marie Fox) of a special issue on legal embodiment for the *Medical Law Review* (2008).

Morgan Healey

Morgan Healey received her undergraduate degree in Gender and Women's Studies at Connecticut College in the United States in 2003 and subsequently moved to Ireland to pursue her postgraduate education. She graduated from UCC in 2004 with an MA in Women's Studies and is now a PhD student in Women's Studies/Sociology at the University of

Limerick. Her doctoral research investigates how Irish women politicians, currently serving in both houses of the Oireachtas, construct their own gendered political subjectivity and the impact this has on the promotion of a more feminist-centred agenda, particularly focusing on the topic of reproductive rights. She is also a member of the Cork Women's Right to Choose Group.

Dr Deirdre Madden

Deirdre Madden is a graduate of UCC (BCL 1987, LLM 1988, PhD 2000) and was called to the Bar in 1989. She has been a lecturer in the UCC Law Department since 1992. Her research interests and publications are primarily in the area of Medical Law. Her textbook, *Medicine, Ethics and the Law,* was published by Butterworths in 2002. Dr. Madden was a member of the Commission on Assisted Human Reproduction 2000-2005.

Dr Sandra McAvoy

Sandra McAvoy teaches Women's Studies in University College Cork. Her research interests include the history and politics of reproductive rights in Ireland and her published articles include "Before Cadden: Abortion in Mid-Twentieth Century Ireland", in Keogh, O'Shea and Quinlan (eds.), *The Lost Decade: Ireland in the 1950s*, Mercier, 2004; and "Sexual Crime and Irish Women's Campaigns for a Criminal Law Amendment Act 1912-1935", in Valiulis (ed.), *Towards New Histories in Ireland: Writing Gender History*, Irish Academic Press, 2008.

Dr. Peter Morriss

Peter Morriss teaches in the Department of Political Science and Sociology, NUI Galway. He is the author of *Power: A Philosophical Analysis* (1987; second edition 2002), and several articles on the concept of power. His main teaching area is in political philosophy; he is particularly interested in the interaction between political philosophy and law, on which he has published several articles (most recently on marriage, in *Irish Political Studies*, December 2007). Another interest is Korean politics: he teaches a course in this area, and has published articles in political science and sociology journals, particularly on South Korean electoral politics. Among his many other research interests is the history of the law on abortion in England and Ireland, particularly in the nineteenth century.

Dr Siobhán Mullally

Siobhán Mullally is a graduate of the European University Institute, Florence (PhD), the London School of Economics (LLM) and University College Cork BCL. She has taught at UCC since 1995 and previously lectured at the University of Hull, UK and at the University of Peshawar, Pakistan. She has held visiting appointments at Cornell Law School, Harvard Law School (Human Rights Fellow), Sydney Law School and at the National University of India Law School. Siobhán has published widely in the fields of human rights law; immigration and refugee law; gender and law. She is currently the Director of an IRCHSS funded three year project on Gender Equality, Multiculturalism and Religious Diversity. Siobhán has worked as an adviser and consultant on Gender and Human Rights to UN bodies and to international NGOs in Timor-Leste, Kazakhstan, Pakistan, Afghanistan and Kosovo. In August 2007, she was appointed to an international team of experts to review the UNDP Justice System programme in Timor-Leste. She has recently acted as an advisor to UNDP and the National Ombudsman on Human Rights in Kazakhstan. She is currently the Chairperson of the Irish Refugee Council and is Editor of the Irish Yearbook of International Law. She is Co-Director of the Centre for Criminal Justice and Human Rights in UCC.

Jennifer Schweppe

Jennifer Schweppe is a Lecturer in Law at the University of Limerick. Prior to her current position, she worked as a Legal Researcher in the Office of the Attorney General and the Law Reform Commission. Her research interests are in the areas of criminal justice and procedure and family law.

Dr Lisa Smyth

Lisa Smyth is a lecturer in Sociology at Queen's University Belfast, where she teaches modules on gender, culture and reproduction. Her research interests cover gender and reproduction, gendered national/cultural identities, moral politics, feminism and intimate citizenship. Her book *Abortion and Nation: The Politics of Reproduction in Contemporary Ireland*, was published by Ashgate in 2005, and examines the shifting dynamics of abortion politics in the Republic of Ireland since the early 1980s. She has also published work on the cultural politics of sex education and abortion debates in Northern Ireland, as well as on pro-breastfeeding campaigns. She is currently working on the moral grammar of reproduction for women (forthcoming 2010 *Women and Reproduction: Society, Morality and Recognition* Palgrave Macmillan) and is planning work, with Martina McKnight, on everyday life for mothers in post-conflict Belfast, as part of a large ESRC-funded project on Conflict in Cities and the Contested State, a collaboration between Queen's, Exeter and Cambridge Universities.

Dr Eimear Spain

Eimear Spain graduated with a PhD from the School of Law at the University of Limerick. Her research interests are in the area of criminal law, particularly the application of emotion theory to the criminal law. Her PhD explores our understanding of the defences of duress and necessity in the criminal law, placing particular emphasis on these defences while examining theories of justification and excuse, the basic aims of the criminal law and the role of emotions in legal theory. She was awarded a Government of Ireland Research Scholarship for the Humanities and Social Sciences in 2005.

INTRODUCTION

> The issue of whether the unborn have a right to life or whether women have a right to have an abortion are moral issues on which there are profound differences and deeply held views throughout the contemporary world (*Attorney General v X,* 1992: 15).

This book is a collection of essays assessing the impact of Article 40.3.3° in Ireland over the last twenty-five years. In this time, what has come to be known as "the abortion issue" in Ireland has never been far away from the public consciousness. It is interesting, however, that Article 40.3.3° does not mention the term "abortion" at all: what it does is acknowledge the right to life of the unborn, and to obligate the State to respect and defend that right, with due regard to the life of the mother. When the Bill was going through the Houses of the Oireachtas, Senator Mary Robinson presciently stated:

> The basic flaw in this amendment is that it is so uncertain in its scope and so potentially contradictory in its meaning and so potentially damaging to existing practices in the area of family planning and medical treatment… (Foley and Lalor, 1995: 240).

This book will address Article 40.3.3° in a broader manner than has heretofore been done. It will go beyond the traditional "anti-abortion" rhetoric and address the question of what protecting the "right to life of the unborn" means in Ireland today.

What follows is a brief background to some of the constitutional and legal issues which form the basis of the discussion in the various essays in this book.

The Evolution of the Right to Life of the Unborn Child in Ireland

The law relating to abortion in Ireland evolved primarily from the English common law. While abortion of the "quickened" foetus had long been a misdemeanour at common law, under Lord Ellenborough's Act of 1803 abortion of the quickened foetus became a felony (Kingston and Whelan, 1997: 52). This distinction between a quickened and non-quickened foetus, which is an echo of the Aristotelian doctrine of delayed animation, came from the biologically inaccurate view that the foetus was not alive until it moved. The Offences against the Person Act, 1837 ended this distinction between a quickened and not-quickened foetus, and the current statute law as regards abortion in Ireland is to be found in sections 58 and 59 of the Offences against the Person Act, 1861.

These sections provide:

> 58. Every woman, being with child, who, with intent to procure her own abortion shall unlawfully administer to herself any poison or other noxious thing, or shall unlawfully use any instrument or other means with the like intent, and whosoever, with intent to procure the miscarriage of any woman, whether or not she be with child, shall unlawfully administer to her or cause to be taken by her any poison or other noxious thing, or shall unlawfully use any instrument with the like intent shall be guilty of felony…
>
> 59. Whosoever shall lawfully supply or procure any poison or other noxious thing, or any instrument or thing whatsoever, knowing that the same is intended to be unlawfully used or employed with intent to procure the miscarriage of any woman, whether she be or be not with child, shall be guilty of a misdemeanour …

Although the law in England and Wales has changed substantially since then, most notably with the introduction of the Abortion Act 1967, this nineteenth century statute has remained valid law in Ireland for nearly 140 years, and its legitimacy was re-emphasised by section 10 of the Health (Family Planning) Act, 1979.

The fact that abortion was illegal in Ireland up to 1982 was seemingly incontestable. While the unborn child had no explicit constitutional rights under Irish law, there were a number of judicial statements over the years which indicated that the judiciary was willing interpret the Constitution as including protection for the unborn. In *McGee v Attorney General* (1974), Walsh J, having emphasised the right to family privacy, restricted this right, stating:

> … any action on the part of either the husband and wife or of the state to limit family sizes by endangering or destroying human life must necessarily not only be an offence against the common good but also against the guaranteed personal rights of the human life in question (1984: 381).

In 1980, Walsh J made another obiter statement in the case of *G v An Bord Uchtala* (1980), where he stated:

> [A child] has the right to life itself and the right to be guarded against all threats directed to its existence whether before or after birth … the right to life necessarily implies the right to be born, the right to preserve and defend (and to have preserved and defended) that life (1980: 69).

McCarthy J in his dissenting judgement in the 1984 case of *Norris v Attorney General* (1984) relied not on any unenumerated right to life, nor on the doctrine of family privacy, but on the Preamble to the Constitution, which he believed:

> … would appear to lean heavily against any view other than that the right to life of the unborn child is a sacred trust, to which all the organs of government must lend their support (1984: 103).

It seemed that there was no question at that point in time other than that the judiciary believed that there was an unenumerated right to life of the unborn child in the Irish constitution.

However, developments in family law of the United States of America made certain elements of Irish society question this faith of the judiciary. The interpretations of the right to privacy in earlier cases[1] were broadened in the infamous case of *Roe v Wade* (1973), which essentially

---

[1] See *Griswold v Connecticut*, which held that a statute criminalising the use of contraceptives by married couples to be unconstitutional as a violation of their right to privacy. This ruling was extended to non-married women in the case of *Eisenstadt v Baird*.

granted American women the right to choose to have an abortion. The court re-iterated the fact that privacy is a fundamental personal right. The extension of the right to privacy set out in the earlier cases to cover family matters was, in the opinion of Blackmun J, "broad enough to encompass a woman's decision whether or not to terminate the pregnancy".

Shocked by the American decision, and with the guarantee of family privacy as outlined in the *McGee* ruling fresh in the minds of anti-abortion activists, the anti-abortion element of Irish society set up a pressure group, the "Pro-Life Amendment Campaign" (PLAC), the aim of which was to give the unborn child a right to life under the Irish constitution. Summing up the fears of this campaign, Deputy Noonan, the Minister for Justice at the time of the Dáil debates surrounding the Eighth Amendment, said:

> It has become apparent that judicial decisions concerning abortion can alter fundamentally what had been accepted to be the law, even to the extent of introducing what is virtually a system of abortion on demand (Foley and Lalor, 1995: 240).

There can be no doubt but that these concerns were based on the *Roe v Wade* decision, which was based on an article of the American Constitution not dissimilar to the right to privacy enshrined in the Irish Constitution in Article 40.3.

The constitutional referendum was ultimately held on 7 September 1983, and the people voted to insert the Eighth Amendment into the constitution by a majority of 755,423 to 324,977. The Amendment became Article 40.3.3° of the Constitution on 7 October 1983, which from 1983 to 1992 read:

> The State acknowledges the right to life of the unborn and, with due regard to the equal right to life of the mother, guarantees in its laws to respect, and as far as practicable, by its laws to defend and vindicate that right.

Post-Amendment: SPUC and Abortion Information[2]

The Society for the Protection of the Unborn Child (SPUC), formerly known as the Pro-Life Amendment Campaign, has had a huge impact on the shape of Irish "anti-abortion" law. Following their success in the amendment campaign, they became the self-appointed guardians of the unborn in Ireland. They were referred to by Finlay CJ in the case of *SPUC v Coogan* (1989) as "an incorporated body, limited by guarantee ... formed with the object of protecting human life, particularly that of the unborn" (1989: 740). In the immediate aftermath of the Eighth Amendment, SPUC began a legal campaign which sought to define the boundaries of Article 40.3.3º. This campaign took the form of three highly publicised cases, *Attorney General (SPUC) v Open Door Counselling Ltd and the Dublin Well-Woman Centre Ltd* (1988), *SPUC v Coogan* and *SPUC v Grogan* (1989). These cases dealt generally with the issue of "abortion information", i.e. information given to pregnant women or to the general public which contained details on abortion clinics in Great Britain. SPUC was generally successful, being a party to cases heard in the Irish Supreme Court, the European Court of Human Rights and the European Court of Justice. Ultimately, their campaign ended with the publication of the Regulation of Information (Services outside the State for Termination of Pregnancies) Bill, 1995 after the 1992 constitutional amendments.

The "X" Case

Ruth Riddick, founding member of Open Line Counselling, commenting on the effect the *X* case had in Ireland, said, "it was the first time that a human face had been put on abortion in this country ... this little girl "X" was someone everybody identified and sympathised with" (Holden, 1994: 59).

The "little girl" in question became pregnant as a result of unlawful carnal knowledge. Understandably distraught, her parents decided that it would be in the best interests of all concerned for the girl to travel to England to terminate her pregnancy. It was this decision, made by thou-

---

[2] For a detailed examination of the legacy of SPUC, see Kingston, Whelan and Bacik (1997).

sands of Irish women every year, that precipitated the most contentious and public legal debate in Ireland's history.

Knowing the pregnancy to be a result of rape, the parents contacted their local Gardaí to enquire about the possibility of having DNA tests carried out on the aborted foetus so as to determine its paternity. Unsure of the law relating to the relatively new process of DNA testing, the Gardaí contacted the DPP to ascertain the evidential status of such information. The DPP in turn informed the Attorney General of the intention of the family to travel to abort the foetus, who had in fact already left the jurisdiction. The Attorney General sought an interim injunction seeking the immediate return of the family to Ireland, in the belief that he had a duty under Article 40.3.3° to protect the unborn child from an unconstitutional abortion. The family returned to Ireland and the case came before Costello J in the High Court.

Having been granted an interim injunction, the Attorney General sought an interlocutory injunction against the defendant, seeking to restrain the defendant, or any agent acting on her behalf, from interfering with the right to life of the unborn, from leaving the jurisdiction for nine months, and from procuring or arranging a termination of the pregnancy.

In the High Court, Costello J granted the order sought by the Attorney General, and injuncted the defendant, or any agent acting on her behalf, from interfering with the right to life of the unborn, from leaving the jurisdiction for nine months, and from procuring or arranging a termination of the pregnancy. His decision was based, *inter alia*, on the fact that the risk to the life of the unborn was "real and imminent", whereas the risk to the mother's life was not one in which surgical intervention was necessary to save the life of the mother. Rather, the risk to the life of the mother was one of self-destruction, a risk "of much less … magnitude than the certainty that the life of the unborn will be terminated" (1992: 12) if the order were not to be made. The case was appealed to the Supreme Court.

The Supreme Court decided by a 4–1 majority that the Constitution envisaged abortion being constitutionally permissible in certain limited circumstances, and that X, satisfying these circumstances, could travel to England for an abortion. The family, much relieved, travelled to England, and arranged for X to have the abortion which was now permissible under Irish law.

Irish law has always recognised that there are certain circumstances where termination of a pregnancy is permissible. This situation arises where the termination is the indirect result of life-saving medical treatment for the mother.[3] The question the Supreme Court had to answer in the *X* case was whether there were any other circumstances in which the termination of pregnancy might be permissible under the Constitution.

In interpreting the Eighth Amendment, Finlay CJ first had to address the question of how to reconcile the two competing rights. He decided that the rights were to be interpreted harmoniously, holding that the true test to be applied in interpreting Article 40.3.3° and reconciling the rights was:

> [I]f it can be established as a matter of probability that there is a real and substantial risk to the life, as distinct from the health, of the mother, which can only be avoided by the termination of her pregnancy, such termination is permissible (1992: 53-54).

He found that the risk of suicide in this case was indeed a risk to the life of the mother.[4]

McCarthy J agreed that the rights should be interpreted harmoniously. He accepted the test laid down by the Chief Justice, with a small discrepancy; McCarthy J avoids the life/health debate by referring to a "real and substantial risk attached to her *survival*" (1992: 80). He had no

---

[3] This is known as the doctrine of double effect. Kingston, Whelan and Bacik (1997: 56), explain the doctrine:

> [W]here an action (or means) has two effects (or ends) one of which, the principal effect, is desired, and one of which, the subsidiary effect, is not desired … [t]he principal effect, must necessitate the means adopted (if another means could be used which would bring about the principal, but not the subsidiary, effect it must be used). Furthermore, the moral benefit of the principal effect must outweigh the moral repugnance of the subsidiary effect.

[4] One of the more interesting aspects of Finlay CJ's judgement is that he makes a distinction between a risk to the *life* as opposed to the *health* of the mother. Particularly with reference to a case like this, where the risk is psychologically based, it is difficult to see where a difference between a risk to the life and the health of the mother can be made. Macnaghten J stated this dilemma succinctly in the case of *R v Bourne,* where he stated

> What then is the meaning to be given to the words "for the purpose of preserving the life of the mother". There has been much discussion in this case as to the difference between danger to life and danger to health … I confess that I have found it difficult to understand what the discussion really meant, since life depends upon health and it may be that health is so gravely impaired that death results.

problems with accepting a risk of self-destruction as a risk coming within the ambit of the test.

The decision to let the young girl in the *X* case travel to England to have an abortion was seen by most to be the only solution in the case. After the case the legal position regarding abortion in Ireland was that abortion was constitutionally impermissible except where there was a real and substantial risk to the life, as opposed to the health, of the mother, which risk included that of suicide.

The Aftermath of the *X* Case

After the *X* case, therefore, the legal position regarding abortion in Ireland was that abortion was constitutionally impermissible except where there was a real and substantial risk to the life, as opposed to the health of the mother, which risk was to include the risk of suicide. However, there was still a section of Irish society which believed in the absolute sanctity of unborn life, and it was utterly outraged at the decision of the Supreme Court. The case precipitated a rash of academic opinion, two constitutional amendments and its effect is still felt today, with many issues still as alive today as they were fifteen years ago.

Constitutional Amendments

The *X* case precipitated a further three Constitutional referenda in 1992. The Minister for Justice at the time, Deputy Flynn, introduced the debate in the Seanad saying:

> Each of the three Bills proposes to amend subsection (3) of section 3 of Article 40 of the Constitution and their combined effect would be to deal with the various issues that arise from the decision of the Supreme Court in *(The) Attorney General v. X* and some other Supreme Court decisions on A40.3.3° in so far as it relates to provision of information… (Foley and Lalor, 1995: 268).[5]

The three amendments put forward in the referenda were:

[5] For an in-depth analysis of the Amendments and the Dail and Seanad Debates at the time, see Foley and Lalor (1995: 267-275). See also, Kingston,Whelan and Bacik (1995: 180-187).

> 12. It shall be unlawful to terminate the life of an unborn unless such termination is necessary to save the life, as distinct from the health, of the mother where there is an illness or disorder of the mother giving rise to a real and substantial risk to her life, not being a risk of self-destruction.
>
> 13. This subsection shall not limit freedom to travel between the State and another state.
>
> 14. This subsection shall not limit freedom to obtain or make available in the State, subject to such conditions as may be laid down by law, information relating to services lawfully available in another state.

The Twelfth Amendment was defeated by a two to one majority. The Thirteenth and Fourteenth Amendments were passed and inserted into Article 40.3.3° of the Constitution accordingly.[6]

The "Abortion Information Act"

In order to regulate how "abortion information"[7] was to be disseminated under the Fourteenth Amendment, the Regulation of Information (Services outside the State for Termination of Pregnancies) Act, 1995 was introduced. Under section 3 of the Act, it is unlawful to publish or procure the publication of abortion information to the public unless the information "relates to services provided in a particular place or to persons providing them in a particular place" and "the information is truthful and objective and does not advocate or promote, and is not accompanied by any advocacy or promotion of, the termination of pregnancy". Under section 5 of the Act, information given following a request by a woman may not advocate the procurement of an abortion in any way, and coun-

[6] For an analysis of the effect of the Amendments on Irish law, see Kingston, Whelan and Bacik (1997: 187-226).

[7] Abortion Information, or "Act Information" as it is referred to in the Act, is defined as information that "(a) is likely to be required by a woman for the purpose of availing herself of services outside the State for the termination of pregnancies, and (b) relates to such services or to persons who provide them."

sellors or doctors giving information to a client must give all the alternative options to abortion to the client.[8]

Government Reports

In 1996, the Constitution Review Group produced a report which set out difficulties surrounding the abortion question. The Group made a number of recommendations, and the report was followed by the Green Paper on Abortion. The Green Paper sets out at the beginning what the situation regarding abortion in Ireland was at that time:

> Constitutionally, termination of pregnancy is not legal in this country unless it meets the conditions laid down by the Supreme Court in the X case; information on abortion services abroad can be provided within the terms of the Regulation of Information (Services outside the State for Termination of Pregnancies) Act, 1995; and, in general, women can travel abroad for an abortion (1999: 3).

However, there were still a number of issues left to be resolved, and in response to the Green Paper the Government formed a Committee to address the question of abortion in Ireland, and to recommend what approach should be taken by the Legislature. The findings of the Committee were published as the Fifth Progress Report of the All Party Oireachtas Committee on the Constitution. In the Report, it was accepted that crisis pregnancies are a very live issue in this country.[9] Amongst other things, the Committee recommended that a three-stage strategy should be implemented to deal with the abortion issue. This involved a preventative widespread education campaign, as well as making other options to abortion more attractive and providing post-abortion counselling. The Committee came up with three alternatives to address the abortion issue. The first, essentially, concentrated on the three-stage strategy, and advocated no change to the legal status quo. The second supported a legislative programme to regulate the issue, and the third maintained that

---

[8] See, sections 3-8 of the Act for the various prohibitions and restrictions on the dissemination of Act Information.

[9] The Committee referred to Mahon, Conlon and Dillon (1998: 31), which indicated an abortion rate of 5.6 per 1000 in 1995 in Ireland.

a constitutional amendment was the only option to finally put a close to this long-running saga.

The Twenty-Fifth Amendment of the Constitution (Protection of Human Life in Pregnancy) Bill, 2001

The explanatory memorandum accompanying the Twenty-Fifth Amendment of the Constitution (Protection of Human Life in Pregnancy) Bill, 2001 stated:

> The purpose of [the Bill] is to provide for the amendment of the Constitution to state that the proposed Protection of Human Life in Pregnancy Act, 2002, shall be the law on abortion in the State.

One of the key proposals in the Bill was to remove suicide as a grounds for termination of pregnancy. Once again, the proposed amendment was rejected, and the position on abortion in the state remains unclear as ever.

Conclusion

The Constitutional position in Ireland is firmly anti-abortion; however, it is interesting that one refers to the situation of the unborn child in Ireland as one that is "anti-abortion", as opposed to "pro-foetus", or even "pro-life". This is because, up to now, abortion is the only manner in which the foetus has been considered in Irish law.[10] While the Eighth Constitutional Amendment is framed in positive terms, historically it has been interpreted in quite a negative fashion, *prohibiting* the dissemination of "abortion information" and *preventing* a young girl travelling to England. It remains to be seen if the Amendment will be used in a positive sense, in terms of introducing policies of foetal protection and foetal rights into Irish law. Further, the question arises as to what extent the State is obliged to protect the equal right to life of the mother, and what internationally respected reproductive rights are protected at a Constitutional level. This book will examine Article 40.3.3° from a new perspec-

[10] The one exception is the explicit right to succession under a will in section 2 of the Succession Act, 1965, which says, "Descendants and relatives of a deceased person begotten before his death but born alive thereafter shall, for the purpose of this Act, be regarded as having been born in the lifetime of the deceased and as having survived him".

tive, asking what obligations the State is under to protect unborn life, and to protect the mother of that unborn life.

Bibliography

All Party Oireachtas Committee on the Constitution (2000) *Fifth Progress Report: Abortion* Dublin: Stationery Office.

Constitution Review Group (1996) *Report of the Constitution Review Group* Dublin: Stationery Office.

Department of An Taoiseach (1999) *Green Paper on Abortion* Dublin: Stationery Office.

Foley J.A. and Lalor, S. (eds) (1995) *Annotated Constitution of Ireland* Dublin: Gill and MacMillan.

Holden, W. (1994) *Unlawful Carnal Knowledge – The True Story of the Irish "X" Case* London: HarperCollins.

Kingston, J., Whelan, A. and Bacik, I. (1997) *Abortion and the Law* Dublin: Round Hall, Sweet and Maxwell.

Mahon, E., Conlon, C. and Dillon, L. (1998) *Women and Crisis Pregnancy* Dublin: Stationery Office.

Cases

Attorney General v X [1992] IR 1.

Attorney General (SPUC) v Open Door Counselling Ltd and the Dublin Well-Woman Centre Ltd [1988] IR 593.

Eisenstadt v Baird 405 U.S. 438 (1972).

G v An Bord Uchtala [1980] IR 32.

Griswold v Connecticut 381 U.S. 475 (1965).

McGee v Attorney General [1974] IR 284.

Norris v Attorney General [1984] IR 36.

Roe v Wade 410 U.S. 113 (1973).

SPUC v Coogan [1989] IR 734.

SPUC v Grogan [1989] IR 753.

Part One

THE POLITICS OF ARTICLE 40.3.3°

1

FROM ANTI-AMENDMENT CAMPAIGNS TO DEMANDING REPRODUCTIVE JUSTICE:

The Changing Landscape of Abortion Rights Activism in Ireland, 1983-2008

Dr Sandra McAvoy

New technologies are transforming abortion rights activism in Ireland. Members of pro-choice groups blog and keep in contact through email lists. Web pages make links with international networks instant. At the time of writing, one of the Safe and Legal in Ireland Campaign's three short videos, in a series entitled *Stop the Silence, End the Stigma*, is ranked the second most watched posting on YouTube in Ireland. In these videos Irish women and men discuss abortion; talk about the problems facing Irish women forced to travel to Britain, often accessing abortion some weeks later than women in other countries; about the stigma that still silences them on their return; and about Irish politicians' avoidance of responsibility for this women's health and rights issue.[1] New developments in networking were clear too, in April 2008, when the Council of Europe discussed a report on access to safe and legal abortion in its member states, prepared by its Committee on Equal Opportunities for Women and Men. The report highlighted the restrictive abortion laws in Ireland, Andorra, Malta, Monaco and Poland and the trauma suffered by women forced to participate in abortion "tourism", which can mean late

---

1 At: http://www.youtube.com/profile_videos?user=SafeAndLegalIreland&p=d.

abortions, or clandestine abortions. It called on member states to decriminalise abortion.[2] Several Irish groups used traditional lobbying methods before the debate, including a letter to Council members from civil society groups such as One Family, the Dublin Well Woman Centre, Women's Aid and the National Women's Council of Ireland,[3] and lobbying emails to Irish Council of Europe delegates from Cork Women's Right to Choose Group and Choice Ireland. The use of a video letter, distributed to selected European Council members by the Safe and Legal in Ireland Campaign, was an innovation.[4] In it a senator, a doctor and a lawyer described the legal situation in Ireland and its impact on women, including, as lawyer Catherine Forde says, that women who suffer rape and incest and "women who may have wanted pregnancies, but whose pregnancies have resulted in foetuses that are incapable of separate existence, must scurry like criminals to a foreign jurisdiction to have abortions there".

This chapter examines aspects of abortion rights activism in Ireland during the past three decades, including resistance to the insertion of Article 40.3.3°, the clause banning abortion, in the Irish constitution in 1983. It also looks at some of the arguments made by, and actions taken by, those involved in highlighting the problems the ban has caused for Irish women in the twenty-five years since. What abortion rights "activism" means is subtly different in different political contexts. The term "activist" might apply to the outspoken women and the doctors, lawyers, politicians and others who opposed the 1983 prohibition; to those who found ways to provide information and counselling services; to those who wrote about abortion during the stringent censorship of the 1980s; or to the women and men who have held banners, leafleted, protested, lobbied and canvassed during more than thirty years. This chapter does not focus on elected political figures like Mary Robinson and Ivana Bacik who have made important stands on abortion rights, but on those who

---

[2] Parliamentary Assembly, Doc. 11537, 17 March 2008, *Access to safe and legal abortion in Europe.*

[3] At http://safeandlegal.blogspot.com/2008_04_01_archive.html.

[4] "A Message from Ireland for Members of the Parliamentary Assembly of the Council of Europe", at: http://www.youtube.com/watch?v=X7LcTnIC8Yc.

work on the issue at grass roots level. It draws on materials relating to Dublin- and Cork-based groups. The aims of those involved in activism may vary. A unifying focus is the demand for the removal of Article 40.3.3º, the decriminalisation of abortion in Ireland, and the possibility of dealing with this complex, personal and private issue as a women's health or choice matter.

Access to Fertility Control

Before looking at developments in the 1980s, it is useful to remember how the legalisation of contraception was resisted during the 1970s and that, at the beginning of that decade, access to reliable contraception was as divisive an issue as abortion became at its end. Doing so helps to place in context the backlash against liberal reforms that resulted in a campaign for a constitutional ban on abortion. Contraceptives were criminalised in Ireland under section 17 of the Criminal Law Amendment Act 1935, legislation that brought Irish law into line with Catholic Church teaching. Importing and sale of contraceptives was punishable by a fine of up to £50 and/or up to six months in prison. Unlawful abortion was, and remains, a crime in Ireland, punishable by up to life imprisonment under sections 58 and 59 of the Offences Against the Person Act 1861. Fertility control methods acceptable to the dominant church, the Roman Catholic Church, such as the Billings method, were promoted. Publications judged as advocating birth control had been censored since 1929. Those with the knowledge and means to access contraceptives imported them from abroad during the period of the ban, but the 1970s was a period of change and one in which an Irish women's movement began to flex its muscles and demand access to fertility control.

As early as 1969, a group of doctors, nurses and lay supporters opened the Fertility Guidance Company (later the Irish Family Planning Association (IFPA)). This Dublin family planning clinic was the first in Ireland to offer advice on contraception. Its doctors could prescribe the pill, but other contraceptives had to be imported illegally (Solomons, 1992: 23-31). Other sympathetic doctors also quietly prescribed the contraceptive pill on the pretext that it was a menstrual regulator and by 1978 the Irish Medical Association estimated that some 48,000 women were using it (Hug, 1999: 116). There was a gulf between law and practice but the battle to legalise contraceptives was drawn out across the decade, with a majority of politicians resisting change.

Increasing numbers of Irish women accessed legal abortion services in Britain too. In 1973 it was reported that 1,193 had given Irish addresses (Hansard Parliamentary Debates, 1974: cols. 544-545), but by 1983 the annual figure (considered an underestimate as some used British addresses) had risen to 3,677: approximately 10 per day.[5] As there were cultural taboos on discussion of such matters, not surprisingly, there was little public demand for abortion rights. In 1976, however, the radical feminist group Irish Women United (IWU) listed "the right to a free, legal and safe abortion" among the requirements to end women's "exploitation" and "oppression" published in its journal *Banshee* (Connolly and O'Toole, 2005: 32). Though they published this statement, group members recognised that the climate was not right for pro-choice activism and their focus from 1976 to 1979 was on women's right to free and accessible contraception.

Political pressure to legalise contraception built gradually during the 1970s. In 1971 members of the Irish Women's Liberation Movement famously waved contraceptives under the noses of embarrassed Dublin customs officials on their return from a day trip to Belfast. In the same year, Senator Mary Robinson made her first attempt to introduce a private member's bill on the issue. In 1972, the Report of the Commission on the Status of Women drew on international agreements on the rights of parents to decide the numbers and spacing of children to support a recommendation that birth control should be available for those with no moral objections to its use (Commission on the Status of Women, 1972: 223-225).[6]

Change began with a successful legal challenge. Mary McGee was a mother of four children, including twins, all born within a twenty-three month period. She developed toxaemia during her pregnancies and suffered a stroke during one. Her case provided an example of how denial of access to reliable contraception could impact on a woman's health.

---

[5] http://www.ifpa.ie/abortion/iabst.html.

[6] Agreements quoted were: the 1968 UN Teheran International Conference on Human Rights proclamation and the 1969 UN Declaration on Social Progress and Development.

Advised against becoming pregnant again, she was fitted with a diaphragm, however an attempt to import a spermicidal jelly through the post ended with its confiscation by customs officials. Mrs McGee challenged this seizure and in 1974, the Supreme Court ruled that she and her husband had a constitutional right to make the private decision to limit the size of their family (*McGee v Attorney General*, 1974).

This case did not clarify the issues of sale and access within Ireland. A 1974 Fine Gael-Labour coalition attempt to legislate on foot of the *McGee* case failed because many politicians in the proposing as well as the opposing parties, including the Fine Gael Taoiseach Liam Cosgrave, voted against it. In a state in which the Catholic Church remained a dominant force – one that taught that every sexual union should be open to "the transmission of life" – politicians knew that flouting Church teaching might be politically damaging. Even with knowledge of the threat pregnancy could pose to women like Mrs McGee, an overwhelmingly male Dáil rejected the bill by 75 votes to 61 (Hug, 1999: 106-108).

From 1976, radical feminist group Irish Women United (IWU) put its energies into the Contraception Action Programme (CAP), supported by trade and student unions and some Labour Party and socialist groupings. The campaign called for free, legal and accessible contraception and the introduction of sex education in schools and colleges, including information on birth control (Connolly and O'Toole, 2005: 59). In a visible campaign, CAP volunteers distributed condoms free from stalls in Dublin and Cork and in community centres in working class areas. It took considerable courage, energy and commitment for women with limited campaigning experience to make this sustained and public stand. While in Cork the police occasionally confiscated stocks,[7] a change in public attitudes was becoming obvious. A network of family planning clinics had sprung up in Dublin, Cork, Limerick, Galway, Bray and Navan, offering advice and providing contraceptives (Keogh, 1994: 333).

By the end of the decade, legal change was overdue but when it came it was designed to restrict rather than liberalise access to contraception. Under Fianna Fáil Health Minister Charles Haughey's Health (Family

---

[7] Interview with Glenys Spray, February 2008.

Planning) Act 1979, the "private" decisions of citizens would be mediated by their doctors. Contraceptives would only be available on prescription and the doctor issuing this was to reassure himself that they were required for "*bona fide*" family planning purposes: that is, that they were for use within marriage. The influence of those who associated fertility control and promiscuity was clear.

The legislation eased the situation for middle class couples, but contraceptives were not provided free under the General Medical Services (GMS) scheme, by which those on low incomes accessed free medical services. Challenging this, Cork Labour Party TD Eileen Desmond was scathing about the government's lack of concern for women's "human rights or for women as persons": for "underprivileged women, women living in overcrowded homes, in bad homes or women suffering the tensions of having to share those housing conditions with in-laws" (*Dáil Debates*, 1979, vol. 313, cols. 1294-1295). It was 1995 before contraceptives – though not condoms – were made available free of charge to medical card holders (Hug, 1999: 139). The new law fell far short of the CAP demand for free and accessible contraception. Its restrictions also meant that campaign members could no longer work distributing condoms at community level and the group disbanded, though some members became involved in setting up the Women's Right to Choose Group.

Abortion

Why was there a focus on abortion at the beginning of the 1980s? Throughout the 1970s lay Catholic fundamentalist groups marshalled their forces to resist both the legalisation of contraceptives and a movement in support of what became known as the "liberal agenda". As Girvin points out, rapid socioeconomic change during the 1960s and 1970s and "emerging secularist trends" had fuelled challenges to the Catholic Church's dominance (Girvin, 1986: 61). By the end of the 1970s the women's movement had gained ground, highlighting issues such as violence against women, sexual violence, and discrimination in family, employment law and pay scales, as well as demanding access to contraception. A movement to legalise divorce was growing and attitudes to women who bore children outside marriage and to their children were slowly changing. Some of those who sought a constitutional amendment banning abortion saw changing attitudes to reproductive rights issues as the first stages in the onslaught of a "promiscuous society". They believed that their campaign was "the last line of defence against the encroaching moral decadence of Europe" (Arnold and Kirby, 1982: 13).

O'Reilly traces the origins of the backlash that resulted in the 1983 constitutional ban on abortion to 1973, when the Irish Family League was founded. Further groups emerged during the decade, including umbrella organisation the Council of Social Concern. O'Reilly also provides an insight into the role played by the secretive lay Catholic organisation the Knights of Columbanus, whose members occupied influential positions in Irish social and political life. For such groups, the finding in the *McGee* case (1974) that couples had a right to make private decisions on family limitation rang alarm bells. A similar result in the United States case of *Roe v Wade* (1973) led to recognition of a woman's right to choose abortion (O'Reilly, 1992: 19-29; Hesketh, 1990: 1-37).

Was a challenge to Irish abortion law likely? The Women's Right to Choose Group (WRCG) was founded in Dublin in late 1979. Its aims included the "decriminalisation of abortion, open referral for abortions at hospitals and health centres, and the removal of all social and economic discrimination against single mothers" (O'Reilly, 1992: 54). By 1980 the WRCG had established the Irish Pregnancy Counselling Centre, held a number of public meetings and organised a seminar with international speakers at Trinity College, Dublin. By 1980 too, the Dublin Well Woman Centre referred around 1,000 women a year to British abortion services (Riddick, 1994: 140-161; Hesketh, 1990: 4-5). Both the WRCG and Well Woman Centre were small organisations, but they broke the silence on abortion. To conservative groups they were a threatening presence that might make Irish women's access to abortion a live issue.

Grounds for Abortion

There were other aspects to the abortion issue than a woman's right to choose, though before the campaign for a referendum began there was little public space in which to discuss them. One issue was a lack of clarity in the 1861 legislation. It referred to "unlawful" abortion, with an implication that there might be "lawful" abortion. In a September 1981 *Irish Times* article, Dooley-Clarke, a lecturer in medical ethics in University College Cork, considered the moral arguments against and for abortion. While accepting that abortion was "generally immoral", she concluded that it might be justifiable in exceptional cases: when a woman's life was at risk, when a pregnancy resulted from rape and in cases such as anencephaly. Pointing out the "divergence between … our expressed national attitude and … our actual practice" on abortion, Dooley-Clarke argued that the issue should be dealt with by updating the 1861 legislation so that "physicians would not have to 'second guess' the legal consequences of interventions and wonder whether 'acting in good faith' passes legal muster if the woman's life is clearly threatened by a pregnancy" (*The Irish Times*, 1981).

There is evidence that abortion on limited medical grounds was practiced in Ireland before 1983. The Catholic Church permitted "indirect" abortion in cases of ectopic pregnancy and uterine cancer, on the ground that the intention was the removal of a diseased organ, although the effect was the death of a foetus. In his book *Pro Life? The Irish Question*, Jewish obstetrician Solomons suggested some "exceptional cases" in which he and some non-Catholic colleagues might have considered terminating pregnancies before 1983:

> Some were clear-cut: cancer of the womb or breast, severe heart disease, obstetrical histories indicating a dangerously high risk, acute psychological disorders, and other conditions such as renal failure and hypertension that had not responded to treatment and that an experienced physician considered would affect the life-expectancy of the mother (Solomons, 1992: 72).

That the positions of the major non-Catholic religious groupings differed from those of the Catholic Church became obvious during the amendment campaign. Although anti-abortion, the Protestant Churches argued that it was a legislative rather than a constitutional matter. The Church of Ireland, for example, made clear its acceptance that cases "of strict and undeniable medical necessity" did arise in which termination of pregnancy might be justifiable (Arnold and Kirby, 1982: 61-73; Hesketh, 1990: 59-70). Chief Rabbi Dr David Rosen explained that in Jewish teaching "the sanctity of the life of the mother was above that of the embryo" (*The Irish Times*, 1983e). A 1983 eve of poll report in *The Irish*

Times on the agonised death of Sheila Hodgers, denied cancer treatment in Our Lady of Lourdes Hospital in Drogheda because she was pregnant, provided a glimpse of what the amendment might mean for Irish women (*The Irish Times*, 1983d).

The Pro-Life Amendment Campaign

How could an issue like abortion become a constitutional matter? During 1980 a Pro-Life Amendment Campaign (PLAC) was established with Catholic Doctors Guild members, representatives of the Council of Social Concern and of the Irish branch of a British organisation, the Responsible Society, at its core. It aimed to insert a clause in the Irish constitution that guaranteed the right to life of an embryo from conception. Before the formal launch of the PLAC, in April 1981, the Society for the Protection of Unborn Children (SPUC) became involved. The early 1980s was a period of economic downturn and political turmoil with three changes of government between 1981 and 1982. It was not difficult to pressurise politicians who were desperate for votes and under the impression that opposition to abortion was an issue the majority of the population agreed on. PLAC gained the support of the two men who alternated as Taoiseach and opposition leader in this period: Fianna Fáil's Charles Haughey and Fine Gael's Garret Fitzgerald. Labour politician Conor Cruise O'Brien cynically summed up their involvement as "nothing to do with the right to life, except the right to life of politicians" (Arnold and Kirby, 1982: 15).

It proved difficult to word a constitutional ban. Following a failed attempt by the Fine Gael government to introduce a version that allowed for changing attitudes and legislative amendments in the future (Hug, 1999: 152), in April 1983 the Dáil agreed a clause originally proposed by Fianna Fáil in 1981:

> The State acknowledges the right to life of the unborn and, with due regard to the equal right to life of the mother, guarantees in its laws to respect and, as far as practical, by its law to defend and vindicate that right.

That this wording was ambiguous was understood when the Referendum Bill passed through the Dáil. In February 1983, the Attorney General,

Peter Sutherland, had issued a warning that the term "unborn" might be broadly interpreted to mean either that abortion was prohibited from conception or that it was permitted until the point of viability. He also emphasised that the wording could prevent doctors from intervening in cases where pregnancy threatened the life of a woman, since they would be required to show equal regard for the life of the "unborn" (*The Irish Times*, 1983a). Knowing this, a majority of Deputies voted for it. That they found it impossible to draw back from putting what they were warned was a flawed wording to the people suggests something of the influence of pro-amendment groups and of the Catholic hierarchy that supported them. The date set for the referendum was 7 September 1983. The political campaign that ended that day is recognised as the bitterest and most divisive in recent Irish history. Those who opposed the amendment, however, did so from a range of perspectives, with many making clear that they opposed abortion.

Arguments against the Amendment

As Hesketh points out, Fianna Fáil Taoiseach Charles Haughey's original announcement, in March 1982, that a referendum would take place was condemned by a number of organisations focused on women's rights, including the Well Woman Centre, the Irish Family Planning Association, the Council for the Status of Women, the Women's Right to Choose Group and the Irish Council for Civil Liberties (Hesketh, 1990: 58). It was June 1982, however, before a coordinated Anti-Amendment Campaign (AAC) was launched, more than a year after the launch of the PLAC. The AAC involved a broad platform of individuals and groups, including politicians, particularly socialist politicians, journalists, academics, lawyers, doctors, non-Catholic clergy, writers, actors and artists.[8] Professional organisations, such as Doctors Against the Amendment, Academics Against the Amendment and Lawyers Against the Amendment gave further weight to the campaign. In Cork city, for example, more than 80 per cent of lawyers opposed the amendment (*The Irish Times*, 1983b).

---

[8] For a list of campaign sponsors, see Hesketh (1990: 391-392).

The AAC's strategy was to attack the amendment and appeal to a broadly liberal element in Ireland. Arguments used fell into five categories: that abortion should be a legislative and not a constitutional matter; that the amendment would create legal and medical confusion, threaten current medical practice and women's lives and make some methods of contraception illegal; that it was a waste of public money and would not reduce the numbers travelling to Britain for abortions; that a more worthwhile project would be improving the conditions experienced by unmarried mothers and their children; that, as discussed above, the amendment was sectarian, opposed by the main Protestant churches and the Chief Rabbi, a blow to progress towards a pluralist society and an indicator to Northern Irish Protestants that Rome still ruled the Republic. An additional argument was that, far from prohibiting abortion, the wording of the amendment could be interpreted as permitting it (Hesketh, 1990: 279-285).[9]

On women's rights the AAC's central arguments were that women's right to life would be subordinated to the right of the "unborn" from conception; that a number of methods of contraception, including the IUD, might become illegal as they prevented implantation in the womb, that women's right to travel abroad for abortions might be restricted, and that referral agencies and family planning clinics in Ireland might be injuncted (Hesketh, 1990: 279-282). A Cork campaign notice also listed the possible denial of the "morning-after pill" to rape victims and of cancer treatment to pregnant women (*The Cork Examiner*, 1983b).

The Women's Right to Choose Group (WRCG) played a role in initiating the AAC, but made a pragmatic decision to mute pro-choice demands and work within a broader liberal platform (Hug, 1992: 148-149). Some members refused to accept a subordination of women's rights arguments and were concerned about the AAC's middle class focus and failure to organize at local level as the PLAC had done (Hesketh, 1990: 279-282). These activists formed the Women's Right to Choose Campaign (WRCC), and highlighted women's rights and directly attacked the motives of those who lobbied for the amendment:

---

[9] Arnold and Kirby (1982) contains press materials covering a range of arguments.

> The Women's Right to Choose Campaign believe [sic] that this Constitutional amendment campaign represents a reactionary and anti-democratic movement to counter the progressive liberalization of opinion within Irish society. Nor is the title 'pro-life' for this amendment an honest one. The campaign is anti-abortion only, and to be consistently pro-life it would also have to call for the ending of legal discrimination against children born outside marriage and oppose capital punishment. Furthermore, the blatant disregard for the welfare of women (whose rights are always deemed secondary to those of the fertilized ovum, embryo or foetus) inherent in the attitudes of its leading supporters, raises the question of what it means to be genuinely pro-life (WRCC statement, Arnold and Kirby, 1982: 17).

Glenys Spray, who had been active in the CAP and became part of the AAC in Cork, Ireland's second city, was not inhibited about stating that she was pro-choice but found that:

> People were given very simplistic messages and saw people who were pro-choice as demonised. We were portrayed in a certain light and stereotyped as certain types. The opposition also stereotyped themselves as caring, Catholic, concerned. You were brave to mention the word "abortion", never mind "choice" as it was immediately like a rag to a bull. My employer was phoned and that was the experience of others too.[10]

In August 1983 AAC supporter Maureen Curtis Black, founder of the Cork Citizens' Advice Bureau, spelled out a number of reasons for voting no in a *Cork Examiner* feature. In her conclusion, she related PLAC to the subordination of women and indifference to their lives and health: "But then it is only women who are at risk – and women, especially married women, don't count in Ireland" (*The Cork Examiner*, 1983a). At a September 1983 Dublin press conference other prominent women expressed anger at the exclusion of women's concerns and experiences from the debate. Journalist Nell McCafferty noted opposition leader Charles Haughey's failure to mention "women", "pregnant", or "moth-

[10] Interview, February 2008. See also *The Irish Times* (1983c).

ers" in a pre-referendum broadcast. Sylvia Meehan, of the Employment Equality Agency, spoke of her anger at the "utter contempt for women" shown by a bishop who used the "cheap American-coined phrase 'the most dangerous place for a baby is in its mother's womb'" and Louise Asmal, of the Anti-Apartheid movement, suggested: "This amendment contains within it the concept of revenge against sexually active women" (*The Irish Times*, 1983f).

The final days of the campaign were sometimes violent. Arthur Leahy recalled events in Cork city and county where canvassing, postering, leafleting and public meetings were organized from a pay-phone in the recently established Quay Co-op:

> Many activists in the national campaign had political experience … but in small towns some individuals made brave stands … it is difficult now to give a real sense of what it was like or of the stress caused by threats of violence. In the city campaign members worked in groups because they were targeted by particular, very violent, families.… Every house in the city was leafleted and there was a tremendous sense of togetherness. As they called from door to door in rural and city areas reactions varied. Some people screamed and shouted … others were interested to know what it was all about; and then there were many who felt that they were being given space to talk about their own stories for the first time and drew the canvassers into their lives. There was a sense of scratching the surface and finding that the social problems of the real Ireland affected most families in some way … one of the successes of the campaign was that it opened up a range of issues including the problems faced by single parents (CWPA, 1993: 10-11).

There was evidence of apathy and confusion among voters (Hug, 1999: 150). Confusion may have increased when in his eve-of-referendum broadcast, Fine Gael Taoiseach Garret Fitzgerald warned that the amendment wording was indeed so ambiguous that he could not advise voters to endorse it (*The Irish Times*, 1983g). The Catholic Bishops urged parishioners to support the amendment. Only 54.6 per cent of the electorate went to the polls, however. Of these 66.45 per cent voted for the constitutional prohibition on abortion and 33.87 per cent voted against. This meant that only 35.79 per cent of the electorate voted the Eighth Amendment to the Constitution into place (Girvin, 1986: 76).

Pro-choice activist O'Neill was clear on what the campaign had meant to her:

> A copy of the "foetus road show" video being handed to my 10 year old daughter by a "concerned" neighbour with the instruction that she should then talk to me about it. Stones being thrown at my window because I had pro-choice leaflets there.
>
> It meant raising money for working class women to go to Britain for abortions, taking their children into our homes for the duration of the visit – pretending that Mammy was gone to a funeral – holding pub quizzes, and running limited draws, as well as running sales of work and raffles under a range of weird and wonderful names to preserve anonymity.
>
> It meant supporting those same women during subsequent referenda when they heard the hate brigade becoming more and more virulent. It meant the Mansion House pro-choice rally and being spat in the face in the name of Jesus. It meant having my phone cut off for non-payment of the bill.
>
> It ultimately meant that, as a working class activist, that my resolve to support women in the face of this opposition grew stronger and stronger – a resolve that makes me determined to continue fighting for the repeal of the Eighth Amendment (O'Neill, 2003: 8).

For a brief period abortion had been publicly discussed and consciousness had been raised that it was a legal fertility control option, though one accessed outside Ireland. Victory for the Catholic fundamentalists, however, marked the end of political progress for the pro-choice movement. The WRCG and WRCC disbanded. Riddick states that, in 1990, "consideration of women's moral right to choose has been virtually abandoned" (Riddick, 1994: 143). As well as the draining nature of the campaign, a lack of networking on choice may have been an issue. Horgan recalled that a range of local AAC action groups had pro-choice activists at their core. This was certainly the case in Cork and Horgan suggests it was so in areas like Sligo and Donegal (Horgan, 2003: 16). After

1983, however, the focus of pro-choice activists was practical: enabling women to choose by providing non-directive counselling and information on abortion services abroad.

Resisting Censorship

In the late 1980s and early 1990s the Eighth Amendment was used by SPUC, in the way predicted during the anti-amendment campaign, to injunct and close down abortion information providers. In 1986 two services were targeted: Open Line Counselling (OLC) – a telephone counselling and information service established in June 1983, when financial pressure closed the Irish Pregnancy Counselling Service – and the Dublin Well Woman Centre (Riddick, 1994: 143). In 1988 SPUC initiated a case against the officers of three student unions (Union of Students in Ireland, and the unions in University College Dublin and Trinity College Dublin) because they included abortion information in student handbooks. Connolly noted the sense of demoralisation experienced by pro-choice activists in this period when it appeared the backlash against the advances of the women's movement and liberalisation was succeeding (Connolly, 2002: 173-176). Nevertheless, the right to choose movement remained alive at community level. New organisations responded to the closing of counselling services. A "Defend the Clinics" campaign emerged and in 1987 supported the establishment of the Women's Information Network, an underground non-directive helpline, staffed by trained volunteers. Important links were maintained with the London-based Irish Women's Abortion Support Group (IWASG), an Irish women's collective established in 1981. The IWASG provided information, made clinic appointments and provided practical support for Irish women forced to travel (Connolly and O'Toole, 2005: 72; Bacik, 2004: 112-114; Smyth, 1992a: 47-56).

Censorship intensified after the SPUC legal actions. Some British newspapers and magazines were banned because they advertised abortion services and books and British telephone directories were removed from library shelves.[11] It was impossible, however, to prevent the circula-

---

[11] A speech by academic and activist Ailbhe Smyth, at a June 1992 Cork Repeal the Eighth Amendment Campaign meeting, captures a sense of this time (Smyth, 1992b).

tion of pamphlets such as Horgan's *Abortion: Why Irish women must have the right to choose* (Horgan, 1990), or the Cork Abortion Information Campaign's (CAIC) 1991 44 page challenge to censorship: *Censored: Ireland's Abortion Reality, Including a Guide to Services for Irish Women*. This booklet discussed abortion law, medical issues around abortion, explained the methods used in abortion and provided a detailed guide to "support, counselling and referral organizations" and contact details for British clinics. It commented on clinics ("Nice and friendly, easy to locate", "more expensive but very friendly") and added information on family planning, post-abortion counselling and check-up services. On its cover was a young woman, her mouth stopped by a gag on which the word "censored" was emblazoned. The publication was a powerful statement of women's resistance.

The counselling services case was forwarded to the European Court of Human Rights (ECHR) but there was a long wait for a hearing. In 1991 the case against the students was dealt with in the European Court of Justice (ECJ), where abortion was defined as a "service" legally available in several European Community (EC) states. As the students did not have a commercial relationship with an English clinic, however, the court concluded that, in their case, the ban on information did not breach European law. The case was returned to the Irish courts (Hug, 1999: 160).

The ECJ ruling did imply that if an Irish organisation had such a link, it could provide information legally (Hug, 1999: 157-160; Bacik, 2004: 114).[12] It seemed possible that EC law might be used to bring change in Ireland. By chance, negotiations on the Maastricht Treaty were under way. Late in 1991, with no public discussion – and clearly advised by anti-abortion groups – the Fianna Fáil government forestalled any such move by having a protocol entered in the Treaty to the effect that European decisions would not "affect the application in Ireland of Article 40.3.3°" (Hug, 1999: 172). Within a week of signing the treaty, in February 1992, an abortion crisis emerged the implications of which still reverberate more than fifteen years later.

---

[12] Senator Ivana Bacik was one of the TCD students prosecuted.

The *X* Case

In February 1992, the Attorney General, Harry Whelehan, sought and was granted a High Court injunction preventing a 14-year-old girl, who had been raped, from travelling to England for an abortion. One implication of the judgment was that women intending to travel for the purpose of abortion might be detained and forced to continue their pregnancies. The immediate impact of the case was to raise national awareness that the constitutional prohibition could impact cruelly on real, vulnerable women and young girls, including one, as in the *X* case, sexually abused and so devastated by her pregnancy that she was suicidal. An *Irish Times* editorial captured the sense of shock at the judgement:

> What are we now to compare ourselves with? Ceausescu's Romania? The Ayatollah's Iran? Algeria? There are similarities.
>
> The implications of Mr Justice Costello's judgement, delivered and circulated yesterday, may be little short of catastrophic for the health and safety of Irish women, for the very concept of individual bodily rights, for the role of the State as a protective and benign organism … (*The Irish Times* 1992a).

The day following the judgment, several hundred protestors gathered outside the Dáil. The *Irish Times* recorded slogans on their posters, including "Ireland Defends Men's Right to Procreate by Rape" and "Referendum '83, Vote in Haste, Repent at Leisure". The newspaper also carried a photograph of a banner calling for "Abortion Information Now" but, in compliance with the 1986 ruling on information in the counselling service cases, with the service phone number on it blanked out (*The Irish Times* 1992b).

A new campaigning phase had begun and numerous activist groups emerged into the public space. Protests were held in cities and towns around the country. The Dublin Abortion Rights Group (DARG) called on protestors to march in O'Connell Street, Dublin, and an estimated 10,000 participated (Bacik, 2004: 117). The Supreme Court overturned the High Court's decision (*Attorney General v X*, 1992). It found that, as the girl was suicidal and this constituted a genuine risk to her life, a termination was permissible, even one performed in Ireland. It also ruled that if no such risk existed, access to information and possibly travel could be prevented in the interests of safeguarding the rights of the "unborn". This suggested the possibility that pregnant women might be detained at ports or airports, while the protocol to the Maastricht Treaty would prevent any appeal to EC laws guaranteeing freedom of travel. The Treaty had to be ratified during 1992 and the upcoming referendum provided a further focus for abortion rights activists in organisations such as the CAIC, Dublin Abortion Information Campaign (DAIC), and the Repeal the Eighth Amendment Campaign (REAC), which had sister organisations in Cork and Waterford.

DAIC reacted to the *X* case by distributing a leaflet, headed "Women have the right to choose. Scrap the 8th Amendment". It carried phone numbers for the Women's Information Network and British clinics. DAIC leaflets calling for a vote against Maastricht also carried contact numbers and listed a range of reasons why women chose abortion (including not being able to afford more children, threats to health, contraception failure and the need for chemotherapy in cancer treatment), and warned voters that if they voted "yes" the government might renege on a recent promise to hold a referendum on travel rights and information. An internal DAIC document suggested that "Maastricht should not be seen as an end in itself, rather as a chance to raise the arguments" (DAIC document, 1992).[13] In May 1992, however, to ensure that the travel issue did not affect voting on the Treaty, a "solemn declaration" was signed by the European partners. It stated that the Protocol would not limit travel to, or information on services in, member states. At a June 1992 Cork Women's Political Association meeting, anger was expressed that it had ever been possible to attach to the Treaty a Protocol on which there had been no public discussion and that was intended to deprive Irish women of rights enjoyed by their European sisters. A press release issued after the meeting called for a "no" vote in the referendum, the removal of the Protocol and the establishment of travel and information rights (CWPA: 1992a). The Treaty was ratified in a June referendum.

A REAC leaflet on Maastricht had argued that:

---

[13] I am most grateful to Alan Mac Simon of the Alliance for Choice for allowing me access to a range of materials from this period.

> If the government is really serious about giving women these rights, then it must act in Ireland. It must lift the injunctions on abortion information and non-directive counselling … so that Irish women are in no doubt where they stand (REAC leaflet, 1992).

In August 1992, however, the SPUC case against the students returned to the Irish courts. A permanent injunction was granted, restraining them from providing abortion information. At this stage the constitutional position on travel and information remained unclear.

Though REAC supported women's right to choose, there was internal debate on the issue (REAC conference agenda, 1992). A September 1992 discussion paper listed some of the reasons why women who contacted the Dublin Women's Information Network sought abortions:

> ... fear and shame of being pregnant, poverty – large families and employment, recuperation from illness, illness itself, battering of the woman and/or her other children, rape, incest, age, intake of medication or x-rays during early pregnancy (REAC discussion paper, 1992: 1).

Its author, Joan O'Connor, argued that abortion should not be discussed in a vacuum but in relation to how Irish society failed women:

> [the] severe lack of childcare facilities, little or no support for single parents (financial or emotional) and the availability of work for women with children often forces women into making decisions on their lives which ultimately they do not wish to make (REAC discussion paper, 1992: 1).

It suggested that support for a right to choose also involved campaigning "on childcare, contraception etc." and demanding that there should be fewer crisis pregnancies and fewer abortions. By Autumn 1992 a campaign on travel and information was underway, and the Discussion Paper also suggested that supporting women's right to choose should not be a condition of REAC membership (REAC discussion paper, 1992: 2).

Another Restrictive Proposal

In September 1992 it emerged that, in a confidential communication with the Government, members of the Second Commission on the Status of Women had recommended that Article 40.3.3° should either be deleted or amended to guarantee travel and information rights (*The Irish Times* 1992d). It also became clear that the Government would put three, rather than two, constitutional amendments to the people in November 1992: those on freedom to travel and the right to information on services legally available in other states, and – despite the outpouring of public sympathy for Ms X – one designed to ensure that in future a suicidal girl would be denied access to abortion in Ireland. The wording of this third amendment was also designed to prevent the Supreme Court from interpreting the Eighth Amendment as permitting abortion to protect the health of a woman:

> It shall be unlawful to terminate the life of an unborn unless such termination is necessary to save the life, as distinct from the health, of the mother where there is an illness or disorder of the mother giving rise to a real and substantial risk to her life, not being a risk of self-destruction.

The November 1992 vote, held on the same day as a general election, provided a new focus for activism. An October ruling of the ECHR, in the counselling services case gave impetus to the pro-information campaign. The ban on abortion information was found to be "disproportionate". It created a risk to the health of women for whom, for example, difficulty in accessing information meant late abortion, or inability to access post-abortion check-ups (Hug, 1999: 159). This was a vindication of those who had provided support and counselling for more than a decade.

On 12 October 1992 the Council for the Status of Women (CSW) issued a press release stating that "women were angry listening to linguistic contortions on the question of abortion, to a debate that frequently did not respect women's own judgement". It argued that "the line between life and health cannot be defined and should not be drawn" and that the fact that a suicidal woman was genuinely at risk should be recognised (CWPA, 1992b). Abortion rights activists called for "yes" votes on travel and information and a "no" on what was euphemistically known as the "substantive" issue: the clause further limiting abortion rights. A CWPA press release suggested that the proposed amendment denied women "the possibility of honest dialogue with their doctors, might be used to delay or deny treatments for health-threatening illnesses, and shirked issues such as rape, incest, and physical problems such as the development of anencephaly" (CWPA, 1992c).

Voters rejected the proposal to roll back the *X* case judgment and distinguish life from health, but voted for the travel and information amendments. No legislation followed and rumours circulated that a draft bill would make the life and health distinction, despite the electorate's decision, and that it would limit access to information. This provoked further actions. The CWPA sent a detailed statement to the Minister for Health on access to information arguing that "a woman's emotional health is indistinguishable from her physical health" (CWPA, 1993: 25-27). The statement was used to lobby Munster TDs. In this period too, stickers giving counselling service contact details appeared on toilet doors in colleges, pubs and clubs. Some activists wore the phone numbers on T-shirts or jackets. In Cork, three were prosecuted when, in what they called "a deliberate act of civil disobedience", they pasted posters with helpline numbers at prominent points in the city. The charge was littering and the fine £300 each (*The Cork Examiner*, 1994).

One cause of delay was resistance by anti-abortion groups who opposed any attempt to end censorship and argued that information legislation would be ruled unconstitutional because it implied a threat to the "unborn". Another problem was tension on the issue within the Fianna Fáil-Labour coalition. After a November 1994 change of government, new Fine Gael Minister for Health Michael Noonan published the Regulation of Information (Services outside the State for Terminations of Pregnancies) Bill. Under it, abortion information could only be provided in the context of a non-directive counselling session, regardless of the woman's wishes on this. Doctors were not permitted to make abortion appointments for women or to forward letters of referral to clinics abroad. Counselling restrictions did not apply to anti-abortion counselling and the use of scare tactics against vulnerable women by "rogue" counselling agencies would arise within the next decade. An advance was that public funding was provided for a range of counselling agencies including Dublin Well Woman Centre, Cherish and Irish Family Planning Association – which would develop advocacy roles – as well as anti-abortion organisations LIFE and CURA. For women outside Dublin, however, accessing information and counselling was and remains an issue only partly alleviated by access to the internet.

1996–2001

Between 1996 and 2001, abortion occasionally hit the headlines. In 1996 the Report of the Constitution Review Group suggested that Article 40.3.3° should be amended (Constitution Review Group, 1996: 273-279). Recognising the difficulties this involved, it recommended at least "the introduction of legislation covering such matters as definitions, protection for appropriate medical intervention, certification of 'real and substantial risk to the life of the mother' and a time limit on lawful termination of pregnancy". In May 1997, a new umbrella group, the Alliance for Choice, added its voice to calls for legislation and condemned politicians who had "shown scant regard for the equal right to life of women" (Alliance for Choice, 1997). In November 1997, the issues of rape, suicide and under-aged victims were again highlighted in the *C* case (1998). The Eastern Health Board sought permission to take a child in its care, who had been raped and was suicidal, to England for an abortion. The High Court permitted her to travel, because under the *X* case test, there was a real and substantial risk to her life.

Publication of a 1998 study, *Women & Crisis Pregnancy*, provided new evidence on the reasons why Irish women chose abortion and raised issues such as access to reliable contraception and information on how to use it (Mahon, Conlon and Dillon, 1998). In 1999 the Fianna Fáil government published a *Green Paper on Abortion* and in 2000, the *All-Party Oireachtas Committee on the Constitution, Fifth Progress Report: Abortion* was published. Some organisations involved in pro-choice activism gave oral evidence to the committee, including Abortion Reform, Cork Women's Right to Choose Group (CWRCG) and Catholics for Choice. Absent from the State's consultation process, however, were the more than 100,000 Irish women who by 1999 were known to have had abortions. In 2000 too, the Irish Family Planning Association published *The Irish Journey*, a moving collection of testimonies by women who travelled abroad for abortions and the first book to give voice to a group that had been silenced in Ireland (Ruane, 2002).

A new dynamic entered abortion rights activism in 2001when pro-choice groups took the initiative – rather than reacting to anti-choice moves – and invited the Women on Waves project to Ireland. The visit of Dutch doctor Rebecca Gomperts's floating abortion clinic to Cork as well as Dublin received huge publicity and provided a forum for discussion of women's right to information, reliable fertility control and to choose abortion. Reactions from the hundreds of people who visited the boat in both venues were positive and many took the opportunity to consult with the on-board obstetrician.[14] There was a sense of a sea-change in attitudes. The scale of the problems, including financial ones, facing those trying to access abortion services abroad, however, came as a shock to pro-choice volunteers staffing telephone information lines during the visit. Some women had got deeply in debt with moneylenders to pay for travel, accommodation and British clinic fees.

One important development from that visit was the establishment of a new organisation, Doctors for Choice, designed to "encourage political advocacy by pro-choice doctors nationwide, and to provide practical medical information to all doctors treating patients travelling abroad for abortion services" (Doctors for Choice, 2002). Another result of the Women on Waves visit was the building of a network of women's organisations and rights activists who formed the nucleus of umbrella group the Alliance for a No Vote (ANV) later in 2001, when the Fianna Fáil and Progressive Democrat coalition government proposed another restrictive constitutional amendment.

2002–2008

The Human Life in Pregnancy Bill was unveiled in October 2001. It contained two familiar proposals already rejected by voters in 1992: the rolling back of the *X* case judgement so that a woman who was suicidal as a result of a crisis pregnancy would not be permitted to have an abortion in Ireland; and a provision permitting abortion to save the life, but not the health, of a woman. In addition, a woman who attempted abortion and

[14] The author participated in this initiative.

anyone who helped her do so faced up to twelve years imprisonment (a reduction of the life sentence under the 1861 legislation). The hypocrisy of measures designed to continue criminalising women who had abortions or self-aborted in Ireland, when 6,391 women (19 a day) had travelled to Britain for abortions in 2000, was focused on in Alliance for a No Vote (ANV) press releases and leaflets (ANV materials, 2000-2001). Also highlighted was Ireland's two-tier system in which only those with sufficient funds could choose abortion abroad.[15] The Alliance became the central organiser of an anti-amendment campaign that included street demonstrations, picketing government party events, leafleting, media liaison, setting up photo opportunities and providing speakers for interviews. The amendment was also opposed by opposition parties Fine Gael, Labour and the smaller parties on the left, by umbrella group the National Women's Council of Ireland, and by the Irish Council for Civil Liberties (*The Irish Times*: 2002b; 2002c; 2002e). The Women's Health Council, a statutory body, criticised the government's proposals and its failure to discuss them with its women's health advisory body (*The Irish Times*, 2002a).

Calls for a right to choose were muted in an activist campaign focused on defeating the referendum, though women like Cathleen O'Neill (whose views on the 1983 campaign are quoted above) made principled stands on this issue in media interviews. The most potent voice to emerge from the referendum campaign was that of Deirdre de Barra, a woman who declared that she was against "abortion on demand", but whose personal experience highlighted the draconian nature of the government's approach. In a much publicised letter to *The Irish Times*, she conveyed a sense of the trauma a forced journey to Britain imposed on her when, during a much wanted pregnancy, she found that the foetus she carried was suffering from a chromosomal abnormality and would not survive after birth. She spoke of the "inhumane treatment of women in this State" and of her feeling of violation arising from it (*The Irish Times*: 2002d).

The restrictive 2002 proposals were defeated. In the years since then, the State has done nothing to define the circumstances in which abortion

[15] From materials in the possession of the author.

is legal in Ireland. Reporting critically on the Irish situation in April 2008, the Council of Europe's Human Rights Commissioner stated that the Irish authorities had informed him "that there were currently no plans to legislate for abortion on the grounds of the X case".[16] The sometimes hypocritical actions of the State in facilitating abortion in Britain while banning it in Ireland, and the impact of current policy on women, were accurately summed up in the 14 April 2008 letter to the Council of Europe from organisations that deal with women in crisis pregnancies:

> We have observed that the Government in the Republic of Ireland facilitates access to abortion abroad by providing some women with funds or documents necessary for travel. However, migrant women often face delay, considerable bureaucratic hurdles, and a loss of privacy while obtaining permission to travel. On occasion the State has denied women permission or the necessary papers to travel abroad for an abortion, or has delayed to the point when a woman's pregnancy has advanced too far to obtain a legal abortion. In recent years health care providers have found evidence of a return to illegal, unsafe abortion not seen since the early 1950s. Such illegal activity has been seen mainly among an immigrant population who face greater restrictions on travel and often lack funds.
>
> On a daily basis our organisations witness how a woman's age, her emotional state, and her other life circumstances affect her decision whether to carry a pregnancy to term and her ability to do so. Yet the laws restricting abortion disregard all such factors.[17]

How can abortion rights activists work to change such a situation? They have begun to look outside the state for support, to international human rights bodies such as the UN's Committee on the Convention on the Elimination of All Forms of Discrimination Against Women (CEDAW). Three organisations, the CWRCG, the IFPA, ICCL, and a coalition of

---

[16] Report of the Commissioner for Human Rights, Mr Thomas Hammarberg, on his visit to Ireland, Strasbourg, 30 April 2008, CommDH(2008)9, section 5.2, para. 78. Report available at: http://www.coe.int/t/commissioner/Activities/visits_en.asp.

[17] Available at http://safeandlegal.blogspot.com/2008_04_01_archive.html. Letter signed by Family Planning Association of Northern Ireland, IFPA, National Women's Council of Ireland, One Family, Dublin Well Woman Centre and Women's Aid.

groups involved in the Women's Human Rights Alliance (WHRA), sent reports to the CEDAW committee in advance of Ireland's appearance before it in 2005. The Committee's concluding comments expressed concern about Ireland's "very restrictive abortion laws".[18] In addition, individual women are using legal routes outside Ireland. Deirdre de Barra brought a case to the European Court of Human Rights, though in 2006 it was ruled inadmissible as she had not exhausted legal channels in Ireland.[19] At the time of writing three further cases await decisions on admissibility. With termination of pregnancy recognised as the commonest gynaecological procedure Irish women experience (Favier, 2008: 19) and with access to abortifacient drugs, such as RU486, through the internet, it is likely that more legal challenges will follow.

New lobbying and activist groupings have emerged. The Alliance for a No Vote has become a revamped Alliance for Choice. In 2005 the Safe and Legal in Ireland Campaign was launched. It aims to end "the hypocrisy of exiling women in crisis pregnancy that choose to have an abortion". Its website also indicates that the campaign involves "various strands, including a litigation strand, a public awareness strand and a national and international advocacy strand" and that it supports the women who have taken their cases to Europe. Activism within Ireland has increased with groups like CWRCG and Choice Ireland becoming visible with regular street stalls, workshops and leafleting. Choice Ireland pickets "rogue" abortion information services alleged to provide misleading information to women seeking counselling. A catalyst for this renewed activity was outrage at the 2007 court case involving Miss D, a teenage girl in the care of the State. Carrying an anencephalic foetus, she was forced to go to court for permission to travel outside Ireland for a termination.

Abortion rights activists have focused on different issues over 25 years. Some have opposed measures designed to make Ireland's abortion laws even more draconian, others have maintained a discourse on women's reproductive rights, or provided information, counselling and practical support for women in crisis pregnancies. Most support women's right to choose. Forced to look outside Ireland for remedies, some are

---

[18] Concluding Comments: Ireland, CEDAW/C/IRL/CO/4-5, para. 38.

[19] *D v Ireland* (application no. 26499/02).

coming to grips with new concepts, including ideas around reproductive justice; that legalising "choice" is meaningless if women do not have the means to exercise it; and that "reproductive rights must be embedded in human rights and social justice frameworks" (Sherk, 2008: 6). They work to end the criminalisation and stigmatisation of women and, to borrow the words of the April 2008 Council of Europe resolution, to establish "effective access to safe, affordable, acceptable and appropriate abortion services" in Ireland.[20] Our legislators seem impervious to these ideas, still content to turn a blind eye and let Britain, the Netherlands and Spain cope with our problems. For a new generation of activists, one that does not remember the defeat and backlash of the 1980s, that public representatives end the hypocrisy and recognise international standards on reproductive health, and on women's right to make reproductive choices, is essential. Meanwhile, there can be few stronger statements of the subordination of Irish women than that, regardless of their circumstances, they are forced to "scurry like criminals" to access abortion facilities abroad. Because it is used against women in this way, because it is interpreted as equating the rights of an embryo from the moment of conception with those of a pregnant woman, for abortion rights activists, repeal of the Eighth Amendment remains the key demand.

Bibliography

Archive Material

The Alan MacSimon Private Collection:

Alliance for Choice (1997) Information Pack, 14 May.

ANV materials: (2001-2002) Leaflet "No abortions here, says Bertie – even if you've been raped and you're suicidal" and Press Release "Picket of the Dáil in protest at railroading of abortion Bill", 28 November 2001.

DAIC document (1992) untitled but with "Presentation by Andrew Flood to D.A.I.C. 24/3/1992" written on by hand.

DIAC leaflets (1992) "Women have the right to choose. Scrap the 8th Amendment" and "Some reasons why women have abortions".

---

[20] Quoting from Council of Europe Resolution 1607 (2008), Access to safe and legal abortion in Europe.

REAC leaflet (1992) "Never Again: Repeal the 8th Amendment Campaign for information and choice."

REAC discussion paper (1992) Joan O'Connor "Women's Right to Choose" 1 September.

REAC conference agenda (1992) "Repeal the Eighth Amendment Campaign National Conference 4th October. Royal Dublin Hotel. Final Agenda."

Cork Women's Political Association materials:

CWPA (1992a) Cork Women's Political Association Minutes 8 June.

CWPA (1992b) Council for the Status of Women press release "Women's Lives and Health Must be Protected" 12 October.

CWPA (1992c) Press Release: "CWPA urges a no vote on the abortion issue" 18 November.

CWPA (1993) "CWPA Submission to the Minister for Health" in *VOW: Voices of Women*, November edition, pp. 25-27.

Doctors for Choice (2002) Leaflet: "Doctors striving to make comprehensive reproductive health services, including contraception and abortion available in Ireland."

Books and Journals

Anonymous (1991) *Censored: Ireland's Abortion Reality, Including a Guide to Services for Irish Women* Cork: Cork Abortion Information Campaign.

Anonymous (2003) *20 Years of the 8th Amendment* Dublin: Alliance for Choice.

Anonymous (2003a) "The Quay Co-Op and the 1983 Campaign" in *VOW: Voices of Women* Cork Women's Political Association Journal, 8th Amendment Special Edition, Cork: Cork Women's Political Association, pp. 8-9.

Arnold, M. and Kirby, P. (1982) *"The Abortion Referendum": The Case Against*, Dublin: Anti-Amendment Campaign.

Bacik, I. (2004) *Kicking and Screaming: Dragging Ireland into the 21st Century* Dublin: O'Brien.

Connolly, L. (2002) *The Women's Movement: from Revolution to Devolution* Basingstoke: Palgrave.

Connolly, L. and O'Toole, T. (2005) *Documenting Irish Feminisms: The Second Wave* Dublin: Woodfield Press.

Favier, M. (2008) "GPs and the silence around abortion" in *Forum*, May edition, pp. 19-20.

Galligan, Y. (1997) *Women and politics in contemporary Ireland: From the margins to the mainstream* Washington: Pinter.

Girvin B. (1986) "Social Change and Moral Politics: The Irish Constitutional Referendum 1983" in 34 *Political Studies* 61.

Hesketh, T (1990) *The Second Partitioning of Ireland: The Abortion Referendum of 1983* Dun Laoghaire: Brandsma Books.

Horgan, G. (1990) *Abortion: Why Irish women must have the right to choose* Dublin: Bookmarks Ireland.

Horgan, G. (2003) "… pushing the abortion issue aside was a mistake…" in *20 Years of the 8th Amendment* Dublin: Alliance for Choice.

Hug, C. (1999) *The Politics of Sexual Morality in Ireland* London: Macmillan.

Keogh, D. (1994) *Twentieth-Century Ireland: Nation and State* Dublin: Gill and Macmillan.

Mahon, E., Conlon, C. and Dillon, L. (1998) *Women & Crisis Pregnancy* Dublin: Stationery Office.

O'Neill, C. (2003) "… raising money for working class women to go to Britain for abortions …" in *20 Years of the 8th Amendment* Dublin: Alliance for Choice.

O'Reilly, E. (1992) *Masterminds of the Right* Dublin: Attic Press.

Riddick, R. (1994) "The Right to Choose: Questions of Feminist Morality (1990)" in Smyth, A. (ed.) *A Dozen Lips* Dublin: Attic Press.

Ruane, M. [introduction] (2000) *The Irish Journey: Women's Stories of Abortion* Dublin: Irish Family Planning Association.

Sherk, K. (2008) "Reproductive rights, sexual rights and human rights", *a/the abortion magazine* Winter, pp. 6-7, available at: http://www.ipas.org/ Publications/asset_upload_file661_3322.pdf .

Smyth, A. (1992a) *The Abortion Papers: Ireland* Dublin: Attic Press.

Smyth, A. (1992b) "The Politics of Abortion in a Police State" in Smyth, A. (ed.) (1992) *The Abortion Papers: Ireland* Dublin: Attic Press.

Smyth, A. (ed.) (1994) *A Dozen Lips* Dublin: Attic Press.

Smyth, L. (2005) *Abortion and Nation: The Politics of Reproduction in Contemporary Ireland* Aldershot: Ashgate.

Solomons, M. (1992) *Pro Life? The Irish Question* Dublin: Lilliput Press.

Newspapers

The Cork Examiner (1983a) "Reasons to Vote No", 24 August.

The Cork Examiner (1983b) Pre-referendum advertisement, 7 September.

The Cork Examiner (1994) "Abortion poster trio fined £900", 18 February.

The Irish Times (1981) "Divergence between Theory and Practice", 11 September.

The Irish Times (1983a) "Attorney General rules out wording", 16 February.

The Irish Times (1983b) "600 lawyers are opposed to amendment, says group", 1 September.

The Irish Times (1983c) "McCarthyism seen in letters to employer", 1 September.

The Irish Times (1983d) "Sheila Hodgers – a case in question", 2 September.

The Irish Times (1983e) "Opposition by Chief Rabbi", 5 September.

The Irish Times (1983f) "Women shut out from debate", 6 September.

The Irish Times (1983g) "Taoiseach warns on wording", 6 September.

The Irish Times (1992a) "Descent into Cruelty", editorial, 18 February.

The Irish Times (1992b) "Protestors march on Dáil", 18 February.

The Irish Times (1992c) Supreme Court judgments published 6 March.

The Irish Times (1992d) "Proposals on right to advice, travel", 28 September.

The Irish Times (2002a) "Women's Council not asked for advice", 4 February.

The Irish Times (2002b) "Council for Women calls for No vote", 18 February.

The Irish Times (2002c) "ICCL urges No vote over implications for women", 21 February.

The Irish Times (2002d) Letters to the Editor, 25 February.

The Irish Times (2002e) 15 Groups combine to oppose proposals", 27 February.

Official Publications

All-Party Oireachtas Committee on the Constitution (2000) *Fifth Progress Report: Abortion* Dublin: Stationery Office.

Commission on the Status of Women (1972) *Report to the Minister for Finance* Dublin: Stationery Office.

Constitution Review Group (1996) *Report of the Constitution Review Group* Dublin: Stationery Office.

Green Paper on Abortion (1999) Dublin: Stationery Office.

Hansard, Parliamentary Debates (1974) House of Commons 28 June

Cases

A and B v Eastern Health Board and C (the "*C* case") [1998] 1 IR 464

Attorney General v X (the "*X* case") [1992] 2 IR 1.

Magee v Attorney General [1974] IR 284.

Roe v Wade (1973) 410 US 113.

2

FROM RIGHTS TO COMPASSION:

The D Case and Contemporary Abortion Politics

Dr Lisa Smyth

Introduction

It is well-known that the Republic of Ireland's economic, social and political fortunes have changed dramatically in the years since the momentous events of the *X* case in 1992 (Kuhling and Keohane, 2007; O'Sullivan, 2007a). A relatively successful peace process has been negotiated in the North, and the South experienced significant economic success in an era when other economies were stagnating or going into decline. The society became a destination for refugees, asylum seekers and economic migrants for the first time during these years, as the economy began to thrive and the European Union was enlarged, driving debate over questions of entitlement and belonging through the lens of "race" and ethnicity, in ways that have also reconfigured public debate over gender, nationhood and reproduction (Fletcher, 2007; Harrington, 2005; Mullally, 2005; Tormey, 2007). The status of women in the society has undergone important change during these years. Increased levels of economic activity, delayed motherhood and smaller family size have transformed the gender order in some respects, while reinforcing inequalities around access to key resources such as childcare, income, and citizenship more generally (O'Sullivan, 2007b).

This chapter is concerned with exploring the dynamics of contemporary debate on women's reproductive choices and rights in this somewhat transformed arena. It will focus on the events of April and May 2007 as the case of "D", a 17-year-old in the temporary care of the state, seeking to terminate her (much wanted) pregnancy after a diagnosis of severe foetal abnormality,[1] became yet again a focus of public debate on abortion access within the state. The Health Service Executive (HSE), which was responsible for her care, sought to prevent her from travelling to Britain for an abortion when a social worker became aware of her intentions. D was told that she could not leave the country without permission, and that were she to try to do so, she would be arrested. Her social worker wrote to the Gardaí, requesting that she be prevented from travelling abroad, and attempts were made to prevent her being issued with a passport. D applied to the High Court to contest the HSE's right to prevent her from travelling, drawing her situation to public attention (Sheehan, 2007).

The discussion, in what follows, of the framing of the issues this case raised in the public domain is aimed at considering the continuities and discontinuities in the dynamics of contemporary abortion politics in the society. What is of interest is the shifting moral grammar shaping the debate, and specifically the frames which contributors adopted in presenting intelligible arguments aimed at persuading a public audience (Ferree et al., 2002; Honneth, 1995). A key tension in this case was the apparent conflict presented by Article 40.3.3° between the state's duties to defend both the right to life of the "unborn", and the right to bodily integrity of minors in its care.[2] The case illustrates the ongoing tensions between changing characterisations of Irishness, and the social dynamics of access to reproductive rights, particularly for national minors in the care of the state.

---

[1] Her foetus was diagnosed with anencephaly, a condition where part of the brain is missing. A baby born with this condition would be unlikely to survive for more than three days.

[2] Indeed, legislation protecting children is very much aimed at protecting their bodily integrity.

Public Debate on Foetal Abnormality, Minors and Abortion

The *D* case emerged against a background of ongoing public and legal deliberations, both within the state and beyond, over the meaning of Article 40.3.3°. Significantly, there had been a previous *D* case (2006), where the State's abortion laws were challenged in the European Court of Human Rights (ECHR) by a woman whose 12-week scan showed that one of the two foetuses she was carrying had died, and that the other was suffering from a fatal abnormality. She had been forced to travel to England for an abortion, and subsequently took a case against the State. The challenge was unsuccessful because she had not exhausted the remedies available in the domestic courts before going to Strasbourg. However, the State did argue that had she sought a domestic remedy, it was likely that she would have been successful (*D v Ireland,* 2006). Indeed, the ECHR, which usually manages to avoid intervening in political debates over abortion access, had recently ordered Poland to compensate a woman for refusing her an abortion, on the grounds that her rights had been violated by the uncertainty of the decision-making process which regulates access to abortion in that country (Harrington, 2007). This case had received some news coverage in Ireland (e.g. Hennessy and Smyth, 2007; O'Hanlon, 2007).

The 2007 case of D, described above, again refocused public and political attention on the question of legal abortion access within the parameters of Article 40.3.3°. Although the courts had dealt with requests for legal abortions in situations of severe foetal abnormality, as well as cases of minors in their care experiencing crisis pregnancy, the specific features of this story marked it out as quite unlike any of the previous cases. D's situation opened up an important and telling debate about the moral standing of abortion in cases of terminal foetal abnormality. News reports of the story illustrate a number of key themes which will be outlined in detail below.

As already mentioned, this case involved a young woman carrying a foetus which was very unlikely to survive long after birth. Neither of the possible natural outcomes of this pregnancy, namely stillbirth or a live birth closely followed by death, could be simply presented in public debate as preferable to terminating the pregnancy, although some efforts were made to do so. While the case received widespread media attention, both within Ireland and beyond, it did not, unlike the landmark *X* case, present a moment of national crisis where the moral values of the nation were perceived to have been captured and exposed by an episode in one young woman's reproductive life.[3] Instead, this became an opportunity for expressing compassion and sympathy for D, which she herself clearly recognised in her comments to the media (English, 2007; McDonald, 2007c).

An examination of the news coverage of the case in the national dailies, particularly the *Irish Independent* and *The Irish Times*, with some supplementary material from the Irish editions of British dailies such as the *Mirror* and the *Sun*, provides an insight into the broader frames employed to define what was at stake in this latest episode in the Republic's abortion politics (Ferree et al., 2002). A reading of national-level daily reporting during this period indicates the predominance of three main frames: the moral character of the collectivity, as discernable through practical responses to human suffering; the social status of the family and (gendered) familial identities; and the emerging prioritisation of medical and health issues in decision-making about pregnancies. These frames were employed in relation both to critics and supporters of the HSE's actions.

Framing Abortion in the National Press

Public outcry against the HSE's efforts to prevent D from travelling for an abortion echoed some of the responses to *Attorney General v X* (1992) in 1992. The state and the nation were criticised as immature, reverting to the perspectives and activities of 1992, prior to the transformations which began to take place later in that decade. There was some recognition that the case would shock a younger generation who had no personal memory of events such as this. There were also numerous explicit and indeed official defences of an absolute right to travel, on the grounds that Ireland is not a totalitarian state (Carolan, 2007b; Farren, 2007). The effort to force D to continue with her pregnancy, whose outcome was

[3] In fact, the Pro-Life Campaign spokesperson Berry Kiely claimed that the public attention the case received illustrated Ireland's democratic culture: "people in Ireland recognise the importance of discussing the issue openly unlike some countries where abortion is almost accepted without question" (Murphy, 2007).

doomed, was regularly characterised as "monstrous" and shameful (e.g. Morton, 2007; O'Kelly, 2007).

The sympathetic tone of much of the reporting was shaped by drawing on D herself as a primary definer of the issues at stake. Her moral and psychological struggle with the situation she faced was reported as an authoritative first-hand perspective on why some women may need or want abortions. Other women who had undergone similar experiences, particularly Deirdre de Barra, were included in the press coverage, such that the moral and political consensus among women who had experienced pregnancies with severe foetal malformation became authoritative in establishing what was at stake (de Barra, 2007; Reid, 2007; Vousden, 2007). This was a new feature of the reporting of abortion politics. Previous coverage had drawn primarily on religious and political groups and actors in establishing frames of meaning, rather than those women or girls at the centre of controversies (Smyth, 2005). The following discussion will explore those frames in this episode, and consider their implications for the broader dynamics of abortion access.

Suffering and Compassion

> It is a cruel twist that having already received the devastating news that her baby will die at birth or shortly afterwards, a pregnant woman should then have to face the reality that there is no help for her in this country. She can, of course, leave and take her problem elsewhere. We don't know anything about that, and we don't want to know. So long as the 6,000 remain anonymous and silent, the sand in which we collectively bury our heads remains comfortably undisturbed. Every so often, though, reality intrudes, invariably in the form of the stark human suffering involved in such cases (Raftery, 2007).

The moral character of the collectivity operated as an important frame in reporting on the case. For example, D's treatment was described as "heartbreaking", involving, as above, "stark human suffering", which involved her grieving for her baby while she was still pregnant (e.g. Sheehan, 2007). The HSE's response to her situation was characterised as "draconian", "unthinkable", "inhumane" and "immoral" (e.g. Muggivan, 2007). The occurrence of this case was perceived as illustrating the hypocrisy of the collective treatment of access to abortion,[4] described as "a Pontius Pilate approach [which allows us to] let England do our dirty work" (Devlin, 2007). As one writer put it, "… the country is effectively sticking its head in the sand and damaging the image of a developed, grown-up state we may now be trying to sell to the rest of the world" (Sullivan, 2007). The need to deal with the traumatic situation D was experiencing with compassion, by allowing her to travel for an abortion, was a very commonly expressed and much reported response to the case.

The comments of one prominent politician, Mary Harney, captured the way in which the case was dealt with, both legally and publicly. As she argued, this was simply a tragic situation, which called for a humane, sensible, compassionate and sensitive court decision (Healy and Donnellan, 2007). This is a very different approach to treating the case as raising important questions about justice and rights, more typical of previous debates. Harney argued that "the people" were not ready for anything more substantive than this, since, as she saw it, they had rejected the "very balanced" approach of 2002, which in fact would have removed suicide as acceptable grounds for abortion, along with foetal abnormality.

The centrality of the call for compassion itself became a matter of contestation both during and after the case. Both liberal and conservative voices in the media articulated their position as "compassionate". Those who would have preferred that D continue her pregnancy to term expressed concern about the moral impact allowing an abortion would have, both on D herself and on the wider society, in ways which reflect previous public debates. From this perspective, allowing an abortion, even in situations where a lethal abnormality has been detected, would involve a lack of compassion for the foetus, denying the dignity and value both of "unborn children" and of disabled persons. The Pro-Life Campaign justified its stance on the case in this way (e.g. Healy and Donnellan, 2007), as did, for instance, Padre Liam Hayes, in a letter to

---

[4] As Vincent Browne put it: "The scale of this hypocrisy remains a monument to contemporary Ireland. We are absolutely opposed to having abortion here but absolutely opposed to any inhibition on Irish people going abroad to have abortions; indeed, we facilitate them by way of as much information as they need to have an abortion" (Browne, 2007).

The Irish Times, where he claimed that allowing abortions in such cases amounted to a form of eugenics which seeks to eradicate disabled people from the population. As he put it, "Every person is a gift. It is not for us to decide who deserves to live or not" (Hayes, 2007).

This question concerning who should be the recipient of compassion was an important theme in much of the public debate over the case reported in the press. While some explicitly contested that this case involved allowing abortion on grounds of likely disability (Colgan, 2007), the issue of disability remained a central question of much of the reporting of the case. For example, coverage of the views of Declan Keane, Master of the National Maternity Hospital in Dublin, who favoured providing access to abortion in Ireland in cases such as D's involving foetal anencephaly, was framed in terms of whether abortions should be available when disability is likely. The prominence of this sort of concern is indicated by his defence that "… abortion in such cases would not lead to a free-for-all where women might abort babies when a scan showed they had a minor disability, such as a cleft palate" (Walsh, 2007).

While some, such as those quoted above, articulated absolutist perspectives on the issue, there was also reportage of more complex considerations of the interactions between compassion and rights. For example, *The Irish Times*, the newspaper of the liberal middle-classes, published a letter from a woman who had spent twenty years working with profoundly disabled children, who described her position on abortion as pro-choice, despite her moral difficulties with it. For O'Connor, the media coverage of the case was encouraging simplistic binary thinking in ways which were counterproductive for practicing and encouraging compassion. As she explained:

> There is no belittling the difficult journey, the tears, the exhaustion experienced by parents of a disabled child, but one thing is certain: they are not helped by a knee-jerk reaction in the media. Compassion and the freedom to act compassionately are what are needed here for the HSE, for the judiciary and above all for the young women [sic] and her family (O'Connor, 2007).

Indeed, the suffering D endured was reported as not disconnected from the activities of campaigners on both sides of the reproductive rights divide. For instance, the *Irish Independent* portrayed D and her mother as direct targets of anti-abortion and pro-choice activists during the High Court hearings, describing how individual activists sought to establish contact with them, somewhat unsuccessfully. The determination of activists to "pursue" the suffering figure at the centre of this case was directly commented on: "No court order, it seems, can place Miss D beyond the reach of those who wish to pursue her as she endures her horrific ordeal" (McDonald, 2007b). It would seem that political activists, in their pursuit of principle, were lacking in compassion. The ongoing significance of compassion, and the way in which it operated in this debate in contrast with the pursuit of rights, can be seen, for instance, in a reflective article by conservative journalist Kevin Myers, four months later, in an opinion piece directed at feminists entitled "You got your wish, sisters ... and it has killed off compassion" (Myers, 2007).

The primacy accorded to compassion as a key moral value in the debate involved downplaying questions of rights and responsibilities. While some supporters of the HSE's action in this case articulated their position in rights terms (see Cooney et al., 2007), arguing, for instance, that the right to life could not be compromised by judgements about the quality of that life, it tended not to dominate the reporting. There was some consideration of D's right to bodily integrity in the coverage, driven not least by D's own articulation of this frame, which was sympathetically reported on by commentators who supported her entitlement to end her pregnancy (McDonald, 2007c; O'Malley, 2007):

> An articulate and intelligent young woman, she is furious that women should feel under pressure to plead a mental illness [to avail of abortion under the X Case ruling] to exercise autonomy over their bodies. "Who are these people in the courtroom that can make my decision. It is my body. They (the HSE) don't own my body. I own my body. I was angry over the way the HSE were treating me. I was nothing," she said (*Irish Independent* 2007b).

The question of rights also emerged in criticisms of the HSE's action against D as an unjust criminalisation of those who were not old enough or wealthy enough to travel abroad to terminate fatally malformed pregnancies. *The Irish Times* reported that the HSE had funded seven abortions for women whose pregnancies were "incompatible with life outside the womb" during the previous year (Carolan et al., 2007). The language of the United Nations Declaration of Human Rights was used to condemn the action taken against D as a form of "cruel and unusual punishment" (Article 5). From this perspective, the right to travel should not be compromised by age or by being in temporary state care. For some, this question of D's rights over her pregnancy marked Ireland out as problematic in European terms, a view that was reflected in the arguments of some letter writers to the liberal *The Irish Times*: "[i]n any other European country her right to an abortion would be unquestioned in those circumstances" (Farren, 2007).

Overall, the politics of rights in the case of D was dominated by those sympathetic to her efforts, and critical of the actions of the HSE. While conservative perspectives on abortion access in cases of severe foetal malformation did articulate their position in rights terms, this was not a prominent feature of the reporting. Principled anti-abortion arguments remained in the background of much of the compassionate reporting, which constructed D's case, and others like it, as exceptions to the otherwise firm principle which defines abortion as immoral.

Families, Mothers, Fathers

The second frame shaping public debate on the *D* case can be described as a concern with the social status of the family and its gendered constituent identities. This was articulated in a number of ways, including the publication of expressions of solidarity from sympathetic mothers who had been through similar pregnancies.

For example, Deirdre de Barra wrote a letter to *The Irish Times* expressing her sympathy with D's situation, and criticising politicians and the HSE for their failures with respect to abortion access for cases of severe foetal abnormality (de Barra, 2007). She had unsuccessfully challenged Ireland's abortion laws through the European Court of Human Rights after being forced to travel abroad to end a much wanted third pregnancy because of a diagnosis of chromosomal abnormality "incompatible with life". She had spoken publicly of her experience during the 2002 abortion referendums, one of the few women to have done so, in making a case for limited access to abortion in Ireland in circumstances similar to her own (see e.g. Vousden, 2007). This public stance has established her as an important voice whose interventions in abortion politics will be reported, enabling her to set the terms of debate to some extent. Her letter, like many others, called for a humanitarian response to the situation, and its publication reinforced the primacy of women's experiences of ill-fated pregnancies in shaping the frame of the debate.

The support D received from her boyfriend, the father of the foetus, also played a relatively prominent role in framing the case in familial terms (see e.g. Carolan, 2007a). His support went from taking legal proceedings against the HSE on her behalf, to helping her come to terms with the diagnosis:

> When she first learned her unborn child would not survive outside the womb for more than a few days, Miss D said she could not bring herself to look at her stomach. However as her boyfriend would go to touch it, she would temporarily forget the awful prognosis and begin imagining her baby's christening (Heffernan, 2007).

The support from her boyfriend also included planning a family in the longer term. D was reported as saying, "[w]e just wanted to be set up as a family until we heard the news" (Maguire, 2007).

The press interest in the role of D's boyfriend can be understood as part of a larger media and public interest in active, committed fathering (Wall and Arnold, 2007). This angle made the story more newsworthy, as it provided a clear contrast with the more usual abortion stories involving fathers who are either sexual predators who victimise young girls, as in the *X* and *C* cases, or simply absent, as in popular narratives of crisis pregnancy (e.g. O'Brien, 1998).

D herself was characterised during the hearings as an admirable person who was struggling to overcome the conditions of her early family life. Her own father had been largely absent and her mother had become a heavy drinker. D had been taken into state care after "an incident" with her mother which had resulted in her trying to commit suicide (Carolan, 2007a). Nevertheless, her mother did ultimately support her daughter in her efforts to bring her pregnancy to an end. D was portrayed as "assertive", for instance, in the court room with her mother, in refusing to declare herself suicidal, in confronting the HSE and in asserting her right to bodily autonomy in a difficult context. The media presented her as a product of a broken family trying nevertheless to establish a family of her own (*Irish Independent*, 2007b).

While the relationship with D's mother was portrayed as difficult, it was nevertheless an important source of support for her: "'This was a chance to start my own family; to make things right and not make the mistakes like my mother,' she said, fondly stroking her mother's hand and acknowledging their difficult journey together" (*Irish Independent*, 2007b). This was unlike her relationship with her own absent father, who was reported as having left the family when she was three weeks old, and with whom she had no contact. So, while D was from a less than idyllic family, she nevertheless drew support from both her boyfriend and her mother, and was reported to be actively planning a family of her own in the longer term.

The significance of love in familial relationships, particularly those between mothers and their children, was an important aspect of this frame. Those who supported D's efforts to obtain an abortion referred to the idea that babies should be wanted or loved if they are to "have the life [they] deserve" (Pimm, 2007). This theme was also employed by anti-abortion perspectives. For example, conservative journalist Breda O'Brien argued that the predicted brevity of D's baby's life span could not justify an abortion: "You don't need a complete brain to give and receive love – all you need is a heart" (O'Brien, 2007).

D reportedly characterised herself not as a suicidal teenager, as in the *X* and *C* cases, but instead as a mother-in-waiting, who had welcomed her unplanned pregnancy despite the initial shock, and who was distraught at not being able to raise her first child. Her maternal disposition was underlined, as the *Irish Independent* reported that "[s]he would love to have a baby 'tomorrow' and plans to get pregnant next year" (McDonald, 2007c). This did not mean that she would forget her first pregnancy, but would incorporate it into her future family's narrative.[5]

---

[5] Mother of seven Collette O'Loughlin publicly recounted her efforts to do this also. She had given birth to a baby with anencephaly, who lived for three days: "Thomas was part

The first step in doing this was to bury her first baby in Ireland, following a medical rather than a surgical abortion in Britain. She reportedly chose a medical abortion because she perceived it as more humane, another sign of her maternal orientation towards her foetus:

> There were pictures of babies who had been aborted and I didn't like the way it was done. My baby deserves more than that [...] So I am going to be induced and I will get to hold my baby. I'll go through labour like a normal woman. If it breathes when it comes out, I will be able to get a birth certificate (*Irish Independent*, 2007b).

This desire to give her baby a public identity, through her hope that she could acquire a birth certificate, but also through her plans to buy "baby-doll" clothes in which to dress her infant, can again be interpreted as a motherly effort to do her best for her "unborn" in the most adverse of circumstances.

The press portrayal of D as a maternal figure extended to coverage of her plans for burying her baby's remains:

> [s]he wants to have the burial in Ireland so "I don't forget that it is my child. And to my next child, I want to tell my child it did have a brother or sister" (McDonald, 2007c).

The connections being made here between the national territory, burial and remembering are noteworthy. It would seem that having an abortion outside of the country carried a risk of forgetting or at least of distance. Bringing the remains back to Ireland for burial provided a way of ensuring that the baby's position in the family's narrative could be assured, not least because of its burial in a family grave. D reportedly said that "she does not want the baby to be interred in an 'angel plot'[6] but in a normal plot where, in the future, she too can be buried alongside her child" (Heffernan, 2007).

The close connections between nationhood, the family and abortion, established during previous episodes in the abortion conflict, are recon-

---

of our family and always will be. We have pictures of him in his little coffin, and it is there with all the other photos of the kids who are all grown up now" (Reid, 2007).

[6] This is the term given to burial plots for stillborn infants.

figured here in such a way as to allows a young woman and her aborted "unborn" to affirm their national and familial identification and belonging through a rite of mourning and burial on the national territory.[7] While this might appear to be a significant reconfiguration of the previously established links between the family and the nation which excluded abortion, D's self-identification as maternal and familial, despite her teenage status, and the public construction of the ending of her pregnancy not as a voluntary abortion but as a necessary early medical inducement of labour and birth, were central to this narration of a national, familial, public and sympathetic abortion story.

"Let Doctors Decide"

Finally, a medical and health-oriented frame was employed, again by those on both sides of the political divide on this issue. This had been an emerging frame in public debate on abortion since the late 1990s (Smyth, 2005). Medical language was prominent in debating the case, such as the characterisation of D's pregnancy as "incompatible with life" (de Barra 2007), or talk of the use of "futile effort to support a life by such extraordinary means" (Muggivan, 2007).

The emerging significance of a medical frame could also be seen, for example, in the reported complaints from the Masters of the Maternity Hospitals that medical opinion had been sidelined in the HSE's actions against X. Also, the possible psychological damage that D may have been exposed to, either by allowing her to abort her pregnancy (e.g. Corkery, 2007; Dillon, 2007) or by refusing to allow her to do so, was an important focus for discussing abortion access in terms of health and medicine. As the Chair of conservative organisation Family Solidarity argued:

> Instead of subjecting her and her unborn child to a serious medical procedure, upsetting her system and leaving her with both physical and mental sequels, it would be far better to allow matters to take their natural course, and to support her until her baby was born naturally and inevitably died. The aftermath of that

[7] Indeed, mourning has been described as a foundational narrative of Irishness. See Witoszek and Sheeran (1998).

> would be far less damaging to the health of Miss D (Ó'Halmháin, 2007).

The medical framing of the issues did not provide a route for avoiding moral debate, but instead depended on the deploying of a moral distinction between acceptable "therapeutic" abortions for health reasons on one hand, and unacceptable abortions for reasons of personal "choice" on the other (*Irish Independent*, 2007c; Raftery, 2007). While this was not entirely new, it became more prominent in debating the morality of abortion in cases of severe foetal malformation. This distinction was adopted by D herself, allowing her to confer a positive meaning on her experience (McDonald, 2007a), and consequently gained wider currency in the public debate. For example, the *Irish Independent* reported that "Miss D [...] gave birth to her unborn infant last week" (2007a). Thus, "abortion" continued to be castigated as an extreme form of immorality on a par with murder, while some support seemed to emerge for "induction" for women carrying doomed pregnancies, who were constructed as deserving of public sympathy and compassion. However, such a distinction required women ending pregnancies by "induction" to go through significant pain. An *Irish Independent* journalist characterised D's choice as follows: "[s]he will endure the pains of labour and the heartbreak of delivering a dead or dying baby" because of her concern to do her best for her baby: "[d]oing the right thing is paramount to Miss D" (2007b).

This distinction enabled the continued narrative of Ireland as an anti-abortion nation (Fletcher, 2001; Smyth, 2005), at least for viable pregnancies which women choose to end. In situations where medical opinion indicates that a pregnancy is not viable, a pragmatic and compassionate approach can be legitimately adopted to help alleviate physical suffering or trauma.

Conclusion: The Moral Grammar of Contemporary Abortion Politics

While the 2007 *D* case had the potential to re-interpret Article 40.3.3° to allow for legal abortion in cases of fatal or severe foetal abnormality (O'Loughlin and McDonald, 2007), this did not happen. What happened instead was a re-assertion of the existing constitutional position established in the *X* case, namely, that the right to travel cannot be compromised by the right to life of the "unborn".

This examination of press coverage of the issues raised by the *D* case suggests that contemporary abortion politics has taken on some new characteristics, while also reproducing some of the key dynamics of previous debates. In this episode, the frames of meaning were primarily defined, for the first time, by the voices of women who have experienced pregnancies involving severe foetal malformation. However, this did not result in a debate about the extent to which women might have decisional authority over their pregnancies. While D's assertion of entitlement to make decisions about her body was reported, a more general rights frame was not prominent. Instead, compassion was established as a dominant moral value, enabling exceptions to be made to the principled opposition to abortion articulated by key figures in this story, including D herself, along with Deirdre de Barra and others. The diagnosis of foetal anencephaly at the heart of this story facilitated the employment of a medical frame, which supported a broader moral distinction between abortion by choice and abortion (or inducement of labour) for therapeutic medical purposes when "incompatibility with life" is diagnosed.

Abortion continues to operate as an important marker of collective morality in the state. The daily national press coverage of the issues raised by the *D* case reflect ongoing tensions between claims to moral unity and certainty on the one hand, and gendered, aged, classed and racialised experiences of those apparent certainties on the other, as the state and its agents seek to balance competing duties of care to girls, young women, their "unborn" foetuses, and their familial aspirations.

Bibliography

Browne, V. (2007) "Abortion debate resurfaces" *The Irish Times* 2 May.

Carolan, M. (2007a) "Girl seeking abortion challenges HSE" *The Irish Times* 1 May.

Carolan, M. (2007b) "State lawyers insist Miss D does not require HSE permission or court order to travel" *The Irish Times* 8 May.

Carolan, M., Houston, M. and O'Brien, C. (2007) "AG tells court girl has right to travel for abortion" *The Irish Times* 2 May.

Colgan, F. (2007) "Letter to the Editor" *The Irish Times* 9 May.

Cooney, J., McDonald, D. and O'Loughlin, A. (2007) "No such thing as a right to abortion, says archbishop" *Irish Independent* 2 May.

Corkery, N. (2007) "Letter to the Editor" *The Irish Times* 7 May.

de Barra, D. (2007). "Letter to the Editor" *The Irish Times* 8 May.

Devlin, M. (2007) "I'm afraid we need another abortion referendum" *Irish Independent* 3 May.

Dillon, M. (2007) "Letter to the Editor" *The Irish Times* 7 May.

English, G. (2007) "Brave fight for a determined young girl" *Daily Mail* 10 May.

Farren, G. (2007) "Letter to the Editor" *The Irish Times* 2 May.

Ferree, M.M., Gamson, W.A., Gerhards, J. and Rucht, D. (2002) *Shaping abortion discourse: democracy and the public sphere in Germany and the United States* Cambridge: Cambridge University Press.

Fletcher, R. (2001) "Post-colonial fragments: Representations of abortion in Irish law and politics". 28 *Journal of Law and Society* 568.

Fletcher, R. (2007) "Reproducing Irishness: Race, Gender, and Abortion Law". 17 *Canadian Journal of Women and the Law* 365.

Harrington, J (2007) "Poland's anti-abortion policies: John Harrington explains how the European Court of Human Rights has been drawn into a political controversy over Polish abortion laws" *Morning Star* 1st June.

Harrington, J.A. (2005) "Citizenship and the Biopolitics of Post-Nationalist Ireland" 32 *Journal of Law and Society* 424.

Hayes, L. (2007) "Letter to the Editor" *The Irish Times* 4 May .

Healy, A. and Donnellan, E. (2007) "Abortion not election issue – Harney" *The Irish Times*.

Heffernan, B. (2007) "This baby is the world to me – I feel this is just a normal human being" *Irish Independent* 12 May.

Hennessy, M. and Smyth, J. (2007) "European court ruling in Poland abortion case could affect law here" *The Irish Times* 21 March.

Honneth, A. (1995) *The struggle for recognition: The moral grammar of social conflicts* Cambridge, Mass.: Polity Press.

Irish Independent (2007a) "Harrowing ordeal nearly destroyed me, says teenager" 22 May.

Irish Independent (2007b) "'The HSE doesn't own my body — I own it'" 12 May.

Irish Independent (2007c) "Indications that State is now ready to accept right to therapeutic abortions" 2 May.

Kuhling, C. and Keohane, K. (2007) *Cosmopolitan Ireland: Globalisation and Quality of Life* London: Pluto Press.

Maguire, S. (2007). "Miss D will have op 'within days'; she will buy clothes for baby and have christening; convinced her child is a little girl." *Sunday Mirror* 13 May.

McDonald, D. 2007a "Abortion should remain illegal says pregnant teen" *Irish Independent* 12 May.

McDonald, D. (2007b) "Even in the Four Courts, tormentors won't let her be" *Irish Independent*

McDonald, D. (2007c) "Miss D, My Story" *Irish Independent* 12 May.

Morton, O. (2007) "Letter to the Editor" *The Irish Times* 2 May.

Muggivan, J.J. (2007) "Letter to the Editor" *The Irish Times* 3 May.

Mullally, S. (2005) "Citizenship and family life in Ireland: Asking the question 'Who belongs'?" 25 *Legal Studies* 578.

Murphy, S. (2007) "Why did they drag the poor girl to court? Judge accuses HSE of putting Miss D through needless ordeal" *Daily Mail* 10 May.

Myers, K. (2007) "You got your wish, sisters ... and it has killed off compassion" *Irish Independent* 31 August.

O'Brien, B. (2007) "Consensus over disabled baby's fate a worry" *The Irish Times* 5 May.

O'Brien, E. (1998) *Down by the river* New York: Plume.

O'Connor, I. (2007) "Letter to the Editor" *The Irish Times* 9 May.

Ó'Halmháin, L. (2007) "Letter to the Editor" *The Irish Times* 7 May.

O'Hanlon, E. (2007) "Abortion debate cannot be reduced to a catchphrase about women''s rights" *Irish Independent* 25 March.

O'Kelly, E. (2007) "Shadow of men in black looms over a girl's fate" *Irish Independent* 6 May.

O'Loughlin, A. and McDonald, D. (2007) "Legal crisis fear as teen seeks UK abortion" *Irish Independent* 1 May.

O'Malley, T. (2007) "Previous D case may prove relevant to current abortion case" *The Irish Times* 3 May.

O'Sullivan, S. (2007a) *Contemporary Ireland: A Sociological Map* Dublin: University College Dublin Press.

O'Sullivan, S. (2007b) "Gender and the Workforce" in O'Sullivan, S. (ed.) *Contemporary Ireland: A Sociological Map* Dublin: University College Dublin Press.

Pimm, M. (2007) "Letter to the Editor" *The Irish Times* 3 May.

Raftery, M. (2007) "Burying our heads in the sand" *The Irish Times* 3 May.

Reid, L. (2007) "Let girl abort, says mother who bore the same pain" *Irish Independent* 3 May.

Sheehan, M. (2007) "Legal trauma almost over, Miss D set to face into her terrible grief" *Irish Independent* 6 May.

Smyth, L. (2005) *Abortion and Nation: The politics of reproduction in contemporary Ireland* Aldershot, Hants, England; Burlington, VT: Ashgate.

Sullivan, K. (2007) "Letter to the Editor" *Irish Independent* 8 May.

Tormey, A. (2007) "'Everyone with Eyes Can See the Problem': Moral Citizens and the Space of Irish Nationhood" 45 *International Migration* 69.

Vousden, P. (2007) "I was sent to a strange hospital in a foreign city just another Irish statistic; the haunting testimony of a woman who suffered the same ordeal as Miss D" *Daily Mail* 11 May.

Wall, G and Arnold, S (2007) "How involved is involved fathering? An exploration of the contemporary culture of fatherhood" 21 *Gender & Society* 508.

Walsh, A-M. (2007) "Dissenting patients opt to leave pro-abortion consultant's care" *Irish Independent* 11 May.

Witoszek, N. and Sheeran, P.F. (1998) *Talking to the Dead: A Study of Irish Funerary Traditions* Amsterdam-Atlanta GA: Rodopi.

Cases

A and B v Eastern Health Board and C [1998] 1 ILRM 464 (the *C* case).

Attorney General v X [1992] 1 IR 1 (the *X* case).

D v Ireland Application Number 26499/02.

3

"I DON'T WANT TO GET INTO THIS, IT'S TOO CONTROVERSIAL"

How Irish Women Politicians Conceptualise the Abortion Debate

Morgan Healey

On the twenty-fifth anniversary of the Eighth Amendment to the Irish Constitution, the relevance and repercussions of Article 40.3.3° remain a pertinent and pressing topic for discussion. Looking back over the last twenty-five years, economic prosperity and the shifting, fluid nature of "global capital" have signalled profound changes within the cultural and political landscape of the Irish nation. While such changes have helped to challenge certain aspects of what has historically been a conservative and traditional discourse in Ireland, the topic of abortion continues to be a controversial and emotive issue, and one I would argue speaks directly to the positioning of women in Irish society. Thus, as a feminist researcher I am continually interested in understanding the role the state plays in constructing notions of womanhood, motherhood and the nation around this issue; and more specifically how the intersection of such discourses affect the positions taken up (or resisted) by Irish women politicians.

As such, this essay takes largely from my just completed field work interviews[1] with 17 out of 35 (or about 50 per cent) currently serving women

[1] These were semi-structured interviews conducted over the period from February 2007 to December 2007. As there was a general election held in June of that year, not only did

TDs and Senators to examine some of the discursive frames utilized by this small population of women. Initially, the work suggests that Irish women politicians, as both women and legislators, express a range of positions and ambiguities when it comes to the topic of abortion. Therefore, I beg the question: How do Irish women politicians make sense of the discourse surrounding abortion and construct their own position on it?

In an effort to answer this question, this essay is broken down into three parts. First, the concept of "frames" as defined by Ferree et al. (2002) in their comparative study between abortion discourses in Germany and the United States is used to produce a framework for understanding some of the ways abortion discourse has been constructed in Ireland. Second, the pro-life and pro-choice frames combine within these women politician's positionality on the issue will be shown to create a third frame: "contextual sympathy". And finally, how the vitriolic, historic legacy of the abortion debate in Ireland persists in the memories of these women and would appear to silence or prohibit further discussion of the topic will be addressed.

Framing Irish Abortion Discourse

In the work of Ferree et al. (2002) on how certain frames of abortion became accepted and normalised public discourse in Germany and the United States, they define "frames" as "central organising ideas that provide coherence to a designated set of idea elements" (2002: 105). As I understand this concept, frames construct the parameters of the argument; they set up what language and meaning is included based on social/cultural standards and conversely what is deemed outside the bounds of such constructions. Consequently, there is never just one frame that dominates within public discourse, particularly when looking at such a controversial issue like abortion. In their research, Ferree et al. (2002) highlight eight such abortion frames.[2] While arguably elements of each

---

my pool of possible interviewees change but the interviews were divided between pre and post election. However while there was a shift in women politicians over my period of research only one woman that I interviewed before the election is no longer in politics; thus 16 out of 17 are currently serving in either house of the Oireachtas.

[2] Ferree et al. (2002: 107-8) further separate these eight frames into two categories: rights and other frames. Under the rights heading there is foetal life (anti-abortion direction),

can be seen to varying degrees in the Irish context, for my own simplifying purposes just two will be used here: the pro-life (encompassing foetal rights and social morality) frame and the limited[3] pro-choice (women's rights and bodily integrity) frame. Consequently, as public opinion has shifted away from the absolutes of the debate, it will be argued that a third frame has emerged in the positionality of Irish women politicians; one which situates the majority in this "grey" area in between the two. This is referred in this chapter as the "contextual sympathy" frame.

Critically, in seeking to understand the current context for abortion in Ireland, there will be a brief exploration as to how these first two frames have been constructed and normalised. Historically, there have been a number of social/cultural and political factors in Ireland that have influenced the dominance of an Irish pro-life frame. As Oaks (1999, 2002), Smyth (1998, 2002, 2005) and Martin (2000) have argued in their respective works on the Irish abortion debate, in constructing a pro-life, pro-foetus stance in moments of contestation over abortion, what continually gets reaffirmed is a particular notion of an "authentic" Irish identity brought on by a post-colonial past. This pro-life mentality has conventionally sought to construct the Irish identity as traditional, rural and Catholic; juxtaposed against notions of a liberal, Protestant and British coloniser (Oaks, 2002: 10). Abortion was seen as eroding an exceptional form of Irish Catholic morality (under the guise of the absolute protection of the "unborn") as liberalising/global forces have begun to take hold in Ireland. Thus, these external pressures helped to construct abortion politics in Ireland as the site for negotiating the Irish national identity through the control of women's bodies and reproduction.

---

balancing (neutral direction), women's rights (pro-abortion direction) and individual and state (pro direction). The other frames include – social morality (anti-abortion direction), effects on society (neutral direction), pragmatic consequences (pro-abortion direction) and social justice (pro-direction). The authors cite that within each frame one can see elements of what they characterise as the anti, pro and neutral positioning but that usually one idea dominates over the others; thus next to each category is the predominate direction of the frame.

[3] I use the term limited pro-choice because, up until recently, particularly with regard to public discourse, the advocates of pro-choice have done so in constrained and specific ways, usually arguing for reform and legislation within the confines of the judgment in the *X* case (1992).

As a result of this emphasis on Catholic morality and the "sanctity of life" in Irish abortion discourse, the pro-life frame has had a profound and lasting affect on how people conceptualise and talk about the issue. This is exemplified in the 1983 Amendment which, as Smyth argues, came to be constructed by establishing three key elements: the association between colonised nationhood and the image of the vulnerable male foetus; equating the anti-amendment campaign with the destruction of the nation through their perpetuation of modernity and feminism; and then juxtaposing that position with an association of the anti-abortion campaign with the heroic republican tradition (Smyth, 2005: 71). Thus, in Ireland the abortion debate is not merely about balancing the rights of the pregnant woman with that of her foetus, but is a site of continued contestation over a particular definition of Irish identity.

While the pro-life frame has traditionally and largely defined the language and direction of the debate in Ireland, the limited pro-choice frame has had moments of success in trying to instantiate women's bodily integrity and responsible decision-making into the abortion equation. As *Attorney General v X* (1992) highlighted, abortion was not as black or white as the pro-life contingent had sought to frame it – either between those who valued all life and "baby killers". Exemplifying not only moments when extenuating circumstances had to be taken into consideration, but also the possibility of women being interned within the nation-state, what became apparent to many were the unexamined repercussions of the Eighth Amendment. As Fletcher (2001) claims, the *X* case signalled an important change in the abortion law discourse from one which "constructed abortion as an absolute threat to Irish cultural values, to recognising abortion as a medical service for which women can travel to England" (2001: 584). Thus, while not completely equalising the predominance of one frame over another, the *X* case did allow for greater and broader construction of who was affected by such laws and what was at stake in decisions relating to crisis pregnancies.

In tangent with these socio-cultural factors that have influenced the predominance of one abortion frame over the other, there are also political factors that have helped to perpetuate such beliefs. Historically, unlike other European countries, Ireland has not had a strong left-right distinction in their political parties or institutions. As Fahey, Hayes and

Sinnott (2005) explain, this weakness dates back to the formation of the Republic in the early twentieth century:

> Given the overwhelming agrarian nature of the southern economy the material basis for any owner-worker cleavage in the newly independent Irish Free State was extremely weak. Moreover, the dominance of an ideologically conservative Catholic Church made the political climate particularly inhospitable to the politics of the left (Fahey, Hayes and Sinnott, 2005: 13).

Subsequently, the new Irish parties were divided more along the cleavages produced by the Pro- and Anti-Treaty sides, and subsequently the partitioning of Ireland, than along any strong socialist/capitalist distinctions. Thus, unlike other countries where abortion and other liberal social changes have been pushed and advocated for by left-wing parties, there has been no such phenomenon here in Ireland. Consequently, this has perpetuated not only the more conservative pro-life frame amongst the legislators because of the traditional nature of the two centre parties, but has meant that left parties, like Irish Labour, are marginal and not in positions to promote a more liberal agenda.

With that said, however, as Irish culture interacts and intersects to a greater degree with global influences and capital, these frames have begun to shift and become more multifaceted. The debate is no longer defined in absolutes and as recent opinion polls[4] suggest, the Irish acceptance of abortion is contextual and complex. As will be highlighted in the next section, Irish women politicians' positioning on the issue can not simply be referenced by the historical pro-life frame. As I have argued, traditionally the constraints of the abortion discourse have been set, particularly for women politicians, as a choice between one side or the other. Yet, as I will show, their arguments draw on elements of both frames, carving out a space for themselves in the grey areas in between the two. It is these internal battles of trying to make sense of the issue

---

[4] See the 2007 TNS mrbi poll commissioned by the DHR, on behalf of the Safe and Legal (in Ireland) Abortion Rights Campaign. This shows that the majority of people favour making limited abortion services available in Ireland in most situations, except in cases when a "woman decides it is in her best interests" (only 43 per cent agreed and 51 per cent disagreed with this position).

while also not wanting to alienate an electorate that I will focus on in the next section.

The Positioning of Irish Women Politicians on Abortion

Having briefly set the scene and frames for the abortion debate here in Ireland, the next issue to be addressed is how women politicians construct their own positionality on the debate and how they utilise both elements of the pro-life and limited pro-choice frames to create this "contextual sympathy"[5] frame. A sample of quotes from the women will be set out, highlighting the various ways they combine these two initial frames and then move onto one particular example, that for me, really exemplified the "contextual sympathy" frame.

Many of the women, when asked how they would characterise the abortion debate today, described the cultural changes that have occurred in Ireland over the last twenty years. Particularly, they cited the lessening of a Catholic hegemony and its relationship with the state as having altered an absolute pro-life frame. And while many of them still asserted that they would be fairly conservative on the issue and did not support a situation where there would be "abortion on demand" in Ireland; there was an acknowledgement of extenuating circumstances, the need for compassion and a woman's right to bodily integrity. Thus, listening to each woman speak, I got a sense that not only were they cautious in their construction of their argument, but in many instances while still using the framework of the pro-life campaign their arguments were far more nuanced and employed some pro-choice language surrounding women's autonomy and bodily integrity.

Politician One said:

> You know I would want to have a humane attitude to abortion whereby there would be certain circumstances in which it would be allowed but I wouldn't want abortion on demand either, you

---

[5] While not wanting to spend too much time on this notion of "sympathy", I also do not wish to leave it undefined or uninterrogated. In this context, I take from Sandra Bartky's (1997) use of Max Scheler's term "*Mitgefuhl*" or "feeling-with". Thus defined, sympathy both allows for the recognition and feeling of someone else's experiences, while, at the same time, maintaining the distinction between the one who feels and the one who feels-with.

> know. And maybe that's a product of just, you know, living in Ireland but I'd say the sort of lobby that would look for abortion on demand, you know, at a relatively early stage of the pregnancy would be very small in Ireland I'd say.

She then went on to clarify her position a bit more stating:

> It is so specifically about a woman's body. And even though obviously men are involved in the decision making process I would … I mean it is … I think even though a man's positioning maybe as the father of the potential child has to be a big part of the decision I think ultimately it has to be a woman's decision.

The argument here centres on a humane and sympathetic approach to abortion, where women's decision-making is paramount to the debate, while simultaneously sliding back into the pro-life language of abortion on demand, citing this as a product of living in Ireland. Interestingly, and this was a comment made by several other women, she puts the onus back onto the general public, stating that she believed that abortion on demand would only be supported by a small percentage of Irish people. The assumption here appears to be that this notion of "abortion on demand" is antithetical to Irish cultural values and that her disavowal of it is in line with the general public.

Similarly, another woman stated:

> I must say now just to be clear about this I mean I am not in favour of abortion on demand and I never have been. As I said I think that debate in Ireland is evolving. I think you know the whole issue of women having personal choices which they make and the whole issue of them being advised and being counselled is the really important issue and the core point. And I certainly don't … I think the opinion in Ireland is changing but I think certainly a lot of women in Ireland of my age would probably be conservative enough on the issue. For instance I don't at all agree with late abortion. I think I would be absolutely opposed to it. So just to be clear about that (Woman Politician Two).

Echoing the previous speaker, this woman also argues for women's personal choice on the issue of abortion while pointedly making sure that I knew exactly her position on the topic: against abortion on demand. However, while in the last example the woman centred her argument on women's decision-making, this politician widens the argument by emphasising the need for counselling and advice in crisis pregnancy. She also makes reference to a generational shift on the issue, believing her age group (40 and above) would be fairly conservative while the opinion of younger people is evolving.

Yet another woman positions herself again using the definitive statement of not being an advocate of "abortion on demand" while recognising the need to provide abortion services here in Ireland in certain circumstances and allowing women the right of choice:

> But I mean I don't want to sound like somebody who's looking for abortion on demand because I'm not. But I do think we need to recognize that medical circumstances and other circumstances whatever … that I firmly believe in a woman's right to choose and that we should be providing services. And you know limit them out but I'd love an honest debate about it. And we never ever get that. I do think there is a slight shift in it's not as militant or as reactionary as it used to be (Woman Politician Three).

While another politician specifically stated that she would consider herself to be pro-choice:

> Women did not have for a long time the right to say, "Well look it's my body and what I want to do you know" … Now having said that, I'm not necessarily pro-abortion but I would be pro-choice because you know again looking at the situation, looking at what has happened and making a reasoned judgment based on that. I think in the past women were condemned to have babies you know. To live life a certain way (Woman Politician Four).

Interestingly, this woman politician makes the distinction between being pro-abortion and pro-choice (getting away from the term abortion on demand). Having seen the repercussions for women of forced motherhood, she believes that her position on the issue and the basis for her argument centres on reason and rationality. She believes that women should have the means of deciding what they do or do not do with their bodies as otherwise, as she goes onto argue, larger social problems and situations are created.

However, while some women have obviously been influenced by the limited pro-choice frame, exemplified in the examples stated, others clearly positioned themselves within a more pro-life frame. One woman was torn between being opposed to abortion completely and acknowledging that horrible circumstances do happen.

> There would be views on it that in certain circumstances should we have abortion. And we can think of rape or incest…but if you open that door are you opening the door for other abortions? And how do you describe circumstances … I don't know. I can't give an answer to that. I have very strong views myself that in certain circumstances yet I'm very pro-life. And I'd want to save both mother and child is my philosophy. It's a hard one, isn't it? (Woman Politician Five).

This woman specifically states her position as pro-life and utilises the argument of opening up the flood gates to all abortions if you allow for it in particular situations. Similarly, instead of talking about the pregnant woman she uses the term mother, which as Ferree et al. (2002: 277) have noted is indicative of a pro-natalist stance of equating pregnancy with motherhood and negating the individual woman from the equation. However, it is also apparent that she is not completely comfortable with any absolute framing of the issue, citing the difficulty of making these decisions when looking at circumstances of rape and incest.

Another woman, again justifying her position as being in synch with that of the general public, claimed that Ireland is still a rather traditional society and assumedly not ready for a more liberal system like the British:

> I don't support a situation where we'd have abortion on demand for example and I wouldn't be comfortable with that. We currently operate under the *X* case from 1990 which basically allows women freedom to access information and freedom to travel. And I don't believe that … I mean we've had two referenda on abortion since then and the majority of the people didn't want a liberalisation of abortion and I don't think if we had a referendum in the morning

> that the result would be any different. But we are kind of a traditional society in that regard (Woman Politician Six).

Particularly, this woman's position not only argues for the continued construction of Ireland as a traditional society and again against any notion of abortion on demand; but as one of the younger women politicians she seemingly negates the generational perspective of the older woman politician mentioned earlier. In other words, conservatism does not appear to be age dependent.

What I find particularly surprising about this quote is her general lack of knowledge of the debate. Not only does she get the year wrong for the *X* case but she also cites the rejection of the last two referenda as evidence of the public being against a liberalisation of abortion. However, the issues involved in the 1992 and 2002 referenda had nothing to do with advocating for a liberalisation of the abortion system here in Ireland, but specifically dealt with the public's rejection of the then government's desire to role back the ruling in the *X* case and to prevent the use of suicide as an argument for abortion. Thus, while she uses the public as a means of both expressing perhaps her own traditional, pro-life views on the topic and rejecting modernising influences on the debate, her use of the last two referenda as proof of a continued Irish conservatism strikes me as a lack of awareness of the debate in general.

In a similar pro-life frame, another woman uses very clear language to articulate her stance by alluding to the need to preserve life and the rights of the foetus:

> I personally wouldn't be in favour of abortion. Once you have conceived … I would be in favour of course of plenty of contraception and proper sex education for children. But once you conceive another person comes into it and you don't have the freedom to destroy that person cause there is another person. And I don't think your womb is just a place that you can empty at will if there is something in it (Woman Politician Seven).

She argues for the personhood of the foetus and that once conception has occurred, a woman looses the freedom to make life and death decisions for that other person. For this woman politician, foetal rights are paramount and women should not have the right to a termination.

Yet not all of the women expressly positioned themselves, preferring to speak more generally about the debate. One woman expressly used the term "grey" to define the issue. Seeming to waiver back and forth and unwilling or unable to state her own positioning on the topic, she again uses the electorate as a means of side-stepping the issue:

> It's a bit grey. Very much an Irish solution to an Irish problem, but I don't think with the electorate that we have that we are going to change it. And I think the current government recognises that. And so many people go to England for an abortion everyday. And we can't have it here but I think it's … realistically you're not going to change that in the immediate … by referendum and any time you tinker with the Constitution you've ended up in more trouble than you started out and obviously … I think it's … I won't be left alone. Personally, I'm not sure if it should be a legislative issue. I think that's … well the Supreme Court should be legislated … that judgment … I don't think the public are ready for it (Woman Politician Eight).

In this context, I think there are several pertinent points to be made on how she constructs the issue. In the first instance, she signals out the hypocrisy of the situation in Ireland and recognises that England has become a safety net for Irish women seeking abortions. Secondly, she cites the problem of dealing with such an issue constitutionally. I presume that her reference to troubles caused by tinkering with the constitution is an allusion to the Eighth Amendment and the unforeseen consequences of it; arguably referring to it in the negative. And thirdly, when she seems unable to directly state her own position on it she falls back on the public; arguing, like many of the women, that people are not ready for the "substantive" issue to be dealt with.

Thus, from the quotes I have highlighted so far one can see that these women politicians utilise the two frames to express a range of opinions on the topic; more specifically, they highlight the acceptance of abortion as contextual, dependent on the circumstances. Some cover issues regarding the competing rights of foetus and mother; others focused on their position being in line with the feelings of the Irish public and that there was little support for a liberalisation of abortion, while some framed it in terms of personal choice. And while there were varying degrees of acceptance on the issue, few argued in the extreme in one direction or the other.

As a final example of this notion of a "grey" area or "contextual sympathy" frame, I will highlight what I believe was a rather interesting and telling interview and one which expressly uses the notion of sympathy. Initially, the politician was hesitant to discuss the issue of abortion with me. She expressed her position very early on as conservative, sitting on the fence but yet willing to listen to both sides of the argument. However, as we began to discuss the issue more, the intersectionality of frames and subsequently the complexity of her thoughts on the topic began to unfold:

> So I'd have to say I'm sitting on the fence but coming down more with my conservative half than I would be with a liberal half. But my ears aren't closed and I'll sit on the fence and if I hear things that will sway me one way or the another that's how I will be going. And I think that's a good position.

Contextually, she goes on to cite the role that the Catholic Church has played in the traditional framing of conservative abortion politics in Irish society and the affect this has had on the general framing of the topic:

> But Ireland in that context … no we're a predominately Catholic country. You know religion wouldn't be too far away from any of our families … not too long ago that church and state were one. The church is loosening its grip on the State and I'd say in generations to come they might be better equipped to have the debate that we can't have at the moment. So who knows, maybe ten, fifteen, twenty years time that debate would come in. But the only thing I'd say to you is I don't know … I don't care what age I would be I wouldn't like to see abortion on demand in Ireland.

Similar to most of the other women's statements, this politician would not be an advocate of "abortion on demand" here in Ireland. Interestingly, she lends support to the argument that the close relationship between the Church and state has restricted how abortion has been constructed here; and she believes that as this tradition wanes there will be more space for a wider debate.

Consequently, this restricted, traditional pro-life frame of the debate has meant that the Irish have had to "export" abortion to England. She argues that this has created a stigma around the issue and a lack of accessible post-abortion medical resources for Irish women. Compassion and sympathy seems to be a driving force in her narrative, stating that she felt for the women who have to make that journey and believed the debate should listen more to the women who have had abortions:

> I would and maybe we should listen to that big group of people. But they're not the people who are going to come forward because there is a stigma. And you know they are all of our daughters. You know, we're all equal in the eye of the State and yet somebody has to go and leave the country to have something like a termination where you can get information and we have the right to travel. And you must go outside and then it opens the whole debate that if something goes wrong for that woman in the UK [sic] and she comes back medically unwell you know you go a long way in Ireland to get a sympathetic doctor who's going to take over her care. And again you know I'd have … I'd have issues you know maybe I'm saying too much now but I really would have issues around that. I just think that's, from a woman's point of view, that's very unfair. If the shoe was on the other foot and it was a man I'd still be saying the same kind of things. And I would be big enough to say I'll sit down and listen to that woman in the same way I'd sit down and listen to the woman that's carrying the very, medically deformed baby. And you have the medical profession saying the baby isn't going to live. You know should we say let there be pro-choice in those situations and let the woman decide. And, you know, if there was pro-choice that takes away the stigma and I doubt we would have … that the flood gates would open and we would have that many women who would be opting because nobody, no woman makes that … and I don't care what age you are, would make the call too lightly to go and have an abortion. And I think, you know, we should also look at the day when the woman has to do that, that she has somebody to call and come and sit with her and help her in a way and say, "Look, I'm here with you" (Woman Politician Nine).

I chose this particularly long quote because in listening to this woman talk I could almost see her trying to verbalise all the complexities that the topic of abortion brings up. In the first two initial quotes she does not want to appear to go too far in either direction, pro-life or pro-choice. But moving into this last part, she brings up many of the issues that have been left unresolved in the debate here in Ireland.

Particularly, she emphasises the stigma that persists in Ireland for the women who have had abortions outside the country and the injustice they face by not necessarily having access to post-abortion medical treatment. She then moves onto debate the topic of medically deformed foetuses that will not live outside the womb, stating that perhaps there should be choice in those situations. And finally, she negates the belief that choice would open up the floodgates of women running for an abortion, stressing that no woman makes that decision lightly. While not seeking to question her own positionality on the issue as being fairly conservative, I would argue that the compassionate language she uses to describe the debate offers an excellent example of how these two frames have coalesced to form a "contextual sympathy" frame on the topic.

Arguably, what became apparent to me through this research process is that Irish women politicians do not simply position themselves either within the pro-life or limited pro-choice frame. Rather, these women offer a more nuanced and complex argument for their individual positioning. The contested nature of the debate and more specifically the post-colonial insistence on an "authentic" Irish identity constructed through pro-natalist policies continues to hold sway for many of the women. Historically, this frame has been the dominant one and the language that these women use is very much in keeping with that, particularly this notion of "abortion on demand". Yet more saliently, there would also appear to be an increase in the relevance and use of pro-choice terminology regarding women and choices surrounding their bodies. Even within their own narratives, these women offer continuities and discontinuities between how they frame the debate, their personal beliefs and public opinion. Importantly, most of these women did not offer a polarised view on the matter, insisting that they remain in these "grey" areas in between the two.

Silences: Why Irish Women Politicians are Not Vocal on Abortion

In this last section the issue of why these women politicians, as public representatives and in positions of power, do not vocalise or lead on the topic, will be asked. As women and legislators there seems to be a veritable silence on the issue of abortion. These silences will be explained both through the historical memory of previous, bitter debates and the affect this has had on these politicians; and also on a more theoretical level concerning who gets to speak in the public, political arena.

As I progressed through my interviews, what came to the fore time and again was just how previous acrimonious debates around abortion continue to be relevant and hold sway with many of the women currently serving in national politics. The vitriolic and often malicious campaigns of 1983, 1992, 1995 and 2001 has served to not only silence this segment of the population dependent upon electoral support to maintain their jobs; but has also created a palpable atmosphere of fear and intimidation.

In one instance a woman politician described how specifically politicians had been targeted in previous campaigns and argued that very few people want to bring that kind of abuse on themselves:

> I think if you are a rural TD you have a real fear of being targeted. Yeah, I mean women and men were targeted. There are a few Labour politicians who had Youth Defence camped on their gardens of their homes and nobody wants to bring that on themselves. I mean the 1995, and this was just around information, this wasn't about legalising abortion, this was just trying to make information more available … Youth Defence people camped on people's gardens and it has a very intimidating affect on anybody else wanting to speak out. So I don't blame people for not wanting to (Woman Politician Ten).

Sentiments like this were echoed throughout the interviews with women continuously remembering and describing these debates as both nasty and emotive. Arguably as a consequence of this, they expressed trepidation at discussing the topic with me in general and did not feel that at the moment there was a space within the Oireachtas for a debate on the matter.

> I think people are quite frightened about it. They've had a couple of very bad abortion referendums that have gone all over the place; created havoc (Woman Politician Eleven).

> I'm even afraid talking about it. That's how divided this whole thing is. It's a very emotive issue (Woman Politician Nine).

> And you know I'd go so far as to say you know that there is blood spilt every time you mention these kinds of topics (Woman Politician Twelve).

> I think constrained is nearly the way I'd say it; in one way in so far as an ostrich with its head in the sand. It is the quintessential Irish solution to an Irish problem (Woman Politician Three).

One woman actually refused to discuss the topic at all. When I asked her how she would characterise the way reproductive rights have been dealt with in Ireland. She responded with:

> I don't really want to get into this. It's too controversial. I have to be so careful about this. It's a very emotive issue. It's extremely emotive. I have very strong views. I don't really want to talk about it.... I just have such bad memories of the abortion referendum. It was just so divisive and so ... that's why I don't want to talk about it because like it's still not sorted out (Woman Politician Thirteen).

Another woman expressed how her own involvement in the anti-Amendment campaign of 1983 and the nasty nature of that debate as having put her off the topic:

> I think it's very hard to be honest about it, particularly if you are trying to win votes and you know keep your seat. It's very hard to be honest about it, you know. And it's hard to be even believed if you are being honest. People think you have a further agenda either on one side or the other. And I suppose ... I mean it's one of those things that has actually emotionally affected me, you know; cause I was involved in 1983. That was the big one, you know. That was the really painful one where we were really abused, you know.... Maybe I'm not even that objective about it. But it's one

> that people are just not … don't … can't … very few people can talk very straight forwardly about it (Woman Politician One).

I think interestingly this historical memory of these debates continues to haunt these women politicians; not only do they hesitate to broach the topic in the Oireachtas, but the language that they use to describe the events is evocative. Words like *havoc*, *being afraid*, *emotive*, *divisive*, *bad memories* and *lack of objectivity* seem to reflect and reinforce a discourse around the topic of abortion that is defeatist from the start and leaves little room for, as one woman said, straight-forward and honest debate. Even more so, one believed that blood was spilled every time the topic was brought up. And another said that it was like she was fighting a guerrilla war inside the walls of the Dáil every time abortion was brought onto the political agenda. Thus, the imagery that is used by some of these women is both extreme and powerful. I was left with the impression that this is not a topic that many women felt safe discussing and that personally engaging with the topic could be political suicide.

However, I would also argue that more than just bad memories keep these women from specifically speaking out and positioning themselves on the issue. Aside from the fear of possibly alienating an electorate, who most women politicians have constructed as being opposed to the liberalisation of abortion in Ireland, are more theoretical possibilities for their silence.

Returning again to Ferree et al. (2002), they use the concept of "gendered subtexts" to discussion types of participation in the public sphere:

> Public and private spheres have a gendered subtext in which the public realm is a male sphere and its norms and practices reflect this in subtle (and often not so subtle) ways to exclude the 'feminine' modes of participation. The norms and practices governing policy discourse privileges certain forms of presentation over others, and thus selectively disempowers certain categories of speaker (2002: 225).

Like feminist criticisms of the gendered nature of political theory and practice, the gendered subtext of the Irish public discourse (not each woman's positionality) on abortion might still only privilege a certain pro-family, pro-foetus frame and further silences women who have had abortions and particular to this research, the women politicians who do not construct their argument singularly within this pro-life frame.

Similarly, because the Oireachtas is still very much dominated by men and their norms and modes of representation, women politicians may feel that they must conform to certain masculine speech acts that insist on reasonability and disembodied rationality. Young (1996), in her work on institutional forms and styles of deliberation, argues that the norm in parliamentary and judicial structures privileges speech that is "dispassionate" and "disembodied":

> They tend to presuppose an opposition between mind and body, reason and emotion. They tend falsely to identify objectivity with calm and absence of emotional expression (Young, 1996: 124).

Again echoing feminist critics of Cartesian dualisms that have equated men with mind and reason and women with body and emotion, to assert certain ways of deliberating over others might silence those that are not in a dominant position (i.e. women).

Thus, if Young is correct in her assessment that often norms of deliberation "operate as forms of power that silence or devalue the speech of some people", then perhaps woman politicians, and it is not intended to reduce them to a homogenous category, might be excluded from articulating their position on abortion within the institutional structures of the Oireachtas, which favour "norms of assertiveness, combativeness and speaking by the contest rules" (Young, 1996: 124). This would be particularly salient on the topic of abortion and the argument made here is that women politicians use the frame of "contextual sympathy" to articulate their positionality. Arguments that insist on instantiating women's bodies and the use of emotive, sympathetic language could be rendered unintelligible within the norms of speech in the Oireachtas. As such, for women politicians, they may be silenced by such rules of intelligibility or could choose to remain silent on the issue instead of having to transcend their subjective beliefs on the matter in order to make objective claims.

It is argued that while women politicians simultaneously experience silencing by a male institution which designates "appropriate" speech acts within the Oireachtas, they also might exercise their own agency and choose to silence themselves on the topic. If this simultaneity of silencing/silence occurs, then I believe this offers hope for these women politicians to speak out in the future. While not saying that the dominant, male form of the Oireachtas will change, these women who choose not to speak now might have the chance to exercise their agency as the arguments around abortion shift and evolve. As public opinion appears to allow for greater openness in addressing the women who experience crisis pregnancies, the opening of the debate and the change in discourse could arguably allow for women politicians to express themselves to a greater extent in public arena.

Conclusion

Irish women politician's positionality on the topic of abortion arguably operates within the "grey" area between the two frames of pro-life and limited pro-choice; what I have referred to as the "contextual sympathy" frame. This middle ground that the women politicians have constructed for themselves is far more complex and nuanced than either being on one side of the spectrum or the other. Many seem to utilise elements of both the traditional discourses around the sanctity of life and the remaining presence of a Catholic morality, while at the same time acknowledging that extenuating circumstances occur and there is a need for compassion and women's bodily integrity.

However, while their positionalities are not absolute and allow for greater variability on the topic, there is still a sense of fear and definite silence from this contingent of women. It is argued that understanding Irish women politician's positionality on this debate is important because, theoretically, as national representatives they are in positions to effect change one way or the other. And as a feminist dedicated to seeing such changes occur with respect to the position of women in Irish society, this writer firmly believes that examining how Irish women politicians construct the abortion debate themselves is necessary and could lead to greater change in the future.

Thus while on a basic level many women politicians are afraid to lead on the issue and in some instances even to talk about it because of the historically vitriolic and personal tone of the debate; on another, more theoretical level, their silence is also structured by deeper institutional barriers. As Ferree et al. (2002) and Young (1996) have argued, women politicians' silences could be indicative of their gendered, minority status in a field historically dominated by men and masculine norms. Pushing this narrative further, a constant tension between being silenced and choosing to silence oneself could theoretically be experienced by such women. If this is the case, then such a tension could be productive and a hopeful point of intervention. Choice signals some level of agency, and while many women politicians have to negotiate the masculine rules of national politics, there might be room within the expanding and shifting abortion discourse to allow for and make intelligible such contextualised sympathy. As one woman politician said the debate is evolving and arguably in a way that putatively parallels the positionality of Irish women politicians as expressed above. Hopefully, with such changes come new ways of speaking about abortion in Ireland and subsequently a greater opportunity for women politicians to be given the space and acceptability to frame the argument in their own language.

Bibliography

Bartky, S.L. (1997) "Sympathy and solidarity: On a tightrope with Scheler" in: Tietjens-Meyers, D. (ed.) *Feminists Rethink the Self* Boulder, CO: Westview Press.

Benhabib, S. (ed.) (1996) *Democracy and Difference* Princeton, NJ: Princeton University Press.

Fahey, T., Hayes, B. and Sinnott, R. (2005) *Conflict and Consensus* Dublin: Institute of Public Administration.

Ferree, M.M., Gamson, W.A., Gerhards, J. and Rucht, D. (2002) *Shaping Abortion Discourse: Democracy and the Public Sphere in Germany and the United States* Cambridge: Cambridge University Press.

Fletcher, R. (2001) "Post-Colonial Fragments: Representations of Abortion in Irish Law and Politics" 28(4) *Journal of Law and Society* 568.

Martin, A. (2000) "Death of a Nation: Transnationalism, Bodies and Abortion in Late Twentieth Century Ireland" in Mayer T. (ed.) *Gender Ironies of Nationalism: Sexing the Nation* London and New York: Routledge.

Mayer, T. (ed.) (2000) *Gender Ironies of Nationalism: Sexing the Nation* London and New York: Routledge.

Morgan, L.M. and Michaels, M.W. (eds.) (2000) *Fetal Subjects, Feminist Positions* Philadelphia: University of Pennsylvania Press.

Oaks, L. (1999) "Irish Trans/national Politics and Locating Fetuses" in: Morgan, L.M. and Michaels, M.W. (eds.) *Fetal Subjects, Feminist Positions* Philadelphia: University of Pennsylvania Press.

Oaks, L. (2002) "'Abortion is part of the Irish experience, it is part of what we are': The transformation of public discourses on Irish abortion policy". 25(3) *Women's Studies International Forum* 315.

Smyth, L. (1998) "Narratives of Irishness and the Problem of Abortion: The X Case 1992" 60 *Feminist Review* 61.

Smyth, L. (2002) "Feminism and abortion politics: Choice, rights and reproductive freedom" 25(3) *Women's Studies International Forum* 335.

Smyth, L. (2005) *Abortion and the Nation: The Politics of Reproduction in Contemporary Ireland* Hants, UK and Burlington, VT: Ashgate.

Tietjens-Meyers, D. (ed.) (1997) *Feminists Rethink the Self* Boulder, CO: Westview Press.

TNS/mrbi poll (June 2007) "Abortion: A Survey of Public Opinion" Commissioned by DHR, on behalf of the Safe and Legal (in Ireland) Abortion Rights Campaign.

Young, I.M. (1996) "Communication and the Other: Beyond Deliberative Democracy" in: Benhabib, S. (ed.) *Democracy and Difference* Princeton, NJ: Princeton University Press.

Part Two

THE MATERNAL–FOETAL CONFLICT

4

FOETAL PERSONHOOD IN COMPARATIVE PERSPECTIVE

Dr Neville Cox

Introduction

The question of the value which the law should attach to foetal life and the consequent level of protection that it should provide for it is a notoriously unanswerable one.[1] This is for two reasons: first, the moral if not the physical status of unborn life or of any individual foetus is simply objectively uncertain and secondly there is no other context within the human experience in which one human entity (the foetus) so closely and directly affects the existence of another (the mother) as to be, essentially, a human parasite.

These two factors play into but do not determine the debate on this issue. Thus the group that represents what is traditionally known as the "pro-choice" standpoint may argue that the status of the foetus or "unborn life" generally is too morally uncertain to merit any legal protection (let alone protection in the form of a constitutional right) and indeed furthermore, that even if it does possess some nominal moral value this is completely undermined in a legal sense by reason of the parasitical impact of pregnancy on another independent legal person. Equally of course, the side traditionally known as the "pro-life" side may take the

---

[1] See, for example, the concerns in this regard of the US Supreme Court in *Roe v Wade* (1973).

approach that, even if it is not possible to be absolutely certain of the moral status of the foetus or of unborn life, equally *life* generally is the paramount value in our society, and a maximalist approach to this value commits us to affording foetal life, at any rate, the benefit of the doubt of this uncertainty.[2] In other words, the fact that we cannot prove the moral status of the foetus does not mean that it has no moral status, and it would be more consistent with the broad ethic that permeates western society, that we would decide the uncertainty in its favour. Moreover, this viewpoint would presumably argue that the parasitical nature of the foetus is simply irrelevant in determining whether or not to protect it legally, in that it is simply the essence of the reality of pregnancy, and thus if the foetus or unborn life is to be ascribed legal value then realistically this must be in conjunction with, rather than distinct from the parasitical nature of pregnancy.

These competing arguments have appeal both at a rational and at an intuitive level to different people and different societies based on relevant social conditioning factors such as religion, history and culture. So for example it is highly unlikely that the Eighth Amendment to the Irish constitution would have been passed so blithely had the level of dominance of the Roman Catholic Church in Irish social policy not been at the level it was at in 1983.[3] Similarly, it is improbable to say the least, that, a decision such as that of the American Supreme Court in *Roe v Wade* (1973) could have happened, had the emerging concern in 1960s America both with the claims of the feminist movement and with the right to privacy as a mechanism for securing autonomy over matters personal to the individual not taken hold.[4]

The impact of such cultural factors on a nation's abortion law is particularly stark from a German perspective (and much of this chapter will focus on the German approach to the question of foetal life) (Levy and

---

[2] See, for example, Binchy (1992). This is also essentially the conclusion of the German Constitutional Court in *Abortion 1* (1975).

[3] It is similarly unlikely that the popular reaction in favour of the defendant in *Attorney General v X* (1992) would have been as vehement or widespread if the power of the Roman Catholic church in Ireland had not been on the wane at that stage.

[4] See, for example, Mohr (1978).

Somek, 2001; McAllister, 2004; Telman, 1998; Kommers, 1994; see generally Kommers, 1997).

A number of historical and social factors affect German abortion law, but by far the most important is the lingering impact of the shame of the period of national socialism.[5] The Nazi approach to abortion was that it could be enforced if the foetus was of non-Aryan stock, but could be punished by the death penalty if it was.[6] In other words, the value attributed to the foetus was dependent on a eugenic choice deriving from state policy. But this was, of course, merely a derivative of Nazi policy generally, such that selective choices were consistently made as to how valuable any individual life was based on categorisations. In other words, Jews, homosexuals, gypsies etc were categorised as being somehow quasi-human and as a result did not enjoy standard legal protection (Perry, 1998).

The contemporary reaction against this policy, as it plays out in German abortion law has been to say that, in the new German constitutional order as laid down in the Basic Law (essentially the constitution) *no* category of life, however morally uncertain, should be excluded from the general constitutional protection of "life".[7] In other words, the concept of life in Article 2 is given the broadest and most expansive possible definition[8] – and, in two cases, has been held to encompass unborn as well as born life.[9] And even more significantly, this has meant that the most important of all constitutional values in the German constitutional order (namely human dignity[10]) has been deemed to attach to the foetus.

The concern of this chapter, however, is not with the fact of affording constitutional protection to the foetus, but with what it means to do so and it is hoped, by reference to comparative approaches to this issue

---

[5] That this is the case is made clear by the Constitutional Court in *Abortion I* (1975).

[6] See for example http://www.lifeissues.net/writers/air/air_vol16no1_2001.html.

[7] Again this is at the heart of the conclusion of the constitutional court in *Abortion 1* (1975).

[8] In similar vein the Constitutional Court has held that the pivotal protection of human dignity can extend to persons who are dead. See *Mephisto Case* (1971).

[9] See also *Abortion II* (1993).

[10] See generally Kommers (1997: ch. 7).

to inform the discussion about the reality and breadth of the "25 years of protection" that flow from Article 40.3.3°. Two dominant questions (which, it is submitted, are at the heart of the problems with the Irish law in this area) are addressed, namely:

- If it is desired that some constitutional statement be made (as in Ireland) that the "unborn" should receive legal protection, should this be taken to refer to the individual foetus as a matter of individual right, or should it instead be taken as referring to unborn life *in general* and represent a statement that the overall constitutional value of life should cover both born and pre-born life and receive constitutional protection, and
- If either category of entity (the foetus or "life" generally) is to be protected, what form should such protection take and specifically should the parasitical and contingent nature of unborn life be a factor which should influence the answer to this question?[11] In other words, does the unique nature of unborn life (when compared to any other stage of life on the continuum between birth and death) indicate that if it is to be protected effectively, this will of necessity mean that such protection will have to be tailored to the issue, rather than derived from the standard types of legal protection afforded to born entities?

The essential contention of this chapter is that there is no good reason why a legal system cannot have some form of protection for unborn life or the foetus as a normative or constitutional standard, nor indeed why it cannot deem the value of unborn life to be equal to born life. However, if the protection afforded to unborn life is to mean anything in practice, and if it is to accord with widespread popular and intuitive views of justice, then it should be recognised both that what is being protected is far more appropriately regarded as a general constitutional concern with developing life than a right vested in an individual constitutional person.

[11] This is not an inquiry into whether competing rights of the mother can be used to outweigh any putative right of the unborn, but rather whether, irrespective of such competing rights, the protection afforded to the foetus should be conditioned by the nature of pregnancy.

Further, it should be recognised that it is fully legitimate for the state to afford equal rights to unborn life as to the born human, without necessarily committing to the view that the method by which both are to be protected must, therefore, be identical. It is further submitted that it is the popular and judicial failure to realise this, which is arguably the root of the lack of sophisticated analysis of the abortion issue in Ireland as well as the interpretative difficulties which the Courts have faced and the consequent constitutional crises thrown up by Article 40.3.3°.

The Notion of Foetal Protection in Comparative Perspective

The first issue to be discussed then is how best to approach the question of who or what is to be protected by a constitutional clause aimed at protecting unborn life and providing normative underpinning to an anti-abortion law. In answering this question, we will consider both the circumstances under which Article 40.3.3° came to be in the Irish constitution and the dominant motivation of those who advocated for such a change, and also, by way of comparative analysis, one aspect of the approach to unborn life taken by the US Supreme Court in *Roe v Wade* (1973). It will be argued that the individualistic approach to the notion of a foetal person possessed of constitutional rights has in fact undermined the sophistication of analysis and the level of protection afforded to foetal life in both cases.

The Eighth Amendment to the Constitution

The constitutionalisation of Irish abortion law can be traced back to *McGee v AG* (1974) – the pivotal case in which a heroic 27-year-old mother of four who had been told by her medical adviser that another pregnancy would seriously endanger her life, challenged the constitutionality of Irish legislation prohibiting the sale and importation (but not the use) of contraceptives, alleging that it violated her unenumerated constitutional right to marital privacy.[12] The Irish Supreme Court upheld her claim and located a right to marital privacy within both Article 40.3

[12] Section 17(1) of the Criminal Law (Amendment) Act 1971 made it a crime to sell contraceptives, and section 17(3) of the same act included contraceptives in the list of items whose importation was illegal under section 42 of the Customs Consolidation Act 1876.

(personal rights) and Article 41 (Protection of the Family) of the Irish constitution (1974: 322).

The reason why this development appeared to impinge on the Irish abortion situation was because in America the judicial recognition in *Griswold v Connecticut* (1965)[13] of a similar unenumerated right to marital privacy (albeit one encompassing a right to *use* contraceptives), had (however spuriously) been the basis for the majority decision in *Roe v Wade* (1973) some eight years later in which a full constitutional right to have an abortion was recognised. It was argued that Irish abortion law as contained sections 58 and 59 of the Offences against the Person Act 1861 was threatened by the decision in *McGee* in that the Irish right to marital privacy might be used as the basis for an Irish right to an abortion in the same way as was its American counterpart.[14]

However unlikely the possibility that abortion would be foisted on an unwilling public either by the courts (or indeed by developments at a European level), anti-abortion activists set up a Pro-life Amendment Campaign in 1981, to press for a referendum to insert a foetal right to life clause into the constitution of Ireland. Equally the motivations behind such a move clearly indicate that what was sought was in fact the strongest available constitutional bulwark to protect existing Irish abortion law from destructive forces. In other words, the existence of Article 40.3.3° arguably owes more to shrewd political manoeuvring and a buying into popular legal jargon than it does to any philosophical consensus that such a thing as a constitutional foetal person or a foetal right to life is implicit in the concept of ordered liberty as it is understood in western legal theory.

This campaign for constitutional reform, known as PLAC garnered a remarkable level of political support for such a referendum (in which respect it owed a good deal to its ability to stress to politicians the electoral value of being overtly opposed to abortion in an era of intense po-

---

[13] This case was expressly approved in *McGee v. AG.*

[14] See the comments of Professor Binchy in a letter to *The Irish Times* 22 July 1982 where he suggested that: "The dangers to the unborn are not limited to the fact that the constitution affords them neither explicit nor implicit protection, but that the constitution could be interpreted as conferring a broad right to abortion on demand based on a woman's right of privacy in respect of procreation. Such a right if recognised by the courts, would be a constitutionally protected, personal right …"

litical instability).[15] After a good deal of political manoeuvring, the wording for a proposed amendment was suggested by the Fianna Fáil leader Charles Haughey in September 1982, two days before his government fell. This wording, which would become Article 40.3.3° of the Irish Constitution reads as follows:

> The State acknowledges the right to life of the unborn and, with due regard to the equal right to life of the mother, guarantees in its laws to respect, and as far as practicable, by its laws to defend and vindicate that right.

There was, at the time, a certain degree of opposition, both to the concept of such an amendment and also to the wording of this particular amendment which is plainly very broad and very open textured. So for example, phrases like the *unborn*, *due regard*, and *as far as practicable* within the terms of the amendment remain undefined and unpredictable[16] and leave open the most important questions of (a) what is being protected[17] (b) what form such protection should take and (c) how any situation in

---

[15] Between 1981-1982 there were three general elections. Following the June 1981 General Election, both Michael D. Higgins and Jim Kemmy (of the Labour Party), who lost their seats, attributed this fact to their refusal to support a pro-life amendment, and their consequent vilification by PLAC. See Hesketh (1990: 135-136).

[16] Indeed, the Attorney General Mr Sutherland suggested that the amendment as it was worded could lead either to a situation where foetal rights could triumph over those of the mother, or alternatively to a situation where abortion could be permitted in Ireland. The result in the short term was likely to be confusion. As he put it: "Having regard to the equal rights of the unborn and the mother, a doctor faced with the dilemma of having to save the life of the mother knowing that to do so will terminate the life of the unborn, will be compelled by the wording to conclude that he can do nothing. Whatever his intentions he will have to show equal regard for both lives and his predominant intent will not be a factor" (Dáil Debates, vol. 340, col. 473). Prof Binchy, in a reply to Mr Sutherland's comments, said that: "Mr Sutherland has no credibility when he asks us to believe that in passing the amendment we may actually be permitting abortions of unborn children of up to seven months. This assertion dramatically opposed to the purpose of the amendment and directly contrary to the meaning of the text is one which no experienced lawyer could possibly make" (*Irish Press*, 7 September 1983).

[17] Thus it is not clear both whether the "unborn" refers to the foetus/embryo at all stages post-fertilisation, or only after a defined point such as implantation (the position in Germany) or indeed viability (the position in the USA). Moreover, it is not clear whether the phrase refers to each individual foetus and affords rights to all such individual foetuses or whether it refers to unborn life as a general conceptual phenomenon.

which the expressly equal maternal and foetal rights to life were to come into direct conflict should be balanced. It was further argued that the Amendment did little to tackle the causes of unwanted pregnancy and hence of abortion (O'Mahony, 1983: 38, 60) and would do nothing to reduce the huge number of abortions performed annually on Irish women who travelled to England for this purpose (O'Mahoney, 1983: 40).[18] It was contended that instead the amendment represented a gross oversimplification of a complex problem[19] and one which was also sectarian,[20] in that it mirrored the Roman Catholic teaching on abortion, and was opposed by all the other churches in the country.

PLAC, however, rejected these arguments pointing out that Article 40.3.3° was rooted in the terminology of Article 40.3.1° which had received frequent judicial clarification. The possibility of a mother's life being threatened by virtue of a denial of access to abortion was emphatically rejected and it was argued that Article 40.3.3° would not alter existing medical practice.[21] Accordingly, and despite a proposed alternative wording suggested by the Fine Gael leader Dr Fitzgerald,[22] Article 40.3.3° became part of Irish law on 7 September 1983 and, in all relevant case law between 1983 and 1992, it was interpreted both by the High Court and the Supreme Court (albeit in judgments where there was a notable absence of sophisticated constitutional interpretation of the terms of the clause) as representing a complete ban on any manifestation of abortion, seemingly irrespective of whether the impugned action was proven to have any negative impact on any individual foetus.[23]

---

[18] See http://www.ifpa.ie/abortion/iabst.html for a statistical account of the numbers of Irish women having abortions in Ireland.

[19] Thus O'Mahony (1983: 58) says: "What I fear is a constitutional amendment which would be simple, neat but wrong."

[20] See Hesketh (1990: chs. 2 and 3).

[21] This point was emphasised at the "1,000 doctors for the amendment" conference held in TCD on 2 September 1983.

[22] The new wording, drafted by the Fine Gael A.G. Mr Peter Sutherland, read as follows: Nothing in the constitution shall be invoked to invalidate any provision of a law on the grounds that it prohibits abortion.

[23] See *AG (SPUC) v Open Door Counselling* (1988), *SPUC v Grogan* (1989). See also Friedman (1988).

What is significant about the Irish debate for the purposes of this chapter is the absence of any sophisticated analysis of whether it was actually appropriate to regard the foetus as a constitutional person or a rights possessor and what the new requirement to defend and vindicate the right to life of this new constitutional entity would mean in practice. As has been mentioned, the terms of the Eighth Amendment owe more to political strategising (and possibly an overly simplistic conversion of the belief that the foetus was a moral person into the statement that it was, thereby, a legal person) than to anything more esoteric. Yet there was also little popular questioning of whether an individual foetus could and should be regarded as a constitutional person let alone a rights possessor.

This is arguably because in 1981 in Ireland the ongoing impact of Roman Catholicism on social policy meant that, for many if not most people, it was taken as a given that the "unborn child" was in fact nothing less than the younger version of a real child, and thus that, in light of the fact that the real child was possessed of rights, it would defy logic to deny such rights to its younger counterpart. In other words the uniquely contingent and parasitic nature of unborn life was simply irrelevant. Moreover, Irish constitutional law affords rights to individuals rather than to groups or to values, and hence the notion of not regarding each individual foetus (from whatever point, though probably no later than implantation) as an individual rights bearer was an alien one. Moral superiority breeds a kind of confidence, and it was easy for people in the Ireland of the time to regard the global uncertainty as to the status of the foetus as being evidence, not of the fact that the issue might be uncertain but of the fact that the rest of the world was heading the way of Sodom and Gomorrah. Thus the popular view at the time was undoubtedly that Article 40.3.3° quite appropriately gave the individual foetus a right to life just as it gave its "born" sibling a right to life and at the same level of value as the right of its born mother.

Quite what this clause would mean in practice was simply not discussed at the time despite the fact that this was manifestly uncertain, and particularly if it enshrined the personhood of every foetus conceived in Ireland. Did it, for example compel the Irish government to take measures to stop the thousands of Irish women who travelled annually for abortions from doing so in order to protect the thousands of Irish foetal persons who were being killed? And given that it was well known that such procedures were taking place in England, did the clause require Ireland to take international action against England for licensing the mass homicide of Irish citizens? And most importantly of all, did the clause require the Irish government to take the step taken by the German government in 1974[24] of assessing in a sophisticated and searching way whether the foetus would be better protected by a mechanism other than an unworkable statutory ban on abortion or was it merely to exist as a rather useless statement of intent? These questions which were so vital to understanding the constitutional position in this area were never answered, and into the vacuum fell the defendant in *Attorney General v X* (1992).

Roe v Wade (1973)

In *Roe v Wade* the applicants had asked the US Supreme Court to invalidate the anti-abortion laws of all relevant states on the basis of a somewhat speculative constitutional right of a woman to choose whether or not to have a child which would, itself stem from the then controversial right to privacy originally "discovered" in *Griswold v Connecticut* (1965). This the court duly did. It was then faced with the argument from the State of Texas that, whether or not such a putative right existed, it should be restricted having regard to the compelling state interest in protecting foetal life.

As is well known, the Supreme Court having stated that it did not wish to impose one theory of life on the nation proceeded to impose one theory of life on the nation (Morgan, 1979; Faux, 1980; Cox, 2000: 237). The logic adopted by the court had two central themes:

- First, the view was taken that if such a compelling interest in foetal life was to be found, this would only and could only be the case if the foetus was a constitutional person possessed of constitutional rights.
- Secondly, and on this basis, the court concluded that the foetus was *not* a constitutional person, and that it could not represent a compelling state interest which would restrict the maternal right to an abor-

---

[24] The Abortion Reform Act of 1974 represented a major change in policy on the part of the German legislature on the question of abortion.

tion until the third trimester of pregnancy at which point it would (theoretically) be viable.[25]

The second of these conclusions is not of relevance for this chapter, but the first merits some further consideration. Whether or not the foetus is a constitutional person in the United States, it is surely a criticism of *Roe* (and arguably a consequence of what Glendon terms "Rights talk"[26] – that is, the overuse of the language of rights as a means of political point scoring) that the Supreme Court did not address the question of whether, even if the foetus is *not* a person, nonetheless the value of life as a social value should be factored into the discussion[27] (and irrespective of whether it could amount to a compelling state interest justifying a restriction on the mother's constitutional rights).[28] And it is arguable that in not

---

[25] The logic of the trimester scheme has been explicitly rejected in later cases which have continued to uphold *Roe v Wade* (1973). See *Webster v Reproductive Health Services* (1990) and *Planned Parenthood v Casey* (1992).

[26] See Glendon (1991) and Werner (1996).

[27] Thus, as Representative Robert Drinan said in 1980: "However convenient, convincing or compelling the arguments in favour of abortion may be, the fact remains that the taking of life even though it is unborn, casts at the very heart of the principle that no one's life however unwanted and useless may be terminated in order to promote the health or happiness of another human being" (Destro, 1975: 1338).

[28] As Ely (1973: 926) puts it: "... the argument that foetuses lack constitutional rights is simply irrelevant. For it has never been held or even asserted that the state interest needed to justify forcing a person to refrain from an activity, whether or not that activity is constitutionally protected must implicate either the life or the constitutional rights of another person. Dogs are not persons in the whole sense nor have they constitutional rights but that does not mean that the state cannot prohibit killing them … that the life plans of the mother … may prevail over the state's desire to protect the foetus simply does not follow from the judgement that the foetus is not a person." He went on to point out that while draft cards were not persons, the Supreme Court had recently declared that they merited constitutional protection (in that it had been declared illegal to burn ones draft card in the case of *United States v O'Brien,* 1968). Tribe, in response, says that a government may not protect such interests in a way that makes the exercise of a fundamental right impossible (1988: 114). Furthermore, as he points out, the exercise of no constitutional right necessitates the killing of animals, the operation of the fundamental right to abortion inherently involves the termination of the life of the foetus. It is submitted that this response is not wholly satisfactory. Ely's point is not that, for example, the right to freedom of association is constitutionally suspect because it may involve the burning of draft cards. His point quite simply is that constitutional rights *have* been required to submit to interests short of constitutional personhood, and therefore the simple determination by the Supreme

considering the question of whether life as a value, rather than the specific life of the specific foetus, might be a compelling interest, the Supreme Court decision in *Roe v Wade* can be regarded not as good or bad, or even right or wrong, but simply incomplete.[29] As Destro points out, in all cases of federal discrimination, where black people were deemed not to be citizens, for example, no one ever suggested that this absence of citizenship meant that they were entitled to *no* legal protection, and:

> If one rejects the dubious legal distinction which lies at the heart of the Supreme Court decision in Roe, it becomes extremely difficult to square the notion of abortion on demand with contemporary social thought which still considers Human life as an affirmative value (1975: 1336).

This last criticism of *Roe v Wade* represents, I would suggest, a broader criticism of many approaches to the abortion issue, including the approach taken by Irish constitutional law, namely that in stressing the language of foetal rights and focusing on each individual foetus as a distinct beneficiary of such rights, the debate runs the risk of missing the point. No doubt the reality of getting one's claim heard means that one must on occasion simplify and distort one's claim, but it is surely self-evident that, on a global scale, the question of whether abortion should be lawful is considerably more complicated and less certain than the question of whether murder should be lawful, precisely because of the nature of foetal life and the nature of pregnancy. Hence the approach of many anti-abortion organisations (however well intentioned) of showing slides of a new born baby and then working backwards through the stages of embryonic development to give the desired impression that the foetus is simply a compact version of a human being is inevitably logically suspect. After all, to quote Thompson (1971), a planted acorn will turn into

---

Court in *Roe* that the foetus was not a person did not suffice as a legal justification for deeming foetal life not to be compelling in the first two trimesters.

[29] Dworkin argues that the degree of value to attach to any form of life is a personal value judgement, of almost religious proportions, and as such, had the court assessed the issue and found that unborn life as a quantity was not a compelling interest, whilst he might have disagreed with their conclusion, this would not be a reason why it was a bad decision (1995: 160-168). It did not, however, and thus, it is submitted, the decision may be classified as quite simply a bad one.

a tree but that does not make it a tree (and indeed one might add, it does not make it as valuable as or more valuable or less valuable than a tree).

This does not mean that the individual foetus is not valuable (nor does it even mean that some people may choose to value it by classifying it as a person). Furthermore, it does not necessarily mean that we must adopt Dworkin's "detached" view, that the only reason to afford value to the foetus is because it is alive and life is a social value, or the view of English (1989: 83) to the effect that the concept of foetal personhood is so vague and so widely and badly argued on both sides of the debate,[30] that it should simply be removed from the abortion equation, if for no other reason than because in respect of it, no definite conclusion is possible.[31] The point is merely that the process of arguing that the individual foetus should be possessed of rights because born humans are possessed of rights and the foetus may in time become a born human presents itself as a clear line of analysis when in fact it requires several dramatic twists of logic. Moreover, once again it must be stressed that there is nothing in the traditions and conscience of the people that grounds the concept of foetal personhood or a foetal right to life, not is such a concept by any means implicit in the concept of ordered liberty.

It is arguable, moreover, that many (though by no means all) Irish people who supported the Eighth Amendment at the time of the 1983 referendum did not appreciate the consequences of affording constitutional status and constitutional rights to each individual foetus. That this is the case is evidenced by one of one of the most striking aspects of the events surrounding the *X* case, namely the number of people, in various fora, who said that whereas they voted for the Eighth Amendment,

---

[30] See Tooley (1983).

[31] English says: "Biologically a human being develops gradually. We shouldn't expect there to be any specific time or sharp dividing point at which the person appears on the scene. For this reason I believe our concept of a person is not sharp or decisive enough to bear the weight of a solution to the abortion controversy" (1989: 86). Glendon, on the other hand, worries that a statement that a foetus is not a legal person is a very bad message to give to society. Thus she says that: "Legal specialists may understand that to say that a foetus is not a 'person' within the meaning of the Fourteenth amendment says nothing at all about the essential nature of a foetus for other purposes…. But as *Roe v Wade* is filtered through the communications media to popular consciousness the statement by the highest court of the land that a foetus is not a 'person' has great potential for being misunderstood …" (1991: 60-61).

equally they would emphatically support the defendant's right in this case to have an abortion – or at least to travel for one. The reason why this is striking is because it is strange, if people genuinely believed that a foetus is a kind of mini-person possessed of constitutional rights, that they would regard its mother's rape or age as reasons why she should be allowed to kill it. This dichotomy is, of course, not one that merely arises in Ireland, but the question as to *why* people who genuinely believe in a foetal right to life would also make an exception where pregnancy is caused by rape or where the mother is young or vulnerable received surprisingly little analysis both during and in the wake of the events surrounding the *X* case, yet it is a poignant one.[32] After all, if the foetus *is* genuinely a constitutional person then presumably the age of its mother or the crimes of its father cannot alter this status one whit.

It has been suggested that the reason generally why people who would normally be in favour of a rigid anti-abortion law yet would tend towards favouring a "rape-based exception" to this law is because of an intuitive view that in as much as (in our system) legal responsibility derives from one's causal actions,[33] and in as much as an involuntary action cannot be the legal cause of an event, so therefore a woman whose actions cannot be seen as a (partial) legal cause of pregnancy should not be required to be burdened with the responsibility of dealing with the pregnancy.[34] Yet this analysis (while arguably providing a correct explanation as to why people *do* favour such a "rape exception") does not really explain why a person who vehemently believes that the foetus is a constitutional person would equally vehemently rail against the injustice of a situation where that constitutional person is not permitted to be killed simply because its mother did not have any causal responsibility for its existence. For such a person, this kind of situation should be one to which normal principles of causation do not apply in that the relevant causal action (the sexual act)[35] did more than cause a factual result, rather

---

[32] It is accepted of course that for many people, the fact that the foetus is conceived as a result of an act of rape should not ground an exception to a law against abortion.

[33] See generally Hart and Honoré (1985).

[34] See, for example, Cox (2006).

[35] For a different view of the cause of pregnancy see McDonagh (1996).

it caused a person to come into being and this should be enough to justify such suspension of principles. Similarly, it can surely not be the case that persons who believe in a foetal right to life but favour a rape based exception to an abortion law do so because of an intuitive view that the foetal person is somehow less valuable and hence merits less protection than its mother, for if this was the case then presumably this would also justify abortion in cases where a mother's career (for example) would be undermined by her pregnancy.

It is submitted (albeit cautiously) that in fact the reason why people who professed to believe that the individual foetus was a rights possessor still felt that the defendant in the *X* case should be entitled to an abortion is because for such persons what is at stake in pregnancy from the standpoint of both mother and foetus is something which is simply too complex to be appropriately dealt with exclusively through the language of rights.[36] This is not to say that an individual foetus cannot be afforded moral status (including possibly the moral status of personhood) just as it is not to say that the concept of an unwanted pregnancy does not throw up the gravest concerns for personal autonomy for a woman, but merely that the issue is in fact more easily resolved by regarding it as a clash of social values or social concerns, and not a clash of rights.

The point is that without a doubt, from an Irish perspective and for whatever reason, unborn life is something which represents a most important social value whether or not an individual foetus can properly be regarded as a rights possessor. It is only the contemporary obsession with the language of rights that would suggest that a statement that "unborn life is a social and constitutional value but the individual foetus is not a rights possessor", devalues unborn life in any sense. Moreover, if we take this approach (i.e. that unborn life is a constitutional value, but that the foetus is *not* a rights possessor) as our starting point we have a more fitting and consistent explanation of why people who are otherwise anti-abortion would permit a rape based exception because (by reason *inter alia* of the absence of causal responsibility on the part of the mother in such a case as well as the view that, having suffered as she suffered, it is inappropriate for the law to impose further suffering on her) it is per-

[36] See, for example, Cox (1999).

fectly reasonable to see the social value of life being frustrated rather than enhanced where a raped woman (or possibly any woman) is forced to carry an unwanted pregnancy to term.

This is not to say that unborn life cannot be constitutionally enshrined, nor that the Irish people of 1983 and 1992 did not intend for this to happen. It is merely a suggestion that the manner in which it was enshrined – and parliamentary debates from the time indicate that this was almost certainly a case of affording a civil right to each individual foetus as a "lone rights bearer"[37] – owed more to the fact that the language of individual rights was and is the fashionable legal language of the time than to any genuine philosophical logic.

In this respect, the approach of the German Constitutional Court to the issue of unborn life is instructive. The language of the Constitutional Court on this issue is broad and expansive, as it deems the general constitutional protection of life to cover unborn life because of a reluctance to "devalue" any category of human life or to deem it to be outside the ambit of constitutional protection.[38] Equally, however, the court never suggested that each individual foetus was an individual rights bearer (even though this is the approach taken in the context of questions involving born life). In other words, whereas it deemed unborn life to be constitutionally protected it tailored the fact of such protection to the entity in question.

Put simply, it makes sense to use the mechanism of individual constitutional rights to protect individual born humans who operate in a physically independent and individual manner and who are demonstrably capable of enjoying and exercising such rights. It does not, however, make sense to afford similar protection to human foetuses whose lives are inextricably linked to those of their mother, whose developing moral status is uncertain at any particular point in pregnancy and who are not demon-

[37] See Glendon (1991: ch. 3).

[38] Thus in *Abortion 1* the Constitutional Court held that "Article 2(2) guarantees the right to life to everyone who "lives"; no distinction can be made between individual stages of the developing life before birth or between prenatal and postnatal life. "Everyone" within the meaning of Article 2(2) of the Basic Law is "every living human being" so, expressed otherwise, every human individual possessing life; "everyone" therefore also includes the yet unborn human being …"

strably capable of enjoying or exercising rights. And very importantly, there is no suggestion that by declining to protect the foetus as an individual rights bearer, the German Constitutional Court was in any way suggesting that the protection which it afforded would be somehow inferior in quality to that which would have arisen if such individual rights had been recognised. It was merely implying that the protection in question would be more effective as a constitutional recognition of a general communitarian value in life in all categories rather than as a right attaching to one individual pre birth life.

The Manner by which the Unborn Should be Protected

More stark still as far as the Irish experience of protecting the unborn is concerned, is the question of the form such protection should properly take. Once again the analysis of this issue by Irish courts is considerably less sophisticated than that emerging from their German counterparts. In reality, moreover, such lack of sophistication as far as the Irish law is concerned, owes much to the lack of searching analysis referred to earlier in deciding what is actually to be protected in a clause like Article 40.3.3°. In other words, it is the view of the courts that Article 40.3.3° protects an individual foetus as a rights bearer that has conditioned its view of how such a right should best be protected.

The central contention which will be made here is that far from enhancing the protection afforded to the foetus by treating it like a mini-person, and by seeking to prevent abortion as one prevents murder (that is by simply rendering the act illegal), this may in fact offer a reduced protection, and this is because of one vital reality, namely the fact that prohibitive anti-abortion laws, of themselves simply do not work. Hence in cases of controversy, the net effect of drawing a protection for the foetus by analogy with a protection for the life of an adult will be results which are either absurd or, alternatively, do not actually deal with the reality of the matter in hand. That this is the case is demonstrated by a second remarkable aspect of the *X* case – a case which involved both a constitutional issue and an issue which was plainly very close to the hearts of many people in the country – namely that there was a gross disparity between the popular and the legal view of what the case was actually about.

Let us review the facts. The Attorney General seeks to injunct a 14-year-old alleged non-consensual sexual act victim from travelling to England to terminate a pregnancy. One consultant psychiatrist who had not been cross examined[39] suggested that she might attempt suicide if forced to continue with her pregnancy, although there was no particular critical analysis of the claim.[40]

Now from a colloquial or popular standpoint this will always be remembered as the case about the young rape victim who wanted an abortion and who, in the views of many, should have been entitled to have one. Yet neither the girl's age nor the manner by which the foetus was conceived had any bearing on the way in which the case was legally resolved. Indeed, all that was relevant *from a legal perspective* was the morally less relevant and unevidenced claim that she might commit suicide.

This clash between the popular and judicial view of what the case was about derives both from the manner in which Article 40.3.3° was framed and also from the judicial view of how to defend and vindicate the rights of the unborn as was required under the clause. The unquestioned view of the judiciary was that, despite the unique nature both of unborn life and of the abortion debate, the foetus should be regarded and should be protected in the way in which the rights of any other constitutional person are protected. In other words, just as the right to personal property is protected by laws which prohibit people from violating that right, (for example larceny laws) so also logically, the right to life of the unborn should be protected by laws which prohibit people from violating that right – that is to say laws which prohibit abortion.

So, therefore, both the High Court and the Supreme Court in the *X* case proceeded on the (superficially logical) assumption that the primary step in protecting unborn life was for the law to prohibit abortion, and, in this case to prohibit the young girl from travelling to have an abortion. Hence the questions which the judges asked themselves was whether,

---

[39] In the Supreme Court, Hederman J alone concluded that the level of evidence presented to support the claim of suicide was simply insufficient to justify setting aside the constitutional right to life of the foetus (1992: 64-70).

[40] In fact, some research (see for example http://www.bmj.com/cgi/content/full/313/7070/1431) indicates that induced abortion is a considerably greater trigger for suicide than childbirth.

given the defendant's allegedly suicidal tendencies, it would be appropriate to put this protection in place but *not* whether this was the appropriate method of vindicating and defending unborn life in the first place. And there was no mention of the rape or the age of the girl because, in the context of a situation where the courts regarded themselves as facing a standard question of constitutional rights balancing of the kind that might arise between two born humans, they were, quite simply, irrelevant. After all, constitutional law generally (and the Eighth Amendment specifically) does not permit Party A's constitutional rights to be violated at the behest of Party B either because Party B happens to be in a situation of vulnerability or because Party C has somehow wronged Party B. Thus, the case was left as one where, by reason of the terms of Article 40.3.3° and the manner in which the courts saw the protection it provided as existing, the competing rights to life of mother and foetus – expressly deemed to be equal – were pitted against each other in an impossible struggle, precisely because the court took the view that if such rights were to be *equal* this must of necessity mean that the manner in which they were to be protected must be identical.

Yet there is no good reason why this should be the case. Rights can be equal without necessarily meaning that they must be protected in the same way. Indeed the fact that unborn life *is* a unique form of life completely distinct from "born" or "complete" life would surely suggest that the traditional language of *inter partes* rights balancing was inappropriate in the context of the abortion issue as it would mean that the "protection" afforded to unborn life under Article 40.3.3° would be unfocused, unsophisticated and inadequate.

In this respect, perhaps the defining characteristic of German constitutional law in this area is that whereas the protection afforded to unborn life is a very strong one (and has been deemed by the German Constitutional Court to be superior to any rights of the mother to dignity, autonomy or personality) equally the legislature has been given a discretion as to how best to protect this life. The approach taken by the Legislature since 1974 has been that because of the reality of crisis pregnancies, unborn life will be better protected by a law which, whereas it does not explicitly prevent a woman from having an abortion in certain circumstances will require that, prior to having such an abortion, she undergoes mandatory independent counselling in which she is informed that what she is doing is going against German social policy, than it would be by a blunt criminal law based prohibition on abortion. Indeed the policy of the legislature since 1974 has been to seek to reduce the number of abortions performed annually but this has entailed *increasing* the number of circumstances in which a woman could, legally, have an abortion, and the Constitutional Court has said that the essence of this policy does not infringe the German constitutional protection of unborn life precisely because the unique nature of that life means that it need not and should not be protected in the same way as the law protects born life.

Thus the German approach to "protection" of unborn life is innovative and issue-specific. So, for example, the Constitutional Court has also said that it was incumbent upon the Legislature, in defending unborn life, to have regard not merely to legal but also to socio-political mechanisms for doing so. Hence the counselling requirement works in tandem with the further policy of positively encouraging a woman to continue with a pregnancy by reference to the strong German social welfare system which seeks to ensure that no woman is obliged because of financial concerns to have an abortion.

On one level, this approach seems almost hypocritical. After all, on the one hand, the Constitutional Court says that unborn life is constitutionally protected, but on the other it has endorsed a situation where the intentional destruction of that life is, in a very broad range of circumstances, either legal or, at worst non-punishable. Yet the reason why this approach may appear to us to be hypocritical is again because we are constrained in our approach to the protection of *unborn life* by our expectations of the inappropriate mechanisms which are traditionally used to protect born life, and a more focused look at the issue may lead us to the view that the German approach actually does represent a stronger protection for the unborn than does the normal use of prohibitive criminal law.

Take the case of any woman who is pregnant but does not want to be. All the evidence shows that, wherever one goes, the existence of a criminal law prohibiting abortion simply will make no difference to her decision whether or not to terminate her pregnancy.[41] Such laws are notoriously unenforced against women who have abortions because they are notoriously unenforceable. In other words, the Irish statutory prohibition on abortion, while possibly representing a statement of principle is of no practical relevance whatsoever (especially in light of the fact that abortion is legal in the UK and travel to receive such a legal service is protected as a matter of EC law).[42]

Yet if that same woman was to attend at counselling where she was told of the financial benefits to which she would be entitled should she carry her pregnancy to term, and warned that the State thoroughly and constitutionally disapproved of what she did, this might, for any number of reasons, possibly have the effect of swaying her in the direction of not having an abortion.[43] This is not to say that such counselling would always result in a woman not having an abortion, but simply that by being tailored to meet the practical realities of the unwanted pregnancy situation, it would be more likely to have success than would something as blunt, inappropriate and useless as a prohibition on abortion.

I should stress that I am not advocating recourse to the approach of the German Legislature in this area (and indeed that such an approach proceeds on the basis of the conclusion of the German Constitutional Court that the protection of unborn life outweighted any interests of a mother in her personal autonomy – a conclusion that will be objectionable to many). Even in a jurisdiction, like Ireland, where the right to life is constitutionally enshrined, I confess that whereas I think a law prohibiting abortion is a fallacious thing, I also think that a law imposing counselling requirements of this kind is a complete travesty for its paternalis-

---

[41] It is notable that the Irish abortion statistics (relating to the number of abortions performed on Irish women in England) show no particular variance in 1983 (the year of the original constitutional amendment) and 1992 (the year of the *X* case). See http://www.ifpa.ie/abortion/iabst.html.

[42] *SPUC v Grogan* (1991).

[43] Thus in *Open Door Counseling v Ireland* (1993), the European Court of Human Rights had concluded that the activities of the applicant which had been injuncted by the Supreme Court in the interests of protecting the unborn, might actually have had the effect of persuading some women *not* to have an abortion.

tic overtones and for its susceptibility to abuse.[44] It is surely inconceivable that such an approach would be in place if only men could get pregnant. In my view, however, what remains of intense importance as far as the German law is concerned (and indeed what could be of huge benefit to its Irish counterpart with its express constitutional mandate to protect unborn life) is the conclusion from the Constitutional Court that a genuinely effective protection for the foetus will be one which is tailored to meet the precise concerns of the issue at stake rather than one which proceeds unthinkingly and by analogy with non-analogous situations.

Conclusion

The Eighth Amendment *does* protect the unborn, yet the 25 years of such protection have done little, in practical terms, to protect the unborn, while continuing to represent one of the last two constitutional bastions of a confessional legal system that legislated for but did not listen to women.[45] It has proved, in practice, to be a clause that benefits no one and hurts everyone and one which has produced some stunningly counterproductive results.[46] The reality of crisis pregnancies must surely tell us that if such "protection" is genuinely to be of benefit to the unborn in terms of reducing the Irish abortion rate, it must be in a form which is specific to such reality and above all must involve talking to and listening to the women who are faced with a choice which will so often be impossibly difficult to make.

Bibliography

Binchy, W. (1992) "Pluralism Liberty and the Right to Life" in Whelan, A. (ed.) *Law and Liberty in Ireland* Dublin: Oak Tree Press.

Cox, N. (1999) "The Failure of Rights Talk in the Field of Bioethics" in Junker-Kenny, M. (ed.) *Designing Life?* Aldershot: Ashgate.

---

[44] So, for example, in *Thornburgh v American College of Gynaecologists and Obstetricians* (1986) the US Supreme Court concluded that a similar provision was repugnant to American constitutional law.

[45] The other is Article 41.2 which implies that the constitutionally preferred role for women is within the home.

[46] This would include, for example, the closure of the Open Door and Well Woman counselling agencies.

Cox, N. (2000) "Judicial Activism, Constitutional interpretation and the Problem of Abortion" in O'Dell (ed.) *Leading Cases of the Twentieth Century*, Dublin: Round Hall.

Cox, N. (2006) "Causation, Responsibility and Foetal Personhood" *Northern Ireland Legal Quarterly* 51(4): 579.

Destro, R.A. (1975) "Abortion and the Constitution" *California Law Review* 63: 1338.

Dworkin, R. (1995) *Life's Dominion* New York: Harper Collins.

Ely, J.H. (1973) "*Roe v. Wade* and the Wages of Crying Wolf" *Yale Law Journal* 82: 920.

English, J. (1989) "Abortion and the concept of a person" in Baird, R.M. and Rosenbaum, J.E. *The Ethics of Abortion* New York: Prometheus Books.

Faux (1980) *Roe v. Wade* New York: Macmillan.

Friedman, J. (1988) "On the danger of moral certainty and sacred trusts" *Dublin University Law Journal* 71.

Glendon, M. (1991) *Rights talk: The Impoverishment of Political Discourse* New York: Free Press.

Hart, H.L.A. and Honoré, T. (1985) *Causation in the Law* Oxford: Oxford University Press.

Hesketh, T. (1990) *The Second Partitioning of Ireland* Dublin: Brandsma Books.

Kommers, D.P. (1994) "The Constitutional law of abortion in Germany: Should Americans pay attention" *Journal of Contemporary Health Law and Policy* 10: 1.

Kommers, D.P. (1997) *The Constitutional Jurisprudence of the Federal Republic of Germany* 2nd ed., Durham, NC: Duke University Press.

Levy, R.E. and Somek, A. (2001) "Paradoxical Parallels in the American and German Abortion Decisions" *Tulane Journal of International and Comparative Law* 9: 109.

McAllister, M.C. (2004) " Human Dignity and Individual Liberty in Germany and the United States as examined through each country's leading abortion cases", *Tulsa Journal of Comparative and International Law* 11: 491.

McDonagh, E.L. (1996) *Breaking the Abortion Deadlock* Oxford: Oxford University Press.

Mohr, J.C. (1978) *Abortion in America*, New York: Oxford University Press.

Morgan (1979) "*Roe v. Wade* and the Lessons of the pre-*Roe* case law" *Michigan Law Review* 77: 1724.

O'Mahony, P. (1983) "Medical ethics and the pluralist State" at p. 38 in *Abortion and the Law* Dublin: Dominican Publications.

Perry, M.J. (1998) *The Idea of Human Rights*, Oxford: Oxford University Press.

Telman, D.A.J. (1998) "Abortion and women's legal personhood in Germany: A contribution to the feminist theory of the state" 24 *New York University Review of Law and Society* 24: 91.

Thompson, J.J. (1971) "A Defence of Abortion" *Philosophy and Public Affairs* 1: 47.

Tooley, M. (1983) *Abortion and Infanticide* Oxford: Clarendon Press.

Tribe, L. (1988) *Abortion: The Clash of Absolutes* New York/London: WW Norton & Co.

Werner, U. (1996) "The Convergence of Abortion Regulation in Germany and the United States: A Critique of Glendon's Rights Talk Thesis" *Loyola Los Angelus International and Comparative Law Journal* 18: 571.

Cases

Abortion 1 39 BVerfGE 1 (1975).

Abortion II 88 BverfGE 203 (1993).

Attorney General (SPUC) v Open Door Counselling [1988] IR 593.

Attorney General v X [1992] 1 IR 1.

Griswold v Connecticut 381 US 513 (1965).

McGee v AG [1974] IR 284.

Mephisto Case 39 BVerfGE 173 (1971).

Open Door Counseling v Ireland (1993) 15 EHRR 12.

Planned Parenthood v Casey 505 US 833 (1992).

Roe v Wade 410 US 113 (1973).

SPUC v Grogan [1989] IR 753.

SPUC v Grogan [1991] 62 CMLR 849.

Thornburgh v American College of Gynaecologists and Obstetricians 476 US 747 (1986).

United States v O'Brien 391 U.S. 367 (1968).

Webster v Reproductive Health Services 492 US 490 (1990).

5

Pregnancy and Unwanted Third Party Interference:

A Woman's Rights

Dr Eimear Spain

Introduction

The debate on the right to life of the unborn and the competing right to life, reproductive freedom and bodily integrity of the mother has exercised lawyers, politicians, philosophers and the public at large over many years. The abortion debate has divided societies, none more so than on our own island, as the discourse on Article 40.3.3° highlights. Unfortunately, the extreme nature of this debate has obscured related concerns surrounding harm incurred by a foetus at the hands of a third party acting against the express or implied wishes of the pregnant woman. Moves to recognise criminal sanctions against those who harm the foetus against the wishes of the mother have proven to be controversial. The creation of legislation in these circumstances has been viewed as recognising foetal personhood at the expense of the pregnant woman, creating difficulties for women who choose to terminate their pregnancies, or those who harm the foetus through their lifestyle choices. It is proposed here to take a fresh approach to this controversial area by focusing not on the conflict in rights between the woman and the foetus, but on the interests of the woman in her foetus and her associated rights. This reflects the fact that in situations where a woman chooses to carry a foetus and there is unwanted third party interference in the pregnancy, there is no conflict of interest such as that which occurs in the case of an unwanted pregnancy. The rights of the foetus and woman are aligned and a successful pregnancy is in the best interest of both (Spain, 2006: 16).

There are a number of alternate legislative options available to deal with harm occurring to a foetus before birth and against the wishes of the mother. The first option would be to exclude harm to a foetus occurring in these circumstances from the realm of the criminal law. The second option would be include the foetus within the meaning of "person" for the purposes of the *actus reus* of the crimes of murder or manslaughter. Some jurisdictions specifically recognise the unborn as a person for this purpose; for example, state legislation in Ohio allows a conviction to be secured for the murder or manslaughter of a foetus (Jolicoeur-Wonnacott, 2000). Similarly, at federal level in the United States, the Unborn Victims of Violence Act 2004 allows two separate charges to be brought against an individual who injures or kills a "child *in utero*" in respect of the pregnant woman and her foetus.

Another option would be to recognise a specific offence of foetal homicide, allowing for a charge to be brought in respect of the homicide of the foetus but not a charge of murder or manslaughter. This approach has been adopted in many US states, including Alaska and Georgia, and recognises the State's interest in protecting the foetus without equating born and unborn life. The final option would be to recognise a single victim if a woman and her foetus are harmed, but allow for an increased sanction.[1] The US Motherhood Protection Act,[2] a Democratic alternative to the Unborn Victims of Violence Act 2004, took this approach. This piece of legislation proposed the recognition of equivalent penalties for the termination of a foetus as the Unborn Victims of Violence Act without recognising foetal personhood. The pregnant woman was recognised as the primary victim,

---

[1] Turkey provides for increased penalties for damage to a pregnant woman causing a premature birth: "Art. 456 of the Criminal Code lays down that a person who causes damage to another shall be liable to a prison sentence of between six months and one year; if the victim is a pregnant woman and the damage results in premature birth, the Criminal Code prescribes a sentence of between two and five years' imprisonment.", (2005) 40 EHRR 12, at para. 41.

[2] Proposed by Rep Zoe Lofgren and defeated on 26 February 2004.

thereby guaranteeing "… appropriate penalties in the law without getting us into a volatile, unnecessary debate over abortion" (Stark, 2004).

Right to Life of the Foetus

To date, much of the case law and commentary on the question of how to categorise actions which result in the death of a foetus without the consent of the mother has focused on the right to life of the foetus. Few jurisdictions provide explicit guidance on the issue of harm to a foetus outside the abortion context, and despite the protection afforded the unborn in the Irish Constitution under Article 40.3.3º, it remains unclear whether any criminal proceedings may be taken in this jurisdiction against a person who intentionally or unintentionally harms a foetus against the wishes of the mother. Section 58 of the Offences Against the Person Act 1861 prohibits the intentional procurement of a miscarriage, however there are a number of situations which fall outside this offence. For example, no prosecution would be possible under the 1861 Act against an individual who attacks a pregnant woman with no intent to procure a miscarriage or against one who intends merely to harm the foetus or is reckless as to the danger.[3]

There are differing views on whether a foetus is categorised as a person for the purposes of the *actus reus* of murder or manslaughter in this jurisdiction. The traditional position at common law suggests that personhood begins at birth, therefore the foetus is not considered to be a human being and no conviction for the murder or manslaughter of a foetus is permissible. The law is governed by the "born alive" rule which stipulates that "[a] child must be actually wholly in the world in a living state to be the subject of a charge of murder" (*R v Brain,* 1834*).* Therefore, a child must die following a live birth if a conviction for murder or manslaughter resulting from injuries suffered *in utero* is to be sustained. In the *Attorney-General's Reference (No. 3 of 1994)* (1997) the House of Lords reaffirmed the "born alive" rule. Further, although the court was not willing to recognise the principle of transferred malice for the purpose of a murder charge as the foetus was not a part of the mother, nor was it a person distinct from mother, the Court held that a

---

[3] A foetus who dies during birth is also excluded.

conviction for manslaughter was permissible, indicating that they felt that manslaughter was the appropriate charge in such circumstances.[4]

It has been suggested that the common law position has been altered by the constitutional protection offered to the foetus in Ireland. Article 40.3.3º acknowledges the right to life of the unborn with due regard to the equal right to life of the mother. Charlton takes the view that:

> Since the 8th Amendment to the Constitution on 5 September 1983, it is submitted that the rule of common law which confines the protection of the law, through the offences of murder and manslaughter to children fully extruded from the womb is abrogated (1992: 19).

In *G v An Bord Uchtala* (1980) Walsh J stated: "[t]he right to life necessarily implies the right to be born, the right to preserve and defend (and to have preserved and defended) that life…" (1980: 69).[5] This right to life of the unborn child is normally viewed as a prohibition on abortion, however it may also be important in prohibiting harm which occurs to the unborn against the wishes of the mother. Another consequence of the recognition of the personhood of the unborn, that is, the recognition of the foetus as a person distinct from its mother, is the possibility of the application of the doctrine of transferred malice. It may be that a charge of murder could be brought against one who terminated the life of a foetus, against the wishes of the mother, even if the defendant did not intend to kill the foetus. As Sheikh and Cusack note, the "courts have expressed that mother and foetus are two separate organisms"[6] (1997: 93).

Despite this, some commentators take the view that the common law position persists in Ireland, that is, no criminal sanction is available against one who harms a foetus without intending to procure a miscarriage, unless a child is born-alive (Kingston, Whelan and Bacik, 1997). On this view, Article 40.3.3º has not altered the common law on

---

[4] This ruling has been the subject of criticism. See (1997) "Case Comment", *Criminal Law Review* and Lacey, Wells and Quick (2003).

[5] He continues: "…the right to life itself and the right to be guarded against all threats directed to its existence whether before or after birth …"

[6] See comments of Hederman J in *Attorney General v X* [1992] ILRM 401, at page 442.

this issue and this would appear to be supported by the recent High Court decision in *MR v TR* (2006). In this case, McGovern J held that Article 40.3.3° was enacted with "the purpose of making secure the prohibition on abortion" and interpreted the provision in this context, thereby denying embryos *in vitro* the protection of Article 40.3.3°. If this interpretation of Article 40.3.3° was followed in the future, it seems unlikely that this article would be deemed to have altered the common law position on unwanted interference with the foetus. However, it may be that such a narrow interpretation of Article 40.3.3° is not warranted and we await further clarification on this issue.

Apart from the obvious confusion resulting from a lack of legislative or judicial clarification on the topic, it is clear that leaving the issue to the courts to decide through an interpretation of Article 40.3.3° causes difficulties. The recognition of a criminal offence of this nature would move the court beyond its normal remedies in constitutional cases, damages or injunctions.[7] The courts may also be reluctant to amend the law by interpretation due to the separation of powers and the principle of non-retroactivity. For example, in *Corway v Independent Newspapers* (1999) the court refused to outline the ingredients of the constitutionally mandated offence of blasphemy. However, in *Attorney General (SPUC) v Open Door Counselling* (1988) Hamilton P held that the courts may override concerns relating to the separation of powers and non-retroactivity if necessary to protect constitutional rights. These comments were made in the context of Article 40.3.3°, although they were obiter.

The uncertainty surrounding this area in Ireland is echoed in other jurisdictions and the issue was raised in the European Court of Human Rights recently. In *Vo v France* (2005), a woman challenged the failure of the French State to provide a criminal sanction against a doctor for the unintentional homicide of her foetus. Mrs Vo was six months pregnant when she presented at a French maternity hospital for a routine check-up. However, as a result of an administrative error, a doctor carried out a procedure which ultimately resulted in the death of the foetus *in utero*. The French courts had considered whether the foetus was a "human person" or "another" and therefore whether it fell within the scope of the

[7] See Schweppe (2005).

then Article 319[8] and 221-6[9] of the French Criminal Code. Dr G was found guilty of unintentional homicide in the Lyons Court of Appeal. The Court held that laws permitting abortion did not preclude them from recognising the foetus as a person under the Code:

> … subject to the provisions on the voluntary termination of pregnancies and therapeutic abortions, the right to respect for every human being from the beginning of life is guaranteed by law, without any requirement that the child be born as a viable human being, provided it was alive when the injury occurred (2005: para. 21).

However, this decision was ultimately reversed in the Court of Cassation where Dr G was found not guilty of the unintentional homicide of the foetus.

On an application to the European Court of Human Rights, Mrs Vo contended Article 2 of the European Convention on Human Rights had been violated by the French State.[10] Article 2 of the European Convention provides that "Everyone's right to life shall be protected by law...". The European Court of Human Rights had to decide if the foetus was considered to be a person under Article 2 of the Convention, and if so whether it was afforded the protection of that Article. If these questions were answered affirmatively, the Court would have to decide on whether the member states were obligated to provide a criminal remedy to enforce this right.[11]

---

[8] "Anyone who through his or her inadvertence, negligent act, inattention, negligent omission or breach of regulation unintentionally commits homicide or unintentionally causes death, shall be liable to imprisonment of between three months and two years and a fine of between 1,000 and 30,000 francs."

[9] "It shall be an offence of unintentional homicide punishable by three years' imprisonment and a fine of 45,000 euros to cause the death of another in the conditions and in accordance with the distinctions set out in Article 121-3 by inadvertence, negligent act, inattention, negligent omission or breach of a statutory or regulatory duty to ensure safety or of care."

[10] 17 Judge Court, 14:3 split decision in favour of the Defendant.

[11] The French Government argued that Article 2 of the Convention did not apply to the unborn child and that the defendant had not exhausted all the domestic remedies available to her as required under Article 35(1) of the Convention.

The European Court of Human Rights has been called upon to examine whether the protection for life under Article 2 applies to the unborn foetus on numerous occasions, but the court has consistently refused to provide guidance on whether the foetus is included in the term "everyone" in Article 2.[12] In cases such as *Patton v UK* (1980), *H v Norway* (1992) and *Boso v Italy* (2002), which involved applications by fathers in relation to the procurement of abortions by their partners, the question of the applicability of Article 2 to the foetus was raised. Due to the complex nature of this problem, and a desire to protect the autonomy of individual states, the courts adopted what has now become known as the "even assuming" formula. That is, the courts have held that even assuming Article 2 applies, the individual states had not breached Article 2 by recognising a limited right to abortion. Even if the foetus was a person within the meaning of Article 2, the right to life of the foetus was limited by the mother's interests.

In *Vo v France*, the Court persisted in viewing the issue of unwanted third party interference with pregnancy in an abortion context and held that it was not necessary, on the facts of the case, for them to decide if the foetus was protected by Article 2.[13] The majority decided that even if it was assumed by the Court that Article 2 was applicable, there was no violation of the Convention as the French State had provided adequate civil and administrative remedies, and a criminal remedy was not necessary.[14] However, a number of separate opinions criticised the

---

12 See *Open Door and Dublin Well Woman v Ireland.* This case concerned the distribution of information on abortion. The European Court on Human Rights held that Ireland was in violation of Article 10 of the convention as the injunction granted in the "*wide margin of appreciation"* in relation to morals this was not unfettered. The ECHR came to the conclusion that the Irish State was in breach of Article 10 without coming to a decision on whether the foetus was protected under Article 2 of the Convention.

13 "The Court is convinced that it is neither desirable, nor even possible as matters stand, to answer in the abstract the question whether the unborn child is a person for the purposes of Article 2 of the Convention" (2005).

14 In relation to the second question, whether the position in French law amounted to a violation of Article 2 the majority of the Court found for the defendant on this point and held that a criminal sanction was not the only remedy capable of satisfying Article 2 where the infringement was not caused intentionally. The existing case law suggests that in a case concerning medical negligence, a State may fulfil their obligations by offering a civil remedy or disciplinary measures.

reasoning of the majority and these opinions provide an interesting insight into relationship between Article 2 and the foetus. Although voting with the majority, Judge Rozakis (joined by four others[15]) felt that the Court should have expressly stated that Article 2 was inapplicable as "the life of the unborn child, although protected in some of its attributes, cannot be equated to post-natal life, and, therefore, does not enjoy a right in the sense of 'a right to life', as protected by Article 2 of the Convention" (2005: para. O-I3). In a separate opinion Judge Costa suggested that the Court should have found Article 2 to be applicable but that France had not violated its obligations under the Convention. Judge Costa also expressed the view that a finding that the unborn child is within the scope of Article 2 would not affect the legality of provisions on the voluntary termination of pregnancy in domestic legislation (2005: para O-II12).[16] This conclusion has been expressly supported in national decisions and implicitly supported in the European Court of Human Rights in the case of *Boso v Italy* (2002).[17]

The above discussion illustrates the tendency to examine the issue of unwanted third party interference with a foetus in the context of the right to life of the foetus. The criminalisation of such conduct in a form which equates born and unborn life has proven to be controversial as it is seen as recognising the rights of the foetus at the expense of the woman. However, it could be argued that the possibility of criminal sanctions in these situations is "a valuable method of protecting a pregnant woman's interest in her foetus and not a derogation of her rights" (Spain, 2006: 18). By moving the focus of the debate to the woman's rights, rather than the rights of the foetus, measures criminalising destruction of a foetus

---

[15] Judges Caflish, Fishbach, Lorenzen and Thomassen.

[16] Subject to certain conditions.

[17] It was held: "Even supposing that, in certain circumstances, the foetus might be considered to have rights protected by Article 2 of the Convention, ... in the instant case ... [the] pregnancy was terminated in conformity with section 5 of Law no. 194 of 1978." The majority decision of the Court in *Vo* summarised the *Boso* decision thus: "Even supposing that the foetus might be considered to have rights protected by Art. 2 of the Convention, ... Italian law on the voluntary termination of pregnancy struck a fair balance between the woman's interests and the need to ensure protection of the unborn child."

following third party assaults against the wishes of the woman may prove to be more acceptable.

Rights of the Woman

Rather than perpetuating the confusion of the past, it may be better to take a new approach and examine this issue in the context of a woman's rights, including her right to procreative liberty and to found a family. For example, Wells and Morgan are critical of the Law Reform Commission of Canada for focusing on the rights of the foetus when creating an offence of destroying or injuring a foetus. They suggest that it would be preferable to focus on the interests of the pregnant woman in her foetus and consequently limit liability to third parties (1991: 442).

Contributions in this collection of essays have highlighted the right to reproductive freedom, the right of a woman to choose if, when and how many children she will have. The importance of this right has been recognised by organisations such as the United Nations (Sadik, 1997) and the World Health Organisation (WHO). The WHO suggests that

> [r]eproductive rights rest on the recognition of the basic right of all couples and individuals to decide freely and responsibly the number, spacing and timing of their children and to have the information and means to do so, and the right to attain the highest standard of sexual and reproductive health. They also include the right of all to make decisions concerning reproduction free of discrimination, coercion and violence.[18]

The reproductive rights of a woman are most often discussed as negative rights – the right to avoid reproduction if one so chooses, through contraception and abortion. It is suggested that the right to reproductive freedom, the right to choose, encompasses the right to a carry a child to term if desired: "[i]n addition to freedom to avoid procreation, procreative liberty includes the freedom to procreate – the freedom to beget and bear children if one chooses" (Robertson, 1994: 29). Wells and Morgan note that "a woman may, in addition to her interest in determining whether her pregnancy is terminated, have an equally

[18] See http://www.who.int/reproductive-health/gender/

compelling interest in ensuring the preservation of her foetus" (1991: 431) and "there is no reason why the two should be regarded as incompatible" (1991: 443). In the American context, Robertson has noted that although "there is little explicit law concerning the right to reproduce … dicta in many cases suggests that such a right exists" (1994: 36).

While the right to reproductive freedom has proven controversial in this jurisdiction (Mullally, 2006: 141),[19] the right to marry and found a family under the Irish Constitution has been recognised. The unenumerated right to marry was first enunciated in *Ryan v Attorney General* (1965) and elaborated upon in *Murrray v Attorney General* (1985).[20] In the latter case, a husband and wife who were imprisoned by the State claimed a right to found a family and it was held that the constitution recognised a right to marry and

> … [a]n adjunct to this right, was also the right to beget children which likewise was a personal right protected by Article 40.3.1 of the Constitution.… As with similar such rights this right to marry is not an absolute one and its exercise may be prescribed by legal restrictions, though such restrictions must be reasonable, an example of which would be those which are sustainable in the public interest.[21]

The right to marry and found a family is also recognised in Article 12 of the European Convention on Human Rights: "Men and women of marriageable age have the right to marry and to found a family, according to the national laws governing the exercise of this right." Article 12 does not, however, impose positive obligations on the state to support in economic terms the foundation of a family; rather, "it denoted

---

[19] Mullally (2006) suggests that "[i]n Ireland, women's reproductive health has long been a contested terrain.… The overwhelming concern to define Ireland as 'not England' ensured that women's reproductive autonomy would be sacrificed to a greater good of a post-colonial political project."

[20] A similar decision was reached by the European Court of Human Rights (based on right to marry and found a family in Art 12) in *X v UK*: "The Article grants the general right to found a family; it does not grant that possibility should be available at any given moment" (Fenwick, 2007: 103–4).

[21] See also *Foy v An T-Ard Chlaraitheoir and others* and *Fitzpatrick v K.*

an interference with the ability to found a family and thus prevents the non-voluntary use of sterilisation or abortion" (Fenwick, 2007: 103). It is arguable that, had the focus of the legal argument in *Vo v France* been on the rights of the complainant under Article 12, the outcome of the case may have been different. The European Court has always been reluctant to pronounce upon the question of when the right to life begins, opting instead to respect "the diversity of views on the point at which life begins, of legal cultures and of national standards of protection" (*Vo v France,* 2005: para. 82). Had the right to found a family been considered, this dilemma could have been avoided, and the Court could have moved from the notion of the mother-foetal conflict which seems to surround the debate on the right to life, both in Europe and this jurisdiction. O'Donovan suggests:

> The practical point is that there was a third-party interference with Mrs Vo's autonomy and bodily integrity, with her life plans, with her relationship with her unborn child. To say that this is a question of the child's rights only and that it must be born alive in order to vindicate its rights, is inadequate (2006: 122).

An associated right is the right to bodily integrity which has also been implicitly recognised under the European Convention[22] and under Article 40.3.1° of the Irish Constitution. The right to bodily integrity was recognised by Kenny J in *Ryan v Attorney General* (1965)[23] and in the case of *In Re a Ward of Court (no.2)* (1996). This latter case concerned the withdrawal of artificial means of nourishment and established that

---

[22] *Guerra and Others v Italy*. Walsh J held obiter that "Article 2 also guarantees the protection of the bodily integrity of the applicants. The wording of Article 3 also clearly indicates that the Convention extends to the protection of bodily integrity". Article 8 of the Convention is also relevant. In *Tysiac v Poland*, it was held that "private life includes a person's physical and psychological integrity".

[23] It was held that "… one of the personal rights of the citizen protected by the general guarantee is the right to bodily integrity. I understand the right to bodily integrity to mean that no mutilation of the body or any of its members may be carried out on any citizen under authority of the law except for the good of the whole body and that no process which is or may, as a matter of probability, be dangerous or harmful to the life or health of the citizens or any of them may be imposed [in the sense of being made compulsory] by an Act of the Oireachtas." (Ibid.: 313-314. See also *The State [C] v Frawley*.

one may not be compelled to undergo medical treatment even where a refusal would result in one's death. To compel medical treatment in these circumstances would, the court found, amount to an encroachment upon the individual's right to bodily integrity, as well as his or her right to privacy. Unwanted third party interference with a foetus may similarly be viewed as an encroachment of the woman's right to bodily integrity. O'Donovan suggested that "[i]n a wanted pregnancy the fetus is protected by the mother through her body. Interference by a third party against the will of the mother is a violation of her bodily integrity" (2006: 121). The criminalisation of unwanted third party interference with the foetus "… enhances [the woman's] right to conceive and carry a child free from external interference" and "… to deprive a woman of her future child cannot be seen as anything less than a gross insult to her bodily integrity" (Mason, 2005: 109).

Conclusion

The question of how to accommodate harm which occurs to a foetus in the womb is controversial and complex. Recent moves in the US and Canada[24] to criminalise such behaviour have stirred the passions of their citizens and no doubt any such move in this jurisdiction would prove to be similarly contentious. The decision in *Vo v France* suggests that member states are not obligated under the European Convention on Human Rights to create criminal legislation to vindicate the rights of the foetus against unwanted third party interference, however an analysis of the rights of the woman may point towards a different outcome. It is submitted that the analysis of the constitutional rights of the foetus and the woman in this jurisdiction warrant the provision of sanctions against those who kill a foetus against the wishes of the woman. It is important

---

[24] Canadian Unborn Victims of Crime Bill, (BILL C-484) is currently (May 2008) being considered by the Canadian legislature. Proposed changes to the Canadian Criminal code: s238.1 (1) Every person who, directly or indirectly, causes the death of a child during birth or at any stage of development before birth while committing or attempting to commit an offence against the mother of the child, who the person knows or ought to know is pregnant (a) is guilty of an indictable offence and liable to imprisonment for life and to a minimum punishment of imprisonment for a term of 10 years if the person… (6) An offence referred to in this section committed against a child is not included in any offence committed against the mother of the child.

to acknowledge the inherent value of the foetus and to enact legislation to prevent harm occurring to the foetus, but it is submitted that this does not require the recognition of foetal personhood. Although it has been suggested that legislation which equates born and unborn life for the purposes of the criminalisation of harm to the foetus against the wishes of the mother should not be viewed as a derogation of the rights of the woman, this view continues to persist and diminishes support for legislation dealing with this issue. Rather than focusing on foetal personhood, a right explicitly recognised in our Constitution, the legislature could frame legislation on this issue to focus on a woman's rights and her interest in her foetus. Although the right to found a family, to carry a child to term and the right to bodily integrity are not unlimited, they could form the basis of arguments in favour of protecting a woman from unwarranted interference with her foetus. Legislation framed to focus on the rights of the woman achieves similar aims to that focused on foetal rights while recognising the special nature of foetal life and its nature distinct from born life.

Bibliography

Bateup, C. (2000) "Can Reproductive Rights be 'Human' Rights? Some Thoughts on the inclusion of women's rights in mainstream human rights discourse" 6(2) *Australian Journal of Human Rights* 33.

Casey, G. (2002) "Pregnant Woman and Unborn Child: Legal Adversaries?" 8 *Medico-Legal Journal of Ireland* 75.

Casey, J. (2000) *Constitutional Law in Ireland* Dublin: Roundhall, Sweet and Maxwell.

Charlton, P. (1992) *Offences Against the Person*, Dublin: The Round Hall Press.

Clarkson, C.M.V. and Keating, H.M. (1998) *Criminal Law: Text and Materials* 4th edition London: Sweet & Maxwell.

Cusack, DA, Bacik, I and Binchy, W (1997) "Abortion-Conflicting Rights, Duties and Arguments" 3 *Medico-Legal Journal of Ireland* 82.

Feinberg, J. (1984) *The Moral Limits of the Criminal Law, Volume 1: Harm to Others* Oxford: Oxford University Press.

Fenwick, H. (2007) *Civil Liberties and Human Rights* 4th edition Oxon: Routledge-Cavendish.

Ferner, R.E. and McDowell, S.E. (2006) "Doctors charged with manslaughter in the course of medical practice, 1795-2005: A literature review" 99(6) *Journal of the Royal Society of Medicine* 309.

Jolicoeur-Wonnacott, C. (2000) "The Unborn Victims of Violence Act: Friend or Foe to the Unborn" 17(3) *Thomas M. Cooley Law Review* 563.

Keown, I.J. (1988) "The Scope of the Offence of Child Destruction" 104 *Law Quarterly Review* 120.

Kingston, J., Whelan, A. and Bacik, I. (1997) *Abortion and the Law* Dublin: Round Hall Sweet & Maxwell.

Lacey, N., Wells, C. and Quick, O. (2003) *Reconstructing Criminal Law, Texts & Materials* 3rd edition, London: Lexis Nexis Butterworths.

Madden, D. (1997) "Abortion and the Law – Review and Commentary" 3 *Medico-Legal Journal of Ireland* 103.

Mason, J.K. (2005) "What's in a name? The vagaries of *Vo v France*" 17(1) *Child and Family Law Quarterly* 97.

Moriarty, B. and Mooney-Cotter, A.M. (2004) *Human Rights Law (Law Society of Ireland Manual)* Oxford: Oxford University Press.

Mullally, S. (2006) *Gender, Culture and Human Rights, Reclaiming Universalism* Oxford: Hart Publishing.

Murray, H. (1997) *Using Human Rights Law in English Courts* Oxford: Hart Publishing.

Ni Raifeartaigh, U. (2001) "The European Convention on Human Rights and the Irish Criminal Justice System" 4(2) *Judicial Studies Institute Journal* 20.

O'Donovan, K. (2006) "Taking a Neutral Stance on the Legal Protection of the Fetus, Vo v France" 14 *Medical Law Review* 115.

Plomer, A. (2005) "A Foetal Right to Life? The Case of Vo v France" 5(2) *Human Rights Law Review* 311.

Robertson, J.A. (1994) *Children of Choice: Freedom and the New Reproductive Technologies* Princeton, NJ: Princeton University Press.

Sadik, N. (1997)"The Right to Reproductive and Sexual Health", available at http://www.un.org/womenwatch/directory/reproductive_health_10305.htm.

Schweppe, J. (2003) "Beyond Abortion – The Right to Life of the Unborn Child Under Irish Law" 3 UCDLR 1.

Schweppe, J. (2005) "Revisiting Article 40.3.3: Part One: Third Party Foetal Assault" *Irish Journal of Family Law* 19.

Schweppe, J. (2006) "Pregnant Women and Unborn Children: In Utero Drug Exposure" *Irish Journal of Family Law* 19.

Sheikh, A. and Cusack, D. (1997) "Maternal Brain Death, Pregnancy and the Foetus: The Medico-Legal Implications" 7(2) *Medico-Legal Journal of Ireland* 75.

Smith, J. and Hogan, B. (1999) *Criminal Law* 9th edition, London: Butterworths.

Spain, E. (2006) "Vo v France: Reasonable Settlement or Missed Opportunity?" *Irish Journal of Family Law* 16.

Stark, Congressman P., Addressing the House of Representatives, Thursday, February 26, 2004. Avaliable at http://www.house.gov/stark/news/108th/2004_floor/floor_2004_unbornvictims.htm.

Wells, C. and Morgan, D. (1991) "Whose Foetus is it?" 18 *Journal of Law and Society* 431.

Williams, G.F. (1983) *Textbook of Criminal Law,* 2nd edition, London: Stevens & Sons.

(1997) "Case Comment" *Criminal Law Review* 829..

Cases

Attorney General v X [1992] ILRM 401.

Attorney General (SPUC) v Open Door Counselling [1988] IR 593.

Attorney General's Reference (No. 3 of 1994) [1997] 3 All ER 936.

Boso v Italy (2002) Application No. 50490/99. Decision 05.09.2002.

Corway v Independent Newspapers [1999] 4 IR 484.

Fitzpatrick v K [2008] IEHC 104.

Foy v An T-Ard Chlaraitheoir and others [2002] IEHC 116 at para 142.

G v An Bord Uchtala [1980] IR 32.

Guerra and Others v Italy (116/1996/735/932) 19 February 1998.

H v Norway (1992) Application No. 17004/90. Commission Decision 19.05.1992.

In Re a Ward of Court (no.2) [1996] 2 IR 73.

MR v TR [2006] IEHC 359.

Murrray v Attorney General [1985] IR 532.

Open Door and Dublin Well Woman v Ireland (A/246-A): (1993) 15 E.H.R.R. 244.

Patton v U.K. (1980) (1980) 3 EHRR 408.

R v Brain (1834) 6 C.P. 349.

Ryan v Attorney General [1965] IR 294.

The State [C] v *Frawley* [1976] I.R. 365.

Tysiac v Poland (Application no. 5410/03), 20 March 2007.

Vo v France (2005) 40 EHRR 12.

X v UK Appl 6564/74; D & R 2 (1975).

6

Maternal Consumption of Drugs and Alcohol in Pregnancy: A Child Protection Concern

Liam Curran

Introduction

> Problem drug or alcohol use by pregnant women should be routinely recorded at the antenatal clinic and these data linked to those on stillbirths, congenital abnormalities in the newborn, and subsequent developmental abnormalities in the child. This would enable epidemiological studies to be carried out to establish the relationship between maternal problem drug use and congenital and developmental abnormalities in the child (*Hidden Harm*, 2003).

The above is taken directly from the Advisory Council on the Misuse of Drugs (ACMD) report entitled *Hidden Harm*, which was submitted to the United Kingdom Government in 2003. In Ireland such a recommendation is unlikely to be made or indeed taken seriously. Illicit drug and alcohol use in pregnancy is a grey area of Irish social and legal policy, while the issue of seeking to protect the unborn from harm is even further away from policy development. The professional complexity of offering protection to the unborn in terms of legal, medical and social work practice is one that has gained considerable attention over the past two decades in many jurisdictions outside the Irish state.

It is somewhat of a contradiction within Irish social and legal policy that, given the constitutional status of the unborn in Article 40.3.3°, we do not offer any form of interventionist practice (outside of the abortion decision) to secure and vindicate the life of the unborn. Is it reasonable to assume that Article 40.3.3° was solely inserted into our Constitution on the single issue of abortion, and as such does not concern itself with other forms of protection for the unborn? Where parental consumption of illicit drugs and alcohol are, under medical advice, likely to impair the developing foetus, should the State stand back and exhibit indifference? Or, should State services develop some level of interventions that seek to secure the welfare of both mother and newborn child?

It is perhaps with some concern that we look to our closest neighbour, the UK, where under the Abortion Act 1967 termination of pregnancy is an entitlement up to week 24 of gestation. However, that State still acknowledges its duty to the unborn and has since 1999 offered guidance to multi-disciplinary social care professionals in *Working Together under the Child Care Act 1989* states:

> The legal status of a child before it is born is significantly different to its status post birth. However, if there is reasonable cause to suspect that a child is at risk of harm before it is born, during its birth, or after its birth, it is appropriate to take action to identify and address the risks (1999).

The most recent data for pre-birth registrations in the UK gives a figure of 25,900 children on the child protection register as of 31 March 2005, 310 of which were for unborn children (Department of Education and Skills, 2006).

Research in the UK has shown that this area of child protection of the unborn is fraught with complexity, and is handled very differently in various areas of the UK child protection services (Barker, 1997). It can also be noted that in the United States State legislators are recognising the unborn as a victim for the purposes of imposing criminal sanction on those who harm or impair the development of the unborn. Christie states that such crimes include "vehicular homicide, foeticide or child abuse" (2006: 73). What is emerging in international legal rulings is that the complex area of maternal-foetal conflict is beginning to be addressed, with the rights of the unborn to protection and a safe passage to birth taking centre stage.

Irish literature is beginning to emerge, which is also suggesting the need to consider the welfare and protection of the unborn in circumstances where drugs and alcohol are consumed during pregnancy, both in the medical fields (Barry et al., 2007; Fagan and Keenan, 2006) and in the law (Charleton, McDermott, Bolger, 1999; Schweppe, 2005, 2006). Alcohol and substance use are being increasingly identified as core public health issues generally (Rawaf, 1998; Health Research Board, 2000; Butler, 2002b; Butler and Mayock, 2005) and in pregnancy particularly (King, 1991; Becker and Duffy 2002; Buchanan and Corby, 2005; Schweppe, 2006).

Medical studies conducted in an Irish context (Coghlan et al., 1999; Clarke and Fitzpatrick, 2005; Fagan and Keenan, 2006; Barry et al., 2007; McMillan et al., 2007) all concur that early intervention is imperative to achieving the safe passage of the unborn to a healthy outcome post-birth. Such studies call for a coordinated and focused multi-disciplinary response to the issues of drugs and alcohol during pregnancy, suggesting that multi-agency and multi-disciplinary interventions are imperative in the pre-birth stage in order to address issues of risk and potential harm, and promote the welfare of the unborn. However, the effectiveness of any such intervention can only be assessed if the wider society generally concerns itself with the issue. Evidence, however, would suggest that both on a legal and social policy platform we are still seeking to side-step and dismiss the protection of the unborn as merely a political agenda of pro-life campaigns.

Child psychiatrists at the Mater Hospital, Dublin, suggest that the issue of multi-disciplinary work concerning the use of opiates in "utero" is crucial to the post-birth welfare of the child. Clarke and Fitzpatrick's findings assert that there is a need for better liaison between obstetrics, neonatal, addiction, social work and child psychiatric services to ensure early diagnosis and continuity of care (2005: 123). A further study found that the issue of alcohol harm in pregnancy requires "collaboration of paediatricians, child psychiatrists and other health professionals" (Barry et al., 2007: 18). McMillan et al., when commenting on data showing that 58 per cent of the respondents in a study of the use of alcohol in pregnancy, "did not and would not alter their consumption behaviour even after being informed of the risk by health professionals", concluded that education and prevention services need to be delivered by all health care workers in order to address the social acceptance of such behaviours within Irish culture (2006: 283).

Equally, many commentators and research studies suggest that the real harm and concern for the unborn lies in economic and social disadvantage. The Institute of Public Health in Ireland (IPHI) suggest that "an exploration of the relationships between socioeconomic status and congenital anomaly in Ireland would serve to improve our understanding of the social gradients observed in relation to mortality and low birth weight" (2006: 4). A study by O'Connor, Stafford-Johnson and Kelly of 45 opiate-addicted mothers between 1984 and 1986 attending treatment found significant evidence concerning the psycho-social backgrounds of the women (1998). All were unemployed, all smoked and had left school at an average age of 14. There were high levels of family alcoholism, with over half having fathers classed as alcoholics, and one-third of the maternal parents suffering from depression.

This suggests that the psycho-social needs of pregnant drug and alcohol users are significant factors in assessing issues of concern or harm to the unborn.

The challenge of foetal rights and the rights of pregnant women is complex and difficult for all who operate within the field of medical, legal or social policy interventions. It is a contested area that needs much thought and sensitive understanding.

This research presents the results of a study aimed at exploring contemporary thinking on the subject of harm to the unborn child among health care professionals. It sought participants' views, experiences and practices of their role, when providing services to women who use alcohol and drugs while pregnant, and sought views on whether they had a child protection concern in the course of their duties. The research collected data from four public health nurses, five social workers and five maternity hospital personnel.

Thus, this research sought to:

- Explore practitioners' beliefs, views and experiences in relation to their role when working with pregnant women and the unborn

- Examine what causes professional concerns in relation to the unborn child
- Explore participants' professional responses to pregnant women and the unborn child
- Explore what would enhance multi-disciplinary working in responding to pregnant women and their unborn children.

The study explored these aims from the perspective of 14 frontline practitioners from three key services areas with a collective professional history of 212 years of service. It set out to determine where the concern, if any, existed and how such concerns could be addressed while balancing the rights of both mother and her unborn child. In doing so, it acknowledges the medical, social and legal views on the competing rights of both the unborn and the reproductive autonomy of women to choose how they manage their own pregnancy. The professionals involved within this study have a valid standpoint from which to observe this complex and contentious emerging public health issue. Participants were chosen from three distinct areas of both medicine and social services, as it is now generally accepted that multi-disciplinary practice is key to meeting both the medical and psychosocial needs of drug and alcohol service users. In addressing the issue of alcohol and drug use during pregnancy, the work aims to bring together medical and social models of understanding, in the hope that greater understanding and consistency may be found from a shared understanding of the complex needs of pregnant drug and alcohol users and their unborn children.

Services to Pregnant Women

One of the key themes to emerge from the professionals who engaged with the study was the issue of services to drug and alcohol using pregnant women. This is consistent with Becker and Duffy (2002) and EMCDDA (2006) which suggested that current structures veer heavily in favour of male drug and alcohol users, suggesting that services are patriarchal. Pregnant and parenting women who use drugs or alcohol face particular societal condemnation, which can often lead to women failing to access services, or accessing services too late (Woods, 1994, 2000;

Farrell, 1999; United Nations, 2004), or when accessing services may be confronted by professionals who wish to side-step the issues of addiction and "refer on" (Butler, 2002a). The fear of being judged as unfit to be a mother figures highly in the challenges of services trying to engage women for treatment and education supports. In the executive summary of the UN Report, *Substance Abuse Treatment and Care for Women: Case Studies and Lessons Learned*, it states that the "women encounter significant systemic, structural, social, cultural and personal barriers in accessing substance abuse treatment" (2004: 1). The evidence from the literature that barriers exist within drug and alcohol treatment services, coupled with the current structures and services of ante-natal care programmes, suggest that pregnant women accessing services may encounter multiple difficulties within the very services assigned to help (Abbas, 2007; *The Irish Times*, 2007; WHO, 2006, Collins, 2007).

Several respondents indicated that societal and practical living conditions were significant concerns for women affected by this issue. The way drug and alcohol services are structured was seen by a number of respondents as problematic for women in terms of their ability to access help and education. When asked how social workers might reach the women who are pregnant and using drugs and alcohol, a public health nurse expressed the view that ante-natal care needed to be more accessible. Women who are chaotic in the use of drugs or alcohol tend to be less structured and focused in ways that lend themselves to accessing structured health services. As women tend to keep their drug treatment appointments, it was felt that a holistic approach to the treatment and pregnancy could be best managed within the community drug treatment setting as opposed to the medical setting of hospital:

> I would imagine, you know, having services that are more meaningful to women as in maybe having ante-natal care delivered in drug clinics… I would think more, sort of like locally based services (PHN 7).

In another case the senior social worker talked of having family-friendly services where women who are already parents can access services which will cater for their children while they receive treatment:

> One thing that's been evident is that there's a need for such a facility, a sort of facility which combines childcare with support around addiction, you know, in a safe environment (SW 3).

When asked if we were doing enough to educate on the dangers of alcohol and drugs in pregnancy, one of the medical personnel stated:

> Probably not, because a lot of the people that have this problem are of lower social economic status, they usually have poor education and poor links to the relevant people that maybe able to teach them, so maybe a better outreach programme might be of benefit to target certain people (MH 11).

Such findings reflect previous Irish research carried out by Farrell (1999) which concluded that the "lack of childcare facilities and the fear of being cast as an 'unfit mother' were significant barriers which prevented women coming forward to access treatment services" (2001: 173). Similarly, the research conducted by Butler and Woods found that women suffering from HIV, a significant factor within addiction histories, were less likely to access services due to a fear of being cast as an unfit mother and having their children taken into care by the state. (1992)

Copeland talks of the "double deviant" stereotyping that is attributed to women users because they are often viewed as being sexually promiscuous due to their drug and alcohol behaviour (1997: 186). She goes on to explain that the double deviance is born out of the traditional place that women have occupied within society. The literature suggests that this traditional place for Irish women is held very strongly within Irish social policy (Kiely, 1996; Stopper, 2006). One interviewee suggested that due to this societal pressure, women were often the harshest critic of themselves:

> I think if society would see a woman who's using drugs while they're pregnant as the lowest of the low, and the women who are using drugs when they're pregnant are completely aware of that and would also feel that, you know, not feel that they're the lowest of the low but feel very acutely a kind of the, you know, judgment that was out there, but equally would judge themselves quite harshly as well (MH 12).

A key sub-theme which emerged in the data was the concern of respondents that a significant number of the women who engaged with their services (public health, social work and maternity) were from lower socioeconomic groupings. A recent publication by the Institute of Public Health in Ireland suggest that babies born to opiate-using mothers are "at the lowest end of the socio-economic scale and the risks experienced by these babies are exceptionally high" (2006: 52), a view also echoed by Fagan and Keenan (2006). Clearly, as discussed above by MH 11, those women at the lower end of socioeconomic status are currently identified as hard to engage, and current structures may not be sufficient in addressing the needs of these babies and their mothers who are deemed to be at "exceptionally high risk". Such high risk factors were seen by many of the interviewees as being two-fold: first, the level of substance abuse; and secondly, the environmental factors both before and after birth. A hospital-based social worker spoke of the difficulty of maintaining women in structured ante-natal care:

> Some of them will drop out of their drugs treatment programme, they could be living in a car … you know, ante-natal visits are really low on their priority list (MH 12).

Additionally, the simple fact of ante-natal appointments being offered at the wrong time, and on the wrong day, posed a significant challenge to this hospital service:

> And we discovered two things. Wednesday was before pay day and they didn't have the bus fare to come in, and the other thing was eh, literacy or illiteracy, they knew the letter, they knew the letterhead was the hospital, but they couldn't figure out either the day or the date or the time, now we changed the clinic to a Monday (MH 14).

This evidence does suggest that services are trying to do their best in engaging women with drug and alcohol use. MH 11 in her role as a drug liaison midwife has made significant inroads in working with this client group in the north Dublin region. However, there are currently only three drug liaison midwives within the whole country, and only serving the three main maternity hospitals in the Dublin region. The current liaison midwife of the hospital within this study has in the region of over 80 cases of babies born to methadone maintained parents (MH 14). There are no such services to women who live outside the Dublin region:

> If you go outside of Dublin it's very, [drug use is] more pocketed and all of that then makes it more difficult for the women to access services (MH 14).

The development of a drug liaison post within the Dublin region came about as a result of a need for a specialist post for women living with HIV in the late 1990s. It was in working with this group of pregnant women that the disclosure of drug use prompted the development of the current role, with the first drug liaison midwife role appointed in 1999. This role is seen as pivotal to engaging women who are using drugs while pregnant (EMCDDA, 2006: 35; Scully et al., 2004). Clearly, the development of a national policy on the provision of drug liaison midwife services that engage all maternity hospitals should be a matter of priority by the Health Service Executive.

The development of the service in Dublin is highly regarded by the professionals working in the three areas of service in this study (MH 10, 12. 13, 14, PHN 6 and 7 and SW 1, 2 and 3). This suggests that there are at least some attempts at challenging the old patriarchal structures of drug treatment. However, many obstacles remain in order to truly develop a system whereby women can access services without stigma and blockages (Butler and Woods, 1992; Woods, 2000; Becker and Duffy, 2002; EMCDDA, 2006). The development of women-friendly services is imperative in order to promote early access to prevention and education services. The noted success attributed by interviewees to the drug liaison midwife role suggests that it is possible to build effective working relationships with pregnant substance-using women. However, a consistent theme emerging in the data is the lack of joint working and the provision of wrap-around services to women who are identified as in need of specialist services during pregnancy. The data suggest that there is a lack of consistency amongst the different services, which can have a negative impact. This is consistent with the findings of the UK *Hidden Harm* report (2003), which found that effective treatment of parents can have major benefits for the welfare needs of the child. One of the difficulties of the drug liaison role is the lack of effective consistency when she engages with other services:

> I feel passionate that the women do deserve more consistency and, I mean, through that I would think there would be some more clarity for them and potentially better outcomes for baby (MH 14).

There was also evidence that individual professionals working to the same aim of providing and supporting women with substance abuse issues felt isolated in the task and without any sense of collective support:

> I think, you know, that it will be very useful to actually see what, what other people are saying because sometimes you can seem like a voice in a church, you know, sort of speaking to yourself (SW 3).

Multi-disciplinary Work

One of the prominent themes to emerge in the review of literature was the current poor status of multi-agency or multi-disciplinary relationships in working with women who have drug and alcohol addiction needs (Buchanan and Corby, 2005; McKeganey et al., 2002). Such is the growing level of awareness and concern of the impact that addiction has on the family, the UK Government funded the *Hidden Harm* report in 2003. One of its key finding suggests the reasoning as to why personnel need to work more closely together:

> By working together services can take many practical steps to protect and improve the health and well being of affected children (2003: 3).

Such findings also concur with some local medical studies which have made similar recommendations in an Irish context (Barry et al., 2007; McMillian et al., 2007; Clarke, Fagan and Keenan, 2006; Clarke and Fitzpatrick, 2005) and in academic studies (Woods, 2000; Butler, 2002a, 2002b; Butler and Woods, 1992). Although such findings call for closer working with the issue of substance and women, there is also the complex reality that the work of protecting the welfare of the unborn is emotionally challenging for some professionals as documented by Calder (2003). The challenges of working collaboratively in the delivery of services are peppered with mistrust and unrealistic expectations, according to Buchanan and Corby (2005).

The data from this study would also suggest that there are some significant difficulties and barriers within and between professional groups working in the area of addiction, child welfare and maternity services. Clearly, when considering the issues of the welfare of the unborn, professionals can struggle to engage others with their concerns:

> This mother has two children in care as a direct result of her drug misuse but because she's moved areas, then two community care areas are playing a tennis match, nobody's taking responsibility, there's no accountability, [it's] really confusing (MH 13).

This feeling of not being listened to and having concerns taken seriously was a common theme within the sample interviewed. Tunnard (2002) speaks of positive liaison between different disciplines as vital in the task of protecting and promoting the welfare of children exposed to maternal drug and alcohol use. What is of concern about MH 13's view is that the history of the case did not seem to signify the genuine need for intervention to support this mother and her unborn. Such situations ultimately may lead to unwarranted intervention at birth, the newborn being admitted into care and the parent/child bond being damaged:

> I used to put money on she'll deliver now on Friday of a bank holiday weekend and there'll be, you know, high drama, section 12s, like unnecessary stuff, you know, because of bad management (MH 13).

Barker noted that different responses of professionals were likely to arise as a result of the policies and practices of the child protection agencies and workers attached to those services (1997: 226). Similarly, the view that personality rather than policy was a significant factor within the Irish child welfare services was noted:

> I think that social services in Ireland tend to be a mixed bag of people with their own personal and professional view, and I don't

> think that anybody is seriously addressing a lot of issues that are child protection, let alone this area of the unborn (SW 5).

The public health nurses within the sample portrayed a sense of grievance about the way they would be involved with high risk drug and alcohol cases. Notifications would come from the hospital after the birth, and PHNs would often be told at this stage that concerns have existed from early stages in pregnancy, and that various meetings had taken place. This led to a feeling of mistrust developing between the professions:

> Such and such a one is coming home, she's hepatitis or something else, or the child's on withdrawal symptoms, won't be discharged for three weeks and then the child is dumped out on the district so where do you go to? (PHN 9).

A public health nurse expressed how angry she was at being left out of the loop when asked to engage with a mother who had been under both the addiction services and the drug liaison midwife in the ante-natal stage:

> Because I was very angry at that, you know, finding out there's a meeting tomorrow and I made phone calls and I asked people, you know, why wasn't I involved? And I was told that it wasn't anything to do with me, it wasn't my remit, it wasn't, you know, you know, I was just the public health nurse, it wasn't up to them to involve me, it wasn't their role to involve me and they had dealt with it sufficiently and, you know, that was it (PHN 6).

Clearly this feeling of being excluded could be put down to poor communication. Lack of communication aids the development of mistrust, which ultimately creates difficult working relationships. Buckley (2000) talks of the need for professionals to develop a child-centred approach which can transcend hostilities and tensions between professionals. Similarly, Butler (1996) found that some agencies were perceived of doing what are perceived to be the more pleasant elements of practice, while others are left with the difficult practice decisions. It was also an observation by Butler that non-social work practitioners were unwilling to take on a social policing role. This was not a finding of this study in that, individually, all respondents acknowledged their responsibility to the issues. Another participant talked of the lack of communication between the different disciplines as a primary factor in the frustrations she experienced in working with drug and alcohol "baby cases":

> I often think, because it's a contradiction in terms, I mean, I think as Irish people we're so good at talking and all the rest and yet we're dreadful communicators a lot of the time, you know (PH 8).

What is essential in any partnership role that is endeavouring to protect and promote the welfare of others is the art of communication. Murphy argues that "good communication can help to secure greater involvement by making individuals feel included and confident that they are sufficiently well informed to make useful contributions" (2004: 35). This was echoed in the research:

> I keep coming back to that, but I suppose it does just make you much more aware of, you know, when you're in the picture, the bigger picture and more of the potential problems that might occur (PHN 9).

> Yeah, I have to say I think probably public health nurses in there at the beginning would be quite a good idea, sometimes we forget them (MH 13).

A clear finding from the data is that all the maternity personnel spoke highly of their internal working strategies. Clear multi-disciplinary meetings take place each week; cases where issues of risk as a result of alcohol or drug use are given considerable status and a quick response by all the professionals concerned. This ensures careful management of the cases, and set down clear care plans in respect of the pregnant women:

> Working internally here it's quite good, yeah, quite well balanced and quite well organised (MH 11).

> We will usually be together and there are multidisciplinary meetings, monthly, and then make a plan for her so, it is working quite well so far, we do discuss cases like this patient is at risk, what we need to do and try to help the mother (MH 12).

All five maternity personnel within the study had some level of difficulty when liaising with external agencies – particularly the Health Service Executive. Such external requests, for example, might be a request for a family support worker to maintain the care package that had been started within the maternity hospital:

> I mean, you know, we would hope that in that planning process, for example, if it's home help she needs, or a family support worker, you know, and this used to completely upset me that at 28 weeks we'd be talking about family support worker, baby would be born, spend four weeks in the NICU having a neonatal withdrawal and still no family support worker, like where's the planning involved in that, you know, so I would see that as a huge problem (MH 14).

When asked what they would like to see in place for pregnant substance users in terms of an integrated case management system, one respondent highlighted the difference between social and medical models of care as potential difficulties in achieving an integrated system of shared care:

> I think there's probably a slight disconnection between the social work services and the medical services, you know (MH 10).

Combined with the isolation and non-engaging of public health nurses, and the difficulty in engaging social work services as previously mentioned, a picture emerges of disjointed services and non-cooperative practices. The UN report of 2004 clearly states that appropriate interventions must include a collaboration between the substance abuse treatment sectors and prenatal and child care services. Evidence of joint working and multi-disciplinary liaison from this study suggests that current structures are not meeting the effective treatment and intervention levels that are deemed in research to be best practices (Buchanan and Corby, 2005). The concern of poor interactive mechanisms was also shared by the social work services in a reflection on their own services:

> I am irritated by the way the health board operates anyway, I would have had a much greater sense of working in Scotland and other areas of proper multidisciplinary and multi-agency working (SW 5).

Policy and Procedure

The research found that there was no policy or procedure in operation for the multi-disciplinary working within the field of drug and alcohol use in pregnancy. Currently, there is no assessment framework or guidance to assess the risks or needs in respect of the welfare of the unborn or new-born child. Barker (1997) talks of professional lack of clarity and confusion with regards to the unborn child. The safeguarding of the unborn was a significant concern of all interviewees of the study. However, that application of concerns to practice principles was a difficult transition for some. It also emerged that there was more awareness of the dangers of drug use than alcohol use during pregnancy. Some argued that if we had clear policy and procedure this issue might be addressed:

> I do think it's a fault of the health system authority (HSE) that we tend not to focus too much on alcohol abusers, to the extent as we would drug users… (MH 13).

The feeling of not having any guidance and not knowing what do was expressed:

> It's sad to think that we might need a protocol how to communicate but maybe policy and procedure does again, stipulate certain things that have to be done (PHN 9).

> I would like to see is a consistent approach in terms of policy or guidelines (MH 11).

One local health office in the region has published guidance to professionals in respect of the unborn and concerns.

> If the social worker is satisfied that there are serious concerns we convene a child protection, a pre-birth child protection conference, we invite parents as appropriate in the same way as you invite parents under the same guidance as we would if the child were born (SW 4).

This produces confusion within the other statutory social work services. A social worker in another local health office area talked of needing a mechanism to be put in place in order to have proper multi-disciplinary case conferences:

> … where the hospital would have serious concerns around the level of alcohol or drug misuse, you know, and the associated problems that often come with that, that eh, that there should be some mechanism for establishing a pre-birth conference (SW 3).

Farrell's overview in 1999 stated that assurance needed to be given to female drug users that seeking treatment would not jeopardise their role as mother. It would be difficult to see how such assurance could be given judging by the discrepancies and inconsistencies of current practices. Another social work practitioner, when asked if policy and procedure could help her in her practice, replied:

> Definitely, yeah, because I think again without protocol or procedure every case is dealt with differently, you know, and sometimes that doesn't work at times, but I think that if everyone is very clear about what's going on and the importance of working with an expectant mother, you know, some people would see it as important, some people wouldn't but if there's a protocol and a procedure there, these people have to be worked with, you know (SW 2).

Although some positive policy initiatives have taken place in Ireland over recent years, such as the drug liaison midwife role, there is no clear auditing or evaluation of current service provision for drug or alcohol misusing women. This has led to the Department of Health describing current services being developed "on an ad hoc basis rather than in a strategic national focus" (2006: 68). This belief about an "ad hoc" nature of service was stated on a number of occasions:

> It's all a bit ad hoc, there is, and again it comes back to what I feel is, eh, lack of guidelines or procedures in place and depending who the team leader is, principal social worker it depends on the response (MH 14).

> Would have a drugs liaison midwife to liaise with the local health offices and the care teams but her experiences would be a very

> disjointed, some very positive experiences but very, very negative experiences (PHN 8).

> We have lots of policies but we never get the procedures written so everything is not uniform, a bit ad hoc. Now I would also say that it shouldn't just be for drugs and alcohol because domestic violence should be in there as well because usually that is when the physical violence will start, either when she falls pregnant or if she chooses to leave him so, you know (SW 1).

The issue of domestic violence when considering the welfare of the unborn is considered in a number of international studies (Gilliland et al., 1998; Jasinski, 2001; Humphreys and Stanley, 2006). The correlation between domestic violence and drug and alcohol use is considered as a significant factor in protecting the welfare of a pregnant woman and her unborn child. Foetal harm and possible death have gained considerable attention which has lead to Schweppe (2005) calling on the Irish legislator to revisit the constitutional amendment of 40.3.3° in respect of violence and the unborn. Some main points to surface within the study overall that policy and procedure could assist with include:

- The wide variation in knowledge between professions and within professions as to what constituted risk or welfare issues for pregnant women
- The different roles within the professions with some having responsibility to adults and some to children
- The lack of guidance and shared understanding between professional groupings on what were acceptable or unacceptable behaviours in parenting
- Concerns that mothers may not be able to care for their new born without community-based supports
- Concerns that as designated officers in respect of child protection legislation constituted making a child protection referral where they have concerns that the welfare of the unborn is at risk due to maternal use of substances.

Legislation – How it is Perceived

The participants were asked to consider their understanding of the legislation in respect of concerns for the unborn. How did they view the constitutional status of the unborn and what if any implications this had on their practice? The views ranged from clear accountability to the unborn, with the unborn being treated in a similar manner as the born child, to views that there is nothing that can be done until the child is born. This confusion is replicated within the literature and is consistent with the views expressed by both Schweppe (2005, 2006) and Charleton et al. (1999). Interestingly, what did emerge in the findings is the belief by some that the Child Care Act 1991 does have a mandate to intervene, while others felt it did not. One local health office manager who has direct management responsibility in the child welfare system stated:

> I would have the similar child protection functions as I have for children who are born where risks are identified, during the pregnancy to a child who, as yet unborn, and we proceed accordingly (SW 4).

However, other professionals talked of having their "hands tied" when attempting to intervene where they had concerns for the unborn:

> Yeah, and again it's just, I would feel that our hands are tied in that there is nothing I can do (SW 2).

One respondent talked of the need for a mental/cultural shift in people's thinking about how we address the needs of the unborn. This would be consistent with the developments that are taking place internationally in respect of revisiting the welfare of the unborn.

> I would have these worries so, in other words, in my view, personal view, the child protection system should operate for the unborn as it does for the born child, and that, so that maybe, a mental and cultural shift that we need to make to be more systematic, in how we consider risks for unborn children (SW 4).

Such cultural shifts have for some time been taking place in other jurisdictions, most notably in the United States, which has moved to both punitive responses and child welfare responses where maternal behaviour poses risk to the unborn. In their studies, Alperen and Paone talk of the problematic nature of punitive approaches that have taken place within the US child welfare system (1998). Punitive measures can have the negative effect of preventing women coming forward for help. There was no call for punitive measures from any of the respondents to this study. Indeed, respondents were more in favour of developing services for women rather than penalising them, a view that would be consistent with Fortin, who suggests that statutory coercion by way of criminal sanction is unlikely to persuade pregnant women to have more thought for their unborn (Fortin, 1988: 76), and other studies which show that criminal sanctions deter women from seeking prenatal and substance misuse treatment (Berrien, 1990: 340; Paone and Alperen, 1998: 103):

> Absolutely, yes, yeah, the punitive approach isn't really going to work, women need support not damnation by the courts (PHN 9).

> I suppose it's both actually, it's not just child protection. It's the maternal protection in the first place (MH 11).

The professional interpretation of the constitutional statement of Article 40.3.3° varied from individual to individual in the study. Some viewed it as having no role in day-to-day practice of working with maternal behaviour that may harm the unborn, while others felt quite strongly that we were failing to uphold the constitutional rights of the unborn. The Constitution of Ireland specifically protects the right to life of the unborn, while at the same time ensuring the equal right to life of the mother:

> And it's, you know, until the child is born those rights don't appear to come into play (MH 14).

> I suppose there's a conflict in rights there, and generally I think the situations always go in favour of the parents in that situation in my experience (MH 10).

There was general acceptance that the current system could not intervene, where professionals might have serious concerns for the welfare of the unborn in serious cases of drug and alcohol use. However one professional talked of the inequalities that she perceived in the law. She had personal experience of being involved in a pre-birth case where the court had ordered a mother to undergo medical direction in order to safeguard the welfare of the unborn. These cases have taken place where it was necessary to give certain medications in order to protect the welfare of the unborn:

> You see, part of me in my total cynical way, right, thinks it is so much easier for, you know, super medics to go to a judge and it's sort of a sexier story for want of a better expression (MH 13).

What became clear in discussions on the subject of law and competing rights is that these "rights" cannot be viewed independently of each other, but that some form of compromised intervention is needed. It was generally accepted that respondents felt a sense of unease and frustration in trying to meet the needs of both mother and unborn where concerns were expressed. The concept of a public health approach with a legislative basis, which would incorporate education, further research and a coherent holistic harm reduction treatment option, was the main finding in discussing the legislative base for addressing the problem. Such findings would concur with the literature, where many advocate strongly that non-judgemental accessible services are the key to successful outcomes for children of drug and alcohol misusing parents (Butler, 2002a, 2002b, 2002c; Tunnard, 2002; Woods, 2002; Schroeder, 2000; EMCCDA, 2006; Barry et al., 2007).

> It probably would be a maternal issue, and if you can help the mother to help herself then the baby should be fairly safe after the baby is born (MH 11).

Child Protection or Not?

Health care providers, such as the participants within this study, will sometimes face the difficult responsibility of making decisions that affect their duty of caring for pregnant women in a non-judgemental way. The decision to consider the welfare of the unborn, when trying to engage a mother who is exhibiting behaviour that is endangering that welfare, is loaded with moral, ethical and social responsibility. The absence of clear guidelines that would help professionals caught between their responsibility to the mother and their responsibility to the unborn leave health care professionals without a suitable response that can ease their concerns.

In the research, the ethical struggles of respondents were similar to those ethical principles described by Loewenberg and Dolgoff (1996). This subject of child protection for the unborn is complex, and brings with it the difficulty of balancing the rights and wrongs of professional practice:

> We proceed in practice faced with those ethical dilemmas usually, most usually one is faced with a parent who is seeking assistance and there are times where parents are not seeking assistance (MH 11).

What is evident in the data is that respondents were unanimous in their view that drug and alcohol abuse can harm the outcome of the unborn. Many expressed the view that this harm is more likely in the first trimester of pregnancy, which poses a serious challenge, in that many women might not be even aware of their pregnancy at this stage. It was therefore a belief that any responses given retrospectively are of little use in preventing the short- or long-term effects that research suggests are possible as a result of drug and alcohol misuse in pregnancy. This finding suggests that the most effective protection given to the unborn is maternal protection, and coherent education within wider social policy directives by the Department of Health.

No respondents sought punitive actions to be taken against women who continued to use drugs and alcohol in pregnancy. Respondents were asked if they considered the use of alcohol and drugs in pregnancy as a child protection issue. The following is a sample of the responses given:

> Personally, I think absolutely (SW 5).

> Where one human being's actions or inactions directly impact in a negative way on another human being and that human being is under 18 or pre-birth then it becomes a child protection issue, so yes it is a child protection issue (PHN 9).

> Child protection has a huge role right, eh, it's a role that should be there throughout the entire pregnancy and not just when the child is born (MH 13).
>
> I definitely would consider it to be child protection, yeah, because I think it should be seen as that in the beginning (PHN 6).
>
> I would say yes, there are child protection issues right, you know, just to be the level and I think the early intervention could be the stuff that, you know, ... even if you're reducing the amount of drugs or alcohol would have been consumed during the pregnancy you should be helping the foetus (SW 2).
>
> Yes, it is child protection (MH 14).

The impact of alcohol consumption and illicit drug use during pregnancy on the developmental outcomes for newborn babies has been fully explored within this text. This exploration suggests that the protection of the unborn is a significant social issue, which has to be confronted and addressed in a coherent manner.

However, the study by Collins at the Rotunda offers up evidence that such services are being offered in a haphazard manner (2007: 64). What is also of concern are statistics published by the Department of Health which state that 22.2 per cent of pregnant women wait until the second trimester of pregnancy before presenting for ante-natal care, while 7.9 per cent do not present until the third trimester (2006: 248). When addressing the concerns for the welfare of the unborn, these wider social issues cannot be ignored. The application of current ante-natal strategies in line with those called for by the WHO (2006) and outlined within the study could play a significant part in promoting the welfare of the unborn.

Where concerns persist following ante-natal assessment and advice, practitioners felt there was a need for more formal assessment structure that combined both the medical and social philosophies of protection and welfare. Respondents were informed that the UK child protection system had 310 pre-birth registrations in 2005 (DES, 2006), and were asked if they felt that this was useful tool in intervention or not:

> I think that should happen here (SW 5).
>
> It could, yeah, I think it would be useful, you know, there may be previous child protection issues, or even where the hospital would have serious concerns around the level of alcohol or drug misuse, you know, and the associated problems that often come with that, that, that there should be some mechanism for establishing a pre-birth conference (SW 3).

But respondents also talked about the current ad hoc responses from community care social work services as a major stumbling block to effective intervention, where social work services were feared rather than being perceived as supportive or preventative in their practice. It was clear from several accounts that this ad hoc service was giving mixed messages to parents, who "all knew each other and shared their stories of the social work service" (MH 14). This account is consistent with the findings of Woods (2000a) and Corby (2003), who reported that in child protection services there is still much ambivalence about trying to get the supportive practice correct when working with drug and alcohol abuse in families, while at the same time remaining vigilant in the need to protect from abuse.

It is perhaps interesting to note that as stated in the literature, the subject of the unborn in the United Kingdom has been given its first mention in the reprinted version of *Children First* (1999). In a memo sent to all chief executives by the Child Care Policy Unit in May 2004, concern was expressed by the Department of Health that notifications from other jurisdictions were not being acted upon or were being acted upon too late. It cited cases where pregnant women who had fled other jurisdictions had had their babies and left the maternity hospital before notifications were passed down (Child Care Policy Unit, 2004). The memo closes by emphasising the importance of such information being passed to maternity hospitals without delay.

This clarity of procedure and guidance from the Child Care Policy Unit of the Department of Health, in respect of children conceived outside this jurisdiction, is in stark contrast to the guidance given internally for children conceived and born in Ireland.

Overall Conclusion

A number of key points to emerge from the findings:

- The respondents highlighted the need for drug and alcohol services for pregnant women to be more women-friendly and accessible
- The need for maternity and ante-natal services to be more accessible is also highlighted
- The need for more interaction between the services of adult, child and maternity professionals
- Maternal protection is good child protection
- Services be more supportive and caring rather than being coercive and controlling
- The need for procedural guidance to assist professionals in this complex area of practice
- Less legally-driven and more social services provision with effective supports
- Services are currently delivered in an "ad hoc" manner which is causing frustration to the professionals trying to assist
- That alcohol and illicit drug use in pregnancy is a child protection concern and an issue to be addressed.

The research makes the following seven recommendations:

1. All agencies working with pregnant drug and alcohol users should recognise that they have a responsibility towards dependent children and the unborn. Services should consider whether they could improve the effectiveness of their interventions by adopting a holistic approach to service delivery.
2. The current drug liaison midwife role should be extended so that all drug treatment services nationally can have access to the most appropriate guidance, supports and maternity links. The study would suggest that the appointment of a national drug liaison midwife be

put in place to guide the current system and to campaign for better joined up services to pregnant women.

3. That the HSE in conjunction with the maternity services develop multi-disciplinary training programmes on pre-birth risk assessment. This would facilitate the bringing together of professionals from the different professional groupings to work together on effective, preventive interventions where concerns exist.

4. The Department of Health consider setting up a national advisory group with regional representation to advise and inform on the development of services for pregnant women who use drugs and alcohol during pregnancy. Suggested membership to include GPs, public health nurses, social workers, drug liaison midwives, consultant gynaecologists and community welfare officers and drug treatment professionals.

5. That the Health Service Executive in partnership with the maternity hospitals develop a joint procedure to detail the working relationships and mandatory procedures for dealing with high risk pregnancies due to illicit drugs and alcohol consumption, where there is a concern for the welfare of the unborn.

6. That guidance is issued under the Child Care Act 1991 for appropriate and sensitive measures to protect and promote the welfare of the unborn. That such guidance is universal and consistent in its application.

7. That the HSE Health Promotions Service develop programmes and advertising to educate women who are thinking of becoming pregnant concerning the use of substance use and alcohol during pregnancy. The current HSE promotion on the issues of folic acid in pregnancy is an example of the promotional scale needed on the subject of illicit drugs and alcohol in pregnancy.

Conclusion

This study set out to explore what was termed a "grey area" within Irish social and legal policy. In doing so it sought the views, experiences and concerns of fourteen health care professionals from different walks of life within Irish public services. The study discovered that although this area might be "grey", it is however one that holds serious concerns and anxieties for those professionals.

The analysis has shown that there is a real and pressing issue to be addressed within the development of future social policy in Ireland. The need for women/parent-friendly services are vital in any attempt to protect and promote the welfare and post-birth outcome of children born to illicit drug and alcohol users. Respondents spoke passionately about maternal protection being the best form of protection the services could offer to the unborn. It is also apparent that there are major concerns from the different professionals about the poorly structured services, the lack of shared values and the structural blocks to communication and cooperation that still exist in service provision. The research found that current ad hoc service structures need to be reviewed in the light of both medical and social advances that have being made in recent times concerning the welfare and treatment of pregnant women. The development of greater social awareness that could aid the development of fluid, interlinked health and social services is an imperative, if we are to truly promote the welfare of the unborn.

The task in achieving this requires collaboration at all levels within the structures, which has been well documented by Irish academic, legal, medical and social researchers. Evidence cited in this paper suggest that professionals are very aware and committed to the principals of closer working, but find that the lack of guidance in this area to be a major hindrance to their efforts. The results suggest that services need to address the issue of maternal alcohol and substance use in pregnancy. This can only be done through a strategy of multidisciplinary ownership of this complex challenge. Bridge-building between addiction service, child welfare services, health promotion specialists and the field of obstetrics is essential if we are to truly believe in the old adage – prevention is better than cure.

Glossary

SW 1 – Social Worker, Community Field Work (Children Services)

SW 2 – Social Worker, Community Field Work (Children Services)

SW 3 – Social Worker, Family Addiction Support Service (Statutory)

SW 4 – Social Worker, Service Manager, Child Protection Service (Statutory)

SW 5 – Social Worker, Service Manager, Child Protection Service (Voluntary)

PHN 1 – Public Health Nurse, Community Field Work

PHN 2 – Public Health Nurse, Community Field Work

PHN 3 – Public Health Nurse, Community Field Work

PHN 4 – Public Health Nurse, Community Field Work

MH 10 – Neonate Consultant, Maternity Hospital

MH 11 – Gynaecologist, Maternity Hospital

MH 12 – Social Worker (TL), Maternity Hospital

MH13 – Midwife, Maternity Hospital

MH 14 – Midwife, Maternity Hospital

Bibliography

Abbas, M. (2007) "Antenatal Care in Low Risk Pregnant Women: Modern Medicine" 37(1) *Irish Journal of Clinical Medicine* 52.

Advisory Council on the Misuse of Drugs (2003) *Hidden Harm Report* London: Home Office.

Alperen, J. and Paone, D. (1998) "Pregnancy Policing: Policy of Harm" 9(2) *International Journal of Drug Policy* 101.

Azuma S. and Chasnoff, I.J. (1993) "Outcomes of Children Prenatally Exposed to Cocaine and other Drugs: A path of Analysis of Three- year Data" 92 *Pediatrics* 396.

Barker, R. (1997) "Unborn Children and Child Protection – Legal, Policy and Practice Issues" *Liverpool Law Review,* Vol. X1X (2).

Barry, S., Kearney, A., Lawlor, E., McNamee, E. and Barry, J. (2007) *The Coombe Women's Hospital study of alcohol, smoking and illicit drug use 1998 - 2005*. Department of Health and Children, Dublin: Stationery Office.

Becker, J. and Duffy, C. (2002) "Women Drug Users and Drug Services Provision: Service level responses to engagement and retention" Home Office Drug Strategy Unit, London: HM Stationery Office.

Blondel, B., Pusch, D. and Schmidt, E. (1985) "Some characteristics of antenatal care in 13 European countries" 92(6) *International Journal of Obstetrics and Gynaecology* 565.

Bowen, N. (2007) "Jude aims to protect woman's unborn child" *The Sarnia Observer*, 5 April.

Buchanan, J. and Corby, B. (2005) "Drug Misuse and Safeguarding Children: A Multi-agency Approach" in Carnwell R and Buchanan J (eds.) *Effective Practice in Health and Social Care: A Partnership Approach* Maidenhead: Open University Press.

Buckley, H. (2000) "Interagency Co-operation in Irish Child Protection Work", 6 *Journal of Child Centred Practice* 9.

Buckley, H. (2003) *Child Protection Work: Beyond the Rhetoric* London: Jessica Kingsley Publishers.

Buckley, H. (2005) "Review of Children First: Some Considerations" 3 *Irish Journal of Family Law* 2.

Burns, E., O'Driscoll, M. and Watson, G. (1996) "The Health and Development of Children Whose Mothers are on Methadone Maintenance" 5 *Child Abuse Review* 113.

Butler, S. (1996) "Child protection or professional self-preservation by the baby nurse? Public health nurses and child protection in Ireland". 43 *Social Science and Medicine* 303.

Butler, S (2002a), "Addiction Problems, Addiction Services, and Social Work in the Republic of Ireland" 2 *Journal of Social Work Practice in the Addictions* 31.

Butler, S. (2002b) "Alcohol Consumption and Its Negative Impact on Irish Children and Young People" as cited in *Under the Influence*, Dublin: Barnardos.

Butler, S. (2002c) *Alcohol, Drugs and Health Promotion in Modern Ireland.* Dublin: Institute of Public Administration.

Butler, S. (2002d) "The Making of the Methadone Protocol: The Irish System?" 9(4) *Drugs: Education, Prevention and Policy* 311.

Butler, S (2003) "Paying the Price for Extended Opening Hours: A Comment from Ireland" 10(4) *Drugs: Education, Prevention and Policy* 293.

Butler, S. and Mayock, P. (2005) "'An Irish Solution to and Irish Problem': Harm reduction and ambiguity in the drug policy of the Republic of Ireland" 16 *International Journal of Drug Policy* 415.

Butler, S. and Woods, M. (1992) "Drugs, HIV and Ireland: Responses to Women in Dublin" in Dorn, N, Henderson, S. and South, N. (eds.) *AIDS: Women, Drugs and Social Care* London: Falmer Press.

Calder, M. (2003) *Unborn Children: A framework for Assessment and Intervention* as cited in Calder, M.C. and Hackett, S. (eds.). *Assessment in Child Care Work: Using and Developing Frameworks for Practice* London: Russell House Publishing.

Charleton, P., McDermott, P.A. and Bolger, M. (1999) *Criminal Law* Dublin: Butterworths.

Chasnoff, I.J. (1988) *Drugs, Alcohol, Pregnancy and Parenting* The Netherlands: Kluwer Academic Publishers.

Chasnoff, I.J., Hunt, C., Kletter, R. and Kaplan, D. (1989) "Prenatal cocaine exposure is associated with respiratory pattern abnormalities" 7 *American Journal of Disabled Children* 1556.

Chasnoff, I. (1989) "Cocaine, pregnancy, and the neonate" 15 *Women and Health* 23.

Child Care Policy Unit (2004) Memo to Chief Executives of Each Health Board Region. Department of Health and Children: Dublin

Christie, S. (2007) "Crimes against the Foetus: The Rights and Wrongs of Protecting the Unborn" *Medical-Legal Journal of Ireland* 65.

Clarke, C. and Fitzpatrick, C. (2005) "Psychiatric problems of children exposed to opiates in 'utero' – a descriptive study" 22(4) *Irish Journal of Psych Medicine* 121.

Coghlan, D., Milner, M., Beckett, M., McNally, M., Clarke, T.A., Lambert, I., McDermott, C. (1999) "Neonatal Abstinence Syncrome" 92(1) *Irish Medical Journal* 232.

Corby, B. (2003) "Supporting families and protecting children – assisting child care professionals in initial decision-making and review of cases" 3(2) *Journal of social Work* 195.

Copeland, J. (1997) "Barriers to formal treatment among women who self-manage change in addictive behaviours" 14(2) *Journal of Substance Abuse Treatment* 183.

Cullen, P. (2006) "Fertility treatment Law likely to face delay" *The Irish Times* 16 November.

Daly, M. (2000) "A fine balance: Women's labor market participation in international comparison", in Scharpf, F.W. and Schmidt, V.A. (eds.) *Welfare and Work in the Open Economy* Oxford: Oxford University Press.

Daly, M. and Claver, S. (2005) *Contemporary Family Policy in Ireland and Europe* School of Sociology and Social Policy, Queen's University, Belfast. Available at http://www.welfare.ie/publications/familypolicy/cfpreport.pdf .

Dawson, T.B. (1991) "A Feminist Response to Unborn Child Abuse: Contemporary legal Solutions" 9(2) *Canadian Journal of Family Law*.

Department of Education and Skills (2006) *Statistics of Education: Referrals, Assessments and Children and Young People on Child protection Registers: Year ending 31st March 2005* London: HMSO.

Department of Health (UK) (1999) *Working Together under the Children Act 1989* London: HMSO.

Department of Health and Children (2005) *Health Statistics 2005 Section E. Children in Care and Child Abuse Cases* Dublin: Stationery Office.

Department of Health and Children (1991) *Child Care Act* Dublin: Stationery Office.

Department of Health and Children (1999) Children First: national guidelines for the protection and welfare of children. Dublin: Stationery Office.

Department of Health and Children (2006) *State of the Nation's Children, Ireland 2006* Dublin: Stationery Office.

Enkin, M., Keirse, M.J.N.C., Neilson, J., Crowther, C., Duley, L., Hodnett, E. and Hofmeyr, J. (2000) *A guide to effective care in pregnancy and childbirth* Oxford: Oxford University Press, 3rd Edition.

Fagan, J. and Keenan, E. (2006) Treatment for pregnant drug users available online at *www.dap.ie*.

Fallon, J. (2007) "Women wait until start of fifth month of pregnancy for first antenatal appointment" *The Irish Times* 20 March.

Fallon, J. (2007) "Pregnancy scan delay confirmed in Galway" *The Irish Times* 26 March.

Farrell, E. (1999) "Women, Children and Drug Use" in Moran, R, Dillon, L, O'Brien, M, Mayock, P and Farrell, E with Pike, B (eds.) *A Collection of Papers on Drug Issues in Ireland* Dublin: Health Research Board.

Health Research Board (2000) *Making Knowledge Work for Health: Towards a strategy for research and Innovation for health* Dublin: Health Research Board.

Hogan T.M., Myers, B. and Elswick, R.K. (2006) "Child abuse among mothers of substance – exposed and none-exposed infants and toddlers" 30 *Child Abuse and Neglect* 145.

Home Office (1991) DOH DES Welsh Office *Working Together Under the Children Act 1989* London: HMSO.

House of the Oireachtas Joint Committee on Arts, Sport, Tourism, Community, Rural and Gaeltacht Affairs (2006) *Ninth Report: The inclusion of alcohol in a national substance misuse strategy* Dublin: Stationery Office.

House of the Oireachtas (2006) *Joint Committee on Child Protection* Dublin: Stationery Office.

Humphreys, C. and Stanley, N. (2006) *Domestic Violence and Child Protection: Directions for Practice* London: Jessica Kingsley Publishers.

Institute of Public Health in Ireland (2006) *Unequal at birth – inequalities in the occurrence of low birthweight babies in Ireland* Dublin: Stationery Office.

Jasinski, J.L. (2001) "Pregnancy and violence against women" 16(7) *Journal of Interpersonal Violence* 712.

Kaeser, L. and Figdor, E. (1998) *The Guttmacher Report on Public Policy: Concerns Mount over Punitive Approaches to Substance Abuse Among Pregnant Women* Volume 1. No 5 [online] *www.guttmacher.org* Accessed 31/07/07.

Kennedy, I. (1988) *Treat Me Right: Essays in Medical Law and Ethics* Oxford: Oxford University Press.

Kiely, G. (1996) "Fathers in Families" cited in McCarthy (ed.) Irish Family Studies, selected papers, University College Dublin.

Loewenberg, F.M. and Dolgoff, R. (1996) *Ethical Decisions for Social Work Practice* Itasca, IL: FE Peacock.

McMillan, H., Smaarani, S., Walsh, T.N., Khawaja, C., Collins, P. and Byrne, M. (2006) "Smoking and Alcohol in Pregnancy: Survey in the immediate postpartum period" 99(9) *Irish Medical Journal* 283

Murphy, M. (2004) *Developing collaborative relationships in interagency child protection work* London: Russell House Publishing.

O'Connor, J.J., Stafford-Johnson, S. and Kelly, M.G. (1998) "A review of the characteristics and treatment progress of 45 pregnant opiate addicts attending a National Drug Advisory and Treatment Centre over a two-year period" 157(5) *Irish Journal of Medical Science* 146.

One Family (2005) "Becoming a parent" [online] *www.onefamily.ie*.

Powis, B., Griffiths, P., Gossop, M. and Strong, J. (1997) "The difference between male and female drug users: Community samples of Heroin and Cocaine Users compared" 31(5) *Substance Use and Misuse* 529.

Rawaf, J. (1998) "Public Health and addiction" 11(3) *Current Opinion in Psychiatry* 273.

Schweppe, J. (2005) "Revisiting Article 40.3.3. Part One: Third-Party Foetal Assault" *Irish Journal of Family Law* 19.

Schweppe, J. (2006) "Pregnant Women and Unborn Children – In 'utero' Drug Exposure". *Irish Journal of family Law* 19.

Scully, M., Geoghegan, N., Corcoran, P., Tiernan, M. and Keena, E. (2004) "Specialized drug liaison midwife services for pregnant opioid dependent women in Dublin, Ireland" 26 *Journal of Substance Abuse Treatment* 27.

Seidel, J. and Kelle, U. (1995) "Different Functions of Coding in the Analysis of Textual Data" in Kelle U. (ed.) *Computer-aided Qualitative Data Analysis: Theory, Methods and Practice* London: Sage.

Shankaran S., Fanaroff A.A., Wright, L.L., Stevenson, D.K., Donovan, E.F., Ehrenkranz, R.A., Langer, J.C., Korones, S.B., Stoll, B.J., Tyson, J.E., Bauer

C.R., Lemons, J.A., Oh, W., Papile, L.A. (2002) "Risk factors for early death among extremely low-birth-weight infants" 186 *American Journal ObstetGynecol* 796.

Silverman, D. (2005) *Doing Qualitative Research* (2nd edition) London: Sage.

Society for the Protection of Unborn Children (2006) *Speech by Ms Kathy Sinnott MEP Geneva 28 June* available online at http://www.spuc.org.uk/ lobbying/amnestyforbabies/sinnott.

Stopper, A. (2006) *Monday's at Gaj's: The Story of the Irish Women's Liberation Movement* Dublin: The Liffey Press.

Strategic Task Force on Alcohol (2004) *Second Report* Dublin: Stationery Office.

Tunnard, J. (2002) "Parental Drug Misuse: A review of impact and intervention studies" Research in Practice. Available online at http://www.rip.org.uk

United Nations Office on Drugs and Crime (2004) *Substance abuse treatment and care for women: Case studies and lessons learned* New York: United Nations.

Woods, M. (1994) "Drug Using Parents and their Children: The Experiences of a Voluntary/Non-Statutory Project" 12(2) *Irish Social worker* 10.

Woods, M. (2000a) "The Value of the Strengths Perspective in understanding and responding to alcohol and drugs Problems" 18(1) *Irish Social Worker* 20.

Woods, M. (2000b) "Women, Drug Use and parenting in Dublin: The Views of Professional Workers in the Drug Treatment and Social Work Fields in Illicit Drugs" in Springer and Uhl (eds.) A *Patterns of Use, Patterns of Response, Proceedings of the 10th Annual ESSD Conference on Drug Use and Policy in Europe* Innsbruck: Studienverlag,.

Woollett, A. (2000) "Fit to Reproduce? The Regulative Role of Pregnancy Texts" 10(3) *Feminism and Psychology* 351.

World Health Organisation (2002) *Antenatal Care Randomized Trial: Manual for the Implementation of the New Model* Copenhagen: World Health Organization.

World Health Organisation (2006) *The World Health Report 2006 – Working Together for Health* Copenhagen: World Health Organization.

7

To Intervene or Not to Intervene?

Legal Issues in the Mother-Unborn Child Relationship

Dr Gerard Casey

A (Short) History of Article 40.3.3°

> The State acknowledges the right to life of the unborn and, with due regard to the equal right to life of the mother, guarantees in its laws to respect, and, as far as practicable, by its laws to defend and vindicate that right.

With these words, the Eighth Amendment was inserted into the Irish Constitution as Article 40.3.3° in 1983.

One might wonder, why this amendment and why at this time? In 1965, *Griswold v Connecticut* established a constitutional right to privacy in the United States. Many legal commentators had misgivings about this discovery and found the argument of the US Supreme Court somewhat less than convincing in justifying a constitutional right nowhere mentioned in the United States Constitution. *Roe v Wade* (1973), which removed all restrictions on abortion by the individual US states, was based on an extension of the right to privacy enunciated in *Griswold.* Despite the reservations of many critics on different sides of the abortion debate that there was no necessary logical bridge in respect of privacy between access to contraception (the matter of *Griswold*) and access to abortion (the matter of *Roe*), the US Supreme Court in *Roe* held

(7-2) that the right to privacy "is broad enough to encompass a woman's decision whether or not to terminate her pregnancy" (1972: 159; see Cotter (2002)). When in 1974 the Irish Supreme Court discovered a somewhat similar right to privacy (under the doctrine of unenumerated rights articulated in *Ryan*) in *McGee v The Attorney General* (1974), a fear emerged among those who were opposed to the introduction of abortion into Ireland that a *Roe*-type trajectory might emerge and that, despite the then-current illegality of abortion in Ireland (under the Offences Against the Person Act 1861 sections 58 and 59, undisturbed by *Bourne*-type considerations), abortion could be introduced into Ireland at some future stage.[1] The Eighth Amendment was intended preemptively to prevent this.

Some among those who argued against the adoption of the amendment contended that the meaning of its wording was imprecise. Their opinions would appear to have been justified, at least in part, by the judgments rendered in what has come to be known as the "*X* case" (*Attorney General v X*, 1992). This case concerned a young girl, X, who became pregnant as the result of having been raped. She travelled to England with her mother to have an abortion. The Attorney General, learning of her intention, sought an injunction *ex parte* in the High Court to restrain her from travelling abroad to have an abortion. When X learnt of this she returned to Ireland and appeared in the High Court to resist the injunction. It was held by Costello J that in Irish law one effect of Article 40.3.3° of the Constitution was to restrict one's right to travel abroad for an abortion, and that the danger to the mother's life from a threat of suicide did not outweigh the certainty of the death of the foetus. While the Supreme Court, on appeal, held that Costello J was correct in his judgement that the constitutional provision could be employed to restrict travel abroad, it also held that his assessment of the likelihood of X's committing suicide was wrong in that the risk to X's life was significant and, in the circumstances, outweighed the destruction of unborn life. The court therefore allowed the appeal.

---

[1] It should be noted that two of the judges in *McGee* explicitly stated that, despite the right to marital privacy, abortion still remained illegal (*McGee* at pages 305 and 335).

The Meaning of Article 40.3.3°

The subsequent history of Article 40.3.3° in terms of attempts to clarify its meaning can be seen in the unsuccessful attempts to, in the eyes of its supporters, return to the original meaning (Twelfth Amendment Bill 1992 and the Twenty-Fifth Amendment Bill 2002) and in the successful amendments to permit a pregnant woman's right to travel and to information (Thirteenth Amendment 1992 and Fourteenth Amendment 1992). In the wake of the *X* case, the Twelfth Amendment was proposed to rule out the threat of suicide as a sufficient reason for permitting an abortion. The text of the proposed amendment read:

> It shall be unlawful to terminate the life of an unborn unless such termination is necessary to save the life, as distinct from the health, of the mother where there is an illness or disorder of the mother giving rise to a real and substantial risk to her life, not being a risk of self-destruction.

This proposed amendment was rejected by an unlikely coalition of forces: those who did not wish to limit the legal options provided by the *X* case and those who did not wish to approve, as they saw it, the misinterpretation of the Eighth Amendment by the Supreme Court in the *X* case.

As the result of further pressure to "row back" on the *X* case, the Twenty-Fifth Amendment was put to the people in 2002. A new subsection, 40.3.4°, was to be introduced which would have stated:

> In particular, the life of the unborn in the womb shall be protected in accordance with the provisions of the Protection of Human Life in Pregnancy Act, 2002.

This Act would have been changeable only by the consent of the people in a new referendum, thus making it radically unlike a normal statute. The main provisions of the Protection of Human Life in Pregnancy Bill 2002 were that the threat of suicide, based on the *X* case, would be removed as a ground for abortion (as in the rejected Twelfth Amendment), together with a definition of abortion as the intentional destruction by any means of unborn human life after implantation in the womb. Once again, an unlikely coalition of pro-choice and pro-life forces brought about the rejection of this amendment; the pro-choicers objecting to the removal of the threat of suicide and the pro-lifers objecting to what they saw as the removal of legal protection for the fertilised but non-implanted conceptus. The pro-life movement was divided on the issue, some willing to support the proposal, others not. In the end, the split in the movement was sufficient for the proposal to be rejected by a tiny majority (50.4 per cent to 49.6 per cent).

Some attempts have been made to interpret (and restrict) the application of the term "unborn". One such would limit to the application of the term to the implanted, intrauterine foetus. *MR v TR and Others* (2006) was a case involving a dispute between a husband and wife over three embryos held in storage in which the court held that while the term "unborn" was not defined in the Constitution, given that the clear purpose of the 1983 Amendment was the protection of the foetus within the womb, the term did *not* encompass embryos *in vitro*. The Court found that the question as to whether or not the term "unborn" should include embryos *in vitro* was a matter for the Oireachtas or for a constitutional referendum. In reaching its conclusion the court was impressed with the linkage of Article 40.3.3° with the abortion issue, noting O'Flaherty J's remark (in *Baby O v Minister for Justice*, 2002) that "the enactment of Article 40.3.3° in 1983 did not I believe bring about any fundamental change in our law" and Geoghegan J's comment (in *P J Carroll & Co v Minister for Health*, 2005) that "although courts in this jurisdiction interpret statutes by reference to the words used, they do not do so in a vacuum…"[2]

Another such attempt at interpretation of the term "unborn" occurred in a case before the European Court of Human Rights, *D v Ireland* (2006). This appeared to open up a conceptual space between being a foetus and being unborn:

> There was no legal agreement on when the foetus became an 'unborn' for the purposes of Article 40.3.3°: even the government was rather non-committal on the point (para. 77).

[2] See McGovern (2006).

The Government of Ireland had, in its submission to the Court, put forward the possibility that if a foetus had no realistic possibility of being born alive, it might not be an "unborn" within the scope of 40.3.3°, suggesting that:

> … it was an open question as to whether Article 40.3.3° could have allowed a lawful abortion in Ireland in the applicant's circumstances. The *X* case demonstrated the potential for judicial development in this area.... Accordingly, although it was true that Article 40.3.3° had to be understood as excluding a liberal abortion regime, the courts were nonetheless unlikely to interpret the provision with remorseless logic particularly when the facts were exceptional. If therefore it had been established that there was no realistic prospect of the foetus being born alive, then there was 'at least a tenable' argument which would be seriously considered by the domestic courts to the effect that the foetus was not an 'unborn' for the purposes of Article 40.3.3° or that, even if it was an 'unborn', its right to life was not actually engaged as it had no prospect of life outside the womb (para. 69).[3]

Some Non-abortion Aspects of 40.3.3°

Most of the discussion of 40.3.3° relates to its relevance to the abortion debate. But it should be noted that the Article nowhere explicitly mentions abortion nor in its specific wording gives any indication that it is exclusively concerned with this issue.[4] It is true that, as in *MR v TR*, the courts have identified the 1983 abortion context as partially constitutive of the original meaning of the Article and so denied constitutional protection to *in vitro* and, presumably, pre-implantation embryos, nonetheless, apart from these particular issues, and the ever-contentious issue of abortion, the unique relation between a pregnant woman and her unborn

---

[3] The ultimate source of this idea would seem to have been either the report of the Constitutional Review Group 1996 or a press conference given by the Masters of the three major obstetric hospitals in Dublin on 27 February 2002 or both. See Samiloff (2007); see also Coulter (2006a, 2006b). On this topic, the dissent of Hederman J in the *X* case is especially relevant.

[4] "… [A]lthough the legal situation concerning abortion in this jurisdiction is unclear, Article 40.3.3° of the Constitution raises concerns beyond the abortion issue" (Schweppe, 2006). See also Schweppe (2005) and Spain (2006).

child can give rise to some other significant legal problems to which Article 40.3.3° might be relevant. Such problems as the child welfare issues raised by a pregnant woman's use of illegal drugs or alcohol or tobacco and/or a refusal to accept medical treatment (including blood transfusion) can give rise to a clash between a respect for a woman's autonomy and privacy, on the one hand, and a concern for the welfare of the unborn child, on the other. I propose to examine the approaches to such issues adopted in England, Canada and the USA before returning to consider the possible approach that might be adopted in Ireland.

England

I think it is fair to say that in the matter of potential conflict between the rights of a pregnant woman and her unborn child the English courts come down heavily on the side of maternal autonomy. Kerr recognises that maternal prenatal negligence cases are "... plagued by moral complexity" and that:

> The imposition of a duty of care upon pregnant women will interfere with their bodily integrity, privacy and autonomy rights in a way that it would not interfere with other persons who are not pregnant (2000: 15).

The non-interventionist attitude of the English courts was clearly exhibited in *Re F (in utero)* (1988). In this case, a local authority was concerned that a mentally disturbed, nomadic woman who was pregnant would not take care of or provide appropriate medical attention for her child at and after birth. The local authority made an *ex parte* application to have the foetus made a ward of court. Hollings J refused the application, holding that the court had no wardship jurisdiction over an unborn child. The case went on appeal to the Court of Appeal, which unanimously affirmed his decision. Hollings J was satisfied that "there would be a repugnance on the part of a right thinking person in certain instances to think of applying the principle of paramountcy in favour of the child's welfare at the expense of the welfare and interests of the mother" (1988: 131). Agreeing with Hollings J, May LJ was of the opinion that there would be:

> … insuperable difficulties if one sought to enforce any order in respect of an unborn child against its mother, if that mother failed to comply with the order. I cannot contemplate the court ordering that this should be done by force, nor indeed is it possible to consider with any equanimity that the court should seek to enforce an order by committal (1988: 138).

In this case, there was a clear reluctance on the part of the court to impinge on the woman's autonomy. Ten years later, however, the matter was treated somewhat differently in *St George's Healthcare NHS Trust v S* (1999). This case concerned a 36-weeks pregnant woman who was diagnosed as having pre-eclampsia. She was advised of the need for bed rest and an induced delivery, which advice she rejected. She was admitted to a psychiatric hospital against her will and, still refusing to consent to treatment, had a Caesarean section performed on her, the hospital authorities having applied *ex parte* to a judge in chambers and having received a declaration which dispensed with the need for her consent to treatment. Handing down the judgment of the Court, Judge LJ remarked that, leaving to one side those occasions where the necessity for consent may be dispensed with on the basis of incapacity, it still did not follow that a woman was entitled to put at risk her "healthy viable foetus" (1999: 45). "Whatever else it may be", he said, "a 36-week foetus is not nothing: if viable it is not lifeless and it is certainly human" (*St George's Healthcare*: 45). He cited the words of Lord Hope of Craighead in the *Attorney-General's Reference (No. 3 of 1994)* (1997) to the effect that the Human Fertilisation and Embryology Act 1990 reminds us that "an embryo is in reality a separate organism from the mother from the moment of its conception ... the foetus cannot be regarded as an integral part of the mother" (1997: 267). He put the point at issue very sharply when he asked: "If human life is sacred, why is a mother entitled to refuse to undergo treatment if this would preserve the life of the foetus without damaging her own?" (1999: 46). A good question, and one that deserves, but does not receive, a good answer. Recalling the case of *Winnipeg Child and Family Services (Northwest Area) v DFG* (1996), he cited with approval the opinion of McLachlin J in that case to the effect that:

> To permit an unborn child to sue its pregnant mother-to-be would introduce a radically new conception into the law: the unborn child and its mother as separate juristic persons in a mutually separable and antagonistic relation (1999: 49).

Kennedy and Grubb, authors of a standard textbook in medical law, are of the opinion that the courts "will not force a competent pregnant woman to undergo medical treatment or other interventions for the benefit of her unborn child" (2000: 1505). Others are not so sanguine. Pickworth is of the opinion that the decision of the House of Lords in *Attorney-General's Reference (No. 3 of 1994)* (1997) gives rise to the possibility that English law might follow the example of some jurisdictions in the USA in criminalising those who cause harm to a foetus. Whatever about the merits of the extension of such criminalisation to third parties, Pickworth does not think it advisable to extend such criminalisation to pregnant women, characterising such a policy as "backward-looking, self-defeating and illogical" (1998: 473). Apart from following the example of the United States, there are two other reasons why English law might criminalise those actions or omissions of pregnant women that have the effect of damaging their foetuses. The first is that:

> … the decision [in Attorney-General's Reference (No. 3 of 1994)] shows little reasoning why criminalization of injuries to the foetus born alive should be limited to homicide ... Nor does it necessarily prohibit criminalization of pregnant women who causes [*sic*] the injuries to a foetus (Pickworth, 1998, 475).

The second is that the *Attorney-General's Reference (No. 3 of 1994)*, taken together with some civil cases, demonstrates, in Pickworth's view, "a willingness of the courts at the highest level to condemn maternal treatment of the unborn child" (Pickworth, 1998: 476). Despite the misgivings of Pickworth and some others, I believe it is fair to say that the general tendency of the law in England is towards non-intervention.

Canada

The Supreme Court of Canada ruled in *Winnipeg Child and Family Services (Northwest Area) v G* (1997) that pregnant women whose behaviour can be considered a threat to their foetuses cannot be legally interfered with; in particular, the state cannot force a woman to undergo treatment to protect her unborn child (see Caper., 1997). In the case giving rise to the appeal (*Winnipeg Child and Family Services (Northwest Area) v DFG* (1996)), Winnipeg Child and Family Services asked the Manitoba Court of Queen's Bench to confine "G", who was addicted to sniffing solvents, at a place of safety until the baby was born. As a result of her addiction, two of her previous children were born permanently disabled and were permanent wards of the state. They also asked that she not use what they termed "intoxicating substances" until after her baby had been born. Schulman J, employing the province's Mental Health Act and the doctrine of *parens patria*, ordered the province's director of child and family services to take custody of "G" until she had given birth and, if she failed to complete treatment or left the treatment facility, the province was to be permitted to apply for committal. The Manitoba Court of Appeal threw out the original rulings holding that the findings of the court were not based on the evidence, which included reports of medical expert witnesses, and because the social service agency's action was not taken because of concern about "G" but because of worries about her foetus; the Court of Appeal also held that the existing law of tort and of *parens patriae* did not support the order. The social service agency appealed the question of forcible treatment to the Supreme Court.

The Court heard from the principal parties and eleven interveners. On the facts of the case, there were two questions before the court: (1) Does tort law, as it exists or may properly be extended by the Court, permit an order detaining a pregnant woman against her will in order to protect her unborn child from conduct that may harm the child? (2) Alternatively, does the power of a court to make orders for the protection of children (its *parens patriae* jurisdiction), as it exists or may properly be extended by the Court, permit an order detaining a pregnant woman against her will in order to protect her unborn child from conduct that may harm the child? (1997: para. 9).

The Court reviewed the general position of the law in Canada relating to the unborn child and held that Canadian law, including its law of torts, does not attribute legal personhood to the unborn child (1997: para. 11). Furthermore, the Court held that the issue in dispute, namely, the status of the foetus, "is not one of biological status, nor indeed spiritual status, but of legal status" and, recalling its own findings in *Tremblay v Daigle* said that:

> The task of properly classifying a foetus in law and in science are different pursuits. Ascribing personhood to a foetus in law is a fundamentally normative task. It results in the recognition of rights and duties – a matter which falls outside the concerns of scientific classification. In short, this Court's task is a legal one (1997: para. 12).

The court concluded: "Any right or interest the fetus may have remains inchoate and incomplete until the birth of the child" (1997: para. 16). The court declined suggestions that it was its role and function to extend existing laws beyond their normal parameters. Specifically, it declined the invitation to overturn the born-alive rule or to recognise a foetus's right to sue its mother, refused to recognise causes of action for lifestyle choices that might adversely affect others and, most significantly, denied the propriety of the use of injunctive remedies (such as involuntary confinement) that could have the effect of depriving a woman of important liberties (1997: para. 19). It took this stand on the grounds that such legal changes would create conflicts between fundamental rights and interests and could result in women finding themselves incarcerated and subjected to involuntary treatment for conduct or behaviour that allegedly harmed others. The changes proposed were of such magnitude that they exceeded any legitimate law-making power of the courts (1997: para. 47).

The court went on to make the point that, in effect, given their intimate connection before birth the mother and unborn child are one. If a foetus were to be permitted to sue the pregnant woman the law would be presented with the anomaly of "one part of a legal and physical entity suing itself" (1997: para. 27).[5] In the matter of recognising causes of action resulting from a person's lifestyle choices, the court was clearly of the opinion that there was no sensible way to draw a line, asking:

[5] The Court was citing *Paton v United Kingdom* (1980): 415; cf. Section 29).

> Are children to be permitted to sue their parents for second-hand smoke inhaled around the family dinner table? Could any cohabitant bring such an action? Are children to be permitted to sue their parents for spanking causing psychological trauma or poor grades due to alcoholism or a parent's undue fondness for the office or the golf course? If we permit lifestyle actions, where do we draw the line (1997: para. 33)?

Whatever the difficulties between the parties in a normal legal dispute, such difficulties mount when the parties in a potential adversarial relation are a pregnant woman and her unborn child. The court cited Hoyt CJNB (in *Dobson,* 1997: 336) on the horror of the spectacle of children suing their mothers for smoking or drinking or taking/not taking medicine during their pregnancies where such acts had injured the child in the womb. Were such actions to be permitted, the pregnant woman's autonomy would be severely compromised. If the court were to recognise a duty of care owed by a mother to her child for negligent prenatal behaviour this could "create a conflict between the pregnant woman as an autonomous decision-maker and her fetus" (1997: para. 37). The court resisted arguments tending towards the justification of forcible detention and mandatory treatment (1997: para. 46). It cited from the Report of the Royal Commission on New Reproductive Technologies:

> From the woman's perspective, ... considering the interests of her fetus separately from her own has the potential to create adversary situations with negative consequences for her autonomy and bodily integrity, for her relationship with her partner, and for her relationship with her physician. Judicial intervention is bound to precipitate crisis and conflict, instead of preventing them through support and care. It also ignores the basic components of women's fundamental human rights – the right to bodily integrity, and the right to equality, privacy, and dignity. The potential for intrusions on a woman's right to make choices concerning herself is considerable. The fetus' complete physical existence is dependent on the body of the woman. As a result, any intervention to further the fetus' interests will necessarily implicate, and possibly conflict with the mother's interests. Similarly, each

> choice made by the woman in relation to her body will affect the fetus and potentially attract tort liability (1997: para. 37).

US

In *State v Ashley* (1996), the court, while recognising the singular nature of the relationship between a mother and her foetus, held that "we are not persuaded that based upon this relationship, a mother's duty to her fetus should not be legally recognized" (1996: 1089). The court argued that since there could be no principled objection to holding a mother answerable in negligence to her child *after* its birth, it would be illogical not to provide redress for such injury just because it occurred some hours, days or months before birth. In *Whitner v State* (1997) a woman pleaded guilty to, and was convicted of, criminal child neglect for causing her baby to be born with cocaine metabolites in its system because she took crack cocaine during the last trimester of her pregnancy. The Supreme Court of South Carolina held that it would be absurd to recognise a viable foetus as a person in the context of homicide laws and wrongful death statutes, but not in the context of statutes outlawing child abuse. In arriving at its decision, the *Whitner* court explicitly distinguished itself from the Massachusetts case of *Commonwealth v Pellegrini* (1990) in which the Massachusetts Superior Court had dismissed similar charges against a woman on the grounds that to find a mother criminally liable for such injury would violate her right to privacy. The Court expressed its rationale as follows:

> If … we read Horne [1984] only as a vindication of the mother's interest in the life other unborn child, there would be no basis for prosecuting a mother who kills her viable fetus by stabbing it, by shooting it, or by other such means, yet a third party could be prosecuted for the very same acts. We decline to read Horne in a way that insulates the mother from all culpability for harm to her unborn child (1997: 783).

Actual harm to an unborn child is one thing; possible harm is quite another. Yet this was precisely the point at issue in *In re Unborn Child* (1998). This case concerned a woman, Sierra K, who was found to have permanently neglected her first four children so that they were removed from her care. She had a fifth child, who was born with a positive toxicology for cocaine. After testing positive for crack cocaine, and admitting prenatal drug use, Ms K surrendered this child. The court ordered that she attend and participate in a drug abuse rehabilitation programme, refrain from the use and possession of any illegal drugs, and attend and participate in a parent effectiveness training programme. At the time of the case she was pregnant with her sixth child but had not complied with the terms and conditions of the court order. A petition was filed by the Legal Aid Society of Suffolk County seeking summary judgment that Ms K's unborn child was derivatively neglected based on Ms K's history of drug abuse and child neglect. Counsel for Ms K argued that no legal personality had been conferred on the unborn child. Freundlich J thought otherwise. He noted:

> The courts have moved from the position that no duty is owed to the unborn to allowing recovery for injury to a fetus who is subsequently born damaged or who, after birth, dies due to pre-natal injury (1998: 369).

He added that the Wisconsin Court of Appeals in the case of *State of Wisconsin ex re Angela MW v Kruzicki* upheld as constitutional an order for the protective custody of a viable foetus, which, "by necessity, required the custody of the mother as well" (1998: 370), and concluded:

> It is inconceivable that the legislature would intend a fetus to have property rights and causes of action sounding in tort, but not be protected against threats to its safety or life, from its own mother, while in utero.... It defies logical reasoning that our laws and society would preclude a mother from illegally introducing narcotics and other illegal drugs into her child and yet not protect the unborn child from those same dangers while the child is still in the womb (1998: 371).[6]

These cases raise questions about the nature and extent of society's interest in foetal life, questions that are difficult to answer. Would a woman be open to criminal sanctions if, carrying a foetus she could le-

---

[6] See Gostin (2001) and MacEnzie et al. (1986).

gally abort, she knowingly took drugs that caused severe harm to her child later born alive? Suppose that, having damaged her foetus by taking these drugs, a woman were to try to avoid liability by having a (legal) abortion, would her earlier crime have to be considered as not having been committed? Despite the affirmation by the Supreme Court of the uniqueness of abortion, which leads to it being treated in law in a singular manner, not every court is similarly persuaded that the circumstances underlying wrongful death actions and abortions are clearly and distinctly separate. Siano notes: "Some courts find it difficult to interpret wrongful death statutes to include a nonviable fetus and at the same time allow a woman to willfully [sic] terminate her pregnancy" (1998: 291). Taking everything into consideration, it is difficult to avoid the conclusion that the law in this area is conceptually confused.

Having reviewed a number of significant cases relating to the development of tort law in relation to foetal injury and death, some well known, others not so well known,[7] Hakim concludes that the "recognition of the fetus as a viable entity, with interests and rights separate from and sometimes, conflicting with those of the mother, is now well established in tort law" (1997: 101). The legal recognition of the rights of the foetus, while achieving its first significant foothold in tort law, has now moved beyond this beachhead into the area of criminal law. Though the early attempts to prosecute pregnant women were initially resisted by the courts, Hakim claims that the recent cases of *Whitner*, *Ashley* and *Zimmermann* (1996)[8] are evidence of a trend towards supporting criminal sanctions against pregnant women for injuries caused by them to their foetuses.

> The issues raised by these cases put the rights of the unborn child at direct odds with those of the pregnant woman (Hakim, 1997: 111).

---

[7] *Bombrest v Kotz* (1946); *Renslow v Mennonite Hospital* (1977); *Smith v Brennan* (1960); *Grodin v Grodin* (1980).

[8] Although the ruling of the court of first instance in the *Zimmermann* case was reversed after her article had been published, the points made by Hakim remain essentially unaffected.

The balancing of rights between a woman and her unborn child is given a particular focus in the context of drug use by pregnant women.[9] Does the State have an interest in ensuring healthy pregnancies and, if so, does it have a right to interfere with a pregnant woman's lifestyle (e.g. activities, intake, etc.) to bring this about? Prenatal drug use has been legally proscribed by the use of a variety of statutes that can only have purchase if the unborn is considered to be, for the purposes of the law, a child or person within the terms of such legislation; delivering drugs to a minor, corruption of a minor, or child abuse/neglect. More seriously, there have been charges of manslaughter or assault with a deadly weapon. In most cases, convictions obtained under such statutes have been overturned on appeal to state supreme courts. Only in *Whitner* has the State Supreme Court upheld such a conviction. In general, the state supreme courts have ruled either that the unborn child cannot be considered a child or person under the terms of the relevant acts or, employing rules of statutory interpretation, they deny that the legislature intended such laws to have application to pregnant women in relation to their unborn children.

An important case in this regard is *Ferguson v City of Charleston* (2001).[10] In 1989, some women attending the Medical University of South Carolina (MUSC) for routine prenatal care were secretly tested for cocaine use. This involved the cooperation of the local law enforcement agencies and the hospital. Those women who tested positive were related to the local prosecutors and then were either arrested for criminal child abuse or threatened with arrest for criminal child abuse. Thirty women were arrested over a five-year period, some having given birth, others while still pregnant. In the context of US Constitutional law, the issue this case gives rise to is whether or not such activities by the hospital violated the Fourth Amendment in respect of its prohibition of unreasonable search and seizures. In 2001, the US Supreme Court held that it did.

> *Ferguson* ... raises the question of how society can best deal with the agonizing problem of prenatal substance abuse.... Some states have attempted to criminalize prenatal drug use or treat it

---

[9] See Dailard and Nash (2000). Especially helpful is the tabular representation of laws in different US states pertaining to pregnant women who use drugs.

[10] See Nelson (1998); Humphries (1999, 2001); Hodge (1999); Harris (2000).

> as grounds for terminating parental rights.... But [this] issue ...vividly demonstrates the difficulty policymakers face in attempting to balance the autonomy and bodily integrity of pregnant women with society's interests in ensuring the birth of healthy children.... It raises the question of whether the state can ever be justified in regulating a pregnant woman's behavior in the interest of protecting her fetus and whether such policies potentially undermine the legality of abortion... (Dailard and Nash, 2000: 3).[11]

The courts in all states but South Carolina[12] have been reluctant to stand over the criminal prosecution of pregnant women for prenatal action. Either courts have declined the invitation to extend the scope of existing laws to cover claims of foetal rights, or they have held that the term "child" in such acts does not cover foetuses, nor "parent" a pregnant woman vis-à-vis her foetus, or they have declined to interpret the term "delivery" in respect of controlled substances to cover transmission via the umbilical cord. Several courts have pointed out the obvious dangers of extending existing criminal laws in ways which could criminalise a pregnant woman's smoking, or sports activity, or hazardous employment (Harris and Paltrow, 2003). Nevertheless, up to the year 2000 it was estimated that as many as 200 women had been subjected to criminal prosecution or arrest for illicit drug use, alcohol use, failure to adhere to a physician's instruction or to undergo a caesarean section which, it was alleged, had inflicted harm upon the unborn child (Harris and Paltrow, 2003).

The situation in respect of violations of civil law is somewhat more interventionist. Several states – including Ohio, South Carolina, Con-

---

[11] See also Foley (2002); Toscano (2005); Pulatie (2008).

[12] See Harris and Paltrow (2003). Dailard and Nash note: "To date, no state legislature has adopted a law that creates unique criminal penalties for pregnant women who are addicted to, dependent on, or using drugs" and they add that "while no state has enacted a law specifically criminalizing drug use during pregnancy, prosecutors have relied on a host of criminal laws already on the books to attack prenatal substance abuse ... women who have appealed their convictions to their state supreme court have prevailed in all but one instance.... Only in South Carolina has the state supreme court ... upheld the conviction of a woman charged with criminal child abuse for using cocaine during pregnancy [in *Whitner*]" (2000: 3).

necticut, New Jersey, New York – have employed their child welfare laws to make maternal drug-taking a matter of child abuse or neglect with appropriate civil penalties, including the removal of parental rights. Other states make use of their civil child abuse laws.[13]

In ways that seriously impinge upon a woman's autonomy, some states authorise the civil commitment of women who use drugs while pregnant on the grounds that, in such circumstances, the unborn is an endangered person. As Dailard and Nash point out:

> Minnesota and South Dakota authorize the emergency admission of pregnant women for mandatory drug treatment, including inpatient treatment, for as long as the duration of a pregnancy. The Wisconsin children's code, as amended in 1998, goes so far as to grant the state's juvenile court 'exclusive jurisdiction' over an unborn child when a pregnant woman 'habitually lacks self-control' with regard to alcohol or controlled substances. Because the statute defines an 'unborn child' as a 'human being from the time of fertilization to the time of birth,' the state may intervene and detain a woman throughout her pregnancy if she poses a 'substantial risk to the physical health' of her fetus (2000: 5).

Other state regimes are significantly less intrusive and are geared towards supporting and encouraging women to desist from drug use during pregnancy but not by means of either criminal or civil sanctions.

While arguments can be made on consequentialist grounds on the relative effectiveness or ineffectiveness in respect of foetal health of the more versus the less intrusive state regimes, for our purposes, the interest in such cases derives from their impact upon the autonomy of the pregnant woman. If, as in *Whitner*, a woman can be held criminally liable for behaviour in itself legal (such as smoking or drinking) where such behaviour harms the unborn, what restrictions if any are there on the range of possibly prohibited behaviours?

Minnesota, South Dakota and Wisconsin have enacted laws permitting the civil commitment of women who use drugs while pregnant:

---

[13] For example, Cal Penal Code s. 11165.13; Ind Code s. 31-34-1-10, 11; RI Admin Code s. 03-040-420.II.D.4.a and many others.

Minnesota and South Dakota enjoining mandatory drug treatment, and Wisconsin, under its children's code (amended in 1998) granting:

> … the states juvenile court 'exclusive jurisdiction' over an unborn child when a pregnant woman 'habitually lacks self-control' with regard to alcohol or controlled substances. Because the statute defines an 'unborn child' as a 'human being from the time of fertilization to the time of birth,' the state may intervene and detail a woman throughout her pregnancy if she poses a 'substantial risk to the physical health' of her fetus (Dailard and Nash, 2000: 5).

Ireland

As *Re F (in utero)* showed, English courts appear to be unwilling to adopt or support an interventionist strategy in cases of possible conflict between the rights of pregnant women and the rights of their unborn children; and despite the misgivings of many commentators it is by and large conceded that non-interventionism is still the order of the day in England. In the US, on the other hand, the courts have moved from a generally non-interventionist position to (in *Whitner* and in *In re Unborn Child*) quite a strong interventionist position.

The legal position of the unborn child in Ireland would appear to be constitutionally established. After a series of high profile cases, precisely what is constitutionally guaranteed is a matter of dispute. What are the implications of this constitutional position (however understood) for the matter of incarceration or forced treatment of a pregnant woman in situations where her behaviour or lifestyle is deemed to endanger her unborn child?

In Ireland, in July 2002, a woman who was pregnant and HIV positive refused to undergo treatment that would have had the effect of reducing the risk of transmitting the virus to her unborn child. The President of the High Court, Finnegan J, advised her that if she refused to give birth in hospital he would have to make "serious orders affecting her bodily integrity" (*The Irish Times*, 2002). What could such orders possibly be – forced confinement, 24-hour supervision, or the forced administration of medication? In the event, the woman underwent the medical treatment and the question of the making of the requisite orders became moot.

In 2006, a woman, Ms K, who had just delivered a baby, suffered a massive and life-threatening haemorrhage. She refused to accept a blood transfusion as this was contrary to her religious beliefs (she is a Jehovah's Witness). The hospital sought an order authorising it to administer all necessary treatment, including blood transfusion, to the woman. They sought declaratory relief on the basis of the provisions of Articles 40.3.1°, 40.3.2°, 41 and 42.5 of the Constitution. In the High Court, Abbott J granted orders, on the *ex parte* application of the plaintiffs, authorising the requisite treatment and, if necessary, the restraint of Ms K.[14] According to the newspaper reports, Abbott J accepted that Ms K was competent but nevertheless held that given that her refusal to accept a transfusion would result in her death and the orphaning of her child the interests of her child were paramount. The Constitution required that precedence be given to the welfare of the child. The Constitutional provisions referred to were those in which the State guarantees in its laws to protect, defend and vindicate the personal rights of the citizen (Article 40.3.1°), in particular the life of every citizen (Article 40.3.2°), undertakes to protect the Family (Article 41), and shall endeavour to supply the place of parents where, in exceptional circumstances, the parents fail in their duty towards their children (Article 42.5). It would be extremely interesting to see how an argument based on these provisions would proceed against the argument that could be made for the right of a competent adult to refuse medical treatment, even if such refusal were, in the opinion of medical experts, deemed to be unreasonable.

As it happens, we already have such an argument. In 1995, a case (*In the matter of a Ward of Court* (1996)) came before the Supreme Court in which, *inter alia*, the right of a competent adult to refuse medical treatment was considered.[15] In the High Court, Lynch J had held that:

> … the patient himself being competent, may lawfully decline medical treatment even though not terminally ill which he reasonably considers to be excessively burdensome, having regard to the paucity of benefit to be realised thereby and notwithstanding

[14] For a statement of the facts of the case, see *FitzPatrick and Anor v F K and Anor* [2006]. See also McDonald and Managh (2006) and Donnellan (2006).

[15] See Feenan (1996); Harrington (1995).

> that the absence of such treatment may lead to his death (1996: 94).

Having reviewed the circumstances of the case, Hamilton CJ stated:

> There is no doubt but that the ward, if she were mentally competent, had the right, if she so wished, to forego such treatment or, at any time, to direct that it be withdrawn even though such withdrawal would result in her death (1996: 124).

That such a right is not absolute is implicit in his statement that:

> In the circumstances of this ward there is no conflict between the exercise of these rights and the right to life, which the State is by the Constitution obliged to respect, defend, vindicate and protect from unjust attack (1996: 127).

One must presume that the Ms K decision is to be justified because in her case there was a conflict of rights. Once the principle of paramountcy be granted, what, in principle, is there to prevent any and all limitations of the rights of pregnant women should the court determine such limitation necessary to the welfare of the child?

In the event, the arguments were not made and the law reports in which the facts of the 2006 application are set out concern not the substantive issue of the clash of rights but the procedural question relating to the application of the Watch Tower Bible and Tract Society of Ireland to be joined to the proceedings. Counsel for the Society did make the point that the declaratory relief sought had the potential to transcend the facts of the particular case. It is hard to disagree with this contention, especially as a declaration was sought that Ms K's constitutional guarantee of freedom of conscience and the free profession and practice of religion (Article 44.2.1°) does not entitle her to refuse the medical treatment in question or that, alternatively, her Article 44.2.1° rights must yield to the State's obligations under the previously cited articles. If such arguments were to prevail, we would have sanctioned a highly paternalistic form of intervention. How does this decision sit with the findings of the European Court of Human Rights which, in the context of a case involving a custody dispute, appeared to accept the right of a Jehovah Witness to reject blood transfusions not only for herself but for her children (Enright, 2004). In *Hoffmann v Austria* (1994) the European Court of Human Rights held by a narrow majority (5-4)[16] that the findings of the Austrian national courts had violated Article 8 conjoined with Article 14 of the European Convention of Human Rights (1994: 293, 316). If a person has a right protected under the European Convention of Human Rights to reject such treatment for their legally incompetent dependents, *a fortiori* one would expect that they have should have such a right of refusal for themselves.

Conclusion

The relationship between a pregnant woman and her foetus is unique – not uncommon, but unique. Here I (and I suspect I am not alone) am prey to conflicting intuitions. From a generally libertarian perspective, I am inclined towards non-intervention, especially if intervention has the effect of constraining personal freedom. On the other hand, one's actions are necessarily limited by their effects on others, especially where such action results in bodily harm or, in extreme cases, death. We have child protection laws to prevent the infliction by, *inter alia,* parents on their children. In extreme cases, children can be removed from their parents' control. In the case of pregnancy, however, there is no possibility of such removal yet what is the principled difference in respect of the possible infliction of harm. If such harm would be impermissible *extra utero*, why should it be permissible *in utero*?

In the 2002 case the woman voluntarily underwent the medical treatment and the necessity for the making of the requisite orders became moot so that Finnegan J did not have to make any order affecting her bodily integrity. However, his willingness to make such orders if she had refused to give birth in hospital, taken together with the Ms K case of 2006, would seem to indicate that our courts would be willing to adopt an attitude more consonant with the interventionist American model than with the noninterventionist English and Canadian models. If, in the USA, in a jurisprudential context in which there is no overall agreed upon

---

16 The Commission arrived at the same holding by another slim majority, 8-6 (Hoffmann, 312).

status for the unborn child and in which the unborn child certainly has no specifically protected constitutional status, there are tendencies towards medico-legal intervention then it would seem, *a fortiori*, that interventionism would be facilitated in Ireland by the unique constitutional position of the unborn child. On the other hand, our common law tradition and historically close association with English law would seem to point us in the direction of non-intervention. To intervene or not to intervene – that is the question. What the answer may be one can only speculate.

Bibliography

Annas, George J. (1986), "At Law: Pregnant Women as Fetal Containers", *The Hastings Center Report*, Vol. 16, No. 6, 13-14.

Anon (1993), Report of the Royal Commission on New Reproductive Technologies *Proceed with Care*, Vol. 2, 957-58.

Buckley, Amy M. (1998), "The Primacy of Democracy over Natural Law in Irish Abortion Law: An Examination of the *C* Case", *Duke Journal of Comparative & International Law*, Vol. 9, No. 1, 275-310.

Capen, K. (1997), "Mother's Rights can't be Infringed to Protect Fetus, Supreme Court's Landmark Ruling States", *Canadian Medical Association Journal*, Vol. 157, No. 11, 1586-87.

Casey, G. (2002), "Pregnant Woman and Unborn Child: Legal Adversaries?", *Medico-Legal Journal of Ireland*, Vol. 8, No. 1, 75-81.

Casey, G. (2004), "The "Logically Faultless" Argument for Unenumerated Rights in the Constitution", *Irish Law Times*, Vol. 22 (New Series), No. 16, 46-48.

Casey, G. (2005a), *Born Alive: The Legal Status of the Unborn Child in England and the U.S.A.*, Chicester: Barry Rose.

Casey, G. (2005b), "Are there Unenumerated Rights in the Irish Constitution?" *Irish Law Times*, Vol. 23 (New Series), No 8, 123-27.

Cave, E. (2004), *The Mother of All Crimes: Human Rights, Criminalization and the Child Born Alive,* Aldershot, Hants: Ashgate Publishing.

Chavkin, W. (2001), "Cocaine and Pregnancy – Time to look at the Evidence," *Journal of the American Medical Association*, Vol. 285, No. 12, 1626-1628.

Christie, S. (2006), "Crimes against the Foetus: The Rights and Wrongs of Protecting the Unborn", *Medico-Legal Journal of Ireland*, Vol. 12, No. 2, 65-76.

Cotter, A-M. (2002, "Life Choices – A Comparative Look at the Issue of Abortion in Ireland and North America", *Irish Law Times*, Vol. 20 (New Series), No. 7, 107-11.

Coulter, C. (2006a), "Widening the Grounds for Abortion", *The Irish Times*, 14 July.

Coulter, C. (2006b), "Foetus may not always be an unborn, argues State", *The Irish Times*, 14 July.

Coveney, H. (2007), "Assisted Reproductive Technologies and the Status of the Embryo", *Medico-Legal Journal of Ireland,* Volume 13, No. 1, 14-X.

Dailard, C. and Nash, E. (2000), "State Responses to Substance Abuse among Pregnant Women", *The Guttmacher Report on Public Policy,* December, 3-6.

Donnellan, E. (2006), "Woman in Court Transfusion Case recovering in Hospital", *The Irish Times*, 22 September.

Enright, M. (*2006),* "Dispositional Contracts and Frozen Embryos: Rights for Women?" *Medico-Legal Journal of Ireland*, Volume 12, No. 1, 31-55.

Feenan, D. (1996), "Death, Dying and the Law," *Irish Law Times*, Vol. 14, No. X, 90-X.

Foley, E.M. (2002), "Drug Screening and Criminal Prosecution of Pregnant Women", *Journal of Obstetric, Gynecologic, & Neonatal Nursing*, Vol. 31, No. 2, 133–137.

Gostin, L.O. (2001), "At Law: The Rights of Pregnant Women: The Supreme Court and Drug Testing", *The Hastings Center Report*, Vol. 31, No. 5, 8-9.

Hakim, M.G. (1997), "Mother v. Fetus: New Adversaries in the Struggle to Define the Rights of Unborn Children", *Journal of Juvenile Law*, Vol. 18, 99-111.

Harrington, J.A. (1995), "Constitutional Law – Withdrawal of Treatment from an Incompetent Patient", *Dublin University Law Journal*, Vol. 17 (ns), No. X, 120-X.

Harris, L.H. (2000), "Rethinking Maternal-Fetal Conflict: Gender and Equality in Perinatal Ethics," *Obstetrics and Gynecology*, Vol. 96, 786-791.

Harris, L.H. and Paltrow, L. (2003), "The Status of Pregnant Women and Fetuses in US Criminal Law", *The Journal of the American Medical Association*, Vol. 289, April, 1697-1699.

Hodge, J.G. (1999), "Prosecution of Mother for Prenatal Substance Abuse Based on Endangerment of or Delivery of Controlled Substance to Child," *American Law Reports*, Vol. 70, 5th Series, 461-X.

Humphries, D. (1999), *Crack Mothers, Pregnancy, Drugs, and the Media*, Columbus: Ohio State University Press.

Kennedy, I. and Grubb, A. (2000), *Medical Law*, London: Butterworths.

Kerr, I.R. (2000), "Pregnant Women and the 'Born Alive' Rule in Canada", *Tort Law Review* Vol. 8, No. 1, 713-19.

MacEnzie, T.B. et al. (1986); "When a Pregnant Women Endangers Her Fetus," *Hastings Center Report*, Volume 16, February, 24-25.

Matthieu, D. (1996), *Preventing Prenatal Harm: Should the State Intervene?* Washington, D.C.: Georgetown University Press.

McDonald, D. and Managh, R. (2006), "Jehovah's Witness forced to have Life-saving Transfusion", *The Irish Independent*, 22 September.

McGovern, J. (2006), "A Casenote on *MR v TR* and Others", *Medico-Legal Journal of Ireland*, Vol. 13, No. 1, 42-X.

Meredith, S. (2005), *Policing Pregnancy: The Law and Ethics of Obstetric Conflict*, Aldershot, Hants: Ashgate Publishing Ltd.

Nelson, L.J. (1998), "Criminalization of Prenatal Substance Abuse and Drug Addiction", in Nelson, L.J. Nelson and Marshall, M.F. (eds), *Ethical and Legal Analyses of Three Coercive Policies Aimed at Substance Abuse by Pregnant Women.*

Pickworth, E. (1998), "Substance Abuse in Pregnancy and the Child Born Alive", Vol. 27, No. 4, *Anglo-American Law Review*, 472-80.

Pulatie, K. (2008), "The Legality of Drug-Testing Procedures for Pregnant Women", *Virtual Mentor* (American Medical Association Journal of Ethics), Vol. 10, No. 1, 41-44.

Samiloff, J. (2007), "Conflicting Rights", *New Law Journal*, Vol. 157, No. 7275, 753.

Schweppe, J. (2005), "Revisiting Article 40.3.3°. Part One: Third-Party Foetal Assault", *Irish Journal of Family Law*, Vol. 8, No. 4, 19-X.

Schweppe, J. (2005), "Pregnant Women and Unborn Children – In Utero Drug Exposure", *Irish Journal of Family Law*, Vol. 9, No. 1, 19-X.

Siano, J.R. (1998), "A Woman's right to Choose: Wrongful Death Statutes and Abortion Rights –Consistent at Last", *Women's Rights Law Reporter*, Vol. 19.

Spain, E. (2006), "*Vo v France*: Reasonable Settlement or Missed Opportunity?" *Irish Journal of Family Law*, Vol. 9, No. 2, 16-X.

Toscano, V. (2005), "Misguided Retribution: Criminalization of Pregnant Women who take Drugs", *Social & Legal Studies*, Vol. 14, No. 3, 359-386.

Whyte, G. (2006), "The Moral Status of the Embryo", *Medico-Legal Journal of Ireland*, Vol. 12, No. 2, 77-X.

Cases

Attorney-General's Reference (No. 3 of 1994) [1998] AC 245.

Baby O v Minister for Justice, Equality and Law Reform [2002] I.R. 169.

Bonbrest v Kotz 65 F Supp 138 (DC Cir 1946).

Commonwealth v. Pellegrini, Cas. No. 87970 (Mass. Super. Ct. Oct. 15, 1990).

D v Ireland (2006) 43 E.H.R.R. SE16 ECHR.

Dobson (Litigation Guardian of) v Dobson [1999] 2 SCR 753.

Ferguson v City of Charleston 532 U.S. 67 (2001).

Fitzpatrick & Anor v F K & Anor [2006] IEHC 392.

Griswold v Connecticut 381 US 479.

Grodin v Grodin 301 NW 2d 869 (Mich Ct App 1980).

Hoffmann v Austria (1994) 17 E.H.R.R. 293.

In re Unborn Child 683 NYS S.2d 366 (19 June 1998) (New York Family Court).

In the Matter of a Ward of Court [1996] 2 IR 73.

McGee v Attorney General [1974] IR 284.

MR v TR. and Others [2006] IEHC 359.

P J Carroll & Co v The Minister for Health and Children [2006] IESC 36.

Paton v United Kingdom [1980] 3 EHRR 408.

R. v Bourne [1939] 1 KB 687.

Re F. (in utero) [1988] All ER 193.

Renslow v Mennonite Hospital 367 NE 2d 1250 (Ill 1977).

Roe v Wade 410 US 113.

Ryan v Attorney General [1965] IR 294.

Smith v Brennan 157 A 2d 497 (NJ 1960).

St. George's Healthcare N.H.S. Trust v S [1998] 3 WLR. 936.

State v Ashley 670 So 2d 1087 (1996).

State v Horne 282 SC 444.

State v Zimmerman 1996 WL 858598 (1996).

Toth v Goree 237 NW 2d 297 (Mich 1975).

Tremblay v Daigle (1989) 62 DLR (4th) 634.

Whitner v State 492 SE 2d 777 (SC 1997).

Winnipeg Child and Family Services (Northwest Area) v DFG (Manitoba Court of Queen's Bench, Aug. 13, 1996) File CP 91-01-04256.

Winnipeg Child and Family Services (Northwest Area) v DFG [1997] 3 SCR 925.

Part Three

ARTICLE 40.3.3° AND THE LAW

8

ARTICLE 40.3.3° OF THE CONSTITUTION:

Respecting the Dignity and Equal Worth of Human Beings

Prof William Binchy

In this paper I shall attempt to analyse how Article 40.3.3° fits into the deep structure of the Irish Constitution. I shall argue that it is entirely coherent with that structure and I shall critique some of the judicial interpretations of the provision.

What is the Deep Structure of the Irish Constitution?

Those who seek to mine the depths of the Irish Constitution in order to determine its deep structure come upon a rich treasury. The Constitution rests on a distinctive philosophy involving a network of rights and responsibilities of people relative to each other and to society. Moreover, it has a clear perspective on the existential significance of human life. Whether one admires or abhors this reality, it is impossible to ignore or deny it.

The 1937 Constitution can be regarded as prophetic. It anticipated the great international human rights instruments which began to emerge a decade later. It is premised on rejection of legal positivism, respect for universalism and an understanding of human beings as entities of equal dignity and value, each with a unique worth. Whilst the Constitution articulates a range of rights enforceable again the state, it embraces a wider scaffolding of interpersonal solidarity and the integration of human beings into social relationships beyond simply their relationship with the state.

Before examining the details of the philosophical and normative framework of the Constitution, let me speak in more general terms about what is generally treated with silence or coded language: the existential premises of human rights. Rights language is deeply normative. Natural rights may not necessarily be nonsense upon stilts but they can be verified in no laboratory on earth. They derive their authority from a philosophic perspective. If I say that every human being has inherent dignity, the sceptic may treat this assertion with the disdain that he or she would attach to dogma.[1]

The truth of the matter is that the meaning to be ascribed to human rights discourse and the source of its justification must be found in the realm of philosophy in that area which addresses the most fundamental questions, which some regard as unanswerable and even as incapable of being posed meaningfully. Has life meaning or significance? What is the source of value? Must belief in the worth of every human being be dismissed as meaningless because "rights language" is beyond empirical verification and a product of the speaker's cultural environment?[2] These questions have a particular poignancy in relation to the protection of unborn human beings.

The answers to these questions are crucial because they shape our understanding of human rights in general and of specific human rights such as the right to life, the right not to be subjected to cruel or inhuman treatment, the right to privacy and the right to autonomy. They shape also our determination of who are rights-carriers. Moreover, they inform our interpretation of the concept of human dignity. In short, the existential premises of a particular theory of human rights are far more important than the surface debates that take place so often about the

---

[1] See further Parekh (2007) and Starck (2002).

[2] It is important to have regard to the intensity of contemporary scepticism as to the philosophical and normative foundations for human rights, even among those who see pragmatic and functional merit in resorting to such "rights language". Thus Dembour (2006) observes that she is "…. not merely a human rights agnostic but also a human rights atheist, for I am ready to affirm the non-existence, across the ages, of human rights. Going further, I could even describe myself as a human rights nihilist" (2006: 12).

scope of particular rights where these debates ignore the premises – and the debate about the premises – which shape those rights.[3]

It is of some significance that the Irish Constitution is rooted in a philosophical perspective which embraces a concept of God – not because of any doctrinal implications but rather because God-language explains the existential framework of the particular human rights theory endorsed by the Constitution.[4] On this approach, every human being is a creature of inestimable value; every human life has meaning; human beings have freedom but that freedom must be exercised in accordance with the recognition of one's obligations to others and to oneself. Even non-believers, who regard deism as a foolish self-deceit, would have to acknowledge that this metaphysical perspective shapes the meaning and scope of these rights.

Dignity as a Constitutional Value

It may at this point be useful to note the place of dignity in the Constitution.[5] The Constitution refers expressly to dignity only once, in

[3] One can thus agree to some extent with the observations of Langlois (2005), while not perceiving "philosophical … traditions" as necessarily foreclosing an effective interrogation of the force and merit of those traditions. We are, after all, not mere prisoners of our cultural, political and philosophical past: free thought – even to the point of complete rejection of one's philosophical traditions – is always possible. Langlois contends that: "…the metaphysical account which gives meaning to the term human rights is itself the evolving end-product of a long and complex intellectual tradition. This tradition is inescapably a particularist historical narrative. It is not possible to make sense of human rights, to give them content or meaning or veracity, from any other place than within one or another of the human intellectual traditions. Thus, the existence and universality of human rights do not derive from the capacity of human rights theorists to transcend their human particularity and comment on the nature of the human condition from some place external to that condition – be it a view from nowhere, an Archimedean point or a god's eye point of view. Rather, human rights are established and regarded from within our philosophical, political and religious traditions. These narratives are the only tools we have by which to determine our place in the cosmos. The human intelligence, for all its complexity and wonder, is not able to transcend itself in its bid for self-understanding, other regard and social understanding …" (2005: 383).

[4] For discussion of a similar provision in the Canadian Charter of Rights and Freedoms, see Penney and Danay (2006).

[5] See O'Dowd's wide-ranging analysis (1995) and McCrudden's magisterial review (2008).

the Preamble. Let me quote the Preamble in full so as to enable this reference to be interpreted in its particular context:

> In the Name of the Most Holy Trinity, from Whom is all authority and to Whom, as our final end, all actions both of men and States must be referred,
>
> We, the people of Éire,
>
> Humbly acknowledging all our obligations to our Divine Lord, Jesus Christ, Who sustained our fathers through centuries of trial,
>
> Gratefully remembering their heroic and unremitting struggle to regain the rightful independence of our Nation,
>
> And seeking to promote the common good, with due observance of Prudence, Justice and Charity, so that the dignity and freedom of the individual may be assured, true social order attained, the unity of our country restored, and concord established with other nations,
>
> Do hereby adopt, enact, and give to ourselves this Constitution.

What can one say of the "dignity" here mentioned? It appears to involve a single meaning. Thus, the fact that in ordinary parlance the word "dignity" may be used differently in different contexts has no counterpart in the Preamble.

Let me now turn to consider the judicial articulation of dignity which integrates dignity into the protection of equality under the Constitution. In *Quinn's Supermarket v Attorney General* Walsh J. said that Article 40.1 was:

> not a guarantee of absolute equality for all citizens in all circumstances it is a guarantee of equality as human persons and (as the Irish text of the constitution makes quite clear) is a guarantee related to their dignity as human beings and a guarantee against any inequalities grounded upon an assumption, or indeed a belief, that some individual or individuals or classes of individuals, by reason of their human attributes or their ethnic or racial, social or religious background, are to be treated as the inferior or superior of other individuals in our country (1972: 12-14).

This passage is of crucial importance in providing such a clear acknowledgement of the relationship between dignity and equality. It recognises the radical equality that underlies our inherent value as human beings and seeks to ensure that any inequalities grounded on an assumption or belief that contradicts this equality will not withstand constitutional scrutiny.

These insights, patent in the passage from Walsh J's judgment, were not recognised by judges in many later decisions. The "human personality" doctrine came to be understood, not as a clarion call to scrutinise areas of ingrained prejudice and inequality, but as permitting a wide range of inequalities created by legislation which were not regarded as going to the very core of what it is to be human.[6] The courts should, with benefit, parse more closely what Walsh J had to say. Every society is the accretion of values and power relationships over time.

Anyone who looks at recent Irish social history will be seriously disturbed at the way the some members of our society have been treated: children, in schools and institutions; women, in the home and the workplace; the physically and mentally disabled; the elderly. They have been the victims, not merely of individual injustice but of the passive acquiescence in the *status quo* by those in power. They seem to fit precisely within the language of Walsh J: people subjected to inequalities grounded on the assumption that, by reason of their human attributes or their background they are to be treated as inferiors of others. In all of these cases, human dignity was not assured, contrary to the constitutional mandate. That the assumption was tacit and not driven by specific malice does not subtract from the violation of dignity.[7]

Unborn children were not in the past regarded as inferior to others by virtue of the human attributes of early age, dependency and lack of maturity. International cultural developments, which have affected Ireland and other western European societies, have encouraged the ascription of inferiority to unborn children. This process has been gradual. For a period, the termination of the life of an unborn child by abortion was re-

---

[6] For the most comprehensive analysis of this issue, see Doyle (2006) especially Ch. 2.

[7] I acknowledge that the task of distinguishing between a socially institutionalised assumption of inferiority and a benign but ineffective social policy is difficult and contentious. Nevertheless, few would argue that contemporary Irish social structures are completely free of such an assumption.

garded as presumptively a serious violation of rights, capable of justification or tolerance in a very restricted number of specific circumstances. Over time, abortion has come to be regarded in many societies as a right; unborn children have correspondingly suffered a loss of status. Indeed, in some legal cultures they do not even have the status of inferior human beings: their human character is denied. Whether they should be characterised as property has been mooted, though not widely endorsed. The distance between these developments and the notion of dignity in the Irish Constitution is profound.

The Protection of Rights under the Constitution

Under the Constitution, in the light of its underlying philosophy, human beings are in a relationship of mutual respect which carries with it rights and responsibilities. People must not be treated as mere objects. Crucially, you are entitled to be protected from my directly violating your rights – to life or bodily integrity. I am not entitled intentionally to take your life; nor am I entitled to torture you. Respect for human equality, resting on our human dignity, gives you protection from acts of this kind. Indeed, the current international debate about whether torture may ever be justified reveals the force of these values. There are very pressing utilitarian arguments in favour of torture and even arguments involving a simple proportionality test may seem strong enough to justify torture in extreme cases. Those who wish to argue against torture need to be able to invoke convincing arguments. The naked violation of the "me-you" solidarity on which the Constitution is based offers just such a basis for objecting to torture. In intentionally requiring a person to deny the essence of his or her free will, the torturer is engaging in such a direct violation of interpersonal solidarity as to offend not merely bodily integrity but the values of equality and human dignity. There is nothing sophistical about a constitution based on the insistence that direct violations of rights should not be countenanced.

The Need for the Eighth Amendment

Those who have, however cautiously, followed the path of the argument so far might reasonably ask: if the 1937 Constitution was so wonderful in protecting human equality and dignity, why was there any need for a constitutional amendment in 1983? That is an entirely logical question to which the answer will be found, not in the realm of constitutional theory, but in *realpolitik*.

The truth of the matter, as Dworkin has eloquently explained, is that there is no necessary connection between a constitution and the judicial articulation of its values. Judges can make mistakes (as the appeal process attests); judges can be affected, however unconsciously, by factors external to the internal norms of a constitution; judges may not always fully grasp the philosophical implications of the legal concepts contained in a constitution.

In short, coming up to 1983, in the light of international legal developments, there were good grounds for apprehending that the Constitution, in its original formulation, might not prove capable of withstanding a challenge to legislation prohibiting abortion. The apprehension was of course focused on the issue of abortion but it reflected a wider concern that the Constitution might be interpreted in a way that denied protection to the life of human beings in the early stages, in contradiction of the principle of the equal worth and dignity of every human being.

The Eighth Amendment: Core Concepts

Article 40.3.3°, as introduced by the Eighth Amendment to the Constitution, provided as follows:

> The State acknowledges the right to life of the unbirn and, with due regard to the equal right to life of the mother, guarantees in its laws to respect and, so far as practicable, by its laws to defend and vindicate that right.[8]

What is striking about the language of the Amendment is that it says nothing whatsoever about abortion. It is entirely philosophical in character. It is

---

[8] For a comprehensive analysis of the historical background to the amendment campaign and to the public debate surrounding it, see Hesketh (1990) (Dr Hesketh's book was warmly welcomed by both sides of the debate as an objective, insightful account of events). See also Quinlan (1984), Hogan (1988), Charleton (1992: 350-62), O'Leary and Hesketh (1988: 43-55, 58-9), Chubb (1991: 52-5), Randall (1986), Girvin (1986), Garvin (1987), O'Carroll (1991), Speed (1992: 85), Barry (1992: 107).

premised on two central values: the equality of all human beings and their entitlement not to have their lives directly targeted. In this respect, the Amendment, far from altering the philosophy of the Constitution as originally formulated, endorses that philosophy completely.

The Supreme Court decision in *Attorney General v X*

Let us now turn to consider the decision of *Attorney General v X* (1992). The tragic facts and the holding in the case are well known. By a majority of four (Finlay CJ, McCarthy, O'Flaherty and Egan JJ) to one (Hederman J), it was held that Article 40.3.3° permits abortion where there is a real and substantial risk to the life, as distinct from the health, of the mother which can be avoided only by an abortion. The majority held, further, that this ground was established in the instant case.[9]

Finlay CJ recorded his specific endorsement of the submission that the doctrine of harmonious interpretation of the Constitution involved a consideration of the interrelation of the constitutional rights and obligations of the mother with those of other people "and, of course, with the right to life of the unborn child as well". Such a harmonious interpretation, carried out in accordance with the concepts of prudence, justice and charity, as they had been explained in *McGee v Attorney General* (1974), led Finlay CJ to the conclusion that, in vindicating and defending as far as practicable the right of the unborn to life but at the same time giving due regard to the right of the mother to life:

> the court must, amongst the matters to be so regarded, concern itself with the position of the mother within a family group, with persons on whom she is dependent, with, in other instances, persons who are dependent upon her and her interaction with other citizens and members of society in the areas in which her activities occur (1992: 53).

The Chief Justice stated that, '[h]aving regard to that conclusion', he was satisfied that the proper test was that, if it was established as a matter of

---

[9] On the question whether it was permissible, in other cases, to grant injunctions against travelling abroad to have an abortion, the Court divided somewhat differently. Finlay CJ, Hederman and Egan JJ considered that it was; McCarthy and O'Flaherty J took the opposite view.

probability that there was a real and substantial risk to the life, as distinct from the health, of the mother, which could be avoided only by the termination of her pregnancy, such termination was permissible.

McCarthy J's analysis of Article 40.3.3° was more radical in its ultimate prioritisation of the mother's right to life:

> The right of the girl here is a right to a life in being, the right of the unborn is to a life contingent; contingent on survival in the womb until successful delivery. It is not a question of setting one above the other but rather of vindicating, as far as practicable, the right to the life of the girl/mother (Article 40. s. 2, subs. 2), whilst with due regard to the equal right to life of the girl/mother, vindicating, as far as practicable, the right to life of the unborn (Article 40, s. 3, subs. 3). If the right to life of the mother is threatened by the pregnancy, and it is practicable to vindicate that right, then because of the due regard that must be paid to the equal right to life of the mother, it may not be practicable to vindicate the right to life of the unborn (1992: 79).

In McCarthy J's view, it was:

> not a question of balancing the life of the unborn against the life of the mother. If it were, the life of the unborn would virtually always have to be preserved, since the termination of pregnancy means the death of the unborn; there is no certainty, however high the probability, that the mother will die if there is not a termination of pregnancy. In my view, the true construction of the Amendment, bearing the mind the other provisions of Article 40 and the fundamental rights of the family guaranteed by Article 41, is that, paying due regard to the equal right to life of the mother, where there is a real and substantial risk attached to her survival not merely at the time of application but in contemplation at least throughout the pregnancy, then it may not be practicable to vindicate the right to life of the unborn. It is not a question of a risk of a different order of magnitude; it can never be otherwise than a risk of a different order of magnitude (1992: 80).

McCarthy J considered that the purpose of the Eighth Amendment could be readily identified – it was to enshrine in the Constitution the protection of the right to life of the unborn, thus precluding the legislature from an unqualified repeal of section 58 of the Act of 1861 or otherwise, in general, legalising abortion. The guarantee to the unborn was qualified by the requirement of the regard to the right to life of the mother and made less than absolute by recognizing that the right could only be vindicated as far as practicable.

Echoing the words of the Chief Justice, but elaborating on their scope, O'Flaherty J said that Article 40.3.3° could:

> not, of course, be taken in isolation from its historical background … it must also be considered as but one provision in the whole Constitution. The Constitution has at its core a commitment to freedom and justice. It treats the family with such respect and in language of such clarity and simplicity, that any attempt to summarise or paraphrase it must be inadequate.
>
> Can it be that a Constitution which requires the State to look to the economic needs of mothers is unconcerned for the health and welfare and happiness of mothers? I am certain that reading the Constitution as a whole, as I believe one must do, then the answer is clearly not. A broad dimension must be given to the Constitution and a narrow or pedantic approach to its provisions has to be put aside (1992: 86-87).

The judgments of the majority were to the effect that the words "due regard" and "as far as practicable", in conjunction with an assessment of the totality of constitutional rights and duties of the mother and of others, led to the conclusion that it was permissible to extinguish directly the life of the unborn. In concentrating on the words "as far as practicable" in Article 40.3.3°, these judges ignored the fact that the guarantee of the right to life of all citizens, including the mother, is similarly qualified by a practicability test.

The next major error in the Court's reasoning was to accept the submission of counsel for the Attorney General that Walsh J's remarks in *McGee v Attorney General* (1974) were relevant to the interpretation to be afforded to the terms "due regard" and "as far as practicable". Walsh J was speaking at the highest level of generality on the question of the jurisprudential basis of the natural law rights recognised as anterior to positive law. Walsh J, in a passage not quoted in Finlay CJ's judgment, had identified the natural law thus recognised as a theological concept: "the law of God promulgated by reason and ... the ultimate governor of all the laws of men". The Constitution, he considered, intended the natural human rights to which it referred to be in the theological category "rather than simply an acknowledgment of the ethical content of law in its ideal of justice". Walsh J went on to refer to the fact that, while the Constitution speaks of certain rights being imprescriptible or inalienable, or being antecedent and superior to positive law, it does not specify them. This is so in the case of Article 40.3.

There are clear grounds for interpreting the passage from Walsh J's judgment which the Chief Justice quoted as referring to the court's task of articulating the nature and scope of the unspecified personal rights to which Article 40.3 refers. Walsh J's reference to the virtues of justice, prudence and charity is anchored upon the Preamble to the Constitution. The idea that these remarks give the judiciary a carte blanche to modify a calibration of constitutional rights which the Constitution itself expressly prescribes seems untenable.

Finlay CJ appears to have proceeded on the basis that the concepts of "due regard" and "practicability" should be interpreted by reference to changing social attitudes. The implications of such an approach, not only for abortion law, but also for the law relating to the direct termination of the lives of innocent people who have been born, are significant and controversial.

There was no empirical evidence that social attitudes to the issue of abortion had changed between 1983 and 1992, and the political voices in favour of legalised abortion within the State were, if anything, even fainter in 1992 than in 1983. But let us assume, for the purposes of our analysis, that the opposite was the case and that a clear majority of the Irish people was in favour of legalised abortion in March 1992 on the basis that the unborn's right to life was inferior to that of the mother. What implications, if any, should such a change of values have on the interpretation of the Eighth Amendment?

As a matter of constitutional interpretation it is clear that any such change of values could not have the effect of altering the explicit calibration of equality prescribed by Article 40.3.3°, any more than a clear majority sentiment against the prohibition of divorce legislation could override the express terms of Article 41.3.2°. A court may not seize upon the expressions "due regard" and "as far as practicable" and use them as a channel for replacing the equality of the right to life by a norm of inequality. Such a process violates the requirement of fidelity to the norms unambiguously acknowledged in the Constitution. There is a need here for intellectual honesty at the highest judicial level. The central problem with the majority holding in *X* is that it sought to justify an impermissible alteration of fundamental values by reference to a text that did not warrant such a process.

A wider jurisprudential issue is raised by the Court's reliance on Walsh J's judgment in *McGee*. The idea that fundamental principles of natural law relating to human rights are to be determined by a sense of what the majority of the community at any particular time may favour is one that could very easily slip into a caricature of human rights by opinion poll. If that is what Walsh J envisaged, clearly it would have to be rejected; but that is not, and could not reasonably be interpreted to be, what he was suggesting. What Walsh J would seem to have been rejecting was a sterile ultra-formalistic theory of original intent as a basis of constitutional interpretation. There is no reason to interpret his remarks as warranting the surrender of the judicial obligation to give effect to the natural law principles that underlie the fundamental rights provisions of the Constitution.

It would be wrong to suggest that Walsh J's approach is non-problematic or that it in any sense finally resolves the question of how the courts should discharge this obligation. There is room for much debate on this question, especially in the contexts of the notion of 'prevailing ideas' and the reference to the judges' "training and ... experience". All that the majority of the Supreme Court could contribute to this debate, on the fundamental question of the right to life, was to quote what Walsh J had said, declare that it was relevant to the issues arising in the case, and let the reader infer that the Court must have accepted a radical and unprecedentedly broad interpretation of the role of public opinion in defeating an express provision of the Constitution.

The Court's decision has proved controversial in other respects also. One implication of the judgment is that an abortion would be lawful at any stage of pregnancy. The point here, of course, is not that the life of every viable unborn infant may be terminated on demand or that, where it is alleged that the mother's life is at risk, the viable unborn must in every case be aborted rather than delivered safely. The problem with the Supreme Court decision is that it presents no principled argument against the destruction of the life of an unborn at any stage of the forty weeks' gestation. No doubt, the practicability criterion would point to safe delivery rather than abortion in most instances, but not in all. In a case where a mother asserts a suicidal intent if the child's life is not terminated, nothing in *X* would suggest that a court is obliged to decline to authorise the termination of the unborn life. The fact that the unborn is capable of being born alive is not crucial; the reason the child's life may be taken is that the mother's assertion of suicidal intent takes priority in terms of prescribing solutions. If the problem is characterised as the continuation of the unborn child's life, rather than simply its continuation within its mother's womb, and if the unborn child's right to life is regarded as being in principle capable of direct termination, then the fact that the child is capable of living outside the womb will not, of itself, be a compelling guarantee against a judicial order in favour of terminating its life.

It is worth reflecting on why the Court said nothing about the rights of the unborn at different stages of pregnancy. It could be, of course, that the majority simply forgot to address the question. Another explanation is, however, possible. In other jurisdictions, important legal distinctions are made on the basis of the gestational age of the unborn. Perhaps the most obvious example is the decision of the United States Supreme Court in *Roe v Wade* (1973), which differentiated radically between the rights of the unborn on the basis of the particular trimester in which the abortion takes place. It would have been hard for the Supreme Court in *X* to have engaged in a sliding scale of protection from abortion on the basis of the gestational age of a particular unborn without addressing the question of the value and significance of that life. The Eighth Amendment makes it clear that the lives of all unborn are equally valuable; it does not permit a court to engage in a process of attributing or denying value to a life at any particular stage.

Finlay CJ's judgment may be contrasted with that of McCarthy J in a number of important respects. First, McCarthy J places no emphasis on Walsh J's observations in *McGee* on the interpretation of the natural law and of rights guaranteed by Article 40.3. McCarthy J's understanding of the proper remit of practicability does not profess to depend on a changing social calibration of the virtues of prudence, justice and charity. Secondly, McCarthy J's analytic cornerstone is that *due regard* to the mother's life permits the direct taking of the life of the unborn and that any anxiety about this outcome is neutralised by the practicability proviso.

There is a difficulty with McCarthy J's analysis in this context: no explanation is proffered as to why *due* regard to an *equal* right to life permits or requires the court to favour that life to the extent of authorising the direct taking of the other life. McCarthy J's analysis seems consistent only with the proposition that the mother's right to life is not equal to the right to life of the unborn. That proposition is not in harmony with the Eighth Amendment.

A third feature of McCarthy J's analysis is his rejection of Costello J's conclusion that an injunction should be granted because of the relative magnitudes of the risk to the life of the unborn (which was certain in the case of an abortion) and the mother (which was less than certain). McCarthy J was clearly impressed, and apparently puzzled, by the fact that such an approach would lead to the result that the life of the unborn "would virtually always have to be preserved". It seems that McCarthy J regarded this result as so self-evidently indefensible that some other analysis, permitting the direct destruction of the life of the unborn, had to be preferred.

McCarthy J was right to sense that the conclusion that an abortion was not lawfully authorised could not depend *merely* on a calculating of competing risks. The reason why it is not lawful under the Amendment directly to take the life of an unborn is not reducible simply to that process of calculation; prior values are involved. McCarthy J's error lay in his handling of these values, whereby he gave priority to the mother's right to life, contrary to the specific requirements of the Amendment.

Having criticised the Oireachtas for not having legislated on the subject, McCarthy J went on to pose a series of questions:

> What are pregnant women to do? What are the parents of a pregnant girl under age to do? What are the medical profession to do? They have no guidelines save what may be gleaned from the judgments in this case. What additional considerations are there?

> Is the victim of rape, statutory or otherwise, or the victim of incest, finding herself pregnant, to be assessed in a manner different from others ... ? Does the right to bodily integrity ... involve the right to control one's own body? (1992: 82).

He observed that legislation might be both negative and positive: negative, "in prohibiting absolutely or at a given time, or without meeting stringent tests"; positive by requiring positive action. He observed finally that it was not for the courts to programme society, adding that that was partly, at least, the role of the legislature. The courts were not equipped to regulate these procedures.

What is one to make of all this? Why did McCarthy J raise the possibility of abortion in cases of underage pregnancy, rape, unlawful carnal knowledge and incest and on the basis of the right to control one's own body? How can the absence of legislation be relevant to any of these situations if the Amendment is to be interpreted (as McCarthy J indicated earlier in his judgment) as authorising abortion only in the case of a real and substantial risk attaching to the mother's survival? If one returns to this earlier passage and peruses it carefully, one discovers that McCarthy J did not in fact state expressly that the Amendment authorised abortion only in this case. What he said was that the true construction of the Amendment was that in such a case it might not be practicable to vindicate the right to life of the unborn.

The use of the words "true construction" certainly suggests that the construction should be limited to the stated ground, but it may be argued that it does not require this conclusion. McCarthy J was addressing a case in which the right to abortion on the ground of an asserted risk to the mother's life was being claimed. His conclusion that the true construction of the Amendment was that in such a case it might not be practicable to vindicate the right to life of the unborn did not commit him to holding that it would be practicable in all other cases.

In truth, McCarthy J appears to have been attempting in his later remarks to open up the possibility that the Oireachtas might have power to extend eligibility for abortion to some or all of the cases he mentioned. His profession of the inappropriateness of the courts' function in "programm[ing] society" and the propriety of the legislature's role was no doubt designed to cede to the legislature the primary function of balancing constitutional rights.

O'Flaherty J's judgment also gives cause for reflection. Several features are striking. First, it is noteworthy for its failure to make any reference to the fact that Article 40.3.3° recognises that the unborn child's right to life is equal to that of the mother's. It is fair to observe that a person who read O'Flaherty J's judgment without access to the text of Article 40.3.3° would have no inkling that it recognised such an equal right.

The second noteworthy feature of O'Flaherty J's judgment is that he also envisages legislation providing for abortion in circumstances other than where the mother's life is threatened. As we have seen, O'Flaherty J stated that he believed Article 40.3.3° to be clear in this respect: "Abortion, as such, certainly abortion on demand, is not something that can be legalised in this jurisdiction ... (1992: 87).

We may note here that O'Flaherty J only clearly excluded abortion *on demand* from the legislative programme. Thus, for example, legislation prescribing abortion on grounds such as the mother's health, her young age, rape, incest, or ("perhaps") bodily integrity or privacy could possibly be lawful. O'Flahertv J makes no attempt to distinguish between abortion on demand *de jure* and *de facto*. Relatively few countries expressly authorise abortion on demand and fewer still use language so stark as the term abortion "on demand". What happens in most countries where abortion is legal is that the legislature uses terminology that suggests restrictiveness but in practice results in abortion on demand. This is the experience in Britain, where abortion on demand is available under the rubric of the mother's health, and in the United States, where the mother's right to privacy is the basis for wide-ranging abortion.

Let us consider O'Flaherty J's statement that:

> [t]he legislators when they come to enact legislation must have due regard to the mother's right to life – a right protected throughout the Constitution in any event. Until legislation is enacted to provide otherwise, I believe that the law in this State is that surgical intervention which has the effect of terminating pregnancy *bona fide* undertaken to save the life of the mother where she is in danger of death is permissible under the Constitution and the law. The danger has to represent a substantial risk to

> her life though this does not necessarily have to be an imminent danger of instant death. The law does not require the doctors to wait until the mother is in peril of immediate death (1992: 87).

This passage requires close scrutiny. O'Flaherty J's failure to mention that the mother's right to life is equal to that of her unborn child is here particularly striking. The words "[u]ntil legislation is enacted to provide otherwise" seem crucial. They appear at least consistent with the view that the Oireachtas has power to extend the grounds of abortion beyond life-threatening cases virtually all the way to the terminus of abortion on demand, provided only that it stops just short of that terminus. This notion of legislative power to do what the judiciary cannot is strikingly reminiscent of what McCarthy J suggested less explicitly. O'Flaherty J's words would also seem capable of encompassing a legislative entitlement to restrict, or even exclude completely, the entitlement to abortion stated judicially in *X*. The general tenor of his judgment is not easy to harmonise with this interpretation.

In summary it may be said of the majority judgments that they fail to recognise, or consequently respect, the principles of equal worth and dignity and the entitlement of all human beings to be protected from a direct attack on their life, which characterise the Constitution and the Eighth Amendment.

The sole dissenting judge, Hederman J, saw this clearly. It is worth quoting his analysis:

> The Eighth Amendment to the Constitution was quite clearly designed to prevent any dispute or confusion as to whether or not unborn life could have availed of Article 40 as it stood before the Eighth Amendment. The Eighth Amendment made it clear, if clarity were needed, that the unborn life was also life within the guarantee of protection. It went further, and expressly spelled out a guarantee of protection of the life of the mother of the unborn life, by guaranteeing her life equality – equality of protection, to dispel any confusion there might have been thought to exist to the effect that the life of the infant in the womb must be saved even if it meant certain death for the mother. The death of a foetus may be the indirect but foreseeable result of an operation undertaken for other reasons. Indeed it is difficult to see how any operation,

the sole purpose of which is to save the life of the mother, could be regarded as a direct killing of the foetus, if the unavoidable and inevitable consequences of the efforts to save the mother's life leads to the death of the foetus. But like all examples of self-defence, of which this would be one, the means employed to achieve the self-protection must not go beyond what is strictly necessary.

The most significant aspect of the provisions of Article 40, s. 3 and of the Eighth Amendment is the objective of protecting human life which is the essential value of every legal order and central to the enjoyment of all other rights guaranteed by the Constitution. The constitutional provisions amount to a dedication to the fundamental value of human life. The Eighth Amendment establishes beyond any dispute that the constitutional guarantee of the vindication and protection of life is not qualified by the condition that the life must be one which has achieved an independent existence after birth.

The right of life is guaranteed to every life born or unborn. One cannot make distinctions between individual phases of the unborn life before birth, or between unborn and born life.

Clearly the State's duty of protection is far reaching. Direct State interference in the developing unborn life is outlawed and furthermore the State must protect and promote that life and above all defend it from unlawful interference by other persons. The State's duty to protect life also extends to the mother. The natural connection between the unborn child and the mother's life constitutes a special relationship. But one cannot consider the unborn life only as part of the maternal organism. The extinction of unborn life is not confined to the sphere of private life of the mother or family because the unborn life is an autonomous human being protected by the Constitution. Therefore the termination of pregnancy other than a natural one has a legal and social dimension and requires a special responsibility on the part of the State.

There cannot be a freedom to extinguish life side by side with a guarantee of protection of that life because the termination of pregnancy always means the destruction of an unborn life. Therefore no recognition of a mother's right of self-determination can

> be given priority over the protection of the unborn life. The creation of a new life, involving as it does pregnancy, birth and raising the child, necessarily involves some restriction of a mother's freedom but the alternative is the destruction of the unborn life. The termination of pregnancy is not like a visit to the doctor to cure an illness. The State must, in principle, act in accordance with the mother's duty to carry out the pregnancy and, in principle must also outlaw termination of pregnancy (1992: 71-72).

This analysis brings out clearly the principles of equality and protection from direct attack which underlie Article 40.3.3°.

McGovern J's Judgment in *MR v TR*

Let me now turn to consider McGovern J's judgment in *MR v TR* (2006). In this case, McGovern J interpreted the Eighth Amendment as being exclusively about abortion, leading to the conclusion that human embryos outside the womb were devoid of any constitutional protection. The crucial passage is as follows:

> What clearly emerges from the authorities I have referred to is that the Courts have declared that the Eight Amendment to the Constitution giving rise to the wording in Article 40.3.3° was for the purpose of making secure the prohibition on abortion expressed in s.57 and 58 of the Offences Against the Person Act, 1861 and not to permit abortion or termination of pregnancy except where it is established as a matter of probability that there is a real and substantial risk to the life of the mother if such termination were not effected. The Courts have never, thus far, considered whether the word 'unborn' in Article 40.3.3° includes embryos in vitro. In the *Smeaton*[10] case Munby J referred to a number of commentaries on the issue of law and medical ethics and medical legal aspects of reproduction. He cited a publication called *Post-Coital Anti Pregnancy Techniques and the Law* by K. Norrie who, he said, puts the argument very clearly:

---

[10] *The Queen on the Application of Smeaton v Secretary of State for Health* [2002] 2 FLR 146.

> … The question of when human life begins as a matter of morality, or indeed biology, is not the same as the question of when pregnancy begins for the purpose of the law. Human life may – or may not – begin in a test-tube, but the mere existence of a fertilised egg in a test-tube does not make the woman who produced the egg pregnant… See p. 211.

If Article 40.3.3° and the 1861 Act are concerned with the termination of pregnancy this does not mean that they are concerned with embryos *in vitro*. There has been no evidence adduced to establish that it was ever in the mind of the people voting on the Eight Amendment to the Constitution that 'unborn' meant anything other than a foetus or child within the womb. To infer that it was in the mind of the people that 'unborn' included embryos outside the womb or embryos *in vitro* would be to completely ignore the circumstances in which the amendment giving rise to Article 40.3.3° arose. While I accept that Article 40.3.3° is not to be taken in isolation from its historical background and should be considered as but one provision of the whole Constitution, this does not mean that the word 'unborn' can be given a meaning which was not contemplated by the people at the time of the passing of the Eighth Amendment and which takes it outside the scope and purpose of the amendment …

The Courts have already pronounced on the purpose of the Eighth Amendment to the Constitution. The plaintiff in this case assumes the burden of proving that the word 'unborn' meant something more than the foetus or child in the womb since the clear purpose of the amendment was to deal with the issue of termination of pregnancy. Evidence has been adduced by the plaintiff as to when human life begins, but there is much disagreement on this question among the medical and scientific community and, indeed, among the witnesses in this case. The question of when human life begins is not what the Court is concerned with in the interpretation of Article 40.3.3°. No evidence has been adduced by the plaintiff which would enable the Court to hold that the word 'unborn' in Article 40.3.3° includes embryos outside the womb or in vitro. I have therefore come to the conclusion that the word 'unborn' within Article 40.3.3° does not include embryos in vitro and therefore does not include the three frozen embryos which are at the heart of the dispute between the plaintiff and the first named defendant.

It is not for the Courts to decide whether the word 'unborn' should include embryos in vitro. This is a matter for the Oireachtas, or for the people, in the event that a Constitutional Amendment is put before them …

If the frozen embryos which are the subject matter of this case are not 'unborn' within the meaning of Article 40.3.3° of the Constitution and are not given protection by the Constitution they do not have 'personal rights' under the Constitution.

Since the three frozen embryos are not 'unborn' within the meaning of Article 40.3.3°, this raises the issue as to what protection (if any) is currently afforded these embryos. While there is considerable disagreement as to whether embryos, before implantation in the womb, constitute viable human life, there seems to be almost complete agreement on the fact that, because of their nature, embryos are deserving of respect. I have already referred to the ethical guidelines of the Medical Council. These ethical guidelines do not have the force of law and offer only such limited protection as derives from the fear on the part of a doctor that he might be found guilty of professional misconduct with all the professional consequences that might follow.

The fact that something is not prohibited by the law does not of itself mean that it is morally acceptable to carry out that act. There may be many people who, because of their moral or religious outlook regard the process of IVF as unacceptable even though it is permitted by the law. There are others who see this a great advance in medical science giving the opportunity to infertile couples to have children. In issues such as this there may well be a divide between Church and State, and between one religion and another. It is not for the Courts to weigh the views of one religion against another, or to choose between one moral view point and another. All are entitled to equal respect provided they are not subversive of the law, and provided there are no public policy reasons requiring the Courts to intervene. Moral responsibility exists even in the absence of law and arises out of the freedom of

> choice of the individual. People have many different ideas of morality. Society is made up of people of various religious traditions and none. If the law is to enforce morality then whose morality is it to enforce? The function of the Courts is to apply the law, which are the rules and regulations that govern society. Where these rules and regulations are to be found in Articles of the Constitution they are approved of by the people, and where they are to be found in legislation they are passed by the Houses of the Oireachtas. Laws should, and generally do, reflect society's values and will be influenced by them. But at the end of the day it is the duty of the Courts to implement and apply the law, not morality (2006: 18-23).

I mean no disrespect to McGovern J in observing that his analysis is strikingly unconvincing. The social, political and legal factors that led to the call for an amendment to the Constitution undoubtedly involved a concern that the legislative prohibition of abortion might not withstand a challenge under the Constitution in its original form; the purpose for seeking constitutional change was not simply to rule out abortion but to protect the lives of all human beings at all stages of their lives. That is plain from the extract from Hederman J's judgment which I have quoted. The amendment addresses philosophical and normative issues, not simply a specific issue of legal policy. The idea that the people who voted for the amendment were seeking to remove[11] all constitutional protection from human beings conceived outside the womb is, frankly and with respect, preposterous.

Concluding Observations

My analysis has sought to show that the Constitution, in its original formulation and in Article 40.3.3°, has had a consistent regard for a phi-

[11] It should be borne in mind that the purpose of the amendment was clarificatory rather than transformative. The premise on which both sides of the debate presented their arguments was that the Constitution, in its original formulation, protected unborn human life from destruction. McGovern J's failure to address this dimension is noteworthy as is his failure to clarify whether Article 40.3, in its original formulation, was unaffected or transformed by the Eighth Amendment so far as human beings conceived outside the womb are concerned.

losophy of the equality of value of every human being. The courts have not always understood this. Whatever one's own value preferences, it is possible to identify the values that underlie the constitutional provisions and assess the adequacy of the judicial consideration of them.

Bibliography

Barry, U. (1992) "Movement, Change and Reaction: The Struggle Over Reproductive Rights in Ireland" in Smyth, A. (ed.) *The Abortion Papers* Dublin: Attic Press.

Charleton, P. (1992) "Judicial Discretion in Abortion: The Irish Perspective" *International Journal of Law and the Family* 6: 349-362.

Chubb, B. (1991) *The Politics of the Irish Constitution* Dublin: Institute for Public Administration.

Dembour, M.-B. (2006) *Who Believes in Human Rights?* Cambridge University Press.

Doyle, O. (2006) *Constitutional Equality Law* Dublin, Thomson Round Hall.

Garvin, T. (1987) "The Politics of Denial and Cultural Defence: The Referenda of 1983 and 1986 in Context" *Irish Review* 3(5): 61-81.

Girvin, T. (1986) "Social Change and Moral Politics: The Irish Constitutional Referendum 1983" *Political Studies* 34: 61-81.

Hesketh, T. (1990) *The Second Partitioning of Ireland?* Dublin: Brandsma Books.

Hogan, G. (1988) "Law and Religion: Church-State Relations from Independence to the Present Day" *American Journal of Comparative Law* 25(1): 47-96.

Langlois, A. (2005) "The Narrative Metaphysics of Human Rights" *International Journal of Human Rights* 9(3): 369-387.

McCrudden (2008) "Human Rights and Judicial Interpretation of Human Rights" *European Journal of International Law*.

O'Carroll, J.P. (1991) "Bishops, Knights – and Pawns? Traditional Thought and the Irish Abortion Referendum Debate of 1983" *Irish Political Studies* 6: 53-71.

O'Dowd, T.J. (1995) "Dignity and personhood in Irish Constitutional Law" in Quinn, G., Ingram, A. and Livingtstone, S. (eds.) (1995) *Justice and Legal Theory in Ireland* Dublin: Oak Tree Press.

O'Leary, C. and Hesketh, T. (1988) "The Irish Abortion and Divorce Amendment Campaigns" *Irish Political Studies* 3: 43-62.

Parekh, S. (2007) "Resisting 'Dull and Torpid' Assent: Returning to the Debate Over the Foundations of Human Rights", *Human Rts Quarterly* 29(3): 754-778.

Penney, J. and Danay, D. (2006) "The Embarrasing Preamble? Understanding the 'Supremacy of God' and the *Charter*" *University of British Columbia Law Review* 39(2): 287.

Quinlan, J.A. (1984) "The Right to Life of the Unborn – An Assessment of the Eighth Amendment to the Irish Constitution" *Brigham Young University Law Review* 3: 371-401.

Randall, V. (1986) "The Politics of Abortion in Ireland" in Lovenduski, J. and Outshoorn, J. (eds.) (1986) *The New Politics of Abortion* London: Sage.

Speed, A. (1992) "The Struggle for Reproductive Rights: A Brief History in its Political Context" in Smyth, A. (ed.) (1992) *The Abortion Papers* Dublin: Attic Press.

Starck, C. (2002) "The Religious and Philosophical Background of Human Dignity and Its Place in Modern Constitutions", in Kretzmer, D. and Klein, E. (eds.) *The Concept of Dignity in Human Rights Discourse* London: Kluwer.

Cases

Attorney General v X [1992] 1 IR 1.

McGee v Attorney General [1974] IR 284.

MR v TR [2006] IEHC 359.

Queen on the Application of Smeaton v Secretary of State for Health [2002] 2 FLR 146.

Quinn's Supermarket v Attorney General [1972] IR 1.

Roe v Wade (1973) 410 US 113.

9

ABORTION LAW:

Rights Discourse, Dissent and Reproductive Autonomy*

Dr Siobhán Mullally

Introduction

Women's assertion of reproductive autonomy in Ireland has required the crossing of many borders, both the territorial borders of the State and the jurisdictional borders between international and domestic law. In May 1971, almost 100 women boarded a train in Dublin. They travelled to Belfast, where they purchased large quantities of contraceptives. They returned to Dublin by train, marching illegally through the customs barriers at Connolly Station, waving banners, posters and condom balloons. The "condom train", as it subsequently became known, transgressed many boundaries. In crossing Ireland's disputed border with Northern Ireland and openly flouting the ban on importing contraceptives, the women's movement challenged the borders set by the conservative Catholic consensus in the Republic. They exposed the inequalities between women, North and South, and the closure of Irish society to difference in matters of sexual and reproductive health

---

* Co-Director Centre for Criminal Justice and Human Rights, Senior Lecturer, Faculty of Law, University College Cork. This research forms part of an IRCHSS thematic project on *Gender Equality, Religious Diversity and Multiculturalism in Contemporary Ireland.* An earlier draft of this paper was published as: "Gendered Citizenship and Reproductive Autonomy in Ireland" (2005) 27(1) *Human Rights Quarterly* pp. 78-104.

(Jackson, 1993; Connolly, 2002). This hypocrisy has continued in the abortion debates that have spanned over two decades of legal reform.

Women seeking to terminate their pregnancies have been forced to leave the State and have travelled, usually to the UK, to access safe abortion services. Women have also sought to transgress the borders of domestic law, appealing to international and European human rights standards, pointing to the gender-differentiated nature of Irish citizenship and seeking support for their claim to reproductive autonomy in treaties such as the 1979 UN Convention on the Elimination of All Forms of Discrimination Against Women (the Women's Convention), the 1966 International Covenant on Civil and Political Rights (ICCPR) and the European Convention on Human Rights (ECHR). In the past, women have left the State to access contraceptives. Today, more than 5,000 women travel to the UK, the Netherlands and elsewhere each year, to access safe abortion services.

The *Programme of Action*, adopted at the 1994 Cairo Conference on Population and Development, defined reproductive health as a state of complete physical, mental, and social well-being in all matters relating to the reproductive system, its functions and processes (1994: Ch VII para. 7.2). The 1995 *Beijing Declaration and Platform for Action* reiterates this definition, listing control over sexuality and reproduction amongst women's human rights (1995: paras 94-96).[1] This limited recognition of women's reproductive rights has been hard won and is the subject of ongoing struggle, both at national and international levels (Cook and Fathalla, 1996; Eriksson, 1996; Fleishman, 2000; Glendon, 1987; Cornell, 1995). This article examines the struggle over women's reproductive rights within the context of the abortion debate in Ireland.

Women's reproductive rights in Ireland have long been a contested terrain. As in many post-colonial states, the demarcation of gender roles in Ireland has always been intertwined with debates on national identity (Scannall, 1988; Bradley and Valiulis, 1997; Smyth, 1993; Sheehy-Skeffingtom, 1995; Coulter, 1993). In a struggling nation state, scarred by the trauma of partition and civil war, gender trouble could not be

---

[1] See also CEDAW, General Recommendation 24. Women and Health (Article 12) GAOR Fifty-fourth session, UN Doc.A/54/38/Rev.1, chapter I (1999), para. 23.

countenanced. The overwhelming concern to define Ireland as "not England" led to a search for distinguishing marks of identity, among these, the Roman Catholic religion adhered to by the majority of Irish people (Kiberd, 1996). Nationalist ideologies have always tended to define their groups in either/or terms (Young, 2000: 252). In Ireland, the search for homogeneity and national unity transformed Irish republicanism into a "conservative [...] Catholic nationalist movement" (Browne, 1998: 41-50). This transformation was to have a significant impact on women's citizenship. Defining Ireland in exclusively "pro-life" terms served as a distinguishing mark of Irish identity. Women's reproductive autonomy was sacrificed to the greater good of a post-colonial political project, and women were defined, not by their equal capacity for moral agency, but by their reproductive and sexual functions. When abortion came to the fore as a political issue in the early 1980s, it was debated less on its own terms and more in terms of the consequences it would have for Ireland's inherited religious-cultural traditions (Fletcher, 2001: 574). The Catholic right in Ireland, concerned to preserve the conservative ethos that permeates the Irish Constitution, have portrayed feminism and human rights discourse as a threat to Ireland's sovereignty, and a threat, in particular, to Ireland's "pro-life" and "pro-family" traditions. Debates concerning the family and reproductive rights form the bedrock of the Catholic right's backlash (National Union of Mothers of Ireland, 2001; Neart, 2000, 2001; Smyth, 1993; Smyth, 1990).

To date, there have been five constitutional referenda on the subject of abortion in Ireland – the most recent on 6 March 2002. Despite these repeated referenda and ongoing debate at national level, Ireland's abortion laws continue to be amongst the most restrictive in the world.[2] In recent years, these restrictions have attracted criticism from UN human rights treaty bodies. The Committee on the Elimination of Discrimination Against Women (CEDAW) has called for the full implementation of women's right to reproductive health in Ireland and has expressed concern that women's human rights are being

---

2 For a comprehensive discussion of Ireland's abortion laws, see Kingston, Whelan, and Bacik (1997) and Jackson (1993: 109-129); see also generally Irish Council for Civil Liberties (Women's Committee) (1999).

compromised by the continuing influence of the Catholic Church in official State policy (1999: para. 180).[3] The Human Rights Committee has pointed out that compelling a woman to continue with a pregnancy, particularly where that pregnancy is a result of rape, may violate the prohibition of torture, cruel, inhuman or degrading treatment in the ICCPR (2000: para. 18).[4] The Committee has again recently criticised Ireland's restrictive abortion laws and, citing women's right to access a safe and legal abortion, has called on the State to bring its laws into compliance with the Covenant (2008: para. 13).

The scrutiny of Ireland's abortion laws by UN human rights treaty bodies has led Catholic right groups to mobilise in opposition to the UN human rights agenda. Drawing on the critiques put forward by the Holy See, they have rejected human rights discourse as impoverished, libertarian and peculiarly western.[5] In doing so, they have exposed the dangers to feminism of yielding to cultural claims. In the context of the abortion debate, such claims have meant that where a woman lives determines whether her experience of abortion is that of "a safe, legal method for terminating an unwanted pregnancy or a dangerous, painful and criminal act" (Sundstrom, 1993).

This response from the Catholic right is not unique to Ireland. The Holy See's opposition to an expanding human rights agenda within the UN is well-documented (Centre for Reproductive Law and Policy, 2000; Buss, 2000; Paul, 2000). At the 1995 Beijing conference, the progression of women's rights, particularly in areas relating to reproductive and sexual health, was opposed by an emerging alliance between the Holy

---

[3] The Committee has also expressed concern at the particular hardships experienced by vulnerable groups of women in Ireland. For an asylum-seeking woman, for example, an attempt to leave the State may lead to criminal prosecution (1999: para. 185).

[4] See also *CCPR/C/21/Rev.1/Add.10, CCPR General comment 28. 29/03/2000*, para. 11). The Human Rights Committee has expressed similar concerns in relation to the restrictive abortion laws in Poland. See: Concluding Observations of the Human Rights Committee: Poland, 29/07/99, CCPR/C/79/Add.110. In particular, it has noted "with concern" the strict laws on abortion which lead to high numbers of clandestine abortions with attendant risks to life and health of women (para. 11).

[5] Much of the Catholic right discourse in Ireland draws on the work of US lawyer Mary Ann Glendon. See generally Glendon (1991).

See and conservative Catholic and Muslim states.[6] The Holy See criticised the Declaration and Platform's "exaggerated individualism", the "disproportionate attention" given to sexual and reproductive health and the neglect of the family as a "fundamental societal unit".[7] In its view, this neglect was further evidence that the rich discourse of universal rights was being colonised by an "impoverished, libertarian rights dialect". Similar sentiments have been expressed in the US, where a range of Christian right groups have opposed the application of international human rights law to the family, reproductive health and sexuality. Paul (2000) has described this opposition as a displaced response to the anxiety produced by globalisation. Globalisation has brought with it a sense of economic displacement and loss of control over the nation-state's destiny (Paul, 2000: 7-8). In attempting to regain that control, the Christian right have sought protection for the nation-state's claim to a distinct cultural identity. In Ireland, this claim has clashed in recent years with the economic agenda of a centre-right Government and an expanding economy. The demands of globalisation and participation in the market economy of the European Union, have challenged traditional gendered divisions of labour.[8] Religious-cultural

---

[6]After the draft resolution was adopted, representatives of the following States made general and interpretative statements or expressed reservations: Peru, Kuwait, Egypt, Philippines, Holy See, Malaysia, Iran (Islamic Republic of), Libyan Arab Jamahiriya, Ecuador, Indonesia, Mauritania, Oman, Malta, Argentina, Brunei, Darussalam, France, Yemen, Sudan, Dominican Republic, Costa Rica, United Arab Emirates, Venezuela, Bahrain, Lebanon, Tunisia, Mali, Benin, Guatemala, India, Algeria, Iraq, Vanuatu, Ethiopia, Morocco, Djibouti, Qatar, Nicaragua, Togo, Liberia, Syrian Arab Republic, Pakistan, Nigeria, Comoros, Bolivia, Colombia, Bangladesh, Honduras, Jordan, Ghana, Central African Republic, Cambodia, Maldives, South Africa, United Republic of Tanzania, Brazil, Panama, El Salvador, Madagascar, Chad, Cameroon, Niger, Gabon, United States of America and Canada. The observer for Palestine also made a statement. See: U.N. Doc. A/CONF. 177/20/Add. 1 (1995), p. 157, "Reservations and statements of interpretation".

[7] *Beijing Declaration and Platform for Action*, "Reservations and Interpretive Statements" para. 11. In a statement that reveals a broader agenda, the Holy See criticised the "ambiguous language" of the Declaration and Platform concerning unqualified control over sexuality and fertility, which in its view, could be interpreted as including "societal endorsement of abortion and homosexuality".

[8] In 1971, 60 per cent of women aged fifteen years and over were engaged full-time in "home duties". In 1991, this had fallen to just under 50 per cent. In 1970, women accounted for 28 per cent of the labour force. In 1991, this had risen to just 32.9 per cent.

arguments invoking family values and a "cult of domesticity" have threatened to undermine Ireland's economic expansion and the "Celtic Tiger" project.[9] As a result, such arguments have been increasingly marginalised within political debate. Cultural claims, seeking to protect a distinct religious identity, have instead been channelled into debates on women's reproductive health.

The 1937 Constitution: A Gender-differentiated Citizenship?

Adhering to Roman Catholic teaching on issues relating to the family, sexuality and reproductive health, served to distinguish "Irish laws and

---

Following the rapid expansion of the Irish economy in the 1990s, this figure has now risen to approx. 46 per cent. See generally: First Commission on the Status of Women. Report to Government. Dublin: Government Stationery Office, 1972; Second Commission on the Status of Women. Report to Government. Dublin: Government Stationery Office, 1993; Crowley (1997, pp. 81-96).

[9] The Report of the Second Commission on the Status of Women, published in 1993, called for tax individualisation to eliminate disincentives for married women seeking to enter into employment (1993: 76). Finally, in 1999, in response to increasing labour shortages, the Government finally decided to act, introducing a series of measures including individualisation of the income tax system and tax incentives to encourage women to return to paid employment. This challenge to the traditional gendered division of labour met with opposition. As one commentator noted, "old allies re-emerge[d] to criticise working women" (Holland, M. *Irish Times,* 9 December 1999. See also: *Dáil Debates* Dec. 15th, 1999 *per* Mr John Bruton TD available at: http://www.gov.ie/debates-99/15dec99/sect9.htm) Catholic right groups pointed to the constitutional commitment to recognising and protecting women's lives within the home. Citing article 41.2 of the Constitution, they argued that if women should not be "forced by economic necessity to neglect their duties within the home", economic incentives should not be offered by Government to encourage such neglect. Portrayed as an attack on the family, a devaluation of women's work within the home and possibly unconstitutional, the tax individualisation plan was withdrawn, to be resubmitted a year later modified to take account of the criticisms levied against it. The debate has not ended, however. Incentives to encourage greater female participation in the labour force have been given added momentum by European Union membership and Community strategies to promote gender equality. The European Community framework strategy on gender equality (2001-2005) seeks to promote gender equality in economic life and a change in gender roles and stereotypes (COM, 2000: 335). As a strategy, it conflicts directly with the Christian right's concern to protect women's roles within the home and Ireland's inherited tradition of gender-differentiated citizenship. These concerns have voiced themselves most recently in opposition to the Nice Treaty (Neart, Submission to the National Forum on Europe, 1 Dec 2001). See generally Mullally (2002).

Irish ways" from the "polluting" forces of English law.[10] Article 41.2.2° leaves little room for debate as to the nature of women's citizenship under the Irish Constitution:

> ...the State shall endeavour to ensure, that mothers shall not be obliged by economic necessity to engage in labour to the neglect of their duties in the home.

A commitment to the ideal of "separate spheres", premised on the complementarity of gender roles and a presumption of natural sex differences between women and men, is central to much Roman Catholic teaching (Mullally, 1998, 2006; Dooley, 1998). In his *Letter to Women,* issued prior to the Fourth World Conference on Women at Beijing, Pope John Paul II reiterates the Vatican's commitment to this teaching.[11] In its *Concluding Observations* on Ireland's Combined Second and Third Reports, CEDAW expressed particular concern at the constitutional emphasis on the role of women as mothers and caregivers (1999: paras. 161-201). The UN Human Rights Committee has also expressed concern at the "traditional attitudes" toward the role of women, evident in Ireland's constitutional text (2000, 2008). As a result of these comments, opposition to the liberalising agenda of international human rights law has gathered momentum. In the preparations for the Beijing + 5 review process, a new umbrella body, Neart (meaning strength) was formed, with the stated objective of defending the constitutional recognition of women's roles within the home.[12] Neart prepared an alternative report for the Beijing + 5 meeting, highlighting Ireland's cultural and religious specificity. (Neart, 2000)[13] Neart also distanced itself from Ireland's

---

[10] In the case of *Re Howley* (1940), Gavin Duffy J referred to the Reformation and subsequent common law jurisprudence as "temporary pollutions" that interrupted and distorted the normal flow of "a Catholic common law".

[11] See Pope John Paul's "Letter to Women", 6.

[12] See "New Coalition to Challenge National Women's Council" *Irish Times,* 11 May 2000. Neart comprised over 20 affiliate groups, including Human Life International and National Union of Mothers Working at Home.

[13] See Report on Proceedings, United Nations General Assembly Special Session "Women 2000: Gender Equality Development and Peace". National Forum for Non-Governmental Organisations, Dublin Castle, 10 May 2000 available at http://www.justice.ie.

official report[14] to the meeting and from the submission by the National Women's Council of Ireland (NWCI),[15] which it portrayed as "anti-family" and a threat to Ireland's inherited traditions. Much of Neart's opposition has centred on the abortion debate.

The Abortion Debate: Re-partitioning the State

In 1983, the Eighth Amendment was added to the Constitution, recognising the "right to life of the unborn".[16] The move to introduce a constitutional amendment prohibiting abortion followed the Supreme Court's recognition of a right to marital privacy in *McGee v Attorney General* (1974). There, the Supreme Court concluded that the right to have access to contraceptives was protected as part of the personal right to marital privacy. Anti-abortion activists feared that a right to privacy, broadly interpreted, might be invoked by Irish courts to strike down legislation criminalising abortion. The *Roe v Wade* (1973) decision in the US was preceded by a similar decision of the US Supreme Court.[17] To guard against a similar development in Ireland, the Pro-life amendment campaign (PLAC) was launched in 1981.

PLAC was primarily composed of groups drawn from the Catholic right. The amendment campaign and the bitter debates that ensued have been described as a "second partitioning" of the State (Hesketh, 1990). Although PLAC was careful to employ secular language in its campaign, it clearly drew on a conservative Catholic ethos to support its claim to the absolute inviolability of foetal life (Kingston, Whelan and Bacik, 1997: 4-6). Recognising this, each of the Protestant Churches in Ireland issued statements opposing the proposal for a "pro-life" amendment

[14] Department of Justice, Equality and Law Reform, UN General Assembly Special Session: "Women 2000, Gender Equality Development and Peace", National Report for Ireland, 2000.

[15] The Council is a non-governmental organisation representing over 300 women's groups in Ireland.

[16] Article 40.3.3°, inserted following the enactment of the Eighth Amendment to the Constitution Act, 1983, reads: "The State acknowledges the right to life of the unborn and, with due regard to the equal right to life of the mother, guarantees in its laws to respect, and, as far as practicable, by its laws to defend and vindicate that right."

[17] *Griswold v Conneticut* 381 U.S. 479 (1965).

(Fletcher, 2001: 576). The anti-amendment campaign argued that an absolute constitutional prohibition on abortion would deny non-Catholics equal rights to citizenship in Ireland and would perpetuate a politics of exclusion. PLAC, however, continued to represent abortion as a violent colonial tool threatening the integrity of the Irish nation.[18] Ultimately, the anti-abortion campaign won the day. Significantly, however, the Eighth Amendment also recognised the need for "due regard to the equal right to life of the mother". Almost a decade later, the requirement of "due regard" was to give rise to one of Ireland's most controversial constitutional debates in the case of *Attorney General v X* (1992). Before this was to happen, however, further attempts were made to limit the scope of women's reproductive autonomy. Access to information and women's right to travel came under threat as anti-abortion campaigners sought to entrench an increasingly conservative Catholic ethos in Irish law.

In *SPUC v Grogan and others* (1989) the Society for the Protection of the Unborn Child (SPUC) applied to the High Court for an injunction to prevent student groups distributing information on abortion services available in the UK. The High Court requested a ruling from the European Court of Justice (ECJ) as to: (a) whether abortion was a "service" within the meaning of the Treaty of Rome, and (b) whether student groups had a right under Community law to distribute information concerning abortion services available in other Member States. Departing from the opinion of the Advocate General (1991: paras. 30-38), the ECJ defined abortion "solely in terms of the possible commerce and profit resulting from it" (*SPUC v Grogan*, 1991).[19] Questions relating to fundamental rights were dismissed as raising non-justiciable moral, rather than legal, arguments (1991: paras. 20-21). The Court concluded that the termination of a pregnancy, in accordance with the law of the State in which it was carried out, constituted a service within the meaning of the Treaty of Rome (1991: paras. 20-21).

---

[18] One anti-abortion slogan read: "The Abortion Mills of England Grind Irish Babies into Blood that Cries out to Heaven for Vengeance" (Fletcher, 2001: 577). See also O'Reilly (1992).

[19] For a discussion of the case, see Coppell and O'Neill (1992: 687) and Phelan (1992).

However, the victory was a partial one only. Although the Court was willing to address concerns relating to trade in services, it refused to address reproductive health as a question of human rights. As the student groups had no direct links with the provision of abortion services in the UK or elsewhere, they could not claim the protection of Community law (1991: paras. 25-27).

Although the ECJ's ruling in the *Grogan* case was limited in scope, its potentially liberalising impact on abortion law in Ireland complicated national debates on European integration. As a constitutional referendum on the Treaty of the European Union (the Maastricht Treaty) loomed, the abortion debate became further entwined with debates on national sovereignty. The ECJ's ruling in the *Grogan* case coincided with ongoing negotiations on the Maastricht treaty. Concerned at the possibility of a backlash from anti-abortion groups, the Irish Government added Protocol No 17 to the Treaty, without consulting Parliament. The Protocol sought to protect Ireland's constitutional prohibition on abortion from any change that might be required as a result of EU membership. Before the constitutional referendum on the Maastricht Treaty was to take place, however, a young woman's body became the subject of further contestation between pro-choice and anti-abortion groups.

The *X* case was one of the most controversial cases yet to come before the Supreme Court. International media reported Ireland to be "backward", "barbarous", punitive", "priest-ridden" – a portrayal that did not sit well with the modernising image of an emerging Celtic Tiger economy (Fletcher, 2001). Embarrassed by this potentially damaging attention, the Government undertook to pay all legal expenses arising from X's appeal to the Supreme Court. The Supreme Court lifted the injunction, reversing the High Court's ruling on the substantive question of abortion. Pointing out the State's duty to have "due regard" to the life of the mother, they concluded that abortion was lawful in Ireland where there was a "real and substantial risk" to the life, as distinct from the health, of the mother. The risk to life could include a threatened suicide (1992: 57-58).

The Supreme Court's judgment on the substantive issue of abortion was welcomed by the women's movement. However, its ruling on the right to travel raised widespread concern. The High Court had ruled that the State's duty to protect the life of the unborn amounted to a public policy derogation from the freedom of movement guaranteed under European Community law. The Supreme Court agreed. In its view, the right to travel to terminate a pregnancy was protected only if the mother's right to life was in danger. In the balancing of rights, a woman's right to travel could not, *per se,* take priority over the right to life of the unborn.[20] In the Supreme Court's ruling, we see the limits of the European integration project (Phelan, 1992). Yet again, a woman's body becomes a contested site in the concern to assert an ethno-cultural national identity. The potential restriction on a woman's freedom of movement, and with it the spectre of anti-abortion groups seeking injunctions to restrain pregnant women from travelling abroad, provoked widespread protests.

The protests were particularly worrying for the Irish Government, given the pending constitutional referendum on the Maastricht treaty. Now, it seemed that the addition of Protocol No. 17 to the Treaty may have been misguided. Debate ensued as to whether the Protocol would prevent a reversal of the Irish courts' rulings on rights to travel and to information. Ratification of the Maastricht Treaty was threatened as women's groups mobilised in opposition to the Protocol. In a last ditch attempt to save the ratification process, the Government sought to amend the Protocol so as to exclude any effect that it might have on issues relating to travel or the provision of information. A "Solemn Declaration" was adopted, stating that Protocol No.17 would not have any impact on the rights to travel or information. Prior to the referendum on the Maastricht Treaty, each of the main political parties gave assurances that a further constitutional referendum would be held to resolve the questions raised by the *X* and *Grogan* cases. The assurances succeeded in allaying public fears and the referendum allowing for

---

[20] O'Flaherty J, dissenting on this point, held that restricting a woman's right to travel would interfere to an unwarranted degree with the individual's freedom of movement, the authority of the family and the protection of the dignity and freedom of the individual (1992: 88).

ratification of the Maastricht Treaty was approved by the Irish people in June 1992.[21]

Before a further referendum on abortion could take place, European human rights law was to add its voice to the national debate. On 29 October 1992, the European Court of Human Rights ruled on the challenge brought against Ireland by the Open Door Counselling and Dublin Well Woman centres (*Open Door Counselling v Ireland*, 1993). The absolute nature of the prohibition on abortion information proved fatal and the Court ruled that Ireland had violated Article 10 of the Convention, which protects the right to freedom of expression. Having found a violation of Article 10, the Court held that it was unnecessary to consider the scope of the right to privacy. They also declined to consider arguments concerning the right to life, noting that the applicants had not complained of the substantive prohibition on abortion *per se.*[22] However, in a tentative step towards recognising women's right to reproductive health, the Court did point out that the applicants were providing information on services lawfully available in other States and that those services could be crucial to a woman's health and well-being (1993: para. 76).

---

[21] The Eleventh Amendment to the Constitution Act was enacted, amending Article 29 of the Constitution and thereby permitting Ireland's ratification of the Treaty.

[22] The European Court of Human Rights has not ruled on whether the Convention requires Contracting States to permit a woman to terminate a pregnancy. From the Court's jurisprudence to date, it would seem that Contracting States enjoy a very wide margin of appreciation in regulating abortion. However, the former European Commission on Human Rights has stated that placing a higher value on the "unborn life of the fetus" than on the life of a pregnant women would be contrary to the object and purpose of the Convention. Application No.8416/79, *X v United Kingdom*, admissibility decision of 13 May 1980, 19 D&R 244, 3 EHRR 408 (1980). The Commission supported this interpretation of the right to life, as protected under Article 2 of the Convention, by pointing out that most of the Contracting States allowed abortions when necessary to save the mother's life. In *H v Norway, Application No. 17004/90,* the applicant argued that the Convention must grant the father of a 14-week-old foetus a minimum of rights regarding his unborn child, where the health of the mother is not endangered. The Commission found his application to be inadmissible (19/05/1992). It concluded that any interpretation of the potential father's right under the Convention, in connection with an abortion which the mother intends to have performed on her, must first of all take into account her rights, she being the person primarily concerned by the pregnancy and its continuation or termination. Any possible interference with the applicant's rights under the Convention was justified as being necessary for the protection of the rights of another person.

Less than one month after the ruling of the European Court of Human Rights, a further constitutional referendum on abortion was held. On 25 November 1992, the Irish people were asked to vote on three possible constitutional amendments. The first amendment was defeated. The second and third amendments were both passed, thereby providing constitutional protection for the right to travel and to information. Despite this vote, however, the Government was slow to act. Having secured the ratification of the Maastricht Treaty and fulfilled its promise of a referendum on the *X* case, the Government now failed to introduce legislation clarifying the conditions under which a woman could lawfully terminate a pregnancy in Ireland. In the *X* case, the Supreme Court had condemned as "inexcusable" the Government's failure to enact legislation giving effect to the Eighth Amendment. The Amendment, "born of public disquiet, historically divisive of our people", was, the Court said, "bare of legislative direction" (1992: 92). It was to remain without direction for some time to come.

In 1995, the Government finally introduced legislation allowing for the provision of abortion information.[23] Before it was finally signed into law, however, the 1995 Abortion Information Bill was the subject of a Supreme Court referral (*Re Article 26 and the Regulation of Information (Services Outside the State for the Termination of Pregnancies) Bill, 1995*, 1995). The "Abortion Information" Bill was found to be compatible with the Constitution and was thereby rendered immune from any further challenge. The Supreme Court's concern to recognise the pluralist nature of Irish society was echoed by the Constitution Review Group, reporting one year later. In the 1995 case, invoking the pluralist nature of Irish society, Chief Justice Hamilton concluded that the religious doctrines of one particular faith tradition could not be relied on to determine the limits and scope of fundamental rights. The constitutional text, he said, must be interpreted in the light of prevailing ideas of prudence, justice and charity (1995: 43). The Group concluded that the religious references in the constitutional text no longer reflected a shared sense of national identity (Constitution Review Group: 257-

[23] This was done through the Regulation of Information (Services Outside the State for the Termination of Pregnancies) Act 1995.

259). On the subject of abortion, the Group recommended the introduction of legislation to give effect to the *X* case judgment, concluding that this was the only practical possibility available at that time. Despite the Group's recommendation, however, the Government again failed to act. In the absence of a clear legislative framework, the Irish Medical Council Guidelines continued to exclude a threat of suicide as a ground for terminating a pregnancy (Irish Medical Council, 1998).[24]

The uncertain implications of the *X* case were again brought into focus in November 1997, in the *C* case (*A and B v Eastern Health Board and C*, 1998). The High Court accepted the psychiatric evidence submitted that a real and substantial risk to *C's* life existed, arising from the threat of suicide. The Court concluded, therefore, that a direction authorising travel for the purposes of terminating the pregnancy was lawful. However, in a statement that was to give rise to much controversy, the Court concluded that the constitutional amendment protecting the right to travel prevented injunctions being issued against a woman travelling abroad but did not introduce a new substantive right, as such. On this reading, a court could only authorise travel for the purposes of terminating a pregnancy, if the requirements set out in the *X* case were satisfied, namely that a real and substantial risk to a woman's life existed (1998: 482). The implications of the Court's ruling for children in care were potentially very far-reaching indeed and were certainly not envisaged during the 1992 debates on the right to travel. The High Court was clearly reluctant to recognise C's reproductive rights. A welfarist approach underpins the Court's ruling. In deciding whether the proposed abortion would be lawful, the Court's primary concern was "the welfare of an Irish child in Ireland". The child, C, was firmly situated within the Irish legal system. The constraints that came with Ireland's inherited traditions were to determine the limits of her reproductive rights.

One Step Forward, Two Steps Back: Abortion Reform in Ireland

In 1997, the centre-right Fianna Fáil/Progressive Democrats coalition Government was formed. A minority Government, they were dependent

---

[24] The Medical Council is a regulatory body established by the Medical Practitioners Act 1978.

for support on the votes of four independent TDs. Their support was secured by the promise of yet another abortion referendum. Before any such referendum, a gradual process of consensus-building was to take place. This process began with the establishment of an Inter-departmental Working Group on abortion and the publication of a parliamentary Green Paper setting out a range of legislative and constitutional options available to Government (1999).[25] In an unprecedented response to this process, the Inter-departmental Working Group received 10,000 written submissions from individuals and groups concerned with abortion reform.

The Green Paper was referred to the All-Party Oireachtas Committee on the Constitution. The Committee continued to receive submissions, both oral and written, on the options set out in the Green Paper. The US-based organisation Catholics for a Free Choice argued from a pro-choice Catholic perspective in favour of "Option 7" – permitting abortion on grounds beyond those specified in the *X* case. In its view, published in the *Fifth Progress Report: Abortion* (2000) the other options detailed in the Green Paper represented a narrow continuum of extremely restrictive policy options – from explicit or *de facto* bans on abortion to very limited availability on a case-by-case basis.[26] Ultimately, the Oireachtas Committee was unable to achieve majority support for any one of the options set out in the Green Paper.[27] Despite the absence of consensus,

---

[25] The Green Paper was prepared by an inter-departmental Working Group, charged with considering the constitutional, legal, medical, moral, social and ethical issues surrounding the question of abortion. A Cabinet committee, composed of four men and two women, oversaw the Group's work. Submissions were invited from interested members of the public.

[26] See Catholics for a Free Choice, Submission to the Inter-Departmental Working Group on Abortion, Catholic Options in the Abortion Debate: Reforming Irish Law. March, 1998; *Ibid.* Opening Remarks by Catholics for a Free Choice to the All-Party Oireachtas Committee on the Constitution 12 July 2000, available at: http://www.cath4choice.org/new/pressrelease/071200DublinAbortionReform.htm.

[27] Three options commanded support within the Committee, though not majority support. The first was to leave the legal position unchanged and to focus instead on measures to reduce crisis pregnancies. The second was to introduce legislation to give effect to the Supreme Court judgment in the *X* case. The third was to amend the Constitution so as to protect existing medical practice while at the same time maintaining a prohibition on abortion – in effect rolling back the options opened by the Supreme Court judgment in the *X* case.

however, the Government decided to hold yet another referendum. This time, the Irish people were to be asked to vote on the Twenty-Fifth Amendment to the Constitution, (Protection of Human Life in Pregnancy Bill) 2001.[28] The Bill proposed a prohibition on abortion except in circumstances where there was a risk to the life of the mother. In an attempt to roll back the *X* case judgment, a risk arising from a threatened suicide was excluded as a ground for permitting abortion. A similar proposal had been placed before the people in the constitutional referenda of 1992. This time, however, the foetus's right to life was protected only following implantation in the womb, thereby allowing for the use of contraceptives such as the morning-after pill. A twelve-year prison sentence was proposed for any woman who performed an abortion on herself or for any person aiding and abetting a woman in performing an abortion. In addition, where life-saving abortions were permitted, they would only be carried out in "approved places".

The referendum on the Protection of Human Life in Pregnancy Bill was held on 6 March 2002. It was defeated by the narrowest of margins: 49.58 per cent voting Yes to 50.42 per cent voting No. Only 39 per cent of the electorate voted in the referendum and the results displayed a strong urban rural/divide, with most rural constituencies voting Yes. In an ironic twist of fate, the man convicted of raping the young woman at the centre of the *X* case was again the subject of criminal proceedings. On the day preceding the referendum, he was convicted and sentenced for the sexual assault of a 19-year-old woman.[29] This grim reminder of the trauma that had led to the *X* case litigation may have influenced the electorate. Possibly the decisive factor in the No vote, however, was the split in the anti-abortion movement. Although the Catholic Church mobilised behind the Government's referendum proposal, some members of the anti-abortion movement called for a No vote, because of the Bill's failure to protect human life prior to implantation in the womb.

---

[28] The Bill draws on similar legislation introduced in Poland in 1993, the Family Planning, Protection of the Human Foetus, and Conditions Permitting Pregnancy Termination Act. Prior to 1993, abortion on social grounds was permitted in Poland.

[29] See *The Irish Times*, 5 March 2002.

Despite the defeat of the referendum, however, the prospects of a legislative framework allowing for a limited right to abortion remain remote. The willingness of Government to ignore the rights questions at the heart of these debates was evident in the Taoiseach's comments following the defeat of the referendum on 6 March 2002. He would not, he said, be "in any hurry" to legislate and give effect to the people's decision.[30]

Crossing Borders: International Human Rights Law

Ireland's restrictive abortion laws have been the subject of repeated criticism from UN human rights treaty bodies. The Women's Convention does not mention a right to reproductive health, as such. However, in its General Recommendation on Article 12, concerning women and health, the CEDAW Committee includes reproductive and sexual health within the general protection of women's right to health. Ireland has not entered a reservation to Article 12 of the Women's Convention. Neither has it made any interpretive declarations or reservations to the Cairo Programme of Action or the Beijing Declaration and Platform for Action. And, unlike other State parties to the Convention on the Rights of the Child (CRC), Ireland has not accompanied its ratification of the CRC with an interpretive declaration or reservation concerning the protection of the child before birth. CEDAW has called for full implementation of women's right to health, including reproductive health and has expressed concern that women's right to health, including reproductive health, was being compromised by the continuing influence of the Roman Catholic Church in official State policy (CEDAW, 1999). CEDAW also pointed to the particular hardships experienced by vulnerable groups of women, such as female asylum-seekers, for whom an attempt to leave the territory of the State could lead to criminal prosecution (CEDAW, 1999: para. 185). The UN Human Rights Committee has added its voice to these criticisms and has highlighted Ireland's obligations under Article 7 of the International Covenant on Civil and Political Rights, pointing out that compelling a woman to continue with a pregnancy, particularly where that pregnancy

---

[30] See *The Irish Times*, 15 March 2002 and 26 March 2002.

is a result of rape, may be in violation of the prohibition on torture, cruel, inhuman and degrading treatment.[31] In its Concluding Observations on Ireland's Third Periodic Report under the ICCPR, the UN Human Rights Committee (2008) has recently reiterated its concern regarding the highly restrictive circumstances under which women can lawfully have an abortion in the State. While noting the establishment of the Crisis Pregnancy Agency, the Committee expressed regret that the progress in this regard is slow. Citing Articles 6 (right to life) and 26 (equal protection of the law) of the ICCPR, the Committee concluded that the State should bring its abortion laws into line with the Covenant and should take measures to help women avoid unwanted pregnancies so that they do not have to resort to illegal or unsafe abortions that could put their lives at risk.

In its submission to the Human Rights Committee on Ireland's Third Report, the Irish Family Planning Association pointed to the recent jurisprudence of the Committee, particularly on access to therapeutic abortions (IFPA, 2008). The case of *KL v Peru* (2005) concerned a young Peruvian minor who was denied a termination having discovered that the foetus she was carrying was anencephalic. It was argued that "the refusal to provide a legal abortion service left her with two options which posed an equal risk to her health and safety: to seek clandestine (and hence highly risky) abortion services, or to continue a dangerous and traumatic pregnancy which put her life at risk". The Committee found a breach of Article 7 of the ICCPR, noting that the effects of the denial of a therapeutic abortion on the author of the complaint "could have been forseen". The omission on the part of the State in not enabling the author to benefit from a therapeutic abortion was, in the Committee's view, the cause of the suffering experienced by the young woman. The

---

[31] See also General Comment No. 28, Equality of Rights between Men and Women, adopted 29 Mar. 2000, U.N. GAOR, Hum. Rts. Comm., 68th Sess., 1834th mtg., para. 11, U.N. Doc. CCPR/C/21/Rev.1/Add.10 (2000). The Human Rights Committee has expressed similar concerns in relation to the restrictive abortion laws in Poland. See Concluding Observations of the Human Rights Committee: Poland, adopted 28 July 1999, U.N. GAOR, Hum. Rts. Comm., 66th Sess., 1779th mtg., U.N. Doc. CCPR/C/79/Add.110 (1999). In particular, the Committee has noted "with concern" the strict laws on abortion "which lead to high numbers of clandestine abortions with attendant risks to life and health of women" (1999: para. 11).

Committee referred to its General Comment No. 20, where it noted that the right set out in Article 7 of the Covenant relates not only to physical pain but also to mental suffering, and that the protection is particularly important in the case of minors.[32] Finding a violation of a series of KL's rights (including Article 7, prohibition of torture, cruel, inhuman and degrading treatment; Article 2, failure to provide an effective remedy; Article 17, the right to privacy; and Article 24, the right to protection as a minor girl), the Committee concluded that the State has an obligation to take steps to ensure that similar violations do not occur in the future.

This scrutiny of Ireland's abortion laws has led Christian right groups to mobilise in opposition to the UN human rights agenda. This opposition can be seen in Neart's alternative report to the Beijing + 5 meeting and more recently in its submissions on the Beijing + 10 review process. It can also be seen in the opposition raised by Christian right movements to the Rome Statute for an International Criminal Court, ratified by Ireland on 14 April, 2002, following a referendum and constitutional amendment. Ireland's ratification of the Rome Statute was not accompanied by any reservation or declaration concerning the import of including "forced pregnancy" within the definition of a crime against humanity.

Speaking at the Cairo + 5 review meeting, the then Minister for Health, Mr Brian Cowen, emphasised the importance of recognising that abortion policy and legislation were "a matter for each country to determine for itself".[33] No such defences were raised at the Beijing + 5 review meeting, held just one year later. Addressing the Special Session of the General Assembly, the Minister for Justice, Equality and Law Reform emphasised Ireland's "full endorsement" of the Beijing Declaration and Platform for Action and agreed that there should be no

---

32 General Comment No. 20: Replaces general comment 7concerning prohibition of torture and cruel treatment or punishment (Art. 7), 10/03/92, CCPR General Comment No. 20 (General Comments), para. 5.

33 Brian Cowen, Address at the United Nations Special Session of the General Assembly for the Review and Appraisal of the Implementation of the Programme of Action of the International Conference on Population and Development (30 June 1999), available at www.un.org/popin/unpopcom/32ndsess/gass/state/ireland.pdf.

re-negotiation of the 1995 texts.[34] This difference in approach might be explained by the more ambiguous language in the Beijing Declaration and Platform. It might also be explained by the Government's growing recognition of the difficulties that any such re-negotiation would create. The preparatory process for Beijing + 5 was a difficult one at national level, with Christian right groups repeatedly challenging the tenets of the Beijing texts. The Minister for Justice, Equality and Law Reform was all too aware of the religious-cultural claims that could be raised by States if the original texts were re-opened. Similar difficulties arose in preparations for the Beijing + 10 review process, with the result that Irish Government efforts focused on maintaining the status quo rather than reviewing progress in implementing the Platform. In its submission on the Beijing + 10 review, Neart again emphasised its opposition to CEDAW and to the concept of reproductive rights, repeatedly appealing to the "objective moral order and natural law". Mirroring the strategies of conservative Christian groups at international level, Neart links recognition of reproductive rights with the promotion of "incomplete forms of family" and "reproductive wrongs", and calls for the use of the term "family orientation" in place of sexual orientation in discussions on reproductive or sexual health. The term "right reproduction" was proposed in place of reproductive rights, to ensure that the "objective procreative/unitive basis and natural teleology […] of sex, sexuality and reproduction are clear, to the forefront and protected". The appeals to a "natural teleology" reveal a continuing refusal to shift beyond a conception of rights rooted in conservative Catholic teachings.

In September of 2005, the European Court of Human Rights heard the case of *D v Ireland* (2006). Relying on articles 1, 3, 8, 10, 13 and 14, the applicant D complained about the lack of abortion services in Ireland in the case of lethal foetal abnormality, a situation, she argued, that was unnecessarily exacerbated by the Regulation of Information (Services outside the State for Termination of Pregnancies) Act 1995. The Court found that the applicant's complaints were inadmissible, on the ground

---

[34] Mr John O'Donoghue, Minister for Justice, Equality and Law Reform, Address to the Special Session of the UN General Assembly, "Women 2000: Gender Equality, Development and Peace for the 21st Century" (6 June 2000), available at http://www.un.org/womenwatch/daw/followup/beijing+5stat/statments/ireland6.htm.

of failure to exhaust domestic remedies. The Court further noted that the limitations of the 1995 Act concerned abortion services abroad and had no application to a lawful abortion in Ireland. The Court noted that, at the relevant time, a legal constitutional remedy was, in principle, available to the applicant to obtain declaratory and mandatory orders with a view to obtaining a lawful abortion in Ireland. In arriving at its conclusion, the Court was clearly mindful of the specificity of Ireland's position on abortion. It was particularly important, they said, in a common law system, to allow the courts to develop constitutional protection for fundamental rights by way of interpretation, particularly when the central issue was a novel one, "requiring a complex and sensitive balancing of the constitutionally enshrined equal rights to life and demanding a delicate analysis of country-specific values and morals".[35] The Court also suggested that the right to life of the mother in this case could have allowed for termination of the pregnancy. Specifically the Court concluded:

> […] it is precisely the interplay between the equal right to life of the mother and the "unborn", so central to Article 40.3.3, that renders it arguable that the X case does not exclude a further exception to the prohibition of abortion in Ireland (2006: para. 90).

As the IFPA have noted, the implication, given the Government's refusal to legislate for the *X* case is that the Government considers it the duty of the courts to decide these issues rather than the legislature (IFPA, 2008). However, as we have seen with the *X* case, even when the courts have defined the constitutionally permissible indications for abortion the Government has failed to realise these rights through legislation.

Drawing on international human rights law, the IFPA has launched the "Safe and Legal in Ireland" campaign, calling for the provision of legal abortion services in Ireland.[36] Central to the campaign is a legal challenge against Ireland's abortion laws under the ECHR. The challenge is based on complaints submitted by three Irish women who

---

35 See press release issued by the Registrar: European Court of Human Rights, Inadmissibility Decision in *D v Ireland*, 5 July 2006.

36 See details of the Safe and Legal Campaign, including the pending case *A, B and C v Ireland* at http://www.ifpa.ie/news/index.php?mr=111.

have had abortions in the UK and claim that Ireland's restrictive abortion laws violate the State's duties under articles 2, 3, 8 and 14 of the ECHR.[37] The challenge builds on the growing, though tentative, body of case law under the ECHR safeguarding women's reproductive rights.[38] It follows on the CEDAW Committee's criticism of Ireland's "very restrictive abortion laws"(CEDAW, 2005: para. 35) and the continuing refusal of the Irish Government to provide a legislative framework for abortion in line with the Supreme Court's judgment in the *X* case. This refusal raises questions, at the very least, as to the State's compliance with its positive obligations under provisions such as Article 2 of the ECHR, which has been interpreted as including a duty to protect the life of a pregnant woman.

The limits of the EU integration project have also been tested. The Draft Treaty on a Constitution for Europe, concluded under the Irish Presidency of the EU, was supplemented by a Protocol, providing that the constitutional prohibition on abortion in Ireland would not be affected by the adoption of a Constitution for Europe.[39] Again, we see the limits of the European integration project and the willingness of states to accommodation difference through limits imposed on women's reproductive health. Against the background of this political wrangling, more than 5,000 women will continue to travel abroad each year to terminate their pregnancies. For unemployed women or women earning low wages, this freedom to travel remains illusory. For asylum-seeking women, the freedom to travel does not exist. Travel documents, however, have been provided on an ad hoc basis for asylum-seeking

---

[37] See "European Court to hear women's challenge to ban on abortion", *The Irish Times,* 28 July 2008.

[38] On 20 March 2007, European Court of Human Rights found that the Polish legal framework did not provide an effective mechanism to resolve disagreements as to the availability or legality of therapeutic termination in any case, either between a pregnant woman and doctors or between medical staff themselves. Concluding that Poland had violated Ms Tysiąc's right to respect for private life and noting the severe distress and anguish caused to her, the Court ordered Poland to pay a substantial sum in non-pecuniary damages. *Tysiac v Poland* (Application no. 5410/03), 20 March 2007. In September 2007, the Grand Chamber of the Court announced that it would not be reconsidering the Court's earlier decision.

[39] See Treaty establishing a Constitution for Europe, Protocol on Article 40.3.3 of the Constitution of Ireland, O.J. C 310/377 (2004).

women wishing to travel to the UK to avail of abortion services, raising questions as to the legality of the legislative restriction imposed on travel for such women and conversely, of the legality of the State's ad hoc response. The Irish Human Rights Commission, in its submission to the *CEDAW* Committee on Ireland's *Combined Fourth and Fifth Reports* under the UN Convention on the Elimination of All Forms of Discrimination Against Women, notes that the number of women from immigrant communities seeking the services of crisis pregnancy agencies has risen significantly and that an increasing number of reports of back street abortions amongst immigrant communities are under investigation by An Garda Siochána. For migrant women crossing borders, the search for reproductive autonomy continues.

Migrant Women, Birth and Citizenship

The 1990s witnessed significant changes in Irish society with Ireland becoming, for the first time, a country of net inward migration. Asylum and immigration, rather than emigration and depopulation, became pressing political issues. Increasing immigration coincided with constitutional change, change that was due to peace negotiations in Northern Ireland and a desire for compromise in the ongoing territorial dispute between Ireland and the United Kingdom concerning the status of Northern Ireland. As a result of these peace negotiations and the subsequent Belfast Agreement,[40] the territorial claim to Northern Ireland, enshrined in the Irish Constitution since 1937, was removed, and replaced by a new Article 2 affirming the right to self-determination of the people of Northern Ireland and the entitlement of anyone born within the "island of Ireland" to Irish citizenship.[41] The *jus soli* principle

---

[40] See generally Harvey and Livingstone (1999); Harvey (2001); Harvey (2000).

[41] See Nineteenth Amendment to the Constitution Act, 1998. The full text of Article 2 of the Constitution of Ireland (as amended) reads:

> Article 2
>
> It is the entitlement and birthright of every person born in the island of Ireland, which includes its islands and seas, to be part of the Irish Nation. That is also the entitlement of all persons otherwise qualified in accordance with law to be citizens of Ireland. Furthermore, the Irish nation cherishes its special affinity with people of Irish ancestry living abroad who share its cultural identity and heritage.

recognized in common law and in Irish legislation[42] was given constitutional recognition for the first time. The coincidence of constitutional change with increasing immigration was described by the Irish Supreme Court as an "accident of history" (*Lobe v Osaynde*, 2003: para. 451 per Fennelly J). It is an "accident" that led to significant changes in the concept of citizenship and in the legal protections afforded to migrant families within the State.

In June 2004, a referendum on citizenship was held in Ireland. The referendum and subsequent constitutional amendment led to restrictions being imposed on the constitutionally protected right to citizenship by birth. The citizenship referendum followed a period of heated debate on the meaning of citizenship and the terms on which migrant families would be allowed to remain in Ireland. The debate on birthright citizenship placed migrant women's roles in reproduction at the centre of legal and political debate in Ireland. Migrant women's bodies, their sexuality and childbearing roles became the subject of heightened scrutiny, with newspapers reporting daily on the numbers of migrant women availing of maternity services in Irish hospitals. Introducing the proposal for a referendum on citizenship, the Minister for Justice, Equality and Law Reform highlighted the perceived threat posed to the nation State by migrant women coming to Ireland. "How", he asked, "do we respond?" To require non-national women of child-bearing age to make declarations of pregnancy when arriving in the State was, he said, "clearly unworkable – especially in a common travel area" (McDowell, 2004). The fact that requiring a migrant woman to make a declaration of pregnancy might amount to degrading treatment, a violation of a woman's right to privacy or her right to bodily integrity, did not appear to be a concern.

Of course, the intersection of gender, national identity and reproduction was not new to Ireland. In debates on citizenship and migration, however, the concern to protect the sovereignty of the State and to control immigration trumped "pro-life" and "pro-family" traditions, provoking little response from the Catholic right. Where migrant women have invoked the constitutional protections afforded to

---

42 Irish Nationality and Citizenship Act 1956.

the family or the State's duty to "defend and vindicate" the right to life of the "unborn", the State has been quick to appeal to requirements of comity with other nations and its inherent and universal right to control immigration. Migrant women coming to Ireland and bearing children posed a threat to the racial homogeneity of the nation and to the ever fragile process of nation-building. While postcolonial Irish nationalism celebrated women's roles as mothers, migrant women's reproductive roles were not to be celebrated.

At a time when sovereignty is shrinking, the State acts upon vulnerable categories of migrants (often asylum-seekers) to re-establish and affirm its power to control borders. Lubhéid notes in the Irish context:

> While childbearing by asylum seeker women is represented as a threat to the sovereignty of the nation-state, in fact, their presence has allowed the State to refashion the national imaginary, reinvent itself, and implement new strategies of sexualised, racialised governance (2004: 344).

Although reproduction and sexuality were at the centre of the citizenship debates, the constructions of gender and sexuality that underpinned debates on the need for reform were often ignored by anti-racist and migrant rights campaigners. A moral panic both sensationalised – through their "hyper visibility" – and silenced migrant women coming to Ireland. Migrant women, particularly Black African women, were represented as dangerously fertile foreign bodies, threatening the boundedness of the nation-state. Positioned as "undeserving poor" or "citizen tourists", exploiting the logic of free market citizenship, the embodied migrant women evaded and undermined the State's immigration controls, threatening the integrity of the nation-state. Familiar gender tropes were deployed by the State, as migrant women were "fixed" into pre-defined categories of threat to the national interest. At the same time, the State highlighted the instability linked with migrant women's bodies, the potential to reproduce, and the inability of the State to limit or constrain this potential.

In the citizenship debates in Ireland, women were defined yet again by their reproductive roles and, yet again, the assertion of reproductive autonomy was rejected as a threat to the nation's ethno-cultural identity – an identity that has been revealed both as deeply gendered and deeply racialised. The exclusivity of the family unit that is provided with constitutional protection was also revealed. Migrant families, denied the protection of the State, were not considered to be "indispensable to the welfare of the Nation or the State". Migrant women choosing Ireland as their children's birthplace were presented as threatening to Ireland's claim to racial homogeneity and Irish understandings of "the nation", "the family" and "the citizenry".

The concern to defend and vindicate the rights of the unborn have not been to the fore in challenges to deportation proceedings, where we see an overriding concern with control and protection of the state's territorial borders. In 2002, while anti-abortion and pro-choice debates were dominating the political arena, the rights of the "unborn" were being tested again in Ireland's Supreme Court. The *Baby O* case (2002) involved a Nigerian woman, seven months pregnant and subject to a deportation order from the state, following a failed application for asylum. Taking judicial review proceedings challenging the validity of the deportation order, she argued that the duty to defend and vindicate Baby O's right to life prevented the state from deporting her to Nigeria, where infant mortality rates were substantially higher and the standard of living substantially lower. The Attorney General, acting on behalf of the Minister for Justice, Equality and Law Reform, appealed to the common good, to the need to defend and vindicate the territorial integrity of the state and to the Minister's right to deport failed asylum-seekers. The Court agreed with the submissions of the Attorney General. The threat posed by higher infant mortality rates could not engage the protection of Article 40.3.3° (2002: 23-24). The state's duty to defend and vindicate the right to life of the unborn did not extend to ensuring the health and well-being of Baby O, or even to ensuring a safe delivery. Article 40.3.3° could not be relied on to invoke unenumerated social and economic rights, which the Court held were not implicit within the constitutionally protected right to life. The Court upheld the deportation order and also refused a final application to stay the order pending an appeal to the European Court of Human Rights. If Baby O was born in Ireland, she could claim Irish citizenship. The "common good" required a speedy deportation of the mother and foetus. Again, the narrative of nation was to prove exclusionary. The "pro-life" movement, preoccupied with another referendum on abortion, had little to say in support of Baby O or her mother.

Concluding Remarks

In Ireland, as elsewhere, cultural claims concerning gender identities and roles have been given greater or lesser weight depending on their "fit" with state interests and the ongoing process of nation-building. Lost within these negotiations and compromises is a recognition of the universal legitimacy of women's human rights claims. In recent years, this loss has been most evident in debates surrounding women's reproductive health and the right to access abortion services. The difficulties encountered by feminism within Ireland mirror those encountered within the international human rights movement. Both at national and international levels, the deference paid to cultural claims reveals a gendered division between the public and the private and a willingness to "hive off" the private sphere from public tests of justice and rights. Debates concerning reproductive health have all fallen within the boundaries of the private. Claimed as falling "essentially within the domestic jurisdiction of the state", they have served to underpin the nation-state's claim to a distinct cultural identity.

Within Ireland's constitutional text, we see quite clearly the tensions that arise between, on the one hand, a liberal rights-based democracy and, on the other, a communitarian ethos that appeals to an explicitly Christian (and for the most part Catholic) conception of the common good (Quinn, 1991; Whyte, 1993). For many years, it was presumed that such tensions could be resolved by an appeal to the "ethical values, which all Christians living in the State acknowledge and accept" (*People v Shaw,* 1982 per Kenny J). A politics of presumed consensus prevailed. Given the dominant position of the Roman Catholic Church in the early years of independence, and its role in the drafting of the Irish Constitution, this is not surprising. In more recent years, we have witnessed what Habermas might term a shift from ethnos to demos in legal discourse. This shift, limited though it is, can be attributed to a number of factors. Meeting the demands of globalisation required that Ireland assert itself as a modern European state, capable of feeding the appetite of the Celtic Tiger economy. The Northern Ireland Peace Agreement, concluded on 10 April 1998, required a recognition of the diversity of identities and traditions on the island of Ireland.[43] Irishness could no longer be defined simply as "not English". "Reinventing Ireland"[44] to meet the changing political and economic context meant searching for an identity that would allow greater space for diversity. As yet, however, these changes have not led to greater reproductive autonomy for Irish women.

In its submission to the Inter-departmental Working Group on Abortion, Catholics for a Free Choice argued that even in a predominantly Catholic country laws governing abortion should be formulated on secular, plural, democratic principles.[45] Feminists in Ireland have always sought to move beyond the constraints of particularistic, cultural discourse. Today, as in the early stages of nation-building, however, the challenges raised by feminism have been perceived, not only as hostile to religious-cultural beliefs and practices, but to the very ties that bind the nation-state.

Bibliography

All Party Oireachtas Committee on the Constitution (2000) *Fifth Progress Report: Abortion*, Dublin: Stationery Office.

Beijing Declaration and Platform for Action (1995) U.N. Doc. A/CONF. 177/20. Adopted 15 September 1995.

Bradley, A. and Valiulis, M.G. (1997) (eds.) *Gender and Sexuality in Modern Ireland*, Amherst: University of Massachusetts Press.

Browne, N. (1998) "Church and State in Modern Ireland" in Twomey, P. and Murphy, T. (eds.) *Ireland's Evolving Constitution 1937-1997*, Oxford: Hart Publishing.

Buss, D. (2000) "Racing Populations, sexing environments: The challenges of a feminist politics in international law" *Legal Studies* 20(4):463-484.

---

43 "Agreement reached in the Multi-Party Negotiations", reproduced at (1998) 37 ILM 751 (hereinafter referred to as the Good Friday Agreement). Articles 2 and 3 of the Constitution were revised following the enactment of the Nineteenth Amendment to the Constitution, Act, 1998. See generally Gilbert (1998); Harvey and Livingstone (1999).

44 This phrase is adapted from Kiberd (1996).

45 *Supra* n. 26.

CEDAW (1999) *Concluding Observations of the Committee on the Elimination of Discrimination Against Women: Ireland* UN DocA/54/38.

CEDAW (1999a) *Report of the Committee on the Elimination of Discrimination Against Women on its Twenty-First Session*, U.N. GAOR, 54th Sess., Supp. No. 38, Pt. II, ¶ 180, U.N. Doc. A/54/38/Rev.1 (concluding observations on Ireland).

Center for Reproductive Law and Policy (2000) "The Holy See at the United Nations: An Obstacle to Women's Reproductive Health and Rights" Available at: http://www.crlp.org/pub_art_holysee.html.

Clarke, D.M. (1984) *Church and State: Essays in Political Philosophy,* Cork: Cork University Press.

Committee on the Elimination of Discrimination Against Women (1999) *General Recommendation 24*: *Women and Health (Article 12)* GAOR Fifty-fourth session, UN Doc.A/54/38/Rev.1.

Committee on the Elimination of Discrimination against Women, Thirty-third session, 5-22 July 2005, Concluding comments: Ireland, UN Doc. CEDAW/C/IRL/CO/4-5.

Connolly, L. (2002) *The Irish Women's Movement: From Revolution to Devolution*, London: Palgrave.

Constitution Review Group (1996) *Report of the Constitution Review Group* Dublin: Stationery Office.

Cook, R.J. and Fathalla, M.F. (1996) "Advancing Reproductive Rights Beyond Cairo and Beijing" in Askin, K.D. and Koenig, D.M. (eds.) *Women and International Human Rights Law Vol. 3*, New York: Transnational.

Coppell, J. and O'Neill, A. (1992) "The European Court of Justice: Taking rights seriously?" CML Rev 29:669, p. 687.

Cornell, D. (1995) *The Imaginary Domain: Abortion, Pornography and Sexual Harassment*, New York: Routledge.

Coulter, C. (1993) *The Hidden Tradition: Feminism, Women and Nationalism* Cork: Cork University Press.

Crowley, E. (1997) "Making a Difference? Female Employment and Multinationals in the Republic of Ireland", in Byrne, A. and Leonard, M. (eds.), *Women and Irish Society: A Sociological Reader*. Belfast: Beyond the Pale Publications, pp. 81-96.

Department of An Taoiseach (1999) *Green Paper on Abortion,* Dublin: Government Stationery Office.

Dooley, D. (1998) "Gendered Citizenship in the Irish Constitution" in Murphy, T. and Twomey, P. (eds.) *Ireland's Evolving Constitution 1937-1997*, Oxford: Hart Publishing.

Eriksson, M.K. (1996) "Abortion and Reproductive Health: Making International Law More Responsive to Women's Needs" in Askin, K.D. and Koenig, D.M. (eds.) *Women and International Human Rights Law Vol. 3,* New York: Transnational.

Fanning, R. (1988) "Mr De Valera Drafts a Constitution" in Farrell, B. (ed.) *De Valera's Constitution and Ours*, Dublin: Gill & Macmillan.

Fleishman, R. (2000) "The Battle Against Reproductive Rights: The Impact of the Catholic Church on Abortion Law in Both International and Domestic Arenas" 14 Emory Int'l L. Rev. 277.

Fletcher, R. (2001) "Post-colonial Fragments: Representations of Abortion in Irish Law and Politics" *Journal of Law and Society* 28(4).

Gilbert, G. (1998) "The Northern Ireland Peace Agreement, Minority Rights and Self-Determination" 47 ICLQ 943.

Glendon, M.A. (1987) *Abortion and Divorce in Western Law,* Cambridge, MA: Harvard University Press.

Glendon, M.A. (1991) *Rights Talk: The Impoverishment of Legal Discourse*, New York. Macmillan.

Harvey, C. (2000) "Governing After the Rights Revolution" *Journal of Law and Society* 27: 61-97.

Harvey, C. and Livingstone, S/ (1999) "Human Rights and the Northern Ireland Peace Process" *European Human Rights Law Review* 162-177.

Harvey, C.J. (2001) (ed.). *Human Rights, Equality and Democratic renewal in Northern Ireland*, Oxford: Hart Publishing.

Hesketh, T. (1990) *The Second Partitioning of Ireland: the Abortion Referendum of 1983,* Dublin: Brandsma Books.

Human Rights Committee (2000) *Concluding Observations of the Human Rights Committee: Ireland* UN Doc. CCPR/CO/69/IRL.

Human Rights Committee (2008) *Concluding Observations on Ireland's Third Periodic Report: Ireland* UN Doc CCPR/C/IRL/CO/3.

Irish Council for Civil Liberties (Women's Committee) (1999) *Submission to the UN Committee on the Elimination of All Forms of Discrimination Against Women* Dublin: ICCL.

Irish Council for Civil Liberties (Women's Committee) (2002) *Position Paper on the Abortion Referendum* Dublin, ICCL.

Irish Family Planning Association, *Submission to International Covenant on Civil and Political Rights*, 11 July 2008, available at: http://safeandlegal.blogspot.com/2008/07/ifpa-submission-to-international.html

Irish Medical Council, (1998) *A Guide to Ethical Conduct and Behaviour*, 5th ed. Dublin: Irish Medical Council,

Jackson, N. (1993) "Family Law: Fertility and Parenthood" in Connolly A. (ed.) *Gender and the Law in Ireland*, Dublin: Oak Tree Press.

Kapur, R. (1999) "A Love Song to Our Mongrel Selves: Hybridity, Sexuality and the Law" *Social and Legal Studies* 8(3):353-368.

Kapur, R. and Cossman, B. (1996) *Subversive Sites: feminist engagements with law in India*, London: Sage Publications.

Keogh, D. (1986) *The Vatican, the Bishops and Irish Politics 1919-1939,* Cambridge: Cambridge University Press.

Keogh D (1988) "Church, State and Society" in Farrell B, (ed.) *De Valera's Constitution and Ours (*Dublin, Gill and Macmillan

Keogh, D. (1995) *Ireland and the Vatican: The Politics and Diplomacy of Church-State Relations 1922-1960,* Cork: Cork University Press.

Kiberd, D. (1996) *Inventing Ireland: The Literature of the Modern Nation,* London: Vintage.

Kingston, J. and Whelan, A. with Bacik, I. (1997) *Abortion and the Law,* Dublin: Roundhall Sweet and Maxwell.

Loomba, A. (1998) *Colonialism/Postcolonialism: The New Critical Idiom,* London: Routledge.

Luibhéid, E. (2004) "Childbearing against the state? Asylum seeker women in the Irish republic" *Women's Studies International Forum* 27(4): 335-349.

Martin, F. (1998) "The Family in the Constitution – Principle and Practice" in Murphy, T. and Twomey, P. (eds.) *Ireland's Evolving Constitution 1937-1997,* Oxford: Hart Publishing.

McDowell, M. (1992) "Proposed Citizenship Referendum", *Sunday Independent,* 14 March 2004.

Moghadam, V. (1992) "Patriarchy and the Politics of Gender in Modernising Societies: Iran, Pakistan and Afghanistan" *International Sociology* 7:35-47.

Mullally, S. (1998) "Equality Guarantees in the Irish Constitution: The Myth of Constitutionalism and the Neutral State" in Murphy, T. and Twomey, P. (eds.) *Ireland's Evolving Constitution 1937-1997,* Oxford: Hart Publishing.

Mullally, S. (2002) "Beyond the limits of the Discrimination Model: Promoting Gender Equality" in Barry, E. and Costello, C. (eds.) *Equality Law in Europe,* Dublin: ICEL.

Mullally, S. (2006) *Gender Culture and Human Rights: Reclaiming Universalism* Oxford: Hart Publishing.

Mullally, S. (2007) "Gendered Borders: Reproduction, Family Unity and Immigration Law" in S. van Walsum and T. Spirkerboer (eds.) *Women and Immigration Laws: New Perspectives on Classical Themes,* London: Routledge.

National Forum for Non-Governmental Organisations (2000) *Report on Proceedings. United Nations General Assembly Special Session "Women 2000: Gender Equality Development and Peace"* Dublin Castle, 10 May 2000 available at http://www.justice.ie.

National Union of Mothers of Ireland (2001) "Submission to the Forum on Europe 2001" available at: http://www.forumoneurope.ie as viewed on 17 October 2002.

National Women's Council of Ireland (2000). "Promises Made Promises Broken: Beijing + 5 Alternative Report for Ireland". Dublin: NWCI.

Neart (2000) Beijing + 5: Alternative Report for Ireland available at: http://www.forumoneurope.ie.

Neart (2001) *Submission to the National Forum on Europe* available at: http://www.forumoneurope.ie as viewed on 17 October 2002.

O'Reilly, E. (1992) *Masterminds of the Right*, Dublin: Attic Press.

Paul, J.R. (2000) "Cultural Resistance to Global Governance" *Michigan Journal of International Law* 22:1-84.

Phelan, R. (1992) "Right to Life of the Unborn v Promotion of Trade in Services: The European Court of Justice and the normative shaping of the European Union" MLR 55:670.

Programme of Action of the International Conference on Population and Development, U.N.Doc. A/CONF. 171/13. Adopted 18 October 1994.

Quinn, G. (1991) "Reflections on the Legitimacy of Judicial Activism in the Field of Constitutional Law" Dlí: 29.

Scannell, Y. (1988) "The Constitution and the Role of Women" in Farrell, B. (ed.). *De Valera's Constitution and Ours*, Dublin: Gill and Macmillan.

Sheehy-Skeffington. H. (1995) "Bean na hEireann" in Ward M, (ed.) *In their Own Voice: Women and Irish Nationalism.* Cork: Attic Press.

Smyth, A. (1990) *The Abortion Papers: Ireland.* Dublin: Attic Press.

Smyth, A. (1993) (ed.) *Irish Women's Studies Reader,* Dublin: Attic Press.

Smyth, A. (1993) "The 'X' Case: Women and Abortion in the Republic of Ireland, *Feminist Legal Studies* 1(2):163-177.

Sundstrom, K. (1993) "Abortion: A Reproductive Health Issue" cited in Eriksson M.K. (1996) "Abortion and Reproductive Health: Making International Law More Responsive to Women's Needs" in Askin, K.D. and

Koenig, D.M. (eds.) *Women and International Human Rights Law Vol. 3*, New York: Transnational.

Ward, M. (1983) *Unmanageable Revolutionaries: Women and Irish Nationalism*, London: Pluto.

Whyte, G. (1993) "Constitutional Adjudication, Ideology and Access to the Courts" in Whelan, A. (ed.) *Law and Liberty in Ireland*, Dublin: Oak Tree Press.

Young, I.M. (2000) *Inclusion and Democracy,* Oxford: Oxford University Press.

Cases

A and B v Eastern Health Board, District Judge Mary Fahy and C and the Attorney General [1998] 1 IR 464.

Attorney General v X [1992] 1 IR 1.

Baby O (suing by her mother and next friend I.A.O.) v Minister for Justice Equality and Law Reform and others Unreported Supreme Court Judgment, 6 June 2002.

D v Ireland (2005) Application Number 26499/02.

Griswold v Conneticut 381 U.S. 479 (1965).

Karen Noelia Llantoy Huamán v. Peru, Communication No. 1153/2003, U.N. Doc. CCPR/C/85/D/1153/2003 (2005), available at: http://www1.umn.edu /humanrts/undocs/1153-2003.html.

McGee v Attorney General [1974] IR 284.

Open Door Counselling and Others v Ireland, Judgment of 29 October 1992, (1993) 15 EHRR 244.

The People v Shaw [1982] IR 1

Re Article 26 and the Regulation of Information (Services Outside the State for the Termination of Pregnancies) Bill, 1995 [1995] 1 IR 1

Re Howley [1940] IR 119

Roe v Wade 410 U.S. 113 (1973).

SPUC v Grogan and others [1989] IR 734.

SPUC v Grogan and others [1991] ECR I-4685; [1991] 62 CMLR 849.

10

The State of Abortion Law in Northern Ireland

Dr Karen Brennan

Introduction

> Abortion is legal in Northern Ireland – *in certain circumstances*. It has been said that there is a widespread belief that abortion here is always illegal. If there is such a belief, there is no justification for it. It is wrong and after this case there is no reason that it should persist (*In the Matter of an Application by the Family Planning Association of Northern Ireland for Judicial Review*, 2003: para. 1) (emphasis added).

The Abortion Act 1967 does not extend to Northern Ireland, and the grounds on which abortions may be legally performed there are significantly more restrictive than they are in the rest of the United Kingdom. According to statistics provided by the Department of Health, Social Services and Public Safety (hereafter the DHSSPS), less than 100 abortions, defined as the "interruption of pregnancy for legally acceptable and medically approved reasons", have been performed per annum over the last number of years (Family Planning Association of Northern Ireland, 2007: 1). This, however, is a considerable understatement of the number of Northern Irish women who actually undergo a termination of pregnancy each year. As in the Republic of Ireland, the restrictive nature of the law means that the vast majority of Northern Irish women who wish to obtain an abortion must travel abroad. Every year a significant number of Northern Irish women go to other parts of the UK to avail of the more liberal abortion regime there. For example, according to figures published by the Department of Health in England and Wales (2007), 1,295 abortions were carried out on Northern Irish women in 2006 (Department of Health, 2007: para. 4.2). This figure is probably an underestimate, due to fact that many Northern Irish women who avail of abortion services in England do so in secret and may not provide their real addresses. Thus, as has been noted, Northern Ireland has "a significant 'abortion refugee' population" (Simpson, 1998: 103).

The law on abortion in Northern Ireland has been criticised *inter alia* on the basis that it is uncertain. Lee stated:

> [t]he law on abortion in Northern Ireland is so uncertain that it violates standards of international human rights law. It could not withstand a challenge before the European Court of Human Rights at Strasbourg. The Government should bring forward proposals to clarify the law without waiting for such a defeat (1995a: 16).

Thus far no person has taken such a case, nor has legislation been introduced to cure the law of its uncertainty; the law, then, remains unaltered and, consequently, uncertain. This chapter will address this issue of uncertainty in the law. It will examine a judicial review case taken by the Family Planning Association of Northern Ireland (hereafter fpaNI) in 2003, which drew attention to this problem, and will consider the impact that the outcome of this case will have on the current state of the law and the uncertainty inherent in it. Similar to Lee's conclusion in 1995, it will be argued that the prevailing uncertainty in the law can only be satisfactorily addressed through legislative action. First, however, the law on abortion in Northern Ireland will be outlined.

Current Law on Abortion in Northern Ireland

The law on abortion in Northern Ireland is governed by the relevant provisions of the Offences against the Person Act 1861 and the Criminal Justice (NI) Act 1945, and relevant case-law, including the English case of *Bourne* (1939) and more recent Northern Irish cases decided in the 1990s. The key legislative provision relating to abortion is section 58 of the 1861 Act which provides for the offence of "unlawfully" procuring a miscarriage.[1] This section criminalises any person who intentionally and unlawfully procures the miscarriage of any woman, whether or not she is in fact pregnant; it similarly criminalises pregnant women who intentionally and unlawfully procure their own miscarriage. Anyone found guilty of an offence under section 58 is liable to the most severe penalty available in law: life imprisonment.

Section 25(1) of the Criminal Justice Act (Northern Ireland) 1945, which is the equivalent of section 1(1) of the Infant Life (Preservation) Act 1929, provides for the offence of child destruction which is the intentional destruction of the life of a child who has not yet established an existence independent of its mother, but who is capable of being born alive. This offence covers abortion in the later stages of gestation, usually at 28 weeks or more,[2] and encompasses the destruction of the child up to the point where it can be said to be "born alive", at which stage the killing of the child would be governed by homicide laws. A proviso to section 45(1) of the 1945 Act provides for a defence to a charge of child destruction: "no person shall be found guilty of [child destruction] unless it is proved that the act which caused the death of the child was not done in good faith for the purpose only of preserving the life of the mother." The burden of proof rests on the prosecution; it must prove beyond reasonable doubt that the act in question was not done in good faith for the purpose of preserving the mother's life.

In the 1939 English case of *R v Bourne*, MacNaghten J, in his charge to the jury at the trial of an obstetrician charged with procuring the miscarriage of a 14-year-old girl who had become pregnant as the result of a violent rape, stated that the proviso contained in the English child destruction legislation reflected what "had always been the common law of

---

[1] Section 58 provides: Every woman, being with child who, with intent to procure her own miscarriage, shall unlawfully administer to herself any poison or other noxious thing, or shall unlawfully use any instrument or other means whatsoever with the like intent, and whosoever, with intent to procure the miscarriage of any woman, whether she be or be not with child, shall unlawfully administer to her or cause to be taken by her any poison or other noxious thing, or shall unlawfully use any instrument or other means whatsoever with the like intent, shall be guilty of felony, and being convicted thereof shall be liable to imprisonment for life.

[2] Section 25(2) provides that evidence that the woman has been 28 weeks pregnant would be "prima facie proof" that the child/foetus was capable of being born alive.

England with regard to the killing of an unborn child" (1939: 691). He asserted that although section 58 of the 1861 Act did not specifically incorporate such a proviso, it could be construed as doing so. MacNaghten J found that the word "unlawfully" which is used in section 58 is not "a meaningless word"; he interpreted it as "import[ing] the meaning expressed by the proviso" included in the child destruction legislation (1939: 691). Thus, the offence of procuring a miscarriage would be similarly qualified, and any person who procured an abortion in good faith for the purpose only of preserving the mother's life would not be guilty of an offence under section 58. The jury were directed that the burden rested on the Crown to prove beyond a reasonable doubt that the defendant had not performed the abortion in good faith for the purpose only of preserving the life of the girl; if it failed to do so, the defendant would be entitled to an acquittal (1939: 691).

In relation to the meaning of the phrase "for the purpose only of preserving the life of the mother", MacNaghten J stated that he saw no distinction between a danger to life and a danger to health, "since life depends upon health, and it may be that health is so gravely impaired that death results" (1939: 692). Noting that these words did not mean for the purpose only of preventing the immediate death of the mother (1939: 692), McNaghten J found that they should be "construed in a reasonable sense" (1939: 693-4). He concluded by directing the jury that they could find that a doctor operates for the purpose of preserving a woman's life where he honestly believes "on reasonable grounds and with adequate knowledge, that the probable consequence of the continuance of the pregnancy will be to make the woman a physical and mental wreck" (1939: 694). Mr Bourne testified that, having taken the view that the continuance of the pregnancy would "probably" cause "serious injury" to the girl, he had considered it his "duty" to perform an abortion in this case (1939: 688-9). A medical expert who gave evidence at trial stated that if the girl had given birth to the child, it was likely that she would have become a "mental wreck" (1939: 689). Mr Bourne was acquitted by the jury of the charge of procuring a miscarriage under section 58 of the 1861 Act.

Prior to the introduction of the Abortion Act 1967, Bourne was the main authority on abortion in England and Wales. Whether this English authority was the law in Northern Ireland was clarified in a 1993 High

Court decision, *Northern Health and Social Services Board v F & G*, where *Bourne* was accepted as part of Northern Irish law (McGleenan, 1994: 391-2). The principles derived from this and subsequent High Court cases can be taken to be the law governing abortion in Northern Ireland. There are three cases worth discussing in detail due to the impact they have had on the development of the law on abortion in Northern Ireland. The circumstances of these cases and the legal principles that can be distilled from them will be briefly outlined. Each case which will be discussed involved a pregnant girl/woman who was unable to give consent to an abortion due to diminished mental competence or age; in each case the High Court declared that, in the circumstances, an abortion would be lawful under Northern Irish law.[3]

Northern Health and Social Services Board v F & G (1993), commonly referred to as in *Re K*, involved a 14-year-old ward of court, K, who sought to terminate her pregnancy. K, who had become pregnant after engaging in sexual intercourse with an unknown person at a local disco, had made statements to the effect that she would kill herself and the baby if she was forced to go through with the pregnancy. Psychiatric evidence supported this, finding that the physical and, particularly, the mental risks to the young woman if the pregnancy continued would be significant. For example, one expert noted that K presented a "substantial suicide risk" if the pregnancy progressed (1993: 4);[4] another found that there was a "very real" threat to K's life which justified the termination of her pregnancy (1993: 5); another medical witness asserted that K would, in the words of *Bourne*, become "a physical and mental wreck" if an abortion was not carried out (1993: 5).

In the High Court, Sheil J found that an abortion would be lawful under Northern Irish law.[5] He quoted at length MacNaghten J in *Bourne*

---

[3] McGleenan notes that these cases were "atypical" in the Northern Irish context, as evidently numerous abortions were carried out every year by doctors in Northern Ireland who did not seek authorisation from the courts beforehand (1993: 391).

[4] This reported judgment was obtained on LexisNexis where the page numbers from the report are not provided. Thus, all references to pages in this judgment relate to the judgment as printed from LexisNexis.

[5] It is noted that this is not strictly what Sheil J had been asked to do; in other words, the order sought by the applicant board was not an order seeking a declaration of lawfulness

(1939) and noted the English 1958 case of *R v Newton and Stungo* where Ashworth J affirmed that abortions carried out in good faith for the purpose of preserving the life or *health* (including both physical and mental health) of a woman were lawful. Concluding that this "is and remains the law in Northern Ireland" (1993: 7), Sheil J found that an abortion would be lawful in this case. He stated:

> [h]aving regard to the fact that the minor in this case is insistent that her pregnancy be terminated and having regard to the uncontroverted medical evidence that to allow the pregnancy to continue to full term would result in her becoming a physical and mental wreck, I cannot see any ground upon which any proceedings, criminal or civil, could successfully be brought against any doctor who in good faith carries out the operation to terminate the minor's pregnancy. This court would not countenance giving its approval to an operation which it did not consider to be lawful (1993: 7).

It is worth noting, however, that, despite Sheil J's confidence about the legality of an abortion in this case, no doctor could be found who would carry out this procedure, and K, who was already in hospital recovering from an operation for the removal of her appendix, had to go to England to obtain an abortion. Both consultant obstetricians and gynaecologists who gave evidence at trial, although supporting an abortion in this particular case and registering no conscientious objection to it, stated that they would not be willing to perform this procedure; in fact, it appeared from all the evidence that was given that no consultant would be found in Northern Ireland who would be willing to carry out this operation. The reason for this seems to have been twofold: first, the fact that K's mother, F, had lodged an objection to the abortion; and, second, the medical profession's perception that the law was uncertain. Indeed, it was noted that the view of these medical professionals would not change, even if Sheil J found that an abortion would be lawful in Northern Ire-

---

for an abortion in Northern Ireland in these circumstances, but an order giving them permission to take this minor to England to have her pregnancy terminated there (McGleenan, 1994: 392). Lee opines: "Sheil J bravely chose to consider whether the abortion would be lawful here, as the Supreme Court in *X* focused on whether the abortion would have been lawful in the Republic, whereas in both the *X* and *K* cases the court was really being asked to authorise travel outside the jurisdiction" (1995b: 31-2).

land (1993: 8). This seems curious and it suggests that the profession was not sufficiently confident that the High Court's unambiguous decision on this matter would adequately protect its members against civil or criminal action. Unfortunately, Sheil J did not challenge the view that was taken by the medical profession, nor did he criticise it. He simply accepted the evidence that was given on behalf of the profession, noting simply that it was "regrettable", and granted permission for the girl to travel to Liverpool to have her pregnancy terminated there.[6]

The second key case in the development of the law on abortion in Northern Ireland, *Northern Ireland Health and Social Services Board v AMNH and Ors* (1994), commonly referred to as in *Re AMNH*, came four months after the in *Re K* judgment. In this case, the Northern Health and Social Services Board sought a declaration in the Northern Ireland High Court that it would be lawful to terminate the pregnancy of a severely mentally handicapped adult woman who was ten weeks pregnant. MacDermott LJ granted this declaration. In his exposition of the law, he made a number of significant points. First, he asserted that the phrase "for the purpose only of preserving the life of the mother" was not limited only to "some life threatening situation" (1994: 3).[7] Second, and leading on from this, he stated that the meaning of the word "life" in this context included the mother's "physical and mental health or *well being*" (1994: 3) (emphasis added). Third, he asserted that an abortion could be carried out where "the continuance of the pregnancy would adversely affect the mental or physical health of the mother" (1994: 3). Fourth, he qualified the above, by stating that the adverse effect in question must be "a real and serious one" (1994: 3). Finally, he noted that it would "always be a question of fact and degree whether the perceived effect of non-termination is sufficiently grave to warrant terminating the unborn child". MacDermott LJ also remarked on the uncertainty in the law. He referred to criticism of uncertainty in the law in England prior to the introduction of the Abortion

---

[6] On this point, Lee is critical, stating that Sheil J "might have stood on the dignity of the court" by following-up on this issue (1995b: 31).

[7] This unreported judgment was obtained on LexisNexis where page numbers are not provided. Thus, all page references relate to the document as printed from LexisNexis.

Act 1967,[8] noting that although that piece of legislation may be flawed, it offered "a much more coherent and understandable position than that which continues to prevail [in Northern Ireland]" (1994: 2). He asserted that it would be "in the best interests of not only the medical and legal professions but more importantly of the public at large" if the uncertain legal position in Northern Ireland was "remedied" (1994: 2).

In one sense, MacDermott LJ's judgment seemed to provide for some clarification of the law by, for example, being more specific about the nature of the adverse effect that was required, i.e., that it needed to be "real and serious". However, this decision also casts further doubt on the state of the law. In particular, MacDermott LJ's reference to the "physical and mental health or well being" of the woman suggested a departure from *Bourne* and, potentially, could have resulted in a significant widening of the grounds upon which abortions could be lawfully carried out in Northern Ireland. In addition, as has been noted by Lee, a real threat of suicide does not seem to have been as essential to the decision that the abortion would be lawful in this case, as it was in that of in *Re K* (1995b: 33).

The following year, the High Court made further efforts to clarify the law. In *Western Health and Social Services Board v CMB* (1995), commonly known as in *Re SJB*, Pringle J made a declaration that an abortion would be lawful in a case involving a severely mentally handicapped 17-year-old ward of the court. In his judgment, Pringle J further qualified and explained the law. Pringle J agreed that "life" included both physical and mental health. However, he concluded that by using the term "well being" in this context, MacDermott LJ, in the in *Re AMNH* case, had not meant to imply that "'life' meant something more than physical and mental health such as happiness…" (1995: 2).[9] Essentially, Pringle J halted any potential effort, based on MacDermott LJ's words, to have the law more liberally construed than it had hitherto been.

---

[8] For example, he referred to the case of *Royal College of Nursing v DHSS* (1981), where Lord Diplock described the pre-1967 law as "unsatisfactory and uncertain"; Lord Diplock also commented that although the phrase "physical or mental wreck" was "vivid", it was "unfortunately lacking in precision" (p. 567-8).

[9] This reported judgment was obtained on LexisNexis where the page numbers from the report are not provided. Thus, all references to pages in this judgment relate to the judgment as printed from LexisNexis.

Pringle J further qualified the law on abortion in Northern Ireland, holding that the adverse effect on the woman's physical or mental health must be permanent or long-term; it could not be of short duration. He noted that this is what MacDermott LJ had meant when he referred to "a real and serious adverse effect which would be sufficiently grave to warrant termination" (1995: 2). In relation to the degree of risk required, Pringle J held that in most cases the risk of the adverse effect occurring would need to be a probability, but that in cases where imminent death is the risk in question, a possibility may suffice (1995: 2).[10]

Medical evidence in this case indicated that SJB had no understanding of her own biological functions and, consequently, of the processes of pregnancy and childbirth. In addition, it was noted that SJB would be incapable of caring for a child. A number of medical witnesses noted the probable effects that the continuation of the pregnancy would have on her mental health. For example, one expert, Dr C, opined that there was a very strong possibility that she would have a mental breakdown (1995: 2-3). Pringle J, concluding that an abortion would be lawful, stated that he "… had no hesitation in finding that if the pregnancy were not terminated S would become increasingly frightened by what was happening to her and was beyond her understanding; on delivery the baby would be taken from her and it would be probable that she would suffer a long term psychological trauma which could involve hospitalisation" (1995: 3).

From these cases a number of legal principles governing the lawful termination of pregnancies in Northern Ireland have been distilled. These were set out in the High Court by Kerr J (as he then was), in a judicial review case taken by the fpaNI in 2003. This case is discussed below. The legal principles that are accepted as governing abortion in Northern Ireland are:

---

[10] See also *In the Matter of C.H., A Minor, Down Lisburn Health and Social Services Trust v The Official Solicitor as Guardian Ad Litem of C.H. and L.A.H.* (1995), where, Sheil J, agreeing with Pringle J's exposition of the law, found that an abortion would be lawful in this case. CH, the 16-year-old ward of the court, had threatened suicide in the event of her being forced to continue with the pregnancy. A number of medical witnesses commented on the potential detrimental impact that the continuance of the pregnancy would have on her; for example, it was noted that she would not be able to cope, that she would suffer emotional damage, and that she was at risk of developing a major depressive illness.

1. Operations in Northern Ireland for the termination of pregnancies are unlawful unless performed in good faith for the purpose of preserving the life of the mother;
2. The "life" of the mother in this context has been interpreted by the courts as including her physical and mental health;
3. A termination will therefore be lawful where the continuance of the pregnancy threatens the life of the mother, or would adversely affect her mental or physical health;
4. The adverse effect on her mental or physical health must be a "real and serious" one, and must also be "permanent or long term";
5. In most cases the risk of the adverse effect occurring would need to be a probability, but a possibility might be regarded as sufficient if the imminent death of the mother was the potentially adverse effect;
6. It will always be a question of fact and degree whether the perceived effect of a non-termination is sufficiently grave to warrant terminating the pregnancy in a particular case (*In the Matter of an Application by the Family Planning Association of Northern Ireland for Judicial Review*: 2003: para. 37).[11]

This is the law governing abortion in Northern Ireland. As noted, it has been criticised for being uncertain. This alleged uncertainty poses particular problems due to the fact that it is doctors, in the exercise of their clinical judgement, who are left to apply the law in order to determine whether, in the circumstances of an individual case, a woman can avail of a lawful abortion. In 2003, the fpaNI took a judicial review application which drew attention to this problem. This case and the impact it will have on the law will now be addressed.

---

[11] The principles were put forward by counsel and were accepted by Kerr J as being the current state of the law on abortion. On appeal by the fpaNI to the Court of Appeal, these principles were not challenged as being an accurate reflection of the law (*The Family Planning Association of Northern Ireland v The Minister for Health, Social Services and Public Safety*, 2004). Sheil LJ took the view that they would provide a "good starting point" for departmental guidance (para. 12).

Uncertainty in the Law: fpaNI Judicial Review Case

In 2003, the fpaNI took a judicial review case which highlighted the uncertainty of the law on abortion in Northern Ireland and the difficulties created by this (*In the Matter of an Application by the Family Planning Association of Northern Ireland for Judicial Review*, 2003). In its application to the High Court, the fpaNI sought, *inter alia*, a declaration that the Minister for Health and Social Services[12] had acted unlawfully in failing to provide advice and guidance to women and clinicians on the availability and provision of abortion services in Northern Ireland; in other words, it sought to require the then Minister and her department, now the DHSSPS, to produce guidance on the circumstances in which an abortion could be lawfully obtained in Northern Ireland.[13] The essence of

---

[12] The original case taken by the fpaNI to the High Court was against the Minister for Health and Social Services (now the Minister for Health Social Services and Public Safety). However, by the time this case reached the Court of Appeal Direct Rule has been reinstated and the Secretary of State for Northern Ireland had become responsible for the above minister's old department (now the Department of Health, Social Services and Public Safety, hereafter referred to as the DHSSPS). Thus, for the purposes of the appeal, all of the judges in the Court of Appeal treated the DHSSPS as being the respondent. A number of other parties also intervened on the side of the respondent. They were: Archbishop Sean Brady and the Roman Catholic Bishops of Northern Ireland; the Society for the Protection of Unborn Children, Northern Ireland; Precious Life; and Life (Northern Ireland).

[13] Specifically, the fpaNI alleged that the Minister (or DHSSPS) had, in breach of its general duties under Article 4 of the Health and Personal Social Services (Northern Ireland) Order 1972, failed: (a) to issue advice and guidance to women and clinicians on the availability and provision of abortion services in Northern Ireland; (b) to investigate whether women in Northern Ireland were are receiving satisfactory services in respect of actual or potential terminations of pregnancy; and (c) to secure satisfactory abortion services in respect of actual or potential terminations of pregnancy for women in Northern Ireland (*In the Matter of an Application by the Family Planning Association of Northern Ireland for Judicial Review*, 2003: para. 2-3). The applicant sought a declaration that the respondent had acted unlawfully in relation to each of these alleged failures. At the High Court, the applicant also sought an order of mandamus requiring the respondent to rectify these failures. By the time the case reached the Court of Appeal, the fpaNI no longer sought an order of mandamus due to the fact that the respondent had already established a working group to examine the possibility of producing guidance on the law on abortion (*The Family Planning Association of Northern Ireland v Minister for Health, Social Services and Public Safety and Ors*, 2004: para. 10, per Sheil LJ; see also Fletcher (2005: 132). The focus in this paper will be on the specific claim that the Minister/DHSSPS had failed to discharge her/its duty to issue guidance on the availability of abortion services in Northern Ireland, i.e., on the claim that relates to the matter of the uncertainty about the circumstances in which abortion is lawful in Northern Ireland.

the fpaNI's claim was an alleged lack of clarity in the law, and the consequent confusion among the medical profession about the circumstances in which abortion is lawful. It was argued that the uncertainty in the law meant that women had great difficulty in obtaining legal terminations in Northern Ireland; the main reason for this being the fact that the availability and accessibility of abortion services is left to the discretion of individual doctors who themselves are confused about when they may or may not legally perform abortions. The suggestion appears to have been that the lack of legal clarity created a situation where some doctors were inhibited in making independent medical judgments for fear of criminal prosecution, while others used the uncertainty as an excuse to avoid performing abortions that they had a conscientious objection to. The alleged result of this was considerable inconsistency in the provision of abortion services, with some women being forced to travel to obtain abortions that were actually legal in Northern Ireland.

The fpaNI's application failed in the High Court. Kerr J denied that there was any evidence of confusion about the law. He was of the opinion that any uncertainty about the lawfulness or availability of abortion in Northern Ireland was not due to a lack of clarity about the legal principles outlined above, which he concluded are "clear and are easily absorbed", but was due to reliance on clinical judgement, which meant that it would be "difficult in some circumstances to decide whether the facts of an individual case can be accommodated within the[se] principles" (2003: para. 39). In other words, Kerr J created a distinction between uncertainty about the law or the legal principles, and uncertainty about whether in the circumstances of a particular case an abortion was permitted on the basis of those legal principles; he concluded that it was the latter kind of uncertainty that pertained in Northern Ireland. However, he was of the view that this was not something that could be remedied by the provision of guidelines; this type of uncertainty, i.e., about whether the established legal principles would allow an abortion in particular situations, could only be resolved by a change in the law, either through the development of the current principles by the courts or through legislative reform (2003: para. 13) Kerr J found that guidelines would do nothing to solve the uncertainty about whether the circumstances of a particular case justified a legal abortion because "[s]uch situations do not lend themselves to universally applicable rules"; it would be "impossible to prescribe for every conceivable case where clinical judgment must be exercised" (2003: para. 26).

The fpaNI appealed and, in October 2004, the three judge Court of Appeal unanimously upheld this appeal and granted the appropriate declarations, in the case *The Family Planning Association of Northern Ireland v Minister for Health, Social Services and Public Safety and Ors* (2004).[14] The Court found, *inter alia*, that the DHSSPS had failed to provide adequate guidance to its relevant employees on the law relating to abortion and, consequently, was in breach of the general duty imposed on it by Article 4 of the Health and Personal Social Services (Northern Ireland) Order 1972.[15] In order to fulfil the obligations imposed on it by the 1972 Order, the Court of Appeal strongly indicated that the DHSSPS should consider investigating, amongst other things, the adequacy of abortion services in Northern Ireland, including aftercare services, and, after consultation with appropriate parties and organisations, should consider taking steps to provide guidance on the termination of pregnancy.[16]

Some of the salient points from the Court of Appeal judgments will be highlighted. Campbell LJ found that there was a "strong case" for guidance on the legal principles and that this should be provided to doctors and those who play secondary roles in the termination of pregnancies, as well as to woman who seek such guidance (2004: para. 17). Sheil LJ found that there was uncertainty about the state of the law on abortion

---

[14] As already noted, it was not necessary for the Court of Appeal to make the order of mandamus that was sought at the High Court; see supra at n. 13.

[15] Article 4 imposes a general duty on the DHSSPS to: (a) provide and secure integrated health services in Northern Ireland designed to promote the physical and mental health of the people of Northern Ireland through the prevention, diagnosis and treatment of illness; and (b) to provide and secure the provision of personal social services in Northern Ireland designed to promote the social welfare of the people of Northern Ireland.

It was found that both (a) and (b) covered the provision of lawful abortion services.

[16] The Court of Appeal Order, dated 26 November 2004, asked the DHSSPS to consider what steps it should take to:

> (1) Inquire into the adequacy of termination of pregnancy services provided in Northern Ireland (including aftercare); and
>
> (2) Following such inquiry, and after appropriate consultation with concerned organisations, issuing appropriate guidance (DHSSPS, 2007, News Releases: Department Issues Draft Guidelines on Termination of Pregnancy).

in Northern Ireland, both among medical professionals and the general public, and that this uncertainty could be resolved by the provision of appropriate guidance by the DHSSPS (2004: para. 5). He concluded that the legal principles set out in Kerr J's High Court judgment would be a "good starting point for such guidelines" (2004: para. 12).

Nicholson LJ, noting the legal principles referred to in Kerr J's judgment, concluded that the law was not as clear as it could be and, in particular, that it was not clear to medical professionals and ancillary staff, pregnant women, and even the DHSSPS (2004: paras. 69, 76, 87). This conclusion was based "mainly, but not only" on the fact that the principles "are not expressed in language appropriate to a criminal trial which is what the medical practitioner would be facing" (2004: para. 69). He highlighted various aspects of the legal principles that lacked clarity for the purposes of the criminal law and criminal proceedings, focusing on issues such as the legal and evidential burdens of proof, and the meaning of certain words and phrases, such as "real and serious" and "long-term" (2004: para. 70-5).

It is worth emphasising that Nicholson LJ's judgment was very much in the spirit of clarifying the existing *criminal law* on abortion in Northern Ireland; he was not motivated by a desire to extend the law on abortion or to make it more freely available or accessible to women. In fact, he opined that if guidelines were published, "it would be wrong" to make them available to pregnant women unless they sought them or their doctors considered it necessary to provide them; "[o]therwise, it could regarded as an encouragement [to women] to seek abortion" (2004: para. 84). Further, he asserted that the DHSSPS had a duty to give guidance to women on all of the alternatives open to them when facing a crisis pregnancy, such as the availability of financial support should they decide to proceed with the pregnancy and raise the child, and the option of adoption (2004: para. 86).[17]

There are two issues to be addressed in the aftermath of this case. The first matter is the DHSSPS's effort to issue guidance on the termination of pregnancy. The second issue is the impact that the High Court and Court of Appeal judgments in the fpaNI case will have on the cur-

[17] See also his concluding comments at 2004, para. 117.

rent state of the law and whether guidelines can offer an adequate response to the problem of the uncertainty in the law on abortion in Northern Ireland. These matters will be addressed in the next two sections.

Aftermath of fpaNI Case: DHSSPS Guidance and Assembly Emotion

After the Court of Appeal decision, a working group established by the DHSSPS, which included expert representatives from a range of relevant backgrounds, set to work on the development of guidance on the termination of pregnancy. Draft guidance was published in January 2007. Apart from advising doctors on how to apply the established legal principles, the DHSSPS, in its *Guidance on the Termination of Pregnancy in Northern Ireland* (Draft, January 2007), addresses a number of other matters relating to the provision of abortion services in Northern Ireland, such as, for example, the issues of informed consent, conscientious objection, good clinical practice and service arrangements. The limitations inherent in the guidance given are highlighted in the first paragraph where the DHSSPS makes it clear that the purpose of the guidance is to outline the law relating to abortion in Northern Ireland and to identify good medical practice on this matter. Further, it is stated that the guidelines will not provide prescriptive advice to doctors on when they should or should not perform terminations of pregnancy; it is emphasised that whether an abortion can be performed in any case will depend on the doctor's assessment of the circumstances of that individual case and the application of the legal principles to this (2007: para. 1.1).

The draft guidelines outline the relevant law and set out the key principles that can be distilled from this, as adopted by Kerr J in the fpaNI case (2007: paras. 2.1-2.10). Some guidance is then provided on how individual cases are to be assessed by the clinicians involved (2007: para. 3). For example, assessment of the pregnant woman by two doctors who have previous knowledge of the patient and her medical circumstances is generally recommended, except in situations where the woman's mental health is at issue, in which case assessment by "at least two different doctors is always recommended" (2007: para. 3.1-3.2). In circumstances involving a risk of an adverse effect on a woman's mental health, additional advice is provided (2007: paras. 3.2-3.7). For example, the draft guidance provides a non-exhaustive list of issues that should be considered when assessing a woman's "recent mental state". These matters are: the woman's current mental state; the treatment she is currently receiving; her past mental health history (including any serious suicide attempts); her family mental health history (including a history of suicide); the circumstances of the conception; the familial and non-familial support structures available to her; and her history of previous pregnancies, including any mental health problems that she encountered during pregnancy and postpartum (2007: para. 3.6). The guidelines also state that where the woman has a previous history of "severe and enduring mental illness", a psychiatrist should be involved in the assessment. Further, it is stipulated that while an abortion will probably not be considered in cases where mental illness is the indication, "unless that illness has been pre-existing, severe and enduring", there may be "exceptional situations" where the mental health of a woman, who has no previous mental health history, will need to be assessed by an expert in that area (2007: para. 3.3).[18]

In October 2007, the Northern Ireland Assembly passed a Democratic Unionist Party (DUP) motion opposing the introduction of the draft guidelines. The motion read:

> That this Assembly opposes the introduction of the proposed guidelines on the termination of pregnancy in Northern Ireland; believes that the guidelines are flawed; and calls on the Minister of Health, Social Services and Public Safety to abandon any attempt to make abortion more widely available in Northern Ireland (Hansard Official Reports, vol. 24).

The resistance to the guidelines seems, in part at least, to have stemmed from an evident fear that they would introduce more widespread abortion to Northern Ireland "though the backdoor", something that many members of the Assembly were vehemently opposed to. Many

---

[18] This reference to a "pre-existing" mental illness does not seem to relate to anything that is mentioned in the current legal principles; the DHSSPS appears to have added this is in. The reference to a "severe" and "enduring" mental illness seems to relate to the "real and serious" and "permanent or long-term" requirements that are specified in the law.

of those who spoke took a demonstrable anti-abortion, and indeed Christian, stance. For example, Mrs Iris Robinson (DUP, Chairperson of the Assembly Committee on Health, Social Services and Public Safety), proposing the motion with her colleague Mr Jeffrey Donaldson, stated:

> … I am committed to the sanctity of life, and I am determined to prioritise women's health. That is why I care deeply about abortion. Some people suggest that abortion offers a solution – I simply cannot agree. In truth, abortion does not bring solutions; it brings only pain, heartache, and loss (Hansard Official Reports, vol. 24).

Her party colleague, Mr Easton, stated:

> [a]bortion must be considered only if the life or health of the mother is in critical danger. A moral, and Christian, principle is embedded in the heart of the vast majority of people in Northern Ireland, who consider a child to be a precious gift from God and believe that every child has a right to life from the moment of conception in the womb (Hansard Official Reports, vol. 24).

Mr Pat Ramsey from the Social Democratic Labour Party (SDLP) explained his and his party's position on the matter as follows:

> … as a Christian, the God that I believe in has hopes and a plan for each of us. He loves and values all of us equally, from the moment of conception and right through our lives…. The SDLP position is based on human rights criteria, and the fundamental human right to life clearly takes precedence over all other rights. The SDLP is for the right to live; therefore, it is opposed to any extension of direct termination of pregnancy in Northern Ireland (Hansard Official Reports, vol. 24).

The main objective of many of those who spoke was to assert that any attempt to liberalise the availability of abortion in Northern Ireland would not be tolerated by the Assembly, whether this was through the publication of the DHSSPS's draft guidance or through the extension of the Abortion Act 1967 to that region. A number of Members of the Legislative Assembly (MLAs) expressed adamant opposition to the 1967

Act: it is apparent that they, and their colleagues, were determined to take the opportunity to send a message to Westminster that the Assembly would not countenance any effort to extend that measure to Northern Ireland.[19] This aversion to the 1967 abortion legislation is captured by Mr. Buchanan from the DUP who stated: "…we give thanks to almighty God that, thus far, this Province has been spared from becoming home to such ungodly legislation, which legitimises the murder of the unborn child, on demand" (Hansard Official Reports, vol. 24). This is not the first time in recent years that the Assembly has expressed its opposition to the extension of the 1967 to Northern Ireland,[20] and it seems that, despite repeated assurances to the contrary,[21] the Assembly believes there is a possibility that Westminster will try to liberalise the law on abortion in Northern Ireland, before this becomes an issue for the Assembly to exclusively legislate on.[22]

Unfortunately, it is beyond the scope of this chapter to engage in an in-depth analysis of the October 2007 debate. However, it is worth highlighting that, in relation to the subject of that debate, it appears that many of those who spoke were more interested in expressing their adamant

---

[19] For example, Mr Donaldson, noting that a Liberal Democrat MP was considering proposing an amendment to the Human Tissue and Embryology Bill, which was being debated in Westminster, to extend the 1967 Act to Northern Ireland, stated: "… what better time than now for the Assembly to send a clear signal that it is not in favour of liberalising the law on abortion?" (Hansard Official Report, vol. 24).

[20] The Assembly passed a motion opposing the extension of the Abortion Act 1967 to Northern Ireland in June 2000 (Hansard Official Reports, vol. 5).

[21] Such assurances were noted during the 2007 Assembly debate. For example, the Minister for Health, Social Services and Public Safety, Mr McGimpsey (Ulster Unionist Party, UUP), referred to an assurance that was given by the government in London, prior to the enactment of the Northern Ireland Act 1998, not to amend the law on abortion in Northern Ireland without the consent of the main political parties there. Mr McGimpsey and his party colleague, Mr McCallister, also noted a recent statement made by the Minster of State for Northern Ireland, Paul Goggins MP, to the effect that the Government did not intend to change the law on abortion in Northern Ireland (Hansard Official Report, vol. 24).

[22] It would seem that the Assembly's fear that Westminster will act to extend the 1967 Act to Northern Ireland prior to devolution of justice matters, may not be unwarranted. In July 2008, Labour MP, Ms. Diane Abbott, tabled an amendment to the Human Fertilisation and Embryology Bill, currently being debated in Westminster, to extend the Abortion Act 1967 to Northern Ireland.

opposition to abortion in general, and specifically to the introduction of the 1967 Act to Northern Ireland, than engaging in an informed discussion about the current state of the law and the particulars of the DHSSPS draft guidance. In fact, only a few members expressed any genuine and considered interest in the current law on abortion, including the fact that it is legal in certain circumstances and is an issue that requires urgent clarification. In addition, many of those who spoke gave little consideration to the fact that the draft guidelines resulted from the Court of Appeal's decision in the fpaNI judicial review case and the obligations imposed on the DHSSPS as a result of that case; indeed, only a few MLAs paid any attention to the significance of the origins of the draft guidance. This is not to say that the Assembly was oblivious to the legal situation, but, simply, that a number of those who spoke during this debate chose not to focus on the key legal issues.[23]

The Assembly passed the DUP's motion. The DHSSPS subsequently initiated a formal consultation procedure with the aim of producing more satisfactory guidelines on the termination of pregnancy. The consultation process is currently ongoing.[24]

Impact of fpaNI Case: Restriction and Clarification

The High Court and Court of Appeal judgments in the fpaNI case will have an impact on the state of the law on abortion law in Northern Ireland. First, they serve to emphasise the restrictive nature of the law on

---

[23] For example, a number of MLAs did note that the law required clarification, either by the provision of guidance or the reform of the law; some MLA's also noted that the DHSSPS was not at liberty to ignore the decision of the Court of the Appeal in the fpaNI case and that guidelines were inevitable and necessary. See, for example, comments by Mr McCallister (UUP), Mr Basil McCrea (UUP), Mr Ramsey (SDLP), Mr O'Dowd (Sinn Fein) (Hansard Official Report, vol 24).

[24] See Mr McGimpsey's speech at the end of the October 2007 Assembly debate on the draft *Guidance on the Termination of Pregnancy* (Hansard Official Reports, vol. 24). The DHSSPS issued new guidance for the purpose of consultation in July 2008, (DHSSPS: 2008). At the time of writing, these new draft guidelines were not available for consultation. It is expected that the current consultation process will be completed by October 2008. However, a DHSSPS spokesperson I spoke with in September 2008 was unable to indicate when finalised guidance can be expected. One suspects that due to the difficulties thus far encountered, it may be sometime before definitive guidelines will be published.

abortion in that region. Second, they help to clarify the law in some respects, although the clarification offered is limited. These issues will now be considered.

Restriction

In his High Court judgment in the fpaNI case, Kerr J stated that the grounds for lawful abortion under Northern Irish law approximate to the grounds for abortion that are set out in sections 1(1)(b) and (c) of the Abortion Act 1967 (*In the Matter of an Application by the Family Planning Association of Northern Ireland for Judicial Review*, 2003: para. 41).[25] These subsections provide for abortion on significantly more restrictive grounds than those that are set out in section 1(1)(a) of the 1967 Act, and it has been noted that this comparison to the British legislation could further restrict the law on abortion in Northern Ireland (Capper, 2003: 324; Hewson, 2004: 245). Whether or not the Northern Irish law does approximate to sections 1(1)(b) and (c) of the 1967 Act,[26] it is clear from the principles noted above that the law in Northern Ireland is not as permissive as it is in the rest of the UK. In particular, the grounds on which an abortion may be obtained in Northern Ireland are certainly not as wide as those that are covered by section 1(1)(a) of 1967 legislation. Section 1(1)(a) of the British Act permits an abortion up to the twenty-fourth week of pregnancy where the continuance of the pregnancy would

---

[25] According to section 1(1) of the Abortion Act 1967 (as amended by section 37 of the Human Fertilisation and Embryology Act 1990), an abortion is not unlawful under section 58 of the Offences Against the Person Act 1861, where it is carried out by "a registered medical practitioner if two registered medical practitioners are of the opinion, formed in good faith:

> (a) that the pregnancy has not exceeded its twenty-fourth week and that the continuance of the pregnancy would involve risk, greater than if the pregnancy were terminated, of injury to the physical or mental health of the pregnant woman or any existing children of her family; or
>
> (b) that the termination is necessary to prevent grave permanent injury to the physical or mental health of the pregnant woman; or
>
> (c) that the continuance of the pregnancy would involve risk to the life of the pregnant woman, greater than if the pregnancy were terminated; or
>
> (d) that there is a substantial risk that if the child were born it would suffer from such physical or mental abnormalities as to be seriously handicapped".

[26] See infra at n. 32.

involve a risk, greater than if the pregnancy were terminated, of injury to the woman's physical or mental health (or of injury to the physical or mental health of any existing children of her family). The grounds specified in this section facilitate quite a liberal abortion regime with the vast majority of abortions being carried out under this provision.[27]

In addition, the governing legal principles on abortion in Northern Ireland clearly do not allow for abortion on grounds of foetal abnormality, something which is permitted by section 1(1)(d) of the Abortion Act 1967. This is a point worth emphasising, mainly because it serves to highlight the extent and significance of previous, and possibly existing, uncertainty about the grounds on which abortions are lawful in Northern Ireland. In fact, it appears that in the past there had been a common misconception that foetal abnormality constituted a legitimate ground for an abortion under Northern Irish law, despite the fact that there was no direct judicial authority on this point.[28] Indeed, it seems that until recently many doctors, sharing this view, acted on the erroneous belief that foetal abnormality was the one ground on which they could legally perform a termination.[29]

---

[27] For example, in 2006, 98 per cent of abortions were performed under section 1(1)(a) (Department of Health, 2006: para. 4.2).

[28] For example, prior to the fpaNI judicial review cases in 2003 and 2004, Audrey Simpson from the fpaNI had, in at least two publications, stated that abortion was available in cases involving foetal abnormality (1995: 7; 1998: 99). McGleenan, writing in the early 1990s, noted anecdotal evidence which suggested that abortions were being carried out by doctors in Northern Ireland on grounds of foetal abnormality; he questioned whether, in light of recent jurisprudence, such terminations were actually lawful (1994: 391, 393-4). Lee also notes this issue (1995b: 34).

[29] Francome, in his 1993 study of Northern Irish gynaecologists and their abortion practices, reported that 61 per cent of those surveyed stated that they would carry out a termination where a foetal abnormality had been diagnosed; only eight per cent said that they would not perform an abortion in this situation. The remaining 31 per cent of the group stated that whether they would perform an abortion or not would "depend". It is also worth noting that those surveyed also stated that they would perform abortions on a number of other grounds (e.g. rape), where, in fact, the law would not have permitted this procedure (1994: 392-3). Further evidence that gynaecologists were performing abortions for some foetal abnormalities is found in Nicholson LJ's Court of Appeal judgment in the fpaNI judicial review case. He referred to an anonymous letter that had been sent to the fpaNI in June 1995, in which it was stated that around 25-35 per cent of abortions carried out in Northern Ireland each year were for foetal abnormalities; these terminations were for "major structural abnormalities and genetic disorders" (*The Family Planning Association of Northern Ireland v Minister for Health, Social Services and Public Safety and*

Clarification

The judgments in the fpaNI case clearly identify the governing legal principles and, in doing so, help to clarify the law. Indeed, prior to Kerr J's High Court judgment, the law had not been set out in this manner as a set of accessible legal principles and, presumably, the medical profession had been left to ascertain the law for itself by what could be gleaned from numerous reported and unreported High Court judgments.[30] In light of this, there undoubtedly was much uncertainty about the grounds on which abortions could be carried out, as is evidenced by the foetal abnormality issue mentioned above. The judgments in the fpaNI case, by clearly specifying what the legal principles are, go some way towards ameliorating this problem: it is now plain that abortions are only lawful where the continuance of the pregnancy threatens the woman's life or would adversely affect her health. Consequently, it is evident that abortion for any other reason, such as that of foetal abnormality, is not permitted.

The clarification of the law offered by the judgments in the fpaNI case will be further enhanced when the expected DHSSPS guidelines are published: the governing principles will be more accessible and any advice provided will render certain aspects of the law more understandable and easier to apply by medical professionals who work in this area, at least in some cases. However, it is submitted that, due to the fact that the guidance given must adhere to and reflect the existing law, the clarification promised by the DHSSPS guidelines will be limited. This is because, despite clarification on certain issues, the law on abortion still remains imprecise and ambiguous; it has yet to be adequately defined or explained by the courts.

Ors, 2004: para. 79). In addition, Nicholson LJ noted a letter sent by the Director of Foetal Medicine at the Royal Jubilee Maternity Service at the Royal Maternity Hospital, Belfast, to the DHSSPS seeking clarification of the law on this issue. It was noted in this letter that abortions were carried out at some, but not all, hospitals throughout Northern Ireland in cases involving "lethal abnormalities or abnormalities where there would be a major physical or mental problem for the foetus prior to the stage of viability"; "increasing unease" among medical staff about the legality of this practice was noted (para. 80).

[30] Sheil J criticised this, noting that doctors should not be in a situation where they have to read the case-law on this issue themselves (*The Family Planning Association of Northern Ireland v The Minister for Health, Social Services and Public Safety*, 2004: para. 10).

Indeed, the only jurisprudence available on abortion comes from the 1990s High Court cases referred to above, from which the governing legal principles have been distilled, and the High Court and Court of Appeal judgments in the fpaNI case. However, little explanation of the law is provided in any of these cases. Kerr J did give some indication of his views on the meaning of the Northern Irish legal principles when he agreed with the suggestion that they approximated to sections 1(1)(b) and (c) of the British Abortion Act 1967 (*In the Matter of an Application by the Family Planning Association of Northern Ireland for Judicial Review*, 2003: para. 41).[31] However, apart from this questionable comparison to the British legislation,[32] none of the High Court and Court of Appeal judgments in the fpaNI case, elaborated on the meaning of the legal principles or engaged in an adequate investigation of the matter. In his Court of Appeal judgment, Nicholson LJ emphasised this problem of definition and meaning, but did not attempt to offer an explanation of the law and seems to have assumed that this issue could be resolved by appropriate guidelines (*The Family Planning Association of Northern Ireland v Minister for Health, Social Services and Public Safety and Ors*, 2004: para. 70-5, 87).

It is submitted, however, that due to the fact that it is still unclear what is meant by certain words and phrases that are used in the principles, it is not convincing that guidelines can provide a satisfactory explanation of the current state of the law. For example, it is still not clear what exactly is meant by a "real and serious" and a "long-term or per-

[31] In the Court of Appeal, Nicholson LJ agreed with Kerr J on this point (*The Family Planning Association of Northern Ireland v Minister for Health, Social Services and Public Safety and Ors*, 2004: para. 104). The purpose of this comparison was to determine whether Northern Irish women who travelled to England for an abortion would have been able to avail of abortion services at home.

[32] It may be possible to argue a distinction between a real and serious and long-term/permanent adverse effect on health and section 1(1)(b)'s requirement of a "grave permanent injury" to health. For example, in the Court of Appeal, Campbell LJ remarked on a possible distinction between "long-term" and "permanent" (*The Family Planning Association of Northern Ireland v Minister for Health, Social Services and Public Safety and Ors*, 2004: para. 24). In addition, section 1(1)(b) requires that an abortion is *necessary* to prevent grave permanent injury to the woman's health. Surely this implies a higher threshold of risk than that which is stipulated in the Northern Irish principles, which require probability in relation to the degree of risk involved.

manent" "adverse effect" on a woman's health. What does "real" mean? Does it mean that the threat in question must not be fictitious? Or, does it require something more than that, for example, that the threat is widely recognised as a legitimate medical condition by the medical profession? What does serious mean? Does it simply require that the adverse effect be more than trivial, that it must be significant? Or does it require that the adverse effect be dangerous or severe?[33] How can long term be measured? Is it to be quantified in months or years, or by some other measure? What is an adverse effect on a woman's health? Is it, for example, an identifiable and well-recognised medical condition, something which has a specific diagnostic status, or will something less than this suffice? The words and phrases that have been employed by the courts are ambiguous in meaning and have not been satisfactorily defined; a thorough explanation of the law has yet to be provided. It is doubtful that the DHSSPS can provide adequate guidance when the precise meaning of the legal principles is so unclear. Indeed, it is questionable whether a government department should be left with this responsibility at all.

In summary, while it is now clear what the governing legal principles on abortion are, it is difficult to discern what precisely they mean. DHSSPS guidelines can outline the legal principles and make them available to the medical profession and other interested parties. They can also draw attention to the restrictive nature of the law, emphasising the limited grounds on which doctors may lawfully perform terminations of pregnancy, and highlighting specific grounds on which abortions cannot lawfully be performed, such as, for example, that of foetal abnormality. Such guidelines can also give some assistance to doctors on how to apply the law and, importantly, can give doctors who, in good faith, get the law wrong and perform unlawful abortions some measure of protection against criminal conviction.[34] However, it is not convincing that guide-

---

[33] Kerr J opined that the language used in previous judgments suggested that the effect of the continuance of the pregnancy on the woman would have to be grave (*In the Matter of an Application by the Family Planning Association of Northern Ireland for Judicial Review*, 2003: para. 41).

[34] Sheil LJ noted in his Court of Appeal judgment in the fpaNI case that that DHSSPS guidelines would help eliminate the medical profession's fear of prosecution as it could rely on such guidelines as evidence for a defence of good faith (*The Family Planning*

lines can provide a wholly satisfactory solution to the inherent ambiguities that exist in the law. Due to the fact that the available jurisprudence is meagre, the DHSSPS guidance can offer only partial illumination of the legal principles that stem from the case law. In addition, it is debatable whether guidance given by the DHSSPS can or should tackle the precise meaning of vague words and phrases such as those that are included in the current legal principles. It is suggested that the task of illuminating and clarifying the law is not a job for a government department, but is something for judges or, preferably, the legislature to address.[35]

Conclusion: "Legislate We Must"[36]

The Northern Ireland Court of Appeal has accepted that the criminal law on abortion is uncertain. This is a situation that should not be tolerated, particularly when, in theory at least,[37] medical practitioners face criminal proceedings for performing terminations which fall outside what is permitted by the law. It is imperative, therefore, that the DHSSPS completes its task and finalises appropriate guidance on the termination of pregnancy for the benefit not only of those medical professionals who face difficult clinical decisions, but also those women who seek to terminate their pregnancies in Northern Ireland.

In light of the fpaNI case, the law is now somewhat clearer: for example, we now know what the legal principles are; and, although there may still be much doubt as to when precisely abortions are lawful, there has been some clarification as to when they are not lawful, at least in

---

Association of Northern Ireland v The Minister for Health, Social Services and Public Safety, 2004: para. 9).

[35] Kerr J in his High Court judgment in the fpaNI case made similar comments. He noted that the law could only be clarified by "bringing greater definition to the circumstances in which abortion will be deemed legal". He added that this could only be achieved though reform of the current law (*In the Matter of an Application by the Family Planning Association of Northern Ireland for Judicial Review*, 2003: para. 13).

[36] Taken from Mr O'Dowd's (SF) speech in the October 2007 Assembly debate on the DHSSPS draft *Guidance on the Termination of Pregnancy* (Hansard Official Reports, vol. 24).

[37] Nicholson LJ, in his CA judgment in the fpaNI case, draws attention to the fact that medical professionals have not, in recent times, been prosecuted for this offence (*The Family Planning Association of Northern Ireland v Minister for Health, Social Services and Public Safety and Ors*, 2004: para. 92).

relation to foetal abnormality. The expected DHSSPS guidelines will reinforce this; they will also, to some extent, help to elucidate the law for relevant parties and, in particular, the medical profession. Essentially, department guidelines will ensure that, for the first time, the law will be set out in a readily accessible and coherent way; they will give doctors an indication of the types of issues that should be addressed when applying the law; they will go some way towards assuring doctors that they can protect themselves against criminal prosecution; and they will address other pertinent issues, such as that of conscientious objection.

However, it has been argued that it is unlikely that DHSSPS guidelines can cure the law of all its uncertainty. Thus, while DHSSPS guidelines based on the existing jurisprudence can specify what the legal principles are, it is questionable how much they can do to assist in determining what these principles mean. It is contended that the law is so vague that department guidelines, while helpful, will only go so far to ameliorate the difficulties that exist with the current law on abortion and can be no substitute for legislative reform.

In conclusion, it is suggested that the legislature must act. As criminal justice matters have not yet been devolved, the Assembly currently does not have the authority to legislate on abortion without the consent and approval of the Secretary of State for Northern Ireland. Consequently, abortion remains a matter for MPs at Westminster. It is conceivable that Westminster could extend its abortion law to Northern Ireland; indeed, the recent amendment tabled to the Human Fertilisation and Embryology Bill to extend the 1967 provisions to Northern Ireland indicates there is a will amongst some MPs to act on this issue.[38] Whether this amendment succeeds is another matter. It is worth recalling that on more than one occasion a guarantee has been given to the effect that Westminster will not extend the Abortion Act 1967 to Northern Ireland.[39] This, in conjunction with the Assembly's twice-declared objection to such a move, indicates that it may be too politically contentious for Westminster to pass this amendment.

---

[38] See supra at n. 22. The debate on this amendment is expected to take place in October 2008.

[39] See supra at n. 21.

If Westminster does not take this opportunity to extend the Abortion Act 1967 to Northern Ireland, the task of legislating on abortion will, with the expected devolution of justice matters, fall to the Assembly. What the Assembly is likely to do in such circumstances is beyond the scope of this paper. However, there are two points worth noting. First, in light of the tenor and outcome of previous assembly debates on abortion, it is highly probable that if Northern Irish politicians legislate on this issue, it will be with the objective of ensuring that abortion is only available in very restricted circumstances. Second, it would appear from the 2000 and 2007 Assembly debates on this topic, (Hansard Official Reports, vol. 5, 24), that many MLAs are unwilling to take a reasoned approach to the abortion question. This is a cause for concern. If the delicate and complicated issue of abortion is to be tackled by a legislatively empowered Assembly, the matter must be given mature and careful consideration; the Assembly must resist the emotional stance that it, hitherto, seems to have taken. In essence, if the Assembly legislates, it is crucial that it takes a more constructive approach to the issue of abortion in order to ensure that it does not create even greater problems than those already existing in the current law.

Bibliography

Articles

Capper, D. (2003). "The Condition of Abortion Law in Northern Ireland." NILQ 54: 320.

Fletcher, R. (2005). "Abortion Needs or Abortion Rights? Claiming State Accountability for Women's Reproductive Welfare." *Feminist Legal Studies*. 13: 123.

Francome, C. (1994). "Gynaecologists and Abortion Practice in Northern Ireland."*J. Biosco. Sci.* 26: 389

Hewson, B. (2004). "The Law of Abortion in Northern Ireland." PL: 234

Lee, S. (1995a). "Abortion Law in Northern Ireland: the Twilight Zone." In *The Abortion Law in Northern Ireland: Human Rights and Reproductive Choice*, ed. A. Furedi, 16-26. Family Planning Association of Northern Ireland.

Lee, S. (1995b) "An A to K to Z of Abortion Law in Northern Ireland: Abortion on Remand." In *The Abortion Law in Northern Ireland: Human Rights and Re-*

productive Choice, ed. A. Furedi, 27-45. Family Planning Association of Northern Ireland.

McGleenan, T. (1994). "*Bourne* Again? Abortion Law in Northern Ireland after *Re K* and *Re A*." NILQ 45: 389.

Simpson, A. (1995). "Abortion in Northern Ireland: A Victorian Law." In *The Abortion Law in Northern Ireland: Human Rights and Reproductive Choice*, ed. A. Furedi, 6-15. Family Planning Association Northern Ireland.

Simpson, A. (1998). "Abortion in Northern Ireland: A Problem Exported." In *Abortion Law and Politics Today*, ed. Ellie Lee, 99-109. Palgrave: Hampshire and New York.

Cases

In the Matter of an Application by the Family Planning Association of Northern Ireland for Judicial Review [2003] NIQB 48

In the Matter of CH, A Minor, Down Lisburn Health and Social Services Trust v The Official Solicitor as Guardian Ad Litem of CH and LAH, unreported 18 October 1995, High Court (Family Division), Sheil J (In *Re CH*).

In the matter of SJB (a minor) Western Health and Social Services Board v CMB & Ors., unreported 28 September 1995, High Court (Family Division), Pringle J (In *Re SJB*)

Northern Health and Social Services Board v AMNH and Ors, unreported 21 January 1994, High Court (Family Division), MacDermott LJ (In *Re AMNH*).

Northern Health and Social Services Board v. F & G [1993] NI 268. (In *Re K*).

R (The King) v Bourne [1939] 1 K.B. 687.

R v Newton and Stungo [1958] Crim LR 469.

Royal College of Nursing v DHSS [1981] 1 All ER 545.

The Family Planning Association of Northern Ireland v The Minister for Health, Social Services and Public Safety [2004] NICA 37 (Sheil LJ), 38 (Campbell LJ), 39 (Nicholson LJ); *Family Planning Association of Northern Ireland v Minister for Health, Social Services and Public Safety (SPUC NI and others intervening)* [2005] NI 188.

Assembly Debates

Hansard Official Report, 22 October 2007, vol. 24, available at: http://www.niassembly.gov.uk/record/reports2007/071022.htm#7

Hansard Official Report, 20 June 2000, vol. 5, available at: http://www.niassembly.gov.uk/record/reports/000620.htm

Internet Sources

Department of Health, *Abortion Statistics, England and Wales: 2006* (Bulletin 2007/01, London, 2007), available at: http://www.dh.gov.uk/en/publicationsandstatistics/publications/publicationsstatistics/dh_075697

Department of Health, Social Services and Public Safety, *Guidance on the Termination of Pregnancy in Northern Ireland* (Draft, January 2007), available at: http://archive.nics.gov.uk/hss/guidance.pdf

http://www.dhsspsni.gov.uk/guidance-termination-of-pregnancy-ni-draft-jan07.pdf

Department of Health, Social Services and Public Safety, *News Releases: Department Issues Draft Guidelines on Termination of Pregnancy* (16 January 2007), available at: http://archive.nics.gov.uk/hss/070116h-hss.htm

Family Planning Association of Northern Ireland, Factsheet on Abortion in Northern Ireland (January 2007) available at: http://www.fpa.org.uk/attachments/published/89/PDF%20NI%20Abortion%20January%202007.pdf

11

THE STATUTE LAW ON ABORTION IN IRELAND

Dr Peter Morriss

It is well known that, in the early years of the Irish state, legislation was passed to bring the law more into line with Catholic teaching on a wide range of moral issues.[1] Yet there was no legislation passed to change the law on abortion: the statute law on abortion remains to this day sections 58 and 59 of the Offences Against the Person Act 1861 (24 & 25 Vic. c. 100).[2] That there was no such legislation is puzzling. I cannot solve the

---

[1] The best discussion is Whyte (1980) particularly chapter II. See also Keogh (1986), particularly chapters VI and VII.

[2] The provisions state:

Section 58 Administering drugs or using instruments to procure abortion:

Every woman, being with child, who, with intent to procure her own miscarriage, shall unlawfully administer to herself any poison or other noxious thing, or shall unlawfully use any instrument or other means whatsoever with the like intent, and whosoever, with intent to procure the miscarriage of any woman, whether she be or be not with child, shall unlawfully administer to her or cause to be taken by her any poison or other noxious thing, or shall unlawfully use any instrument or other means whatsoever with the like intent, shall be guilty of felony, and being convicted thereof shall be liable ... to be kept in penal servitude for life ... .

Section 59 Procuring drugs, etc, to cause abortion:

Whosoever shall unlawfully supply or procure any poison or other noxious thing, or any instrument or thing whatsoever, knowing that the same is intended to be unlawfully used or employed with intent to procure the miscarriage of any woman, whether she be or be not with child, shall be guilty of a misdemeanour, and being convicted thereof shall be liable ... to be kept in penal servitude.

puzzle here: I do not yet know why there was no legislation on abortion. But what I aim to do in this article is to refute one possible, and easy, answer: the answer that there is no puzzle as there was no need to legislate since, under the 1861 Act, the law was already in accord with Catholic teaching. That this easy answer is quite widely held can be seen from a throw-away aside on abortion in a recent report by no less a body than the Oireachtas Committee on the Constitution. It writes:

> From the foundation of the state to the enactment of the 1937 Constitution a broad consensus existed regarding the values which should inform law and policies. This led to a close similarity, though not identity, between the laws of the Catholic Church and the state. Until the latter part of the twentieth century, the areas of marriage, homosexuality, contraception and *abortion* were ones in which *the laws of the state supported the teaching of the Catholic Church*… (All-Party Oireachtas Committee on the Constitution, 2006: 37) [my emphasis].

I aim to show that this reading is wrong.

I will do this by concentrating on two questions, on both of which Catholic teaching is sufficiently well-known as not to require any elucidation here. The first is the question of when, in foetal development, does the 1861 Act apply? Specifically, is it illegal to abort a foetus from the moment of conception or fertilisation? The second is to whom does the 1861 Act apply? Specifically, does it apply to doctors performing therapeutic abortions to protect the life or health of the mother? If Catholic teaching were to apply, then the answers to both questions would be "Yes". In fact, the answer is, in each case, "No".

I should say at the start that the support of these answers requires a good deal of detective work. The 1861 Act does not explicitly refer to either point. Further, there is no Irish case law to help us answer these questions, nor was there any relevant English case law before Irish independence. We therefore need to look, in the main, at sources outside those to which lawyers usually refer.

As a preliminary, I will say just a few words about the genesis of the Offences Against the Person Act 1861. As the name implies, it is a Consolidation Act, bringing together a vast range of diverse legislation. The first statute law on abortion is contained in Lord Ellenborough's Act of 1803 (43 Geo. III c. 58). This was repealed in 1828 and 1829, in an early attempt at consolidating parts of the law, usually known as Lord Lansdowne's Act.[3] The next attempt was in 1837;[4] the final wording that has come down to us was passed in 1861. In each case some changes were made in the law,[5] although the general form that the law took remained remarkably constant after 1803.

Because the last three Acts were all aimed at consolidating existing law, there was very little public debate about them: they were mainly tidying-up measures. Unfortunately, there was also little debate about Lord Ellenborough's Act: it remains a mystery why he chose to include the offence of abortion in what was an Act mainly concerned with something quite different.[6] In particular, there was little popular pressure for the introduction of a law on abortion.

So one obvious source of enlightenment on what the law was about – contemporary debates – is of virtually no help to us. We need to look elsewhere. I will now look at my two questions in turn.

1. Does the Act cover the foetus from the moment of conception?

Fortunately, this question has been recently answered for us, in the English case of *R (on the application of Smeaton) v Secretary of State for Health* (2002), which – surprisingly – has received almost no attention in Ireland,[7] although it is a very important case.

---

[3] Offences Against the Person Act 1828 (9 Geo. IV c. 31) section 13 and Offences Against the Person Act 1829 (10 Geo. IV c. 34) section 16, which extended the same law to Ireland.

[4] Offences Against the Person Act 1837 (7 Will. IV & 1 Vict. c. 85) section 6.

[5] I trace these changes in Morriss (unpublished) which is available on request.

[6] The Act was focused on cutting and maiming, but one should not infer any connection between abortion and maiming – the Act is a rag-bag of items on which Lord Ellenborough thought it wise to legislate, including, for instance, setting fire to a house with intent to injure or defraud. In a future article, I hope to shed some light on his decision (fairly late in the day) to include abortion in his Act.

[7] The case was not reported in either *The Irish Times* or *Irish Independent*. It is referred to (without much discussion) in *MR v TR* (2006); the only Irish law review article to

The case concerned the "morning-after pill" Levonelle. Under a statutory order, from January 2001 Levonelle was available for sale by pharmacists in England and Wales without the need for a doctor's prescription. John Smeaton, who was the National Director of the Society for the Protection of Unborn Children, brought an action to declare this statutory order *ultra vires*, as such a sale would be in breach of sections 58 and/or 59 of the Offences Against the Person Act 1861.

Perhaps I should explain at this point that, of course, since 1967 abortion has been legalised in England and Wales. However, this was not done by repealing sections 58 and 59 of the Offences Against the Person Act. Instead, a new law was passed that said that, notwithstanding the Offences Against the Person Act, it would not be an offence if a pregnancy is terminated by a registered medical practitioner who followed an approved procedure.[8] There is no doubt that a pharmacist selling a product without a prescription would not fall under the exemption provided to medical practitioners by the Abortion Act. Since the "morning-after pill" works, it seems, by preventing an already fertilised ovum from implanting, the court had to decide whether preventing such an implantation was indeed illegal under the 1861 Act.

Smeaton's case had two prongs. The first was a matter of legislative interpretation: he argued that the 1861 Act should be interpreted according to the meaning of its terms as understood in 1861. In particular, it was argued that the term "miscarriage" should be construed as it would have been when the Act was passed. The second prong was the claim that in 1861 the legislature would have understood by "miscarriage" any interference with a pregnancy from the moment of conception. Therefore, Smeaton argued, selling the morning after pill without prescription would be illegal under the Offences Against the Person Act 1861.

The Court rejected both arguments. It ruled that an Act such as the Offences Against the Person Act 1861 was "always speaking",[9] and

---

mention *Smeaton* is Power and Shannon (2007), which discusses *MR v TR*. *Smeaton* is also mentioned, in passing, in Casey (2005: 41-2).

[8] Abortion Act 1967 (as amended).

[9] The phrase is that of Sir H. Thring (1878: 32). (The court referred to the identical page 83 of a later, 1902, edition – by the now-ennobled Lord Thring.) It might be worth noting that this brief passage is in a guide to the *drafting* of legislation, not its interpretation.

therefore the Court had to interpret "miscarriage" in its modern sense. It then declared that the modern sense of "miscarriage" did not apply to a pre-implantation embryo: a woman can only miscarry after implantation has taken place. The Court therefore rejected Smeaton's claim.

I am not aware of any Irish jurisprudence on the first of these issues: that of whether Acts of Parliament should carry their original meaning or are always speaking. But, in any case, the Court considered at length Smeaton's second argument, on the (counterfactual) assumption that his first argument had succeeded. And the Court firmly rejected it: it concluded that there was no doubt that, in 1861, the legislators did not think that they were protecting the foetus from the moment of conception.

The Court's argument is very clear, but lengthy: it consists of a mass of detail, rather than a few brief points. I will, therefore, not attempt to summarise it here; but I do recommend it strongly as providing an interesting and compelling argument.

Instead, I will here sketch two points that the Court did *not* mention at all: points which seem to me to make the case for rejecting Smeaton's second argument even stronger.

1A. Lessons from the History of Embryology

The first takes us into the history of embryology.[10] From this we can learn that it is anachronistic to ask what legislators in 1861 might have thought about "the moment of fertilisation"; it is anachronistic since the dominant view of fertilisation in the nineteenth century was very different from ours. If we want to think ourselves back into the minds of nineteenth century legislators, we have to try to understand how they saw the world – and we will find that that understanding is very different from what we now take for granted. So how would they have thought?

They knew, of course, that sexual intercourse was necessary for conception; but it was not at all settled *how* it was necessary. In the nineteenth century (and, indeed, for as far back as we can trace) there were

[10] The most accessible and recent source on this is Pinto-Correia (1997). Earlier works include Cole (1930) particularly ch. 7; Meyer (1939); Gasking (1967), chs. 1, 9-14; Roe (1981); and Farley (1982). Laurence Sterne's *Tristram Shandy* (1759) is a literary extravaganza in which – amongst many other things – Sterne plays with (and takes for granted) these ideas.

three theories of conception. One theory is known as *epigenesis*. This is the view that at conception a new being was created by an amalgamation of male and female gametes. A version of this view is the one that we are familiar with. But, until late in the nineteenth century, few serious scientists believed in epigenesis.

The alternative theories were two different forms of *preformationism*. Preformationism is the view that the new baby is already present, preformed, and just needs a suitable stimulus to start growing. The two versions of preformationism were *spermism* and *ovism*. Spermism held that the baby existed in semen, but – like a seed requiring fertile ground in order to grow – it would only develop in a suitably nourishing environment, which was provided by the mother's womb. Ovism held that the baby originated in the mother; but it required male ejaculate to get it to start developing – just like a seed requires the nourishment of warm spring rain. Throughout the seventeenth and eighteenth centuries, scientists' new discoveries favoured first one and then the other version of preformationism. But epigenesis received much less support until, in 1875, Oscar Hertwig found two nuclei (one male and one female) in the embryo of a sea urchin. But that could not have been anticipated in 1861.

Scientists, then, did not agree on how conception occurred, but they favoured some form of preformationism. Indeed, by the beginning of the nineteenth century scientists had largely given up on the search for the mystery of conception, and had (with what seems like a heavy dose of sour grapes) decided that it was not an important question. Thus, in a well-received medical text at the end of the eighteenth century, the section on conception starts:

> … the first part of the process by which primordial existence is established … is probably involved in too much obscurity to be discovered by the human faculties (Denman, 1794: 199-200).

and ends:

> If we were able to discover the essential properties of the male *semen*, the precise share which the male and female contribute towards the formation of the *embryo*, and the part where the effect is produced, the advantages which would thence accrue in practice do not appear.... But it is happy for us that those things

> which are beyond the comprehension, or which elude the observation of men of plain understandings, are of the least importance in practice: Providence having ordained, that the honest and industrious application of common capacities, should be equal to the exigencies of life, and the duties we owe to society (Denman, 1794:. 207).

Much the same view was taken some fifty years later, in a well-known and comprehensive multi-volume medical encyclopaedia:

> The truth is, "the *how*" of the fecundation is as far from our knowledge today as it was thousands of years ago; this process is still enveloped in what we feel inclined to consider "its sacred mystery". It would be different if we could prove that the spermatozoa really yielded the material foundation for the body of the embryo; that they penetrated the ovum, and were developed into the animal …, or else, that they become metamorphosed into the central parts of the nervous system.
>
> However, we are now convinced that all these assumptions are without any foundation. The import of the spermatozoa must be a very different one. But this is the very point of which we know nothing with any certainty[11] (Wagner and Leuckart, 1847-9: 507).

So what should be clear by now is that the legislators would have had a very different understanding of the process of conception from ours; in so far as they did hold to a theory, it would certainly have been one of the versions of preformationism. But note that the ontological significance of preformationism is very different from that of our view: *we* believe that a completely new person comes into being at the "moment" of conception; the preformationist believed that *an already existing* being started to develop. For the preformationist, conception does not provide the sharp creation of a new person, such as we all now take for granted.

Since the legislators who passed the nineteenth century laws on abortion would have been preformationists (if they were anything at all),

---

[11] See also Thomson (1836-9) and Thomson (1859), particularly pages 137-8. Thomson professed himself similarly mystified as to the process, although he was fairly sure of the truth of ovism.

conception would not have had the deep significance for them that it has for us. It is therefore unsurprising if they showed little interest in conception. So it would be wrong to infer from their silence on the matter that they had any intention for the law to apply as early as conception.

1B. Lessons from Other Areas of the Law

We can also get some insight into nineteenth-century legislators' thinking by enquiring into related areas of the law. Let us look at the legislative response to the killing of a foetus at other stages of its development. At the beginning, there is fertilisation and implantation, and the law at this point is (at best) unclear. But clearly at *some* point in foetal development the abortion laws start applying, making the killing of the foetus an offence.[12] Later, when the child is born, it is considered a full person, and killing it would be murder.[13] But what is surprising is that there was a gap between the offences of abortion and murder: for when the child was *in the process of being born* it was, throughout the nineteenth century, not an offence of any kind to kill it. Thus one would not be committing any criminal offence if one waited for the baby's head to emerge, and then brutally chopped it off – so long, that is, as one was careful to behead the child before it had fully separated from its mother. And this gap in the law's protection of the foetus was not something that was discovered one day by some bright barrister, to be immediately followed by Parliament rushing through emergency legislation to reverse this mistake. This lacuna was well-known throughout the nineteenth century: if one looks at any edition of *Russell on Crimes*, from the first edition in 1819 to the eighth in 1923, one will find the lacuna described in gory detail, citing cases such as *R v Sellis* (1837), the facts of which were much as I have described above.[14] And Parliament – well aware of this

---

[12] In fact, as we shall see, this statement is inaccurate; but it will do for now.

[13] At least, that was the situation in the nineteenth century. The introduction of the different crime of infanticide has complicated the story, but not in a way relevant here.

[14] All editions include the lacuna: the references are as follows. *Russell on Crimes* (1819) Vol. I, pp. 617-9; *Russell on Crimes* (1826) Vol. I, pp. 424-5; *Russell on Crimes* (1843) Vol. I, pp. 485-7; *Russell on Crimes* (1865) Vol. I, pp. 670-4; *Russell on Crimes* (1877) Vol. I, pp. 646-7; *Russell on Crimes* (1896) Vol. III, pp. 7-8; *Russell on Crimes* (1910) Vol. I, pp. 664-5; *Russell on Crimes* (1923) Vol. I, pp. 622-3. In the first two editions, the lacuna is implied rather than specifically mentioned; the appropriate wording seems to

lacuna – did nothing at all about it, until eventually, in 1929, it passed the Infant Life (Preservation) Act, which closed the gap by making it an offence to kill a foetus capable of being born alive.[15]

Admittedly the British parliament was a rather lazy body, and it often failed to pass legislation that it might have thought should be passed. But – surely – at some point during this hundred-year period it would have managed to summon up the energy to remove the lacuna should it have wanted to. Remember that in the 33 years from 1828 to 1861 it managed to amend the existing abortion legislation three times, and throughout this period high-powered Commissions were producing extraordinarily thorough reports aimed at reforming the criminal law. This was not a period of legislative inactivity. So we are forced to the conclusion that, when Parliament passed the 1861 Act governing abortion (and for at least fifty years before and over fifty years after), it was perfectly content that it was no offence to kill a baby that was in the process of being born.

I want to argue that the existence and acceptance of this lacuna sheds a powerful light on the intentions of those who were passing legislation on abortion. It seems to refute entirely any idea that the purpose of the legislation was to protect the life of the foetus. Most modern commentators assume that that must have been at least *one* purpose – even those who claim that it was not the sole or even the main purpose. Thus Munby J, delivering judgment in *Smeaton*, said that it is "common ground" that "one of the purposes of the 1861 Act is to protect the life of the unborn" (2002: para. 55)[16]. But that just beggars belief. It is impossible to believe that a Parliament that happily refrained from protecting the life of a baby being born would nevertheless legislate several times to protect the life of the baby at an earlier stage of development – much less protect it at the two or four cell stage. Parliament certainly did legislate;

---

have been established by the third edition (1843); after that it is expressed in almost identical terms. It might be worth mentioning that S.C. Greaves, the author of the third edition of *Russell on Crimes*, was also the draftsman most actively involved in the 1861 Act (see Greaves, 1861, Preface).

[15] This Act has, of course, no force in Ireland; indeed, the lacuna has never been removed in Ireland. So the Oireachtas's often criticised unwillingness to legislate in this area has the consequence that in Ireland it is *still* not a criminal offence to kill a baby which is in the process of being born.

[16] See also Smeaton (2002: para. 354).

but the purpose behind this legislation could not possibly have been a concern for the life of the foetus.[17]

When we realize this, we can start understanding why the legislation is worded as it is. We need, I think, to read the exact wording carefully (something some commentators seem not to have done). The form that the legislation took in 1803 (followed in all subsequent versions) did not, in fact, make performing an abortion itself a crime. Instead, the crime is doing various things "with *intent* to procure the miscarriage of [a] woman" [my emphasis]. Thus the abortion (miscarriage) element appears only as part of the *mens rea*, and not in the *actus reus*. It follows from this, and was recognized quite early on, that the offence applies just as much when the woman is, as a matter of fact, not pregnant, as when she is: her pregnancy is irrelevant.[18] This element *did* cause some controversy,[19] but it was retained throughout all the versions of the abortion legislation.[20] So someone who does the *actus reus*, with the intent to perform an abortion on a woman who, as a matter of fact, is *not* pregnant, is just as guilty as (s)he would have been if the woman *was* pregnant: pregnancy is just irrelevant. Perhaps I should spell this out a bit further: it is not the case that someone who attempts to perform an abortion on a non-pregnant woman is guilty of the crime of attempted abortion; they are guilty of the full offence usually, but – as we now see – wrongly, called the offence of abortion.[21] On the other hand, it has been claimed in an

---

[17] That, of course, leaves open the question of what *was* the purpose behind the legislation. That is actually a very difficult question to answer; I hope to give a tentative stab at dealing with it in future work. But I can say at this point, both that there is no simple rationale for the legislation, and that protecting the life of the foetus was not a significant rationale.

[18] This was decided in *R. v Phillips* (1811), reversed in *R v Scudder* (1828), and reasserted in *R v Goodhall* [*Goodchild*] (1846), before being explicitly stated in the 1861 Act.

[19] See Morriss (unpublished: pages 9-11) for a more extensive consideration of this issue. Available on request.

[20] The 1861 Act inserted a new clause – which had not been present in the earlier laws – that applied to the woman herself. This new clause required that the woman be pregnant. Maybe because it was placed at the start of section 58, it has served to hide from view the fact that the *main* clause (that applying to people other than the woman) explicitly covers nonpregnant women just as much as pregnant ones.

[21] This consideration seems to be completely overlooked by Annabelle James, in her commentary on *Smeaton*; she claimed that Smeaton's case was bound to fail at the first hurdle, because many people who take the morning-after pill are not, in fact, pregnant,

authoritative source that attempting to abort a foetus that was already dead *was* a crime.[22]

So we see that the nineteenth-century legislation certainly makes it a criminal offence to "perform an abortion" (in scare quotes) on a non-pregnant woman, and also (probably) when the foetus is already dead;

---

and therefore, even if Smeaton won his case, "it would be impossible to tell whether or not a criminal offence had been committed" (James, 2002: 471). That *would* be true for a prosecution of the *woman*, but Smeaton was not interested in that aspect: he was arguing that the *pharmacist*, who sold the pill, would be committing a criminal offence. On that point, any doubts about the woman's pregnancy is *explicitly* excluded by the legislation.

Ironically, though, there *is* a reason why Smeaton's case might be thought not to even get to the starting gate – a reason which is not referred to at all in the judgement. This is that Levonelle is not a "poison or noxious thing" as specified in the Act. (It is not an "instrument or other means", as that applies only to mechanical means of performing abortions.) Indeed, the judge took pains to emphasize how *safe* Levonelle is (*Smeaton* secs. 62-3). The words "poison" and "noxious" in the Act are not redundant. This was established as early as 1862, in one of the first cases on the 1861 Act, *R v Isaacs*. The headnote here states that "it is necessary to prove that the thing supplied is noxious. The supplying an innoxious drug, whatever may be the intent of the person supplying it, is not an offence …". Earlier cases, *R v Phillips* (1811) and *R v Coe* (1834), found the opposite, but they were decided on earlier legislation, which referred at this point, more generally, to "any medicine"; the "poison or other noxious thing" wording was introduced in 1837 and retained in 1861. The issue of whether "poison or noxious thing" would include an abortifacient that does not harm the mother seems never to have come before the courts. It is true that in *R. v Marlow* (1964), Brabin J said "[i]f the substance … is an abortifacient, it cannot be suggested, nor is it, that it is anything but a noxious thing" (1964: 54); and in *R v Hollis and Blakeman* (1873), Bramwell B said "[a] noxious thing within the statute means a thing that will produce the effect mentioned in the statute – that is, a miscarriage" (1873: 467), but both are obiter (and Bramwell's remark is clearly wrong, unless it is read as saying that producing a miscarriage is a sufficient but not a necessary condition for being noxious). Until the development of the morning-after pill, *all* oral abortifacients were poisons and noxious to both mother and baby: they worked by harming both, in the hope, presumably, that the mother but not the baby would survive such harm (see, for instance, *Taylor's Medical Jurisprudence*, 1920, Vol. II: 158). Thus I consider that it could certainly have been argued that Levonelle was neither a poison nor noxious, and that therefore administering it could not possibly be an offence under the 1861 Act.

[22] "It cannot be doubted that the expulsion of a dead child would come under the popular signification of a *miscarriage*; and if the words were strictly interpreted, a prisoner might be convicted whether the child were living or dead …" (*Taylor's Medical Jurisprudence*, 1894, Vol. II: 210). This suggestion is retained in the 1920 edition: "The law uses the term miscarriage, a popular word, and it intends thereby to mean the contents of a gravid uterus, whether such contents be … living or dead …; the thing is the *intent* with which an operation was done or a drug given" (*Taylor's Medical Jurisprudence*, 1920, Vol. II: 179). This reading was not followed when the point came up in *R v Smith* (Norwich Assizes, 1942), by which time it was taken for granted that the purpose of the legislation was to prevent the destruction of the unborn child's life; see *Taylor's Medical Jurisprudence* (1957, Vol. II: 99).

but does *not* criminalise deliberately and intentionally killing a baby that is being born. Thus I suggest that the more that we look at the content of nineteenth-century legislation as a whole, the less plausible it becomes to think of this as motivated by any concern with foetal life.

This may be a matter of some legal significance. In a critique of the *Smeaton* decision, it has been argued that even if the Court was right to interpret the law as "always speaking", any consequent updating should be done by "ascertaining and promoting (or at the very least not restricting) the relevant legislative purpose" (Keown, 2005: 314).[23] The argument then continues that since one such purpose was protection of the foetus, updating should be done in a way that furthers that purpose. If, as I have argued, that was *not* a legislative purpose, then updating should *not* be done to further that purpose.

2. Does the Act apply to doctors?

The short answer here is "No". Again there is a source that demonstrates this clearly; but, again, there is more to be said that strengthens the case still further.

The main source on this question is Keown's *Abortion, Doctors and the Law* (Keown, 1988). Perhaps it should be said here that Keown is – and has been for over two decades – an implacable opponent of abortion. His work provided one of the main planks of SPUC's case in *Smeaton*.[24] Yet Keown has proved beyond doubt that the 1861 Act (and its predecessors) was never applied to medical practice and was never intended to be applied to medical practice. I will not summarise his argument here; I will just refer the reader to it, since it is – as far as it goes – authoritative.

However, there is one point that Keown stresses that is perhaps worth repeating. It is often said that the 1861 Act prohibited abortion absolutely, until the English case of *R v Bourne* (1938)[25] created a de-

---

[23] See further, Keown (2005: 314-8).

[24] Mainly Keown (1984). Keown's argument was rejected by the Court. For his response, see Keown (2005).

[25] This was brought as a test case on the law; Dr Bourne, who was acquitted, was one of the leading gynaecologists of the time. He performed an abortion on a 14-year-old girl who had been raped; the judge declared that abortion would be legal not only if the *life* of the woman was at risk, but if the doctor believed "that the probable consequence of the

fence of intervening to save the life or health of the mother.[26] Keown shows convincingly that that is not the case: all that *Bourne* did was establish what the law had always been, and been known to be. Indeed, the defence that *Bourne* made, and which was accepted by the Court, may well have construed the justifications of abortion too *narrowly* (Keown, 1988). *Bourne* was in no sense an aberration or novel interpretation of the law. The law always did exclude abortions carried out as part of standard medical practice.

Keown provides overwhelming evidence of this claim by citing discussions in medical textbooks and medico-legal sources. But there are also other sources, which he does not give.

One is that this precise question came up in the debates on the Offences Against the Person bill 1828. The Marquis of Lansdowne reported that midwives had expressed concern that their standard practice might be rendered criminal when "they might be compelled to use an instrument according to the most approved principles of the art, in order to save the life of the mother, of which many cases had occurred". The Lord Chief Justice (Lord Tenterden) replied that such a fear was groundless, as "it was quite impossible that … the use of an instrument, in the manner suggested, could possibly bring any man into trouble".[27]

There has, however, been considerable confusion as to *why* therapeutic abortions were legal, if indeed they were.[28] The judgement in *Bourne* might be partly responsible for this confusion. Some have argued that a general defence of *necessity* would justify performing an abortion to save the life of a woman. Whether that would be so is, however, unclear.

---

continuation of the pregnancy will be to make the woman a physical or mental wreck" (1939: 694 per Macnaghton J).

[26] See, for instance, O'Hanlon (1992). O'Hanlon talks of "the state of uncertainty *created* by the decision in *R v Bourne*" (p. 88; my emphasis – PM).

[27] *The Times*, 16 April 1828. This assurance has probably been missed by commentators because it is not in Hansard, whose report finishes immediately before this exchange. It seems that the Hansard shorthand writers had great difficult staying awake during the debates on this Act; the report of the debate on the Second Reading in the House of Commons ends: "A long and desultory conversation then took place on the respective clauses. Several amendments were agreed to, and the bill, with the amendments, was ordered to be reprinted" *Hansard* XIX (1828) cols. 359-60.

[28] A good summary of the state of this confusion is in Kingston, Whelan and Bacik (1997: 61-73).

There is a far clearer reason why therapeutic abortion is legal. That again requires a close reading of the actual Act. Sections 58 and 59 apply only to those who "*unlawfully* administer … any poison" or "*unlawfully* use any instrument" [my emphases].[29] The word "unlawfully" occurs six times in these two sections. Now it may be that, despite its frequent use, the word is simply redundant, and the Act is to be read as if it were not there.[30] I would suggest that, whilst it is certainly not the most helpful expression – for it appears to declare to be unlawful that which is unlawful – it is not redundant. And as a matter of statutory interpretation, words in Acts should be assumed to have a meaning unless no meaning at all can be given to them. Since "unlawful" is a quasi-technical term, a clear meaning can be given to it here: it is lawful to perform therapeutic abortions, and unlawful to perform abortions for other reasons.

This interpretation is given in some later editions of *Russell on Crimes*: "The word 'unlawfully' excludes from the section acts done in the course of proper treatment in the interest of the life or health [*sic*] of the mother".[31] This interpretation seems to me to be correct. Note that many other sections of the 1861 Act contain the word "unlawfully"; thus the section on grievous bodily harm (section 20) makes it an offence to "unlawfully and maliciously wound … any other person". There is no explicit proviso exempting surgeons from this section, but there can be no doubt that when a surgeon takes a knife to a patient to perform an acceptable operation, it is not being done "unlawfully and maliciously",

---

[29] Some such idea was in all the various abortion Acts. In 1803 the idea was expressed more verbosely, as "willfully, maliciously, and unlawfully" in one clause, and "willfully and maliciously" in the other. This became a uniform "unlawfully and maliciously" in 1828, which was reduced to the lone "unlawfully" in 1837.

[30] As argued by Richards (1970: 87-8), amongst others.

[31] *Russell on Crimes* (1910, Vol. I: 830) and (1923, Vol. I: 787). Russell also informs us that "[t]he decisions on criminal use of instruments within sects. 58, 59, are to be found in medical rather than in legal treatises" (1910, Vol. I: 834 and 1923, Vol. I: 790). These passages have a note referring readers to the contemporary editions of *Taylor's Medical Jurisprudence* – which, however, seems somewhat more uncertain on this issue. An earlier edition of *Taylor* seemed less unsure, stating: "A medical man would lay himself open to criminal prosecution if he procured the abortion of a woman at an early stage of pregnancy [that is, before the foetus is viable], except the condition of the mother demanded the operation" (*Taylor's Medical Jurisprudence*, 1894, Vol. II: 208-9).

and so he or she has no reason to fear the Act.[32] Likewise with therapeutic abortions.

One argument has been offered against this reading. It is that in 1846 the Report of the Criminal Law Commissioners proposed inserting a clause explicitly declaring that therapeutic abortions were exempt from the Act;[33] this proviso was not inserted in the eventual Act; therefore its omission should lead us to conclude that no such exemption was intended.[34]

There are, however, several reasons for thinking that this argument is false. If one looks closely at all the various attempts after 1846 to draft the legislation, it seems clear that the writers had severe difficulties in finding a suitable form of words for this proviso. Hence it is reasonable to think that it was dropped as unhelpful and unnecessary, rather than rejected as unacceptable. Another reason that the proviso may have been withdrawn is that its wording might have been thought to be too *restrictive*, for it limits therapeutic abortions to those necessary to save the *life* of the mother, and ignores her *health*. Most medical textbooks refused to draw a distinction between the life and health of their patient – and, as we have seen, some time later a standard authority on the criminal law was interpreting the law (without any explicit proviso) to include an exemption based on a concern for the *health* of the mother. The vaguer wording eventually chosen gave more flexibility to medical practice, and this may well have been a further reason why the explicit statement of the proviso was dropped. In short, the absence of an explicit proviso exempting therapeutic abortions should not be read as implying that no such proviso existed in the law: rather, in 1861 as in 1828, the drafters of the legislation regarded it as too obvious to need stating.

We can, however, dismiss one suggestion for the non-appearance of such a proviso: that in 1861, abortions were so dangerous that it would *never* be in the interests of a woman to have an abortion. This claim has

---

[32] This point is made in *Taylor's Medical Jurisprudence* (1894, Vol. II: 208).

[33] "Provided that no act specified in the last preceding Article shall be punishable where such act is done in good faith with the intention of saving the life of the woman whose miscarriage is intended to be procured" (Her Majesty's Commissioners, 1846: 42).

[34] This has been argued by, amongst others, Richards (1970: 87-8). It is also alluded to in Casey (2005: 38).

been made by Glanville Williams, and has been repeated by many recent writers.[35] It is quite false. Whilst abortions were certainly dangerous, childbirth was also dangerous, particularly when something went wrong. When the pregnancy posed a severe risk to the life or health of the mother, best practice throughout the nineteenth century had always been to endeavour to save the mother by destroying the foetus.[36]

There is a further aspect to this story. I have been referring so far to medical practice in the nineteenth century, at and shortly after the passage of the abortion Acts. But medical practice continued to regard abortion as both legal and therapeutically necessary well into the twentieth century. And it did so in Ireland just as in England and Wales. One of Keown's sources of evidence consists in the teachings embodied in medical textbooks, which can be taken as a guide to what was considered at the time as good medical practice. Several such textbooks were written by practitioners in Ireland, after independence; they include explicit instructions on how and when to perform abortions. I will mention just three, all published in 1936-7 (a time not without significance in Irish constitutional history).[37] All state explicitly that in certain circumstances

---

[35] "In ... the Act of 1861, no exception is expressed for therapeutic abortions. This is not surprising, for the operation was regarded as dangerous only twenty years ago, while in 1861 it would have been ridiculous to call it therapy" (Williams, 1958: 150; see also Williams, 1978: 254). Note that when Williams wrote that passage, "twenty years ago" was 1938, when Dr Bourne – who was certainly in a position to know – regarded the operation as perfectly safe. Williams's quite incorrect assertion has been followed by – amongst others – Charleton (1992b: 361).

[36] See, for instance, the extensive and explicit discussion of this in Churchill (1860, Appendix). For yet earlier textbooks recommending therapeutic abortions as good practice, see (amongst many others) Denman (1794, Vol. II: 170, 241) and Burns (1806: 66). For a large number of further references, see Keown (1988: ch. 3).

[37] The three are Browne (1936), Fitzgibbon (1937) and Solomons and Falkiner (1937). Browne, Fitzgibbon, Solomons and Falkiner were all at the Rotunda Hospital, Dublin; each was Master of the Rotunda, either before (Fitzgibbon and Solomons) or after (Browne and Falkiner) these books were published. They were therefore amongst the leading obstetricians in Dublin at the time. It is perhaps worth adding that all these books are currently in the library of the National University of Ireland, Galway (formerly University College Galway), and would certainly have originally been put there for teaching purposes. These were texts from which Irish medical students would have been taught in the late 1930s and early 1940s.

Toksvig (1937) is a *roman à clef*, in which the main character is based on Bethel Solomons, and in which a recurrent theme is how what he regards as good medical practice is regarded as unacceptable by Catholics. See also Toksvig (1994).

the doctor *should* perform an abortion. Fitzgibbon, for instance, states that in cases of cardiac failure in the early months of pregnancy, it is "best … to terminate the pregnancy" (1937: 381). He then has a section describing how to perform such an abortion, and a long list of conditions that would warrant performing it (1937: 423-6).[38]

Further evidence, if any is needed, was provided by Dr Michael Solomons, who was a gynaecologist and Assistant Master of the Rotunda from 1948 to 1951 (and the son of Bethel Solomons), who has recounted that as a student he saw abortions performed in the Rotunda on such medical grounds as the risk to a mother who had heart disease; part of the teaching at the Rotunda in his time was to describe such medical reasons.[39]

I should perhaps point out that there is absolutely nothing in any of these texts to suggest that the abortions are indirect rather than direct, nor is it suggested that they should be carried out only in circumstances, or in a manner, that might conform to the principles of the doctrine of double effect. These are deliberate, direct, abortions, in which the foetus would be killed in order to remove a likely threat to the life of the mother. Yet there seems to be a recent school of thought in Ireland that such procedures have, miraculously, never occurred here. Commentators as eminent as the

---

[38] Fitzgibbon also says that in the previous three years in an (unnamed) maternity hospital, of 124 cases of hyperemesis gravidarum, 13 required "therapeutic abortion" (Fitzgibbon, 1937: 361). See also Browne (1936: 276-7) (for methods to induce abortion and a brief list of indications when abortion may be induced). See also his discussion of pre-eclampsia, which lists symptoms which "are quite sufficient to warrant immediate induction" (1936: 186); and of hyperemesis gravidarum, when "[i]f the foetus is judged to be still alive induction will save the mother in a case where she would otherwise die, provided it is done at a sufficiently early stage" (1936: 188). Browne adds, cautiously: "The decision to empty the uterus should never be taken without a second opinion. Medico-legal and ethical considerations render such a decision too great to be taken as an individual responsibility" (1936: 189). Solomons and Falkiner, likewise, have a chapter on abortion (Solomons and Falkiner, 1937, ch. X) which starts with a warning that "[i]t is a good rule to follow, never to induce abortion in a doubtful case without consultation with a reliable obstetrician" (1937: 225). There is then also a list of conditions when abortion is warranted, and a discussion of how it should be performed (1937: 239-47). Note that the word "abortion" is specifically used in all three works, along with common medical euphemisms for the same process.

[39] Evidence of Dr M. Solomons, given on 4 May 2000, to the Oireachtas Committee on the Constitution hearings on Abortion (All-Party Oireachtas Committee on the Constitution, 2000: A140).

authors of *Kelly: The Irish Constitution* engage in this wishful thinking, when, after mentioning the *Bourne* judgment, they add:

> One of the more obscure aspects of the debate on abortion is to what extent, if at all, [*Bourne*] represented the law in Ireland. It is clear, however, that it did not affect medical practice in this country, whereby a pregnancy would be terminated only where such result was the *indirect* consequence of an attempt to save the mother's life (2003: 1496-7) (my emphasis).[40]

This is simply wrong, as the authors would have realised if they had bothered to glance through a few old Irish medical textbooks.[41]

There is also considerable evidence not only that therapeutic abortions were taking place in Ireland, but that the Church was well aware that they were. The subject is discussed in a number of Catholic publications. I shall just mention two.

The first is in a little work published in Cork in 1963, with the authority of a Nihil Obstat.[42] The editor, in his brief foreword, is quite clear that illicit abortions are taking place legally:

> Criminal abortion in the sense of an abortion not performed for a therapeutic reason does, of course, exist but the number of doc-

---

[40] There is then a footnote: "This practice reflected the distinction drawn in Roman Catholic moral theology between medical interventions procuring the death of the foetus directly and those which have as a secondary and undesired consequence the termination of the pregnancy. Such a distinction, however, has never been expressly made in Irish law …." (Kelly, 2003: 1497n.) It has also been expressly *not* made throughout Irish medical practice.

[41] Other writers who make this mistake include Charleton and Binchy: see Charleton (1992a: 183-4), Charleton 1992b: 349 and 359-60), and Byrne and Binchy (1994: 166) (in claiming that, before 1983 as well as after, a prohibition of direct abortion, whilst accepting that the death of the foetus might come about as the indirect effect of other treatment, "governed medical practice in the State").

[42] *New Problems in Medical Ethics* (1963). This is a translation of a French work entitled *Cahiers Laënnec*, published by Lethielleux, probably in 1946. It would be interesting to find out why it was translated and published in Ireland when it was. The Nihil Obstat, incidentally, came from the diocese of Westminster. It might be worth noting that Archbishop McQuaid was apparently strongly opposed to the translation of these pamphlets, which perhaps explains why the Nihil Obstat was obtained in England; see Cooney (1990: 281). For a further dispute between Archbishop McQuaid and the Mercier Press on the publication of foreign theological works dealing with abortion, see Cooney (1990: 403-4).

> tors practising it is relatively small, and they are usually, though not always, quite evidently among the dregs of an honourable profession. On the other hand therapeutic abortion is often carried out by specialists of high repute and otherwise unblemished character. Fortunately, as these articles point out, the 'indications' for such interference are becoming fewer as medical science advances (*New Problems in Medical Ethics*, 1963: 9).[43]

Another, perhaps surprising, source is the *Irish Ecclesiastical Record*, a journal intended for priests.[44] Included in this journal is a "Notes and Queries" section, in which "Queries in Theology, Canon Law, or Liturgy" are answered. (The identities of the senders of the letters are not disclosed; from the nature of the questions, most seem to be priests.) A number of these queries are concerned with abortion. Some ask for elucidation of doctrine, which is not here relevant; but several ask for advice on how to respond in the confessional to a doctor who is performing therapeutic abortions. The nature of the questions suggests that these are real, not hypothetical, worries. Perhaps the most useful of these questions, for our purposes, was one from 1940.[45] In the full and informed reply, the clerical respondent[46] states clearly that Catholic teaching and the law of the land are different. For, after stressing at length the importance in canon law of the distinction between direct and indirect abortion, he adds:

> English law is not concerned so much with direct and indirect abortion. It has another distinction between therapeutic and crimi-

---

[43] The editor is (described as) Dom Peter Flood O.S.B., B.A., M.D., M.C.H., J.C.L., Barrister-at-law. Flood was not only in Holy Orders, but had been an eminent doctor and obstetrician in Dublin, who was on the General Medical Council for 14 years (O'Brien, 1979: 41). One of the articles in the book (Portes, 1963), written from a doctor's viewpoint, lists several medical conditions in which therapeutic abortions might be thought to be necessary. It suggests that doctors might be able to adhere to Catholic teaching, but only at some time in the future when medicine will have developed sufficiently that therapeutic abortion will no longer be necessary.

[44] I am very grateful to Mary Harris for drawing these references – and this journal – to my attention.

[45] Anon. (1940). Other questions implying that priests did have to deal in confessional with doctors performing therapeutic abortions include Anon. (1905) and Anon. (1911).

[46] Who signs himself J. McCarthy; presumably this is John Canon McCarthy, who was teaching moral theology and law at Maynooth, and was appointed to the Chair in Canon Law there in 1947.

> nal abortion - a distinction which was very much discussed in a recent case before the English courts. [No case is mentioned, but presumably *R v Bourne* is meant.] Therapeutic abortion is that directly or indirectly procured to save the life or to prevent serious danger to the health of the mother. In all other cases abortion is criminal. It is a felony. Needless to say Catholic teaching condemns direct therapeutic abortion in every circumstance (McCarthy, 1940: 61).

The only thing left unsaid here is that "English law" was also Irish law.

Conclusion

I have argued that the statute law on abortion in Ireland – sections 58 and 59 of the Offences Against the Person Act 1861 – did not conform to Catholic teaching in two crucial areas.[47] First, the law was not originally enacted to protect the foetus, and therefore it does not outlaw the killing of a pre-implantation embryo. Second, the law did not in any way limit approved medical practice, and so did not outlaw therapeutic abortions. Further, it does not recognize the doctrine of double effect, or any distinction between direct and indirect abortion.

It is also clear that the Church was aware that, in one of these areas, practice, as well as law, did not conform to Catholic teaching, since therapeutic abortions were indeed taking place in Irish hospitals. And yet there was, so far as is known on the public record, no attempt to change the law on abortion before 1983. I think there is here a prima facie puzzle as to why such an important area of the law was left untouched, when so much else was changed in the first couple of decades of the Irish state.

Bibliography

All-Party Oireachtas Committee on the Constitution (2000), *Fifth Progress Report: Abortion*, Dublin: Stationery Office.

[47] Perhaps I should point out that I have made no attempt to read the 1861 Act in the light of the Eighth Amendment to the Irish Constitution – for my main interest is in what the law was before 1983. However, my reading of the statute law may well have relevance to the debate whether the Eighth Amendment changed, or merely secured, the existing statute law.

All-Party Oireachtas Committee on the Constitution (2006), *Tenth Progress Report: The Family*, Dublin: Stationery Office.

Anon. (1905), "Craniotomy – is it ever lawful?", *Irish Ecclesiastical Record*, XVII (January-June) p. 86.

Anon. (1911), "Craniotomy and Excommunication", *Irish Ecclesiastical Record*, XXIX (January-June) p. 537.

Anon. (1940), "Direct and Indirect Abortion – Ectopic Pregnancy", *Irish Ecclesiastical Record*, LV (January-June) p. 59.

Browne, O'D. (1936), *A Manual of Practical Obstetrics*, Bristol: John Wright and Sons,

Burns, J. (1806), *Observations on Abortion*, London: Longman, Hurst, Rees, and Orme.

Byrne, R. and W. Binchy (1994), *Annual Review of Irish Law 1992*. Dublin: Round Hall Press.

Casey, G. (2005), *Born Alive. The Legal Status of the Unborn Child in England and the U.S.A*, Chichester: Barry Rose Law Publishers.

Charleton, P. (1992a), *Offences Against the Person,* Dublin: Round Hall Press.

Charleton, P. (1992b), "Judicial Discretion in Abortion: The Irish Perspective", *International Journal of Law and the Family* 6 pp. 349-80.

Churchill, M.F. (1860), *On the Theory and Practice of Midwifery*, 4th ed., London: Henry Renshaw.

Cole, F.J. (1930), *Early Theories of Sexual Generation*, Oxford: Oxford University Press.

Cooney, J. (1990), *John Charles McQuaid: Ruler of Catholic Ireland,* Dublin: O'Brien Press.

Denman, T. (1794), *An Introduction to the Practice of Midwifery*, London: J. Johnson).

Farley, J. (1982), *Gametes and Spores: Ideas about Sexual Reproduction, 1750-1914*, Baltimore: Johns Hopkins University Press.

Fitzgibbon, G. (1937), *Obstetrics*, Dublin: Browne and Nolan.

Gasking, E.B. (1967), *Investigations into Generation 1651-1828*, London: Hutchinson.

Greaves, C.S. (1861), *The Criminal Law Consolidation and Amendment Acts of the 24 & 25 Vict. with Notes and Observations*, London: Stevens & Sons, Sweet & Maxwell.

Hansard XIX (1828).

Her Majesty's Commissioners (1846): "Second Report of Her Majesty's Commissioners for Revising and Consolidating the Criminal Law", *Parliamentary Papers* 1846 [709] XXIV 107.

James, A. (2002), "Definition of 'miscarriage' in Offences Against the Person Act 1861", *Journal of Criminal Law*, 66, pp. 469-72.

Kelly, J.M. (2003), *The Irish Constitution*, 4th ed., by G. Hogan and G. Whyte, Dublin: Butterworths.

Keogh, D. (1986), *The Vatican, the Bishops and Irish Politics 1919-39,* Cambridge: Cambridge University Press.

Keown, J. (1984), "'Miscarriage': A Medico-Legal Analysis", *Criminal Law Review*, pp. 604-14.

Keown, J. (1988), *Abortion, Doctors and the Law: Some aspects of the legal regulation of abortion in England from 1803 to 1982*. Cambridge: Cambridge University Press.

Keown, J. (2005), "'Morning after' pills, 'miscarriage' and muddle", *Legal Studies*, 25, pp. 296-319.

Kingston, J. and A. Whelan (1997), *Abortion and the Law*, Dublin: Round Hall Sweet & Maxwell.

McCarthy, J. (1940), "Reply", *Irish Ecclesiastical Record* LV (January-June) pp. 59-66.

Meyer, A.W. (1939), *The Rise of Embryology*. Stanford: Stanford University Press.

Morriss, P. (unpublished), "The law on abortion: 1803-1861".

*New Problems in Medical Ethics (*1963), Number 4: *Abortion and Narcoanalysis*, Cork: Mercier Press.

O'Brien, E. (1979), "Lunch At Ealing Abbey: A Memory of Dom Peter Flood (1898-1978)", *Journal of the Irish Medical Association*, 72 (16 Feb.), pp. 40-41.

O'Hanlon, R.J. (1992), "The Attorney-General v 'X'. Reg v Dudley & Stephens Reconsidered", *Irish Law Times*, 10, pp. 86-8.

Pinto-Correia, C. (1997), *The Ovary of Eve: Egg and Sperm and Preformation,* Chicago: University of Chicago Press.

Portes, Dr L. (1963), "The Future of Therapeutic Abortion", in *New Problems in Medical Ethics (*1963), Number 4: *Abortion and Narcoanalysis*, Cork: Mercier Press, pp. 11-21.

Power, C. and G. Shannon (2007), "Practice and Procedure", *Irish Journal of Family Law*, 10, pp. 30-31.

Richards, P.G. (1970), *Parliament and Conscience*, London: George Allen & Unwin.

Roe, S.A. (1981), *Matter, Life, and Generation: Eighteenth-Century Embryology and the Haller-Wolff Debate* Cambridge: Cambridge University Press.

Russell on Crimes (1819), Sir W.O. Russell, *A Treatise on Crimes and Misdemeanors*, 1st ed., London: Joseph Butterworth & Sons.

Russell on Crimes (1826), Sir W.O. Russell, *A Treatise on Crimes and Indictable Misdemeanors,* 2nd ed., London: Joseph Butterworth & Sons.

Russell on Crimes (1843), *A Treatise on Crimes and Misdemeanors,* 3rd ed., by S.C. Greaves, London: Saunders & Benning.

Russell on Crimes (1865), *A Treatise on Crimes and Misdemeanors* (4th ed., by S.C. Greaves, London: Stevens & Sons)

Russell on Crimes (1877), *A Treatise on Crimes and Misdemeanors,* 5th ed., by S. Prentice, London: Stevens & Sons.

Russell on Crimes (1896): *A Treatise on Crimes and Misdemeanors,* 6th ed., by H. Smith & A.P. Perceval Keep, London: Stevens & Sons.

Russell on Crimes (1910), *A Treatise on Crimes and Misdemeanors,* 7th ed., by W.F. Craies & L.W. Kershaw, London: Stevens & Sons.

Russell on Crimes (1923), *A Treatise on Crimes and Misdemeanors,* 8th ed., by R.E. Ross & G.B. McLure, London: Stevens & Sons.

Solomons, B. and N.M. Falkiner (1937), *Tweedy's Practical Obstetrics*, 7th ed., London: Oxford University Press.

Sterne, L. (1759), *The Life and Opinions of Tristram Shandy, Gentleman*, London: Penguin, 1997.

Taylor's Medical Jurisprudence (1894): *Taylor's Principles and Practice of Medical Jurisprudence*, 4th ed., by T. Stevenson, London: J & A Churchill.

Taylor's Medical Jurisprudence (1920): *Taylor's Principles and Practice of Medical Jurisprudence*, 7th ed., by F.J. Smith, London: J & A Churchill.

Taylor's Medical Jurisprudence (1957): *Taylor's Principles and Practice of Medical Jurisprudence*, 11th ed., by Sir S. Smith, London: J & A Churchill, 1957.

The Times, 16 April 1828.

Thomson, A. (1836-9), "Generation" in R.B. Todd (ed.), *The Cyclopædia of Anatomy and Physiology* Vol. II, London: Longman, Brown, Green, Longmans and Roberts, pp. 424-80.

Thomson, A. (1859), "Ovum", in R.B. Todd (ed.), *The Cyclopædia of Anatomy and Physiology* Vol. V, London: Longman, Brown, Green, Longmans and Roberts, pp. 1-142.

Thring, Sir H. (1878), *Practical Legislation; or the Composition and Language of Acts of Parliament*, London: Her Majesty's Stationery Office.

Toksvig, S. (1937), *Eve's Doctor,* London: Faber and Faber.

Toksvig, S. (1994), *Irish Diaries 1926-1937*, ed. L. Pihl, Dublin: The Lilliput Press.

Wagner, R. and R. Leuckart (1847-9), "Semen" in R.B. Todd (ed.), *The Cyclopædia of Anatomy and Physiology* Vol. IV, London: Longman, Brown, Green, Longmans and Roberts.

Whyte, J.H. (1980), *Church and State in Modern Ireland 1923-1979*, Second edition, Dublin: Gill and Macmillan.

Williams, G. (1958), *The Sanctity of Life and the Criminal Law*, London: Faber and Faber .

Williams, G. (1978), *Textbook of Criminal Law*, London: Stevens & Sons.

Cases

Irish

M R v T R & Ors [2006] IEHC 359.

English

R (on the application of Smeaton) v Secretary of State for Health ([2002] EWHC 610 (Admin)).

R v Bourne [1939] 1 K.B. 687; also [1938] 3 All E.R 615.

R v Coe (1834) 6 Car & P 403.

R v Goodhall [*Goodchild*] (1846) 2 Car. & K. 293 and 1 Den 187.

R v Hollis and Blakeman (1873) 12 Cox 463.

R v Isaacs (1862) Le. & Ca. 220.

R v Marlow (1964) [1965] 49 Cr. App. R. 49.

R v Phillips (1811) 3 Campb 77.

R v Scudder (1828) 1 Mood. 216 and 3 Car & P 605.

R v Sellis (1837) 7 Car. & P. 850.

Part Four

Reproduction, Medicine, Health and Ethics

12

ARTICLE 40.3.3° AND ASSISTED HUMAN REPRODUCTION IN IRELAND[1]

Dr Deirdre Madden

In vitro fertilisation (IVF) was first introduced into the Republic of Ireland in 1987. At the present time there are nine clinics in operation in Ireland carrying out assisted human reproduction (AHR) services including IVF, insemination and donor programmes. It is estimated that over 2,000 couples are treated annually in Irish clinics, and many more travel to the United Kingdom for treatment.

In vitro fertilisation involves the fertilisation of a woman's eggs by sperm outside the body. The process involves the hormonal stimulation of the woman's ovaries in order to produce a number of eggs in a particular cycle. The eggs are collected and mixed with the man's sperm in the laboratory with the objective of achieving fertilisation of some of the eggs. After an interval of some days, a small number of embryos develop and if considered viable by an embryologist, they are then transferred to the woman's uterus. Other AHR treatments may involve adaptations of the basic IVF treatment, depending on the cause of the infertility, and may include the use of donor eggs and/or sperm or embryos.[2]

---

[1] This paper has been adapted from Madden, D. "Assisted reproduction in Ireland" in Iltis A, Johnson S, and Hinze B. (eds.) (2008) *Legal Perspectives in Bioethics* (New York: Routledge Press) with kind permission of the publishers.

[2] For further explanation of the clinical practice of AHR, see Report of the Commission on Assisted Human Reproduction (2005: ch. 3).

At the present time there is no legislation in effect in Ireland for the regulation of AHR treatments other than the Tissue and Cells Regulations[3] which impose requirements on tissue establishments relating to quality and safety for the donation, procurement, testing, processing, preservation, storage and distribution of human tissues and cells for human application. A tissue establishment is defined as a tissue bank or unit of a hospital where activities of donation, procurement, testing, processing, preservation, storage or distribution of human tissues and cells are undertaken. This includes reproductive cells which are intended to be used for assisted reproduction.

Professional Guidelines

The Medical Council is a statutory body charged with responsibility for protecting the interests of the public in their dealings with registered medical practitioners. The Council was established by the Medical Practitioners Act 1978 and commenced operation in April 1979. A new Medical Practitioners Act was enacted in 2007 and commenced operation in 2008. The principal roles of the Medical Council include: (1) assuring the quality of undergraduate education of doctors, (2) assuring the quality of postgraduate training of specialists, (3) maintaining a register of doctors, (4) providing disciplinary procedures and (5) publishing guidance on professional standards or ethical conduct.

The Medical Council publishes a *Guide to Ethical Conduct and Behaviour* every five years and these guidelines act as a self-imposed disciplinary code for registered medical practitioners.[4] If a complaint is made in respect of an alleged breach of these guidelines, practitioners may be subject to a Fitness to Practice Inquiry. If a practitioner is found to have engaged in professional misconduct there are a number of sanctions which may be imposed, ranging from censure, imposition of conditions, suspension and erasure from the Medical Register.

The Guide states that it is simply an articulation of general principles of ethical conduct against which medical practitioners can measure their

---

[3] Statutory Instrument No. 158 of 2006 (Quality and Safety of Human Tissues and Cells) Regulations.

[4] Available at http://www.medicalcouncil.ie/professional/ethics.asp.

own behaviour. However, the Guide may be indirectly incorporated into law through litigation. In the context of an action for medical negligence, a court could decide that although not of binding legal force in itself, departures from the Guide may constitute a breach of professional duty. It could also be argued that patients have an expectation that medical practitioners will follow the Guide, and this expectation may be deemed to form part of the implied contract between doctor and patient. In the absence of legislation dealing with AHR in Ireland, the Guide currently forms the only source of advice to doctors in this area.

In relation to reproductive medicine (Section F), the most recent edition of the Guide (6th ed., 2004) provides that there is no objection to the preservation of sperm or ova to be used subsequently on behalf of those from whom they were originally taken. Doctors are advised that if they consider treating with donated gametes, they must pay particular attention to the safety issues involved, specifically the source of the donated gametes. They must also advise donors and recipients of the consequences of their involvement in such a treatment.

In relation to IVF, as well as setting out the need for thorough investigation and counselling, the Guide stipulates that "any fertilised ovum must be used for normal implantation and must not be deliberately destroyed". A new addition to the Guide in 2004 also states that "if couples have validly decided they do not wish to make use of their own fertilised ova, the potential for voluntary donation to other recipients may be considered".

Where surplus embryos remain in storage following IVF treatment, and the couple on whose behalf they are stored no longer wish to use them for purposes of reproduction, in theory, there are three possible clinical options. First, the embryos may be removed from storage and allowed to perish. Secondly, the embryos may be donated to another individual or couple for use in reproduction. Thirdly, the embryos could be donated to researchers for embryo or embryonic stem cell research.

In relation to these three options, the Guide of the Medical Council clearly allows the second option to be considered. The first option, i.e. the removal of the embryos from storage without transfer to a uterus, does not appear to be permissible under the wording of the Guide which states that all embryos must be used for normal implantation. Regarding the possibility of donation for research, the Guide stipulates that the creation of embryos for research purposes is unethical and also states that the deliberate destruction of embryos is professional misconduct. If surplus embryos have been donated for research purposes, the ethical imperative is that they must not subsequently be used for reproduction and should be destroyed. As this is contrary to the Guide, it follows that embryo research is also impermissible under the terms of the Guide. Therefore, for those couples who choose not to donate, it would seem it is currently the Council's view that these embryos must be stored indefinitely.

Is There a Constitutional Right to Reproduce?

Ireland has had a troubled history of dealing with issues in the reproductive area and it is to be expected that in any attempt to grapple with the legal issues arising in AHR strong divergences of opinion would be articulated. Although AHR has generally proved divisive in every jurisdiction in which it has arisen for public debate and regulation, there are some specific constitutional tensions in the Irish context that are worth examining in more detail.

Given the constitutional backdrop against which AHR will be dealt, one of the preliminary questions might be whether there is any feature of the Constitution that would enshrine in individuals an enforceable right to reproduce. Although the Irish courts have developed a strong jurisprudence in the vindication of personal rights, these have tended to remain in the area of negative or non-interference rights rather than positive rights that would incur the imposition of obligations on the state. There have been cases in which the state has been attacked for failure to provide educational services or housing,[5] but the courts have tended to take the view that where the vindication of personal rights would involve an adjudication of the fairness or otherwise of the administration of public resources, this would fall within the remit of the executive rather than the judiciary (Morgan, 2001: 62-71). Therefore, while there might be scope for resisting state interference in procreational choices on grounds of a constitutional right to privacy, such as occurred in *McGee v Attorney General* (1974), it does not appear likely that the courts would recognise

[5] See *O'Donoghue v Minister for Health* (1996); *Sinnott v Minister for Education* (2001); *O'Reilly v Limerick Corporation* (1989).

a positive right to procreate that could be used by an individual or couple to oblige the state to provide AHR treatments.

It is also the case that if a couple attempted to resist state interference in a reproductive choice, the court might justify the interference on common good grounds. So, for example, a couple that chose to make an arrangement with a surrogate mother would not likely be successful, on constitutional rights arguments alone, in resisting regulation or interference. The State could argue that, despite the violation of personal privacy rights, prohibition or regulation of such arrangements is necessary on public policy grounds such as protection of public order and morality. The extent to which evidence of harm to the common good might be adduced before the court is questionable in light of the international research studies on the impact of AHR on children and families which, thus far, indicate positive outcomes for both.

The Impact of Article 40.3.3°

The most fundamental difficulty that any regulation of AHR will have to deal with in Ireland is undoubtedly the constitutional protection of the right to life of the unborn. Article 40.3.3° of the Constitution provides acknowledgement by the State of the right to life of the unborn and obliges the State to guarantee in its laws to respect and, as far as practicable, to defend and vindicate that right. The most significant word in the Article for IVF purposes is "unborn". If this word is interpreted to mean the fertilised ovum/embryo, then the rights ascribed to the unborn in the Constitution, specifically the right to life, come into play. Thus, the State would be obliged to respect and, as far as practicable, vindicate such rights since:

> … a child has the right to life itself and the right to be guarded against all threats directed to its existence whether before or after birth…. The right to life necessarily implies the right to be born, the right to preserve and defend, and to have preserved and defended, that life… (*G v An Bord Uchtala*, 1980: 69, per Walsh J).

This would leave certain IVF practices, such as the storage of embryos, and most certainly embryonic stem cell research, open to challenge, as by facilitating storage and research the State could be seen as failing in its obligation to vindicate the embryos' right to life. The issue of the "practicality" of the State intervening to protect the right to life of every embryo is open to question. Such an interpretation would also raise challenges to the constitutionality of certain forms of contraception which are designed to prevent implantation of the embryo in the uterus, such as the morning-after pill.

On the other hand, if the word "unborn" were interpreted as extending only to the embryo after implantation in the uterus, then it would seem that embryo freezing and research would not violate the constitutional provisions. Until recently there was little guidance to be gleaned from the limited constitutional jurisprudence in existence in relation to this article. In the case of *Attorney General (SPUC) v Open Door Counselling Ltd.* (1988) Hamilton P held that the Offences Against the Person Act 1861 protects the foetus in the womb, and "that protection dates from conception". However, it is not clear from the context whether he intended that conception meant fertilisation or implantation; this is a crucial distinction in relation to IVF.

In *Attorney General v X* (1992), the Supreme Court interpreted the constitutional provision to mean that termination of pregnancy was permissible only when it was established as a matter of probability that there was a real and substantial risk to the life of the mother if such termination were not effected. In relation to the question of when the constitutional protection begins, and therefore whether the pre-implantation embryo falls within the scope of the article, there is little to be gained from a reading of the judgments in the case. Given that the facts of the case pertained to an established pregnancy, the court did not have to consider the question as to whether or not the provision applied to the embryo prior to implantation. The language of the court refers to the "life of the infant in the womb", and Hederman J (dissenting) stated:

> The Eighth Amendment establishes beyond any dispute that the constitutional guarantee of the vindication and protection of life is not qualified by the condition that the life must be one which has achieved an independent existence after birth. The right to life is guaranteed to every life born or unborn. One cannot make distinctions between individual phases of unborn life before birth, or between unborn and born life (1992: para. 121).

Unfortunately, it is far from clear from these cases to what extent, if any, the Court would apply the protection of Article 40.3.3° to the embryo outside the womb.

As might be expected, academic commentators differ on the possible interpretation of Article 40.3.3° in this context. Kingston, Whelan and Bacik state that "it cannot be said with certainty whether the protection afforded by Article 40.3.3° to the 'unborn' applies from the moment of fertilisation, the moment of implantation, or from some later date" (1997: 32). The Constitution Review Group stated that the absence of a definition of the word "unborn" creates difficulties in the law and agreed that the word "unborn" seems to imply "on the way to being born" or "capable of being born" and stated that definition is needed as to when the "unborn" acquires the protection of the law (1996).[6]

The Green Paper on Abortion (1999) stated that if it was decided that the "unborn" ought to be defined, there were at least four types of possible definition: fertilisation, implantation, some other specified time after fertilisation, or viability. It was acknowledged that some of these possible definitions pose challenges in relation to current practices including post-coital contraception and IVF. The Green Paper also considered the option of continuing to operate in the absence of a definition and stated:

> Although the difficulties associated with the term 'unborn' cannot be dismissed, they have not troubled the Courts or the medical profession to date. It is significant that in the debate over an amendment to the Constitution in 1991 the issue of defining the term 'unborn' did not feature to a significant extent. It is arguable that much of the difficulty relates to the implications of possible definitions for the whole area of IVF treatment, which, in itself, is not of direct relevance to the Green Paper (1999: para. 7.13).

The All-Party Oireachtas Committee on the Constitution also examined the issue in its Fifth Progress Report on Abortion in 2000, although it did not discuss in detail the difficulties associated with the lack of clarifica-

---

[6] See also the Green Paper on Abortion (1999), which suggests that exclusion of IVF from the protection of Art. 40.3.3° could be anomalous.

tion of the meaning of the word "unborn". In relation to the issue of poscoital contraception, the Committee stated:

> The problem centres on when the unborn comes into being. Some would argue it is when an ovum is fertilised. However, great numbers of fertilised ova are lost in the natural course of things and never become implanted in the uterine wall. As a result some argue that implantation is the decisive event in the development of human life … (2000: 101).

In 1989, Sherlock argued that it was likely that the courts would hold the *in vitro* embryo to come within the protection of the Constitution and, if this were the case, it would rule out embryo research and embryo destruction.

> It would also have implications for infertility treatments involving in vitro fertilisation (IVF) as it would undoubtedly require that all embryos produced would have to be placed in the woman's uterus (1989: 24).

However, the present author argued in 2002 that if the "unborn" means "not yet born" or "with the potential to be born" or "capable of being born" then, in the light of the biological development of the early embryo and the absence of potential in the pre-implantation embryo, it is likely that the pre-implantation embryo does not qualify for constitutional protection (Madden, 2002: para. 6.116).

In 2000, the Minister for Health established the Commission on Assisted Human Reproduction to report on possible approaches to the regulation of all aspects of AHR and the social, ethical and legal factors to be taken into account in determining public policy in this area. The Commission carried out a public consultation exercise and discussed in detail the ethical and legal issues pertaining to IVF and other assisted reproductive treatments. The Commission reported to the Minister in 2005 and recommended, with one member dissenting, that "the embryo formed by IVF should not attract legal protection until placed in the human body, at which stage it should attract the same level of protection as the embryo formed *in vivo*" (2005: 34).

In the absence of clarification in relation to the interpretation of Article 40.3.3º in the context of IVF and the protection, if any, to be afforded to embryos created by IVF, clinics and health professionals worked in a legal vacuum in this regard for many years. The view appears to have been taken that in the absence of clarity, clinics would not be prepared to accede to the wishes of couples whose embryos were stored by them to remove such embryos from storage without transfer to the uterus. This resulted in clinics taking the position that they were obliged to continue to store embryos on behalf of couples for many years, even in the absence of consent to such continued storage by the couple concerned.

The uncertainty in relation to the constitutional status of the IVF embryo also had a consequent effect on embryonic stem cell research (hESC). Such research may be carried out in some other jurisdictions, generally subject to strict compliance with legal conditions and ethical oversight, through the donation of embryos for research by couples who have chosen not to transfer their embryos for reproductive purposes. In some jurisdictions, cell lines have been created from these embryos which are available to researchers. In the Irish context, there is no legislative provision dealing with hESC research either through the importation of cell lines for research or through the donation of IVF embryos for research purposes. Although the Medical Council's Guide to Ethical Conduct, which states that the deliberate destruction is professional misconduct, only applies to registered medical practitioners and not to researchers outside of medical practice, it is expected that IVF clinics would not be prepared to facilitate the donation by couples to researchers as such actions may potentially expose any medical practitioner employed by the clinic to allegations of complicity in embryo destruction.

In 2006 an important opportunity arose for judicial consideration of the interpretation of Article 40.3.3° in the specific context of IVF. This case drew much public and media attention as it was the first case of its kind in Ireland.

MR v TR & Ors (2006)

The facts of this case were that MR and TR were married in 1992 and sought fertility advice from their General Practitioner in 1994. They were referred to the National Maternity Hospital for specialist treatment and subsequently had a son in 1997. Shortly after the birth of the child, MR underwent ovarian surgery as a result of which she sought fertility treatment at an IVF clinic in 2001. In January 2002, the couple attended the clinic and signed a number of documents covering consent to treatment and the cryopreservation (freezing) of the embryos. TR signed a form in which he acknowledged that he was MR's husband and consented to the fertilisation of her eggs and the transfer of three embryos to her uterus. He also acknowledged that he would become the legal father of any resulting child.

As a result of the treatment, six viable embryos were created. Three were transferred to MR's uterus and the remaining three were frozen. MR became pregnant and gave birth to a daughter in October 2002. Marital difficulties arose between the couple and they subsequently separated. The present case arose as a result of the fact that MR wished to have the three remaining frozen embryos transferred to her uterus whereas TR did not wish this to happen nor to become the father of any child that might be born as a result of such a treatment.

There were a number of issues before McGovern J in the case. The first related to the extent to which TR could be held to have agreed to the transfer of the remaining embryos to MR and whether such an agreement was binding on the parties in the circumstances of their marital separation. The second issue related to whether the embryos enjoyed the protection of Article 40.3.3° of the Constitution.

On the first issue, McGovern J held that there was no agreement between the parties as to what would happen to the remaining frozen embryos if the first embryo transfer was successful and resulted in pregnancy. The court held that TR did not give his consent, either express or implied, to the transfer of the frozen embryos and acknowledged that the clinic was unwilling to release the embryos into the custody of MR in the absence of such consent.

In relation to the second issue, the court heard from a number of witnesses who gave their view as to when life begins. Some argued that "from the moment of fertilisation of the ovum by the sperm a new human life begins". Others argued that "it was only when the embryo became implanted in the uterus that the potential to be born existed and that human life began at that point". Yet other witnesses stated that "human life began at the formation of the primitive streak" and others took the view that it was impossible to say when human life begins. In this regard McGovern J stated:

> It is possible for scientists and embryologists to describe in detail the process of development from the ovum to the embryo and on to the stage when it becomes a foetus after implantation of the embryo in the wall of the uterus, but in my opinion, it is not possible for this Court to state when human life begins (2006).

The learned judge went on to acknowledge that the point at which people ascribe human characteristics to genetic material depends on other issues besides science and medicine and is dependent upon one's own moral or religious beliefs. He stressed that it was not the function of the court to choose between competing moral beliefs and that the only issue that he had to decide was whether the three frozen embryos in this case were "unborn" within the meaning of Article 40.3.3° of the Constitution.

In deciding upon this important point McGovern J first stated that in considering the words in Article 40.3.3° the Court could have regard to the legislative history of the constitutional amendment but not to debates in the Oireachtas in order to clarify what was in the contemplation of the people in passing the amendment. He referred to a number of cases mentioned above: *McGee v Attorney General* (1974), *G v An Bord Uchtala,* (1980) *Attorney General v X* (1992), as well as section 58 of the Civil Liability Act 1961 which provides that the law relating to wrongs "shall apply to an unborn child for his protection in like manner as if the child were born, provided the child is subsequently born alive".

He also referred to the Medical Council's *Guide to Ethical Conduct* and Behaviour (2004), outlined above, the Report of the Constitution Review Group (1996) and the Report of the Commission on Assisted Human Reproduction (2005), also mentioned above. McGovern J concluded that there had been:

> … no evidence adduced that it was ever in the mind of the people voting on the Eighth Amendment to the Constitution that 'unborn' meant anything other than a foetus or child within the womb. To infer that it was in the mind of the people that 'unborn' included embryos outside the womb or embryos in vitro would be to completely ignore the circumstances in which the amendment

> giving rise to Article 40.3.3° arose. While I accept that Article 40.3.3° is not to be taken in isolation from its historical background and should be considered as but one provision of the whole Constitution, this does not mean that the word 'unborn' can be given a meaning which was not contemplated by the people at the time of the passing of the Eighth Amendment and which takes it outside the scope and purpose of the amendment (2006).

Consequently, the Court held that the word "unborn" within Article 40.3.3° does not include embryos *in vitro* and therefore did not include the three frozen embryos in this case. McGovern J stated that in the absence of any regulation in this country "embryos outside the womb have a very precarious existence" and that "until the law or the Constitution is changed this issue remains within the sphere of ethics and morality".

At the time of writing, it is understood that this case is under appeal to the Supreme Court. If the Supreme Court upholds the decision of McGovern J, the legal position in Ireland would enable current IVF practices to continue without regulation (other than in relation to technical, safety and quality issues as mentioned earlier). Subject to the provisions of the Medical Council's Guide to Ethical Conduct (which only applies to registered medical practitioners), the legal vacuum would also facilitate pre-implantation genetic diagnosis which removes a cell from the embryo to test for serious genetic disease. Pre-implantation genetic diagnosis is currently not available in Ireland due to the lack of clarity regarding the legal position of the embryo. Given that the Medical Council's Guide currently stipulates that all embryos must be used for normal implantation, it is unclear what legal consequences might follow in the event that an embryo which was diagnosed as affected by a serious genetic disorder was allowed to perish rather than transferred to the uterus. If the High Court decision is upheld, human embryonic stem cell research and other related therapeutic and research applications may also be carried out in Ireland in the absence of regulatory oversight.

If, however, the Supreme Court reverses McGovern J, current practices including post-coital contraception and IVF may be interpreted as a failure by the State to vindicate the right to life of the unborn, and thereby may become unconstitutional. Either option will inevitably raise concern and controversy for the legislature.

European Law

Although the European Union has no regulatory jurisdiction over matters which might be said to fall within the "ethics" of member states, this does not however mean that decisions made by the European institutions cannot influence such matters on a political level. In the decade prior to 1990, the Council of Europe had been working through the Parliamentary Assembly and the Steering Committee on Bioethics, giving responses to advances in medicine and biology. In 1990 it was agreed to begin work on a Framework Convention to set out common general standards for the protection of the human person in the context of the development of the biomedical sciences. However, the European Convention for the Protection of Human Rights and Dignity of the Human Being with regard to the Application of Biology and Medicine (April 1997, known as the Oviedo Convention), has not proved popular among member states. The Convention contains provisions relating to, for example, equitable access to healthcare, prohibition of genetic discrimination, prohibition of sex selection for social reasons and a prohibition on genetic modification other than for therapeutic purposes.

Significantly, the Convention does not contain any consensus as to the status of the embryo. Article 18 deals with embryo research, but merely states that if such research is permissible under national law the embryo must have adequate protection. It does not go on to set out the meaning of "adequate protection" or what these obligations entail for member states. This ambiguous expression has prevented some states from signing the Convention. Ireland has not ratified the Convention as it was believed that this Article was in conflict with Article 40.3.3° of the Irish Constitution. With the recent clarification of this issue in *MR v TR* (2006), discussed above, the decision of the Irish Government as to whether to ratify the Convention now will be of interest.

The regulation of AHR and related therapies across the EU reveals many areas of convergence and divergence. EU states are divided between legislative and non-legislative mechanisms, and between permissive and restrictive approaches. Apart from religious influences in the member states of the European Union, there is also the cultural divergence between member states which may account for the lack of consensus on ethical matters generally, and specifically in relation to the issue of the protection of the embryo and foetus. For example, there is a tradition in some states of encouraging public debate on matters of public importance, and education through the mass media including informative discussions and open forums involving members of the relevant interest groups who may express their concerns freely. Some states have traditionally taken a more paternalistic view of the role of medicine in society, taking the attitude that the professionals know best how to conduct their practice ethically. The argument is that doctors practising reproductive medicine have the same concerns and ethical principles as any other member of the community and it is safe to leave it to professional bodies to self-regulate as to what treatments should and should not be available and to whom.

In each European country similar questions arise with respect to law, medicine and bioethics. But there are differences of a philosophical, economic and social nature which are not easily bridged. The parallel between explosive political change within and across Europe, and the rapid developments in biomedical sciences and their impacts on law, ethics and human rights, gives rise to many challenges. For example, what is the meaning of the right to life and how has this changed through the use of biotechnology? How should difficult issues be resolved – by tolerating moral pluralism or by attempting to reach one dominant approach? Should our laws be accommodating or antagonistic?

It is evident from the diversity of approaches taken to fertility and treatments offered for infertility that national influences tend to play an important role in determining both the way in which the issue is dealt with by the state and also the resolution of the problems encountered. However, due to the difficulties involved in taking national cultural factors into account, it may not be feasible to produce a detailed set of guidelines to which all nations within Europe could subscribe. The most that could be gained from such an exercise, as has arguably been undertaken in the Oviedo Convention, is a written confirmation of the lowest common denominators between the states that would not perhaps advance the ongoing debates on these topics. It also suffers from the difficulty that some states have not signed this Convention due perhaps to perceived national feeling or, in the case of Ireland, to anticipated constitutional difficulties in relation to protection of the unborn.

Perhaps this assortment of controls and ethical principles is in itself a characterisation of a community of states but the danger of such contrasts is that it could lead to bioethical or, more specifically, reproductive tourism. The absence of regulation and ratification of international conventions by some states leaves the way open for research projects and treatments to be attempted in some jurisdictions at perhaps a high cost for those involved. Certainly for citizens of more restrictive regimes the benefits to be obtained by visiting another jurisdiction for treatment services must be persuasive.

Conclusion

Article 40.3.3° of the Irish Constitution 1937 has been at the root of many bitter and divisive debates in this jurisdiction in recent years as politicians, medical professionals, advocates on both sides of the divide and the general public struggle to find uneasy compromises. In the context of assisted reproduction, the difficulties have been compounded by the absence of clarity as to the precise meaning of the single word "unborn" in that Article, and therefore the ambiguity surrounding the State's obligations in this regard. Medical practice, and particularly IVF practice, has developed in a fog of uncertainty as to whether or not the embryos created by means of IVF were subject to the provisions of Irish constitutional law. It is unfortunate that clarification only came through judicial consideration of this issue in the context of a so-called "custody" dispute between a separated couple.

The judgment of Mr Justice McGovern in 2006 in *MR v TR* is to be welcomed for its pragmatic, objective and sensible approach to such a sensitive and unprecedented issue. The judgment clearly states that it is not a matter for the courts to weigh up competing moral beliefs or to make law where none exists. In the absence of legislation or precedent, McGovern J stated that the function of the court is to interpret the words of the Constitution in accordance with the wishes of the people. In his view, there had been no convincing evidence adduced before him that the people, in passing the amendment in 1983, had in contemplation anything other than the foetus in the womb. As a result, he concluded that the embryo outside the womb was not within the meaning of the word "unborn".

Assisted reproduction has enabled many children to be born and families to be created in Ireland in the last two decades. Treatments are currently undertaken by couples and provided by clinics without legal certainty as to their respective rights and responsibilities. It is clear that Ireland will shortly have to face up to the controversial challenge of defining the point at which constitutional protection will begin. Irrespective of the Supreme Court decision in *MR v TR* (2006), the government should consider the implications of Article 40.3.3° for both medical practice and the advancement of scientific research in this country. Perhaps it is time for Article 40.3.3° to be removed from the Constitution and for the legislature to finally provide the regulation that is necessary to bring clarity to the law on assisted reproduction.

Bibliography

All Party Oireachtas Committee on the Constitution (2000) *Fifth Progress Report: Abortion* Dublin: Stationery Office.

Constitution Review Group (1996) *Report of the Constitution Review Group* Dublin: Stationery Office.

Green Paper on Abortion (1999) Dublin: Stationery Office.

Kingston J., Whelan J. and Bacik I. (1997) *Abortion and the Law: An Irish Perspective* Dublin: Round Hall.

Madden, D. (2002) *Medicine, Ethics and the Law* Dublin: Butterworths.

Morgan, D. (2001) *A Judgment too far? Judicial Activism and the Constitution* Cork: Cork University Press.

Report of the Commission on Assisted Human Reproduction (2005) Dublin: Stationery Office.

Sherlock, A. "The Right to Life of the Unborn and the Irish Constitution", XXIV *Irish Jurist* 13, 24 (1989).

Cases

Attorney General (SPUC) v Open Door Counselling Ltd [1988] I.R. 593.

Attorney General v X [1992] 1 I.R. 1.

G v An Bord Uchtala [1980] IR 32.

McGee v Attorney General [1974] IR 284.

MR v TR & Ors [2006] IEHC 359.

O'Donoghue v Minister for Health [1996] 2 IR 20.

O'Reilly v Limerick Corporation [1989] ILRM 181.

Sinnott v Minister for Education [2001] 2 IR 545.

13

Reproductive Justice and Article 40.3.3°

Dr Ruth Fletcher

Introducing Reproductive Justice

Justice is about providing a legal and political framework which enables the exercise of individual freedom in a social context which discourages hardship and poverty and encourages happiness and flourishing (Lacey, 1998: 47; Fraser, 1997; Quinn et al., 1995). Some conservatives and libertarians disagree with this idea of justice and object to any intervention which redistributes social goods to the worse off. But the goal of social justice is intuitively appealing and most acknowledge that a political mechanism such as the welfare state is necessary for the task of maintaining the social conditions within which freedom and flourishing are possible (Baker et al., 2004). Where advocates and practitioners of social justice disagree is on the degree of encouragement or discouragement that is acceptable and on the best means for implementing justice (Mullally, 1998). Reproduction is a key site of justice because the creation of new human beings has contributed to human happiness and flourishing, raised issues of individual freedom about the terms of reproduction, and exacerbated hardship and poverty (Silliman et al., 2004; Petchesky and Judd, 1998; Kennedy, 2004). The goal of reproductive justice perhaps begs more questions than it answers, but is nonetheless worth restating: to protect reproductive freedoms, minimise reproductive hardship and enhance reproductive happiness for humankind. Individual reproducers ought to be free of coercion, assisted in countering the obstacles which poverty and discrimination impose, and valued for their creative and hard-working contributions in bearing and rearing tomorrow's children.

More practically, a reproductive justice perspective reminds us that abortion rights are one aspect of a commitment to reproductive justice, but not necessarily the primary issue for women and men as they reproduce. Reproductive justice advocates are and ought to be as concerned about sterilisation, assisted reproduction, reproductive health services, and childcare laws and policies as they are about abortion (Gerber Fried, 1990). Secondly, a reproductive justice perspective reminds us that women and men are differently situated across sexuality, race, class, ability and nationality as well as gender when it comes to reproductive activities (Roberts, 1997; Silliman et al., 2004). While some struggle against legal assumptions that they will reproduce, others struggle against legal assumptions that they will not.

Adopting a reproductive justice perspective does not entail marginalising abortion rights, not least in a legal context where they have been denied (Kingston, Whelan and Bacik, 1997). Rather the challenge is to think about abortion rights from a reproductive justice perspective. Why and when is the struggle for abortion rights important? And how do abortion rights connect with other sorts of reproductive struggles? Abortion rights are worthy of legal protection because women should have the right to say no to pregnancy and gestational motherhood, and the right to say yes to heterosex. Abortion rights do not mean that foetal life has no value, they mean that foetal life does not always have value of a kind which justifies compelling women to remain pregnant against their better judgment.

Law has an important role to play in a reproductive justice perspective, but so do non-legal measures such as the public funding of quality reproductive services and the training of health professionals (Cook, 2003). Reproductive justice emphasises the values of social solidarity and mutuality in supporting each other in realising our individual goals. Roberts shows, for example, how Black women's reproduction has been legally devalued in a constitutional context which "has elevated reproductive liberty to the level of a fundamental right against governmental interference deserving of the highest judicial scrutiny" (Roberts, 1997:

294). She critiques the concept of a negative right to liberty which requires the state to remain neutral as to competing views of reproductive value against a history of state preference for some forms of reproduction over others. She recognises the value of negative liberty rights in protecting citizens against the imposition of state orthodoxy, but argues that negative liberty rights are insufficient in tackling the implicit but systemic ways in which some women's reproduction is valued more than others. Roberts identifies the values of self-definition and of protection against totalitarian abuse of government power as the key worthy aspects of a negative right to liberty. She advocates a positive conception of liberty and recognition of the connection between liberty and equality. Such a positive conception of liberty "includes not only the negative proscription against government coercion, but also the affirmative duty of government to protect the individual's personhood from degradation and to facilitate the processes of choice and self-determination" (Roberts, 1997: 309). A social justice approach entails prohibiting discrimination by private bodies such as clinics, providing subsistence benefits and public medical care, and prioritising such benefits and services for the more disadvantaged.

Justice and Reproductive Rights

Here I draw on reproductive justice scholarship in two ways, to argue that a conception of reproductive justice should inform legal regulation of reproduction in Ireland and the interpretation, enforcement and reform of Article 40.3.3° in particular. Such a conception of reproductive justice would draw on justice as an underlying principle of Irish constitutional law and seek the interpretation and enforcement of the right to life of the unborn in light of other constitutional and legal interests and not as a trump on those interests. Secondly, I argue that the interpretation of Article 40.3.3° in *Attorney General v X* (1992) and *O v Minister for Justice* (2002) raises questions about the differential protection of the formal right to life of the unborn, just as the formal right to reproductive liberty has been differentially protected along racial and gendered lines in the United States. In an Irish context unborn interests have been elevated to the status of fundamental constitutional rights. Here I am concerned with considering how that constitutional status has been constructed in light of other constitutional interests, such as pregnant women's rights, and secondly in asking whether all unborn interests have been equally valued in law.

Cases like the so-called Baby[1] O case (2002) provide an example of the connection between abortion rights and other reproductive rights, and a reminder that feminists value foetal life, just not as a metaphor for denying women's rights. Although feminists supported Ms O in her efforts to resist deportation it is easy to understand why pro-choice advocates would be concerned at the invocation of the right to life of the unborn in any context (Fletcher, 2005). However, one can support Ms O's right to seek protection of her pregnancy without undermining the claim that women should be allowed access to abortion and assured reproductive freedom. The difficult legal task is not just protecting rights as such, but of weighting rights claims in different factual circumstances. How can a reproductive justice framework help us with that task? At minimum, it would require the identification of the different legal interests which are at stake in a given reproductive context. Secondly, it would offer some guidance as to how to weigh different interests, or adjudicate a conflict where one exists.

The Legal Issues in *X*

The particular legal issue which needed to be decided in *Attorney General v X* (1992) was whether X had a lawful right to terminate her pregnancy, or failing that, whether she had a right to travel to another jurisdiction to obtain a termination that was lawful there. The factual context concerned a fourteen-year-old who had become pregnant through rape[2] and who wanted to end that pregnancy. Her decision together with her parents to travel to another jurisdiction for a termination of pregnancy became known to the authorities when the parents asked whether tissue

---

[1] The legal report and the popular media referred to this case as "Baby O" in a linguistic move which problematically equates unborn foetuses with born babies given that unborn foetuses are located within and nourished directly by the pregnant woman's body, while born babies are not and may have their needs addressed by parties other than the woman who bore them.

[2] At the time, the crime of rape had not been proved in a court of law although the man involved would have been guilty of unlawful carnal knowledge, otherwise known as statutory rape.

from the aborted foetus could be used in a rape trial as evidence. The legal context concerned whether X's decision and right to travel abroad for an abortion could be lawfully infringed by the public authorities given the State's duty to defend and vindicate the right to life of the unborn. The High Court's ruling that an injunction stopping travel abroad during the nine months of pregnancy was warranted under Article 40.3.3° was appealed to the Supreme Court. The government of the day took the unusual step of offering to fund the parents' appeal. The Supreme Court overturned the High Court decision on a 4–1 majority, but not on grounds of X's right to free movement *per se*. Rather X had a right to a termination of pregnancy under Article 40.3.3° because she met the test of there being a real and substantial risk to her life. The risk of X's self-destruction made it impracticable to defend the right to life of the unborn in this instance and therefore any injunction limiting X's movement on grounds of such a defence was unlawful.

In order to come to this decision a number of different arguments were addressed directly and indirectly. The primary claim concerned X's right to abortion, and the extent to which that right was justifiably limited by reference to the State's duty to defend and vindicate the right to life of the unborn. A second claim concerned X's right to travel and again the extent to which that could be limited. Other legal issues which arose but will not be addressed here, concerned X's status as a minor and the legal interests of her parents, the impact of rape or unlawful carnal knowledge on the issues, as well as certain procedural issues concerning the role of the Attorney General and the jurisdiction of the Court to decide the matter.

X's Right to Abortion

The key legal argument in the *X* case concerned the right to abortion when the pregnant woman's life is at risk. The Judges of the Supreme Court assumed they had to defend the idea that Article 40.3.3° could support any right to abortion and did not engage in an open-ended consideration of the scope of Article 40.3.3°. The legal test established by the *X* case is generally regarded as being that there is a right to terminate a pregnancy when there is a real and substantial risk posed to the pregnant woman's life. Although some found this decision surprising because they thought that the Eighth Amendment had produced an absolute ban on abortion, termination for a risk to the woman's life is a logical limit on abortion prohibitions. The more controversial aspect of the ruling was that the risk of self-destruction as evidenced by psychological expertise counted as a real and substantial risk to a woman's life. Part of the reason for the controversy is that the risk is posed not directly by the pregnancy itself, but by the woman's psychological reaction to the pregnancy and by her threatened action to end her own life.

Finlay CJ's articulation of the test for a right to abortion – where there is a real and substantial risk to the life, as distinct from the health, of the mother – is the one that is usually cited as the ratio of the *X* case,[3] although the four judges of the majority adopted slightly different language in their identification of the key legal question. Lawyers representing the defendants and the Attorney General obviously argued for different versions of a risk-to-life test for the right to abortion. Thus, even a consideration of the legal arguments put forward by counsel and judges demonstrates a diversity of possible approaches to and interpretations of the risk-to-life. The test put forward by the defendants was: "if it was established as a matter of probability that the continuation of the life of the unborn constituted a real and substantial risk to the life of the mother then the conflict thus arising should be resolved by preferring the life of the mother" (1992: para. 21). Counsel for the defendants submitted that their suggested test adopted a standard that was more difficult to meet than that which had been adopted in *R v Bourne* (1939) i.e. if the continuance of the pregnancy will endanger the life of the mother *or* make her a physical or mental wreck. They accepted, according to Hederman J, that it would not be sufficient that the woman be made a physical or mental wreck by the pregnancy, rather there had to be a real and substantial risk to her life (1992: para. 70).

The Attorney General argued for the following test: "if it was established in any case that the continuation of the life of the unborn constituted a risk of immediate or inevitable death to the mother the termination of the pregnancy would be justified and lawful" (1992: para. 24). This test was relatively close to the one that had been adopted by

[3] See, for example, Oireachtas Committee on the Constitution (2000: 23).

Costello J in the High Court, when he made the injunction against travel permanent, in the sense that it required a high degree of certainty as to the threat of death. For Costello J there was no right to abortion in this instance because X did not meet his test since the risk to the woman's life was not "certain" and was not of the "same order of magnitude" as the risk posed to unborn life by a termination procedure (1992: para. 19). The Attorney General's test was also close to the one adopted by Hederman J in his dissenting opinion, which sought to deny the appeal against the High Court injunction. Hederman J's view was that it was necessary to show that "the continuance of the pregnancy will, to an extremely high degree of probability cost the mother her life and that any such opinion must be based on the most competent medical opinion available" (1992: para. 128). Since suicide threats could be contained in Hederman J's view, the threat of self-destruction did not indicate such a high degree of probability: "[T]he choice is between the certain death of the unborn life and a feared substantial danger of death but no degree of certainty of the mother by way of self-destruction" (1992: para. 131).

Finlay CJ explicitly rejected the Attorney General's test on the grounds that it insufficiently vindicated the mother's right to life. He concluded that the proper test to be applied was that:

> if it is established as a matter of probability that there is a real and substantial risk to the life, as distinct from the health, of the mother, which can only be avoided by the termination of her pregnancy, such termination is permissible, having regard to the true interpretation of Article 40 s.3 sub-s.3 of the Constitution (1992: para. 37).

McCarthy J also clearly disagreed with the standard set by the High Court and with the Attorney General's interpretation of the proper test for a termination of pregnancy under Article 40.3.3°. He formulated the test in these terms:

> [W]here there is a real and substantial risk attached to her survival not merely at the time of application but in contemplation at least throughout the pregnancy, then it may not be practicable to vindicate the right to life of the unborn (1992: para. 141).

O'Flaherty J put it this way:

> I believe that the law in this State is that surgical intervention which has the effect of terminating pregnancy bona fide undertaken to save the life of the mother where she is in danger of death is permissible under the Constitution and law. The danger has to present a substantial risk to her life though this does not necessarily have to be an imminent danger of instant death (1992: para. 162).

Egan J said:

> [T]he true test should be that a pregnancy may be terminated if its continuance as a matter of probability involves a real and substantial risk to the life of the mother. The risk must be to her life but it is irrelevant in my view, that it should be a risk of self-destruction rather than a risk to life for any other reason (1992: para. 183).

The right to abortion established by the *X* case is therefore a very limited one in the sense that a termination of pregnancy is only justified if the pregnancy is contributing to the probability that the woman will die. The Judges could have adopted a stricter test than the one finally chosen, by limiting risks to life to those imposed by physiological or obstetrical factors and established by medical evidence, or by requiring that the degree of risk meet an imminent death standard. But they chose not to differentiate between psychological and physiological issues in that way and included a probability brought about by psychological trauma and self-infliction of a death risk to a "real and substantial" standard. In so doing the Court relied on expert psychological evidence and on evidence reporting X's views in relation to the pregnancy. However, the Court could also have adopted a less strict test.

The Judges relied primarily on the language of Article 40.3.3° in justifying the test. They also made occasional reference to other constitutional rights which individual women and mothers have, as support for this interpretation of Article 40.3.3°. For example, McCarthy J referred to Article 40 and the fundamental rights of the family guaranteed by Article 41. But he provided no reasons or arguments as to how exactly these other constitutional rights supported the right to abortion. McCarthy J also referred to the right to bodily integrity asking, but not answering, whether this right involves the right to control one's own body (1992: para. 147). The language of Article 40.3.3 and its constitutional context provided interpretative resources, which the judiciary used in unnecessarily restrictive terms. Different applications of Article 40.3.3° were and are open to Irish judges, but they chose, arguably more by default than intention, not to consider a fuller range of possible interpretations.

A key feature of Article 40.3.3°, which the Court relied on in ruling that the right to life of the unborn could be and was limited, was its reference to the need to have "due regard to the *equal* right to life of the mother" and to the fact that the State's duty to defend and vindicate the right to life of the unborn was imposed "as far as *practicable*" (emphasis added). As Egan J noted, the wording of the Eighth Amendment indicates "that an abortion will not in every circumstance be unlawful" (1992: para. 181). These two terms, equal and practicable, are rich in scope and could take on a variety of different meanings depending on the perspective informing them and on the concrete context in which they are applied. Together with the complexity and richness of some of the other concepts raised by Article 40.3.3° and its constitutional context, such as: unborn, State duty, bodily integrity, privacy, familial status and rights hierarchy these terms make the legal meaning of Article 40.3.3° far from clear or obvious. A fuller consideration of their possible interpretation will have to wait another day, but a glance at the literature on the meaning of equality (Mullally, 1998; Baker et al., 2004; Cooper, 2004; Cook and Howard, 2007), for example, indicates the complexity of concepts relevant to the scope of Article 40.3.3°, and the possibility for varied interpretation to accommodate a variety of different factual circumstances.

State Duty to Defend Unborn

Obviously Article 40.3.3° imposes a key limit on any right to abortion that might be derived from the Constitution by imposing a duty on the State to defend and vindicate the right to life of the unborn. The Court assumed that this duty made the unborn's right to life legally equivalent to the pregnant woman's right to life. The judges also assumed that the State duty in Article 40.3.3° was of such a nature as to impose a positive obligation of unborn protection by limiting women's liberty to travel while pregnant, as well as a negative obligation to prevent termination of unborn life, unless justified by other rights. I will address the issue of free movement and travel in the next section, and focus here on the Court's understanding of the right to life of the unborn, and of the State's duty to defend and vindicate that right.

In considering how to reconcile two apparently conflicting constitutional rights, the court heard arguments from the defendant's counsel (1992: para. 70), which differentiated between the legal status of the unborn and the legal status of the pregnant woman by pointing to the contingent and putative nature of unborn life, in the sense of its complete dependence on the pregnant woman for life. Such arguments raise the question of the meaning and scope of the concept of the unborn. This issue has been explicitly picked up by legal developments post-X, and had been raised as a potential problem with the Eighth Amendment during the Referendum debate by the Attorney General of the time, Peter Sutherland, among others.[4] The Commission on Assisted Human Reproduction effectively recommended that the concept of the unborn in Article 40.3.3° be interpreted so as to exclude embryos *in vitro*,[5] and the High Court adopted a similar interpretation in *R v R* (2006)[6] (see further Madden, this volume). The State also argued in *D v Ireland* (2006) that the concept of the unborn could be interpreted so as not to apply to a foetus

---

4 The Attorney General's advice on the Amendment was read into the record by the then Minister for Health, Barry Desmond (Labour), (see Dail Debates, 17 February 1983, col 474) after having been the topic of *Irish Times* reporting on the 16th February 1983. Sutherland had advised that the wording was "ambiguous and unsatisfactory", principally because it failed to define "unborn", which could be interpreted to apply from conception or from viability, and because in posing an equality between pregnant woman and unborn it could restrict medical treatment in the context of pregnancy. Michael Woods, the Minister of Health who had introduced the Bill for the Eighth Amendment before his government fell, noted that the wording did not define the moment at which the unborn's life began, see Dáil Debates, 9 February 1983, col. 1386. See further Smyth (2006: 73-90).

5 See Report of The Commission on Assisted Human Reproduction (2005); Recommendation 16, and further section 6.3 and Appendix 3; available at http://www.dohc.ie/publications/cahr.html

6 McGovern J commented: "I have therefore come to the conclusion that the word 'unborn' within Article 40.3.3° does not include embryos in vitro and therefore does not include the three frozen embryos which are at the heart of the dispute between the plaintiff and the first named defendant" (*MR v TR*, 2006).

which was incapable of independent life after birth, such as a foetus with a lethal genetic abnormality, and the ECtHR accepted that argument.[7]

As the *Green Paper on Abortion* noted in 1999 (para. 7.12) there is theoretically nothing to exclude viability as the moment from which legal protection of the unborn might ensue. As the Green Paper also notes, the constitutional status quo suggests that viability is not the relevant legal criterion, but the possibility has not been addressed in any detail. All of the Supreme Court Judges in the *X* case assumed that Article 40.3.3° applied in the context of X's pregnancy and did not engage in any substantive reasoning about the legal meaning of unborn. By implication, the *X* case decision has excluded viability, or some stage after the first trimester, as a possible starting point for legal protection of the unborn. But technically some stage before the stage of gestation at issue in *X* could mark the beginning point for legal protection of embryos or foetuses *in vivo*. There is obviously obiter and other comment[8] which suggests that the earlier moment of conception, fertilisation or implantation is the relevant point, but these comments may be criticised on various grounds.[9]

But even assuming that legal protection of the unborn applies at early gestational stages, the question still remains as to how to evaluate and weigh any legal rights or interests which attach to an unborn with those that attach to other living beings such as a pregnant woman. The legal recognition of an embryonic or foetal right to life is a starting point

---

[7] "There is, in the Court's view, a feasible argument to be made that the constitutionally enshrined balance between the right to life of the mother and of the foetus could have shifted in favour of the mother, when the "unborn" suffered from a (sic) abnormality incompatible with life" (*D v Ireland*, 2006: para. 90).

[8] In *Attorney General v Open Door Counselling and Dublin Well Woman* (1988: 598), Hamilton P said that statutory protection (sections 58 and 59 of the Offences Against the Person Act 1861) of the unborn began at the moment of conception. The Green Paper interpreted this as meaning the moment of fertilisation (para 7.08). Charleton, McDermott and Bolger (1999) note conception could mean either fertilisation or implantation. See also Sherlock (1989) and Madden (2002).

[9] One such ground is the logical inconsistency in Hamilton P's language. He refers to the "foetus in the womb" as that which has protection and then states that the protection begins at conception. But the foetal stage of development is generally regarded as beginning in the ninth week after fertilisation or eleventh week of gestational age, while conception may refer either to the moment of fertilisation in the fallopian tube, or to the moment when the embryo implants in the womb by attaching to the uterine lining.

rather than a finishing point in legal analysis when it comes to adjudicating how a conflict of rights should be resolved. However, most of the judiciary adopted a fairly superficial approach to the conflict of rights issue as it arose in *X*, with only McCarthy J recognising that the nature of the rights in question might affect the resolution of the conflict.

Finlay CJ noted that the doctrine of harmonious interpretation applied, in light of the concepts of prudence, justice and charity as explained by Walsh J in *McGee v The Attorney General* (1973), and that such an interpretation involved "a consideration of the constitutional rights and obligations of the mother of the unborn child and the interrelation of those rights and obligations with the rights and obligations of other people, and, of course, with the right to life of the unborn child as well" (1992: para. 35). In spite of this promising interpretative opening, which suggested that a range of interests would be evaluated in deciding how to produce a harmonious interpretation of them, we are presented with a conclusion and denied any account of how that conclusion was reached:

> Such a harmonious interpretation… leads me to the conclusion that in vindicating and defending as far as practicable the right of the unborn to life but at the same time giving due regard to the right of the mother to life, the Court must, amongst the matters to be so regarded, concern itself with the position of the mother within a family group, with persons on whom she is dependent, with, in other instances, persons who are dependent upon her and her interaction with other citizens and members of society in the areas in which her activities occur… (1992: para. 36).

O'Flaherty J adopts language which recognises complexity and a range of relevant constitutional interests. He refers specifically to the historical background of the Eighth Amendment, the fact that the Eighth Amendment is but one provision in the Constitution, the core commitment of the Constitution to freedom and justice, the constitutional respect for the family, and the State's constitutional duty "to look to the economic needs of mothers" (1992: para. 161). But he does not provide any reasoned account as to how he has resolved the interaction of all these interests so as to produce the legal test adopted for Article 40.3.3°. Egan J relies solely on the wording of the Eighth Amendment in his reasoning and discusses the issue of rights conflict and his approach thereto only in relation to the conflict between the woman's right to travel and the right to life of the unborn in the context of travelling for a termination of pregnancy, which I discuss below.

Hederman J noted that the Court had to have regard to other provisions of the Constitution in interpreting any Article and took the view that "the objective of protecting human life [was] the essential value of every legal order and central to the enjoyment of all other rights guaranteed by the Constitution" (1992: para. 121). He also considered that there was no relevant distinction between the right to life of the unborn and the right to life of the pregnant woman, and further that the woman had a duty to carry out the pregnancy, with which the State must act in accordance. Hederman J's interpretation of the legal issues was obviously the most conservative. But he also adopted a style of interpretation which identified the key elements of his decision – primacy of human life, a duty to gestate etc. – but did not explain how such interests led to the conclusion he drew.

In adopting a harmonious interpretation of the relevant constitutional interests, McCarthy J preferred to seek the reconciliation rather than the hierarchical ranking of rights (1992: para. 138) and was explicit in differentiating between the status of the pregnant woman and that of the unborn. He said:

> [T]he right of the girl here is a right to a life in being; the right of the unborn is to a life contingent; contingent on survival in the womb until successful delivery. It is not a question of setting one above the other but rather of vindicating, as far as practicable, the right to life of the girl/mother (Article 40 s.3 sub-s.2) whilst with due regard to the equal right to life of the girl/mother, vindicating, as far as practicable, the right to life of the unborn (1992: para. 140).

This is a preferable approach to the complexity of the legal issues as it recognises that an abstract hierarchy of rights does not provide a straightforward solution when applied to the concrete issues, and that a formal equalisation of the interests of pregnant woman and embryo/foetus masks and thus fails to address the actual differences between them.

McCarthy J's opinion is also more useful in its recognition of a positive/negative distinction with regard to legislation when he says that negative legislation prohibits particular activities absolutely or at a given time, while positive legislation requires positive action. He goes on to note that the State could fulfil its role in vindicating the right to life of the unborn by "providing necessary agencies to help, or counsel, to encourage, to comfort, to plan for the pregnant woman, the pregnant girl or her family" (1992: para. 148). In so doing, he raises the question of the scope of the State's duty in vindicating the unborn. Again this is a concept which the Court did not evaluate in any full sense in coming to its decision.

X's Right to Travel

One of the grounds of appeal was that the trial judge was wrong in law and in fact in holding that the Court ought to restrain travelling abroad as an unlawful act as it was not an unlawful act, and such restraint may constitute a curtailment of the defendant's constitutional right to liberty as provided in Article 40.4 of the Constitution. Although this argument was rendered legally redundant by the Court's finding that X had a right to abortion in Ireland, the Court's comments about the right to travel give us further insight into the problems with their constitutional interpretation and reasoning. Three of the five judges gave the obiter view that it would be justifiable to restrict the right to travel where that came into direct conflict with the right to life of the unborn. They did so on the basis that conflicts of rights ought to be resolved by prioritising the right, which was higher up the hierarchy of constitutional rights in their view, that is, the right to life. Two of the five judges were of the view that the right to travel was a type of individual freedom, which ought not to be restricted by the State. In so finding, the majority adopted a conservative approach to the relationship between positive and negative civil rights. They limited a negative right to liberty, to travel in this particular instance, by reference to a positive right to unborn life, without any substantive evaluation of how the relationship between positive and negative rights, or between life and liberty, should be addressed.

Even though Finlay CJ was the Judge who first recognised the right to travel as one of the unenumerated personal rights under Article 40.4,[10] and although he saw it as a fundamental right "closely identified with the characteristics of any free society" (1992: para. 50), he still gave the obiter view that the right to life of the unborn would have to take precedence over the right to travel in cases of stark conflict (1992: para. 53). Egan J was of the view that the constitutional imposition of a positive obligation on the State to defend the right to life of the unborn meant that the right to life had to take precedence over the right to travel *simpliciter*. Hederman J was also clearly of the view that where there was a conflict between the right to travel and the right to life, albeit the foetal right to life, the latter had to take precedence. He noted further that there were other occasions on which persons had their right to travel limited, such as those on bail or those who were wards of court. He said that this case did not concern an issue of criminal law and that there was no question of punishing anyone. Again this is quite superficial reasoning given that the substantive effect of imposing the injunction was coercive and punitive.

In my view, McCarthy and O'Flaherty JJ adopted a better position in substance and approach, but their reasoning could have been more fully developed. They both considered the nature of the liberty right underpinning the right to travel, and the consequences of limiting such a liberty right by reference to an intention to use that liberty to terminate a pregnancy in another jurisdiction. In their view it was not justifiable to deny the right to travel on the grounds that the exercise of travel would infringe the unborn's right to life, because the legal value of liberty ought not to be limited. For McCarthy J it was not a question of a balancing exercise between the right to travel and the unborn's right to life; rather the right to travel could not be curtailed because of a particular intent (1992: para. 153). O'Flaherty J framed the right to travel in terms of "whether officers of the State are obliged to invoke what may be called the police power of the State to interfere with the freedom of the individual, especially the individual's freedom of movement in and out of the jurisdiction?" (1992: para. 164). In his view a decision to grant an injunction interfering "to this extraordinary degree with the individual's

---

[10] See *State (M) v The Attorney General* (1979).

freedom of movement … is impossible to reconcile with a Constitution one of the primary objects of which, as stated in the Preamble, is to assure the dignity and freedom of the individual" (1992: paras. 166-7).

Applying Reproductive Justice

One of the ways in which we can identify the significance of a reproductive justice framework on the legal regulation of abortion, is through the further elaboration of the meaning of the equality principle as it informs Article 40.3.3°. The basic principle of formal equality is that that which is alike should be treated similarly, and that which is not alike should be treated differently. In other words, inequality may be produced by treating similar entities differently and by treating different entities in the same way. Even a basic commitment to formal rather than substantive equality would require an assessment of the two entities that are to be treated equally in order to first establish whether there are any key differences between them. It is arguable that foetus (and embryo) and woman are sufficiently different as types of living beings to merit different treatment in order to avoid the production of inequality. Women have consciousness, while foetuses do not. We know that women feel pain, while the evidence suggests that capacity for foetal pain is unlikely to develop until the third trimester (Royal College of Obstetricians and Gynaecologists, 1997; Lee, S. et al, 2005; Nuffield Council on Bioethics, 2006 at para. 4.19).

The arguments raised in *X* about the different status of a "life in being" as distinct from a "life contingent" could be developed in applying Article 40.3.3°'s direction to have due regard to the "equal" right to life of the mother while vindicating the right to life of the unborn. Having due regard to the equality of the conscious, sentient woman who has constitutional rights to life, bodily integrity, liberty and privacy, while vindicating the right to life of the unconscious, insentient unborn who needs the pregnant woman's body for sustenance, could theoretically be interpreted so as to guarantee the life of the unborn only so far as it does not overly compromise the constitutional interests of the woman. Obviously it would take a considerable change in judicial perspective in order for such an interpretation to become legally feasible, and it may be preferable to remove the Eighth Amendment as a matter of legal reform. But the point remains that the Irish judiciary have chosen a particularly conservative interpretation of the interests at stake in enforcing Article 40.3.3°, one which is at odds with a basic commitment to liberal formal equality principles.

A second set of issues, which could be developed through a reproductive justice perspective, concerns the scope of public duties in defending and vindicating the unborn. Article 40.3.3° has a legal impact not only by regulating pregnant women, but also by imposing duties on the State. In effect, the *X* judgment relied on the public interest in the existence of embryonic/foetal life, as recognised by Article 40.3.3°, when it was considering whether that public interest could limit X's private interest in ending the pregnancy. The main way in which the public interest in embryonic/foetal life was considered therefore focused on the extent to which the State could limit the actions of an individual woman. But that is not the only way in which the State could exercise its duties to defend and vindicate the unborn. Such duties could be realised through the provision of support services for pregnant women in a manner, which values embryonic/foetal and maternal life. Indeed some of the Supreme Court judges, such as O'Flaherty J for example (at para. 166) referred to the need for the State to perform a positive role in the case, rather than a negative one.

Thirdly, a reproductive justice perspective would prefer and develop the view of the minority judgment over that of the majority when it comes to the issue of travel rights and free movement. As is well known, in the aftermath of the *X* case, Article 40.3.3° was amended by referendum in November 1992 so as to incorporate a freedom to travel and a freedom to information. In *A and B v Eastern Health Board and C* (1998) otherwise known as the *C* case, the question arose as to whether a young woman in the care of the State had a right to abortion and to travel abroad in a context where she was suicidal having become pregnant through rape. It therefore fell to the High Court to evaluate the travel issue, among other things, in light of the Thirteenth and Fourteenth amendments as well as the *X* case judgment. One additional aspect was whether a "freedom" had a different legal status to a "right". A freedom is effectively a form of negative right not to have one's liberty proscribed, while a right can have positive as well as negative dimensions in the sense that it may impose a duty of positive action to assist. In the *X* case a majority of the Supreme Court had taken the view that the positive right to life was weightier than the negative right, or freedom, to travel. But as noted above this is inconsistent with any view which takes freedom seriously as a fundamental aspect of human life.

In the *C* case, Geoghegan J seemed to take the obiter view[11] that the freedom to travel trumped as the unborn's right to life had been intentionally restricted by the amendment's adoption of the freedom to travel. This reasoning bases the evaluation of the conflict between rights on the supposed intention of those who passed the amendment. Such reasoning is flawed because it is usual to defend any claim either by reference to either empirical evidence or normative argument. Although Geoghegan J was under no legal obligation to refer to sources such as Dáil debates in seeking to determine legal meaning, his claim about the "people's intention" would be more convincing if he supported it with some evidence. Geoghegan J made no effort to support his interpretation of the intention of the amendment by reference to any evidence as to Parliament's intention in adopting the Bill which put the Thirteenth and Fourteenth Amendments to the people, or to any evidence of popular intention at the time. Evidence of popular intention would be extremely difficult if not impossible to ascertain in a context where the people are law-makers as referendum voters, have a range of different motivations for their voting choices and did not have their motivations and intentions recorded properly at the time. As a result, Geoghegan J was left simply declaring the amendment's intention as if it was common sense, rather than a complex form of wording which could support a number of different interpretations.

In the absence of a sounder evidence base, this kind of reasoning ends up making a normative choice without engaging in normative evaluation of conflicting legal rights. It is arguably better constitutional practice to recognise the different political philosophies and values which inform constitutional provisions (Daly, 2008) historically and normatively, and come to a judgement about how to reconcile them in

---

[11] The decision to permit C to travel abroad for a termination of pregnancy while in the care of the state was based on the reasoning that C met the test in the *X* case and therefore had a right to abortion in Ireland and permission to travel.

the contemporary factual context raised. A reproductive justice perspective would reject such an original intention form of constitutional interpretation on the grounds that it is impracticable as a historical finding and undesirable as a normative goal.

In the *D* case (2007), the High Court was asked to rule on the issue of whether Miss D – who was in the care of the State, whose foetus had a lethal genetic abnormality, and who wanted to travel for abortion services – had a right to travel. McKechnie J is reported as being unequivocal in his opinion that there was no law or constitutional impediment preventing the girl from travelling for the purpose of terminating her pregnancy (*The Irish Times*, 10 May 2007). As there is no reported judgment available, we have to rely on the newspaper reports for an account of his reasoning. His decision that a right to travel should not be limited by the State, through its Health Services Executive, is sensible from a reproductive justice perspective. His interpretative approach appears to have constructed the legal issues as concerning the matter of travel exclusively, and not abortion or the right to life of the unborn. He took the view that "Miss D's right to travel for an abortion was unaffected by Article 40.3.3 of the Constitution", and based his decision on the Child Care Act 1991, saying that "there was no law or provision of the Child Care Act which restrained a child in care from travelling for an abortion or which would support the HSE's claim that District Court permission was required for travel". This understanding seems to accord more with that of McCarthy and O'Flaherty JJ in the *X* case, who thought that the right to travel ought not to be restricted by the State on the basis of the travel's purpose. Although McKechnie J ends up in a position which is defensible from a reproductive justice perspective, it would be preferable to address the conflict of interests directly and find that the State duty in Article 40.3.3° cannot justifiably limit travel rights without sacrificing a legal commitment to basic freedoms.

The Legal Issues in *O*

In the *O* case (2002), the key legal issues concerned the scope of the State's power to deport non-nationals and whether that power was restricted by the State's duty to vindicate the right to life of the unborn under Article 40.3.3° when the person to be deported was pregnant. These legal issues arose in a factual context where a pregnant Nigerian national whose claim for refugee status had been ruled "manifestly unfounded"[12] sought an order quashing her deportation order on various grounds. One of the grounds was that the deportation contravened Art 40.3.3° by failing to protect the unborn. In the High Court, Smyth J had refused the application for the various reliefs claimed in January 2001. But he was of the view that an appeal to the Supreme Court should be taken given that a point of law of exceptional public importance was at issue.[13]

Smyth J therefore granted leave to appeal the refusal of relief in respect of certiorari orders quashing two deportation orders and in respect of a declaration that the first named applicant i.e. Baby O was a person whose constitutional rights would be interfered with by the deportation of the second named applicant i.e. Ms. O, and an order of mandamus requiring the Minister to reconsider deportation in light of the applicant's "changed circumstances" i.e. Ms O's pregnancy. The woman was expected to give birth in May 2002 so an expedited oral hearing was held on 5 and 6 of February 2002. On 14 February the Supreme Court announced that the appeal would be dismissed and that reasons would be forthcoming later. On 6 June 2002 Chief Justice Keane delivered the judgment on behalf of a 5 judge court which agreed with the High Court judge and said that Article 40.3.3° was irrelevant in this context and that the orders in relation to deportation were not procedurally faulty.

The legal arguments which both courts were asked to consider in relation to Article 40.3.3° revolved around the status of the unborn, and the nature and degree of the State's obligations to the unborn in the context of an order to deport a pregnant woman. This case raised for the first time the question of whether the State had a positive duty to protect pregnancy and reproductive health in the context of a wanted pregnancy,

---

[12] The Supreme Court upheld a High Court decision not to grant leave to challenge the validity of deportation orders for failure to give reasons or adequate reasons for the making of the order (*P L and B v The Minister for Justice, Equality and Law Reform and Another*, 2002).

[13] Section 5(3)(a) of the Illegal Immigrants (Trafficking) Act 2000 provides that the High Court's determination of an application for leave to apply for a judicial review shall be final unless the High Court gives leave because its decision concerns a matter of exceptional public importance.

and if so whether and to what extent that duty should compromise the State's power to deport non-citizens. In constructing this claim, lawyers representing "Baby" O were reported as arguing that the unborn is a person under Irish law, that a separate deportation order should have been made in relation to the unborn as a legal entity, and that the State had a duty to do everything practicable to protect the unborn's right to life (Coulter, 2002).

The Supreme Court judgment did not engage with the Article 40.3.3° arguments in any substance and simply declared that Article 40.3.3° was about abortion and was not relevant in a deportation context. Keane CJ agreed with the High Court judge who had stated: "This case has nothing to do with abortion or the right to life of the unborn or what is sometimes referred to as a woman's right to choose" (2002: 8). Keane CJ stated that Article 40.3.3° was intended[14] to prevent the legalisation of abortion, and as the case did not involve the State in seeking to terminate the applicant's pregnancy, Article 40.3.3° was irrelevant. In so doing he narrowed the scope of Article 40.3.3° so that it covers the prohibition of abortion but not the protection of reproductive health. The effect of this is to substantiate the argument that Article 40.3.3° is more about restricting women's reproductive choices than about protecting foetal interests. This interpretation of Article 40.3.3° is unjust in its failure to recognise reproductive health as a value worthy of constitutional protection, and is arguably discriminatory in effectively denying deportees its application.

A Right to Reproductive Health Care

The novel argument which was made on behalf of O in this case was that she had a right not to be deported because deporting her would be a breach of the State's obligation to defend and vindicate the right to life of the unborn under Article 40.3.3°. O's counsel relied on the evidence that the infant mortality rate was 90 per thousand births in Nigeria compared with 7 in the Republic of Ireland, to make the claim that deportation from Ireland to Nigeria would expose O to relatively poor levels of

[14] Keane CJ's reliance on the intention behind the Eighth Amendment may be subjected to a similar critique as that made above of Geoghegan J, when he refers to the intention behind the Thirteenth and Fourteenth Amendments.

pre and ante-natal care. In effect, their argument was that such exposure would subject the unborn to an unacceptable standard of risk and breach the State's obligation to do that which was practicable in defending and vindicating the unborn.

This rather convoluted argument depended on a number of steps for its articulation. First, for this argument to be made out the State's duty under Article 40.3.3° would have to include a duty to sustain a certain minimum standard of reproductive health care. Second, that duty would have to encompass an obligation not to expose human beings to environments which fell below that standard, and that obligation would have to be capable of restricting State power to take action against individuals which would have the consequence of such exposure. In other words, it could be quite difficult to convince a court that all the elements of this argument were legally acceptable or made out on the facts. But the point I am most concerned with here, is the Supreme Court's rejection of the first part of the argument, namely that some right to a minimum standard of reproductive health care could be derived from the State's obligations under Article 40.3.3°.

In rejecting the claim that the State had a duty to protect O's pregnancy from the consequences of exposure to poorer levels of ante and postnatal care the Chief Justice said: "The fact that the standard of ante or postnatal care available to her in Nigeria was less than would be available to her in this country was entirely irrelevant to the legality of her deportation" (2002: 60). The Chief Justice seemed to find it unthinkable that the State may be obliged to address the pre-natal care needs of the unborn. Yet why should an explicit State obligation to vindicate the right to life of the unborn, with due regard to the life of the mother, not include some duty to prevent infringements of a right to basic care? Why should pregnant women who do not wish to be pregnant be the only ones to bear obligations under Article 40.3.3°? In the High Court, Smyth J had stated that the right to life of the unborn did not extend to socio-economic rights such as access to a health or welfare system (Coulter, 2002c). Smyth J could have been responding to the State's argument that this case was really about a pregnant failed asylum seeker seeking access to Irish maternity services. At first instance before the High Court, Birmingham SC was reported as arguing on behalf of the State that this

> … is not a case where the right to life is being put at risk. Instead, however it's dressed up, this is about a person who comes here, puts in a claim for asylum, loses at all stages and says, while that claim is being processed, "I've become pregnant and because the health service here is superior to that in my country of origin, I claim the right to have my baby here" (Coulter, 2002b).

Birmingham clearly represented Ms. O as someone who wants to take unfair advantage of the health service and the legal system, rather than as someone who is acting to defend and vindicate herself and her foetus. In the same moment that the judicial arm of the State denies that there could be a public obligation to provide basic reproductive services as part of a foetal protection law, pregnant women are assumed to bear all responsibility for reproduction privately and individually.

State Power to Deport

The key reason why the Supreme Court found that Article 40.3.3° was not relevant in this context, and moreover did not include a duty to provide basic reproductive health services, was because it constructed the issues as exclusively about deportation and the sovereign power of the State to deport. The Chief Justice stated in response to arguments for O: "[i]f the State's right to deport persons who have been refused refugee status and who have no legal right to remain in the country were thus circumscribed, it would be, in a great range of cases, virtually negated" (2002: 60). Here Keane CJ appears to equate the circumscription of State deportation powers with their negation. But the whole point of guaranteeing rights constitutionally or legislatively is to circumscribe and fetter the State in its exercise of power. But rather than try to find some way to evaluate competing legal interests in this instance – the right to life of the unborn and the power of the State to deport non-citizens – the Chief Justice dismisses the idea that the State's power in this interest could be limited by Article 40.3.3°. The consequence is that the State power to deport is inflated in the same moment that the right to life of the unborn is deflated (see further, Luibhéid 2006).

Counsel for the applicants also argued that if deportation was found to contravene Art 40.3.3° it would necessarily follow that every woman or girl of childbearing age would have to submit to pregnancy testing before she was deported or extradited to a country with less developed pre and postnatal services than are available in Ireland. This seems an unusually coercive and unnecessary interpretation to adopt in considering how best to limit the power to deport in light of pregnancy protection or reproductive health policy. Obviously factual evidence of pregnancy is necessary for a court of law to enforce any rights attached to that pregnancy. But why should the need for evidence of pregnancy in a particular case become the need to test all child-bearing women? Interestingly, Keane CJ comments on the coercive implications of this claim when he says: "No such gross violation of the privacy of women and girls could possibly have been intended by the enactment of Art 40.3.3° of the Constitution" (2002: 60). If compelling pregnancy testing is a gross violation of the privacy rights of women and girls, then so is compelling pregnancy, albeit one that is contemplated by Article 40.3.3°.

Baby O's Alleged Personhood

The positive right to pregnancy and reproductive health care was framed as a right derived from unborn personhood, or more particularly the personhood of Baby O. The language of unborn personhood had not featured in the *X* case. Rather there the emphasis had been on the concept of unborn life, and the duties which derived from the value of life itself, rather than from the status of personhood. But lawyers representing Baby O were reported as arguing that the unborn is a person under Irish law, that a separate deportation order should have been made in relation to the unborn as a legal entity, and that the State had a duty to do everything practicable to protect the unborn's right to life (Coulter, 2002a). They therefore explicitly constructed Baby O as a legal person whose constitutional rights would be interfered with by the deportation of the pregnant woman (Labyani, 2002). In response, lawyers representing the State at first argued in the opening statement that "[I]t is denied that the first named applicant is a person or has a right to legal personality" (Coulter, 2002b). Later, in the wake of controversy over the State taking this position, State lawyers asserted that it was not denying that the unborn had rights, rather the State's argument was that "in the context of these proceedings the rights of the unborn are not distinguishable [from those of the pregnant woman]" (Coulter, 2002b). Although this aspect of the case received considerable press attention as the State's position was questioned, the Supreme Court did not explicitly address the personhood point in its judgment.

In the context of the deportation of a Nigerian woman, the State was happy to argue that foetal rights were not distinct from a woman's rights. This position stands in marked contrast to its explicit representation of the unborn as a distinct legal entity in the context of abortion information law.[15] The State's argument in this regard also contradicts the decisions in the *X* and *C* cases where the unborn's rights were deemed capable of limiting women's rights except the right to life and including the right to travel.

Limiting Article 40.3.3° to Abortion Issues

The Court avoided the task of addressing directly the conflicting interests arguments by limiting the material scope of Article 40.3.3° to the context of abortion and its prohibition. This is a legal trend which is reflected elsewhere, as for example in the context of the legal regulation of assisted conception (Report of the Commission on Assisted Human Reproduction, 2005). Indeed, in the "frozen embryos" case *R v R* (2006), McGovern J noted Keane J's decision in *O* (2002) that Article 40.3.3° applies to decisions concerning the prohibition of abortion. In *R v R* (2006) McGovern J found that Article 40.3.3° applies to embryos *in vivo* and not *in vitro*. But the Supreme Court's ruling in *O* arguably contradicts the face value of the constitutional wording which refers in general terms to the State's guarantee to defend and vindicate the right to life of the unborn. There had also been some obiter comment before the *O* case to suggest that Article 40.3.3° had a wider scope. In the *C* case, Geoghegan J had noted that Article 40.3.3° "quite clearly not merely prohibits abortion but gives a positive right to life to the unborn, subject only to the exception where the mother's life is endangered" (1998: para. 24).

Further judicial elaboration on the meaning and scope of Article 40.3.3° is welcome, as one of the key interpretative issues is its complexity and breadth. But it is noteworthy that the scope of the foetal right is

---

[15] See In Re Article 26 of the Constitution and the Regulation of Information (Services outside the State for the Termination of Pregnancies) Bill 1995 (1995) where the Supreme Court upheld the Bill as constitutional given it was an appropriate balancing of the constitutional interests of the unborn with the those of the pregnant woman.

first explicitly limited by the Supreme Court in a case where it is asserted on behalf of a Nigerian unborn who is being deported. The court did not have to limit the scope of the right in this way in order to produce a similar outcome. It was arguable that the risk to the unborn was too remote on the facts to engage Article 40.3.3° or alternatively to limit the State power to deport. The strong assertion in this instance that Article 40.3.3° applies only to the abortion issue suggests that the constitutional protection of foetal interests is less persuasive when pregnant deportees[16] are before the court.

Applying Reproductive Justice

The *O* case raised a conflict of legal interests on which the Court had to adjudicate. The conflict which was addressed most directly was that between the right to life of the unborn and the power of the State to deport a non-citizen. But the conflict of interests at stake here could have been framed in different legal terms. A more satisfactory strategy from a reproductive justice perspective would have been to see Article 40.3.3° as a positive legal protection of the State's duty to protect voluntary pregnancies, and to assess whether that duty curtailed the State's power to deport a pregnant woman who had failed in her claim to asylum. In O the pregnant woman did want the foetus to continue to exist and so there was a private interest in the pregnancy worthy of legal protection. There was also a public interest in continued existence of the foetus, given the general interest in reproduction. The Supreme Court decided that the woman's interest and the State interest in protecting the pregnancy were not relevant in the deportation context. A reproductive justice perspective would argue that the State cannot just choose to opt out of its duty to protect foetal life. Indeed that duty should apply even more strongly when it is not qualified by a woman's conflicting interest.

The idea that the duty to protect unborn life includes the duty to provide a minimum standard of reproductive health care would fit with a reproductive justice perspective. In denying the constitutional protection of such a derivative duty, the court emphasised private, individual re-

---

[16] See Luibhéid and Lentin (2004) for a more general discussion of the treatment of migrant women in Ireland.

sponsibility for reproduction which is policed by the State. The Court clearly rejected an opportunity to develop a positive conception of the State's duty which would vindicate unborn life by providing a minimum standard of public reproductive health services. At the same time as the court sidelined State duties to provide reproductive health services, it emphasised State powers to deport non-citizens.

From a reproductive justice perspective, both sets of counsel were wrong in assuming that the appropriate scope of the rights protection in this instance turned on the question of whether the unborn was or was not a person. It was possible to argue for legal protection of the pregnancy or the foetal interests in question, without constructing the foetus within O as a legal person. We can accept that a public interest in the health and welfare of women and children implies a legal duty to protect pregnancy and foetal life without relying on ideas of unborn personhood. On the other side, the State could have argued that its obligation to defend unborn rights was not engaged or was justifiably limited without having to frame the arguments in terms of non-personhood. In failing to make these distinctions, counsel allowed popular conceptions of unborn personhood to overtake the legal application of analytical categories.

Conclusion

A reproductive justice framework helps us to contextualise the scope of Article 40.3.3° by reference to the reproductive needs and desires of differently situated pregnant women. Women whose bodies and minds contribute to humankind by sustaining and nourishing foetal life should be supported in so doing. In the same way, women whose bodies and minds tell them that pregnancy is not right in this moment and place should be supported in acting on that judgment. A reproductive justice perspective would seek a shift from the current constitutional position where unborn interests are generally seen as trumps (except where a woman's life is in danger) to a more evaluative consideration of how best to balance public and private interests in women's reproductive roles with public and private interests in foetal life. In that way we can better defend the human process of reproduction against assumptions which have the effect of devaluing feminine and migrant life.

Bibliography

Baker J., Lynch, K. Cantillon, S. and Walsh J. (2004), *Equality: From Theory to Practice,* Basingstoke: Palgrave Macmillan.

Charleton, P., McDermott, P. and Bolger, M. (1999), *Criminal Law*, Dublin: Butterworths.

Cook, R., Dickens, B. and Fathalla, M. (2003), *Reproductive Health and Human Rights: Integrating Medicine, Ethics and Law*, Oxford: Oxford University Press.

Cook, R. and Howard, S. (2007), "Accommodating Women's Differences Under the Women's Anti-Discrimination Convention", *Emory Law Journal* 56: 1039.

Cooper, D. (2004), *Challenging Diversity: Rethinking Equality and the Value of Difference,* Cambridge: Cambridge University Press.

Coulter, C. (2002a), "AG to argue that unborn child is not a person", *The Irish Times*, 9 January.

Coulter, C. (2002b), "State fails to argue foetus is not a person", *The Irish Times*, 10 January.

Coulter, C. (2002c), "Right of Minister to deport upheld by court", *The Irish Times*, 19 January.

Daly, E. (2008), "Hermeneutic Perspectives on Judicial Activism: Dworkin, Constitutional Interpretation and Judicial Law-making", *Cork Online Law Review,* 7: 16-27.

Fletcher, R. (2005), "Reproducing Irishness: Race, Gender and Abortion Law", *Canadian Journal of Women and the Law* 17(2): 365-403.

Fraser, N. (1997), *Justice Interruptus: Critical Reflections on the "Post-socialist" Condition*, New York: Routledge.

Gerber Fried, M. (ed.) (1990), *From Abortion to Reproductive Freedom: Transforming a Movement,* Cambridge MA: South End Press.

Green Paper on Abortion (1999), Dublin: Government of Ireland.

Kennedy, P. (ed.) (2004), *Motherhood in Ireland*, Cork: Mercier Press.

Kingston, J. and Whelan, A. with I. Bacik (1997) *Abortion and the Law*, Dublin: Sweet and Maxwell.

Labanyi, D. (2002), "State Retreats from Saying Unborn Is Not a Person," *The Irish Times*, 9 January.

Lacey, N. (1998)"Theories of Justice and the Welfare State: A Feminist Critique" in Lacey, N., *Unspeakable Subjects: Feminist Essays in Legal and Social Theory*, Oxford: Hart, pp. 46-70.

Lee, S.J. et al. (2005) "Fetal pain: A systematic multidisciplinary review of the evidence", *Journal of the American Medical Association*, 295(8): 947-954.

Luibhéid, E. and Lentin, R. (2004) "Introduction to Representing Migrant Women in Ireland and the EU", *Women's Studies International Forum* 27(4): 293-300.

Luibhéid, E. (2006), "Sexual Regimes and Migration Controls: Reproducing the Irish Nation-State in Transnational Contexts", *Feminist Review*, 83: 60.

Madden, D. (2002), *Medicine, Ethics and Law,* Dublin, Butterworths.

Mullally, S. (1998), "Equality Guarantees in Irish Constitutional Law – The Myth of Constitutionalism and the "Neutral" State" in Murphy., T. and Twomey P. (eds.), *Ireland's Evolving Constitution*, Oxford: Hart, pp. 147-162.

Oireachtas Committee on the Constitution (2000), *Fifth Progress Report: Abortion*, Dublin: Government of Ireland.

Petchesky, R.P., and Judd, K (eds.), (1998) *Negotiating Reproductive Rights: Women's Perspectives Across Countries and Cultures*, London: Zed Press.

Quinn, G., Ingram, A. and Livingstone, S. (eds.) (1995) *Justice and Legal Theory in Ireland*, Dublin: Oak Tress Press.

Report of the Commission on Assisted Human Reproduction (2005), Dublin, Government of Ireland.

Roberts, D. (1997), *Killing the Black Body: Race, Reproduction and the Meaning of Liberty*, New York: Vintage Books.

Royal College of Obstetricians and Gynaecologists (1997) *Fetal Awareness: Report of a Working Party*, London: RCOG Press.

Sherlock, A. (1989) "The Right to Life of the Unborn and the Irish Constitution" *Irish Jurist*, 24: 13 – 25.

Silliman, J., Gerber Fried, M., Ross, L. and Gutierrez, E.R. (2004) *Undivided Rights: Women of Color Organize for Reproductive Justice,* Cambridge MA, South End Press.

Cases

A and B v Eastern Health Board, Fahy and C [1998] 1 IR 464.

Attorney General v Open Door Counselling and Dublin Well Woman [1988] IR 593.

Attorney General v X and Others [1992] IESC 1.

Baby O (suing by mother and next friend IAO) v Minister for Justice, Equality and Law Reform and Others [2002] IESC 53.

D v Ireland (2006) Application no 26499/092.

In Re Article 26 of the Constitution and the Regulation of Information (Services outside the State for the Termination of Pregnancies) Bill 1995 [1995] 1 IR 1.

Magee v Attorney General [1974] IR 284.

MR v TR & Ors [2006] IEHC 359.

P L and B v The Minister for Justice, Equality and Law Reform and Another [2002] 1 ILRM 16.

R v Bourne [1939] 1 KB 687.

State (M) v The Attorney General [1979] IR 73.

14

A "CONSTITUTIONALLY PERMISSIBLE" ABORTION?

The Right to Travel, the Role of the Medical Profession and the Duty of the HSE

Jennifer Schweppe

Introduction

In May 2007 it became clear that yet another young woman in the care of the Health Service Executive[1] (hereinafter referred to as "the HSE") was in the tragic situation of wanting to terminate her pregnancy, but needing to travel to the United Kingdom to do so[2] (*The Irish Times*, 2007a). While two earlier cases which had come before the courts concerned young women who were suicidal as a result of their pregnancy (*Attorney General v X,* 1992; *A and B v Eastern Health Board and C,* 1998)[3], this

---

[1] The Health Boards were consolidated into the Health Service Executive in 2004 under the Health Act 2004. Thus, this essay will refer to Health Boards where the case occurred pre 2004 and Health Service Executive where the case was decided after that.

[2] Judgment in the *D* case has unfortunately not been made available so this essay is based on newspaper reports of the case. This is unfortunate, given the huge importance of the case and the resulting uncertainty in the law. This essay uses reports from the *Irish Times* of the case.

[3] The *C* case concerned a thirteen-year-old girl in the care of the health board. She had been raped and was pregnant, and stated clearly that were she compelled to carry her child to term she would commit suicide. It had already been established in the *X* case, concerning a suicidal pregnant fourteen-year-old girl, that a threat to the life of a woman, including a risk of suicide, was grounds for a termination of pregnancy. The reason for

case was different. It involved a four-month pregnant seventeen-year-old young woman in the case of the HSE whose unborn child suffered from anencephaly.[4] While Miss D was initially happy to be pregnant, when she was told that her unborn child was suffering from this rare condition, she informed the HSE that she wished to travel to the United Kingdom to terminate the pregnancy. The HSE refused to give her permission to travel, and attempted to prevent her from obtaining a passport.[5] Miss D took an action seeking to prevent the HSE from restraining her from travelling to for the abortion. Due to her minority status at law, her boyfriend brought the application on her behalf.

The ultimate pronouncement by the High Court that Miss D was to be allowed to travel to the United Kingdom to have an abortion was unsurprising. There was no prospect of McKechnie J injuncting Miss D from leaving the State for the duration of her pregnancy, and forcing her to give birth to a child which had little or no chance of survival outside the womb. As stated by Minister McDowell, the decision was welcomed as a "humane and common-sense solution" (*The Irish Times*, 2007d). However, the outcome of the case, and the reasoning utilised in it (as it can be discerned without access to a written judgment) has a much wider impact than simply ensuring that seventeen-year-olds whose unborn child is anencephelic can terminate their pregnancies.

As Miss D was the subject of an Interim Care Order, the case is of enormous importance for the purposes of determining the rights and obligations of the HSE in relation to children in its care. The Court granted

---

this is that the termination of pregnancy is to treat the pregnant woman's suicidal tendencies. C sought permission to travel to the United Kingdom to terminate her pregnancy. The Eastern Health Board supported her in this, but her parents objected to her travelling on "moral and ethical grounds". They sought to prevent the Eastern Health Board from arranging for C to have an abortion abroad.

[4] Anencephaly is a condition whereby the brain of the child develops abnormally. Medical opinion stated that the child would survive for a maximum of three days outside the womb.

[5] It is unclear why the HSE refused Miss D the permission sought to travel to the UK to terminate her pregnancy. Reports indicate that it "quietly" facilitated women in a similar position (that is, those whose foetus's had severe abnormalities) to travel to the UK and allowed such women to use the E112 form, which provides refunds for hospital treatments which are not available in Ireland. In these circumstances, the State refunded the costs incurred by these women.

Miss D the right to make decisions in relation to her medical care, and it would appear that neither the HSE nor the Court had any right to limit Miss D's decision making ability. Shannon, speaking in *The Irish Times* downplayed the implications of the *Miss D* case, stating:

> [T]he ruling [will] not lead to children in care leaving the country whenever they felt like it.... [T]he HSE still [have] the power to act in place of the parent on behalf of children under 16 (*The Irish Times*, 2007d).

This chapter will examine the impact of the "Miss D" case from a number of perspectives: first, its interpretation of the travel amendment; second, the interpretation given by the medical profession to the question of when a termination can be carried out in the State; thirdly, the impact of the case on the ability of young people to consent to medical treatment generally; and finally, the impact on the case on the decision-making abilities of young people in care.

Contextualising the "Miss D" Case

The X Case

In the *X* case (1992), where the parents of X supported her wish to terminate her pregnancy, the Court held that the test to be applied in interpreting Article 40.3.3° is:

> [I]f it can be established as a matter of probability that there is a real and substantial risk to the life, as distinct from the health, of the mother, which can only be avoided by the termination of her pregnancy, such termination is permissible (1992: 53-54).

The Court held that as the termination in the case was permissible, Miss X was entitled to travel to the United Kingdom for an abortion. Important to note in this context is that the Court held that Miss X would have been entitled to an abortion in this country. However, this left the question open as to what the constitutional position would be where an individual sought to travel to terminate her pregnancy where the abortion was not constitutionally permissible. The Constitution was further amended in 1992 as a result of the *X* case to provide that the right to life of the unborn child could not be used to prevent a woman from travelling to procure an abortion, and the second paragraph of Article 40.3.3 now reads: "This subsection shall not limit freedom to travel between the State and another state." The question then was, whether the right to travel was an absolute one, or whether there were any constraints on it.

The Impact of the Travel Amendment

Kingston, Whelan and Bacik (1997) consider the travel amendment, and ask whether there are any circumstances under which it would be possible to prevent a woman (whatever age) from travelling to terminate her pregnancy. They concentrate on the issue of whether a husband could prevent his wife from travelling to terminate their unborn child. They are of the opinion that were a husband to seek to restrain his wife from travelling abroad for an abortion, he would probably be granted *locus standi* as having more interest than most in the life of his unborn child (1997: 213-7). The important question to be asked is whether that father would have the right to prevent the woman from travelling. Kingston and Whelan note that the Thirteenth Amendment "states only that nothing in Article 40.3.3° of the Constitution shall affect freedom to travel, leaving open the possibility that other rights, such as those of a husband or putative father, could be relied upon to prevent travel fin order to procure an abortion outside the State" (1997: 214-215).

However, Kingston and Whelan state that the two substantive arguments that would counter such an action are first, that under the ruling in *L v L* (1992) it is not clear whether a husband can automatically invoke the rights of the family against the wife.[6] Secondly, they also they also note that "any rights of the husband in respect of the unborn would have to be balanced against the right of the woman to individual privacy and to individual freedom and dignity, as well as to the independent exercise of the freedom to communicate" (1997: 216). However, they go on to note that if the courts were to find that the woman's rights superseded

---

[6] The *L v L* case involved a woman seeking a beneficial interest in the family home. In the High Court, Barr J found that she was entitled to rights in the property under Article 41, but the Supreme Court found that the wife could not rely on Article 41 against the husband.

those of the unborn and the putative father, it would appear to undermine the prohibition of abortion in the State.

In the *Miss D* case, it would appear from newspaper reports that McKechnie J stated, "Miss D's right to travel for an abortion was unaffected by Article 40.3.3 of the Constitution" (*The Irish Times*, 2007n). Thus, it would appear that the right to travel is bordering on an absolute one: whether a later court would agree with Kingston, Whelan and Bacik that other constitutional rights could be utilised to prevent a woman from travelling is open to question; however, McKechnie J seems to have placed a premium on the right to travel.

The C Case

The *C* case (1998) concerned a thirteen-year-old girl, who was the subject of an interim care order, in the care of the health board. She had been raped and was pregnant, and stated clearly that were she compelled to carry her child to term she could commit suicide. She expressed the wish to terminate her pregnancy. The HSE supported this decision, though her parents disagreed. C and the HSE brought an application to the District Court seeking permission for her to travel to the United Kingdom to terminate the pregnancy. The order was denied in the District Court and appealed to the High Court where Geoghegan J heard the case.

Geogheghan J, having established that for these purposes the termination was a medical procedure for the purposes of the Child Care Act 1991, asked whether he could sanction the decision of the Eastern Health Board to bring C to England to terminate her pregnancy. He was clear in this regard. He stated unequivocally that a court could not sanction the travel of a young person to have an abortion if that abortion was not constitutionally permissible:

> A court of law, in considering the welfare of an Irish child and considering whether on health grounds a termination of pregnancy was necessary must be confined to considering the grounds for termination which would be lawful under the Irish Constitution *and cannot make a direction authorising travel to another jurisdiction for a different kind of abortion* (1998: 478) (emphasis added).

Geoghegan J was of the opinion that, rather than conferring a right of abortion outside of the jurisdiction, the travel amendment "merely prevents injunctions against travelling for that purpose" (1998: 478). This case did not involve an injunction: rather, the case concerned the question of whether the Health Board could facilitate this girl travelling under the terms of the Child Care Act 1991. Geoghegan J went on:

> … the fact that there may be different views as to the importance of the constitutional right to travel does not in my view affect the issue of whether the District Court under the Child Care Act 1991 can actually exercise a jurisdiction authoring travel for a particular purpose, namely, *for an abortion in circumstances where the proposed abortion would not be allowed under Irish law. I think that the court would be prevented from doing so by the terms of the right to life of the unborn expressed in the Constitution* (1998: 479) (emphasis added),

While these remarks are *obiter* it is important to note that Geoghegan J went so far as to say that if, on analysis, the abortion would not have been one that was permissible under the Constitution, he would have granted the order which would have had the ultimate effect of restraining the girl from travelling for an abortion. On the basis of this ruling, it was thought that while parents could lawfully bring their children to another jurisdiction to terminate the pregnancy of that child, where consent of the court was required in order to medically treat a child, or for them to travel, such as children in the care of the Health Board, wards of court and certain children detained under the Mental Health Acts, unless the termination was a constitutionally permissible one, the court could not sanction the treatment and the young person would be forced to bring her pregnancy to term.

Asylum Seekers, the E112 Form and Travel

In *D v Ireland* (2006) submissions by the Government also referred to a case which arose in 1999. Here, a Ukrainian asylum seeker sought an exit visa to stay in her asylum process in Ireland in order for her to travel abroad to terminate her pregnancy. According to the submission, Irish authorities would only allow the woman to travel if she satisfied the criteria as laid out in the *X* case, that is, if her life was at risk. In the High Court, the application was not opposed by the state, and the Court quashed the refusal of the travel visa (2006: para. 71). It was not clarified why the refusal was quashed, nor why, when the case was heard by the Court, the HSE and the State reversed their earlier opposition to her travelling.

Reports also indicate that the HSE "quietly" facilitated women in a similar position to Miss D (that is, those whose foetus' had severe abnormalities) to travel to the UK. Further, the HSE allowed such women to use the E112 form, which provides refunds for hospital treatments which are not available in Ireland. In these circumstances, the State refunded the costs incurred by these women (*Sunday Business Post*, 2008).

***D v Ireland* (2006)**

In a case heard by the European Court of Human Rights, the applicant, D, was pregnant with twins, and was informed that one had stopped developing at eight weeks gestation, and that the other had a severe chromosomal abnormality, Edward's Syndrome, a lethal condition which would lead to the death of the child shortly after birth. D decided to terminate the pregnancy and made arrangements to do so in England (2006: para. 4).

Following the termination, she brought an application to the European Court of Human Rights. She argued that requiring her to travel to procure the abortion amounted to a failure by the Irish state to ensure she was not subjected to inhuman and degrading treatment, as set out in Article 3 of the Convention. Further, she argued that there was a disproportionate interference with her private and family life, as protected by Article 8, due to the information restrictions set out in the Regulation of Information (Termination of Pregnancies) Act 1995. Finally, she argued that her Article 10 rights had been infringed due to the restrictions in the 1995 Act on her treatment by her doctor, particularly the prohibition on her Irish medical team making arrangements or a referral to a clinic in England.

Ultimately, the case was decided on the grounds that D had not exhausted the domestic remedies available to her in Ireland before bringing an application to the European Court of Human Rights. The Irish Government contended that D should have brought an action in the High

Court, seeking a declaration that Article 40.3.3° of the Constitution allowed an abortion in Ireland in the case of a fatal foetal abnormality, along with the necessary ancillary mandatory order (2006: para. 64).

The submissions of the Government as set out in the judgment of the European Court are worth setting out in detail:

> [I]t was an open question as to whether Article 40.3.3° could have allowed a lawful abortion in Ireland in the applicant's circumstances. The *X* case demonstrated the potential for judicial development in this area, and further, the *X* case did not exclude possible evolution in cases such as the applicant's: the foetus was viable in the *X* case whereas in the present case there might be an issue as to the extent to which the State was required to guarantee the right to life of a foetus which suffered from a lethal genetic abnormality … [A]lthough it was true that Article 40.3.3° had to be understood as excluding a liberal abortion regime, the courts were nonetheless unlikely to interpret the provision with remorseless logic particularly when the facts were exceptional (2006: para. 69).

Thus, the Irish Government in 2006 itself made the argument that abortions could be constitutionally permissible where the foetus suffered from a lethal genetic abnormality. However, even though X and C's terminations were constitutionally permissible, they were still required to travel to the United Kingdom to procure these terminations, a point which does not seem to have been developed by the European Court. So, while the Irish government argued that it was constitutionally permissible for terminations to be carried out in this jurisdiction, the fact is that such a termination will not be carried out. The reason for this seems to be Guidelines issued by the Medical Profession in relation to the issue of abortion.

The Medical Council Guidelines

The medical profession responded to the *X* case by publishing a statement relating to guidelines on abortion in 1993.[7] It states:

---

[7] Which were incorporated into the Medical Council's Guidelines in the publication, *A guide to Ethical Conduct and Behaviour and to Fitness in Practise* (1994), at paragraphs 39.03, 30.04 and 39.05 respectively.

> It has always been the tradition of the medical profession to preserve life and health. Situations arise in medical practice where the life and/or health of the mother or of the unborn, or both, are endangered. In these situations it is imperative ethically that doctors shall endeavour to preserve life and health ...
>
> While the necessity for abortion to preserve the life or health of the sick mother remains to be proved, it is always unethical to withhold treatment beneficial to a pregnant woman, by reason of her pregnancy.
>
> Departures from these principles in practice may leave the doctor open to a charge of professional misconduct.

In 1998, the Council issued another set of guidelines, the relevant part of which states:

> The deliberate and intentional destruction of the unborn child is professional misconduct. Should a child in utero suffer or lose its life as a side effect of standard medical treatment of the mother, then this is not unethical. Refusal by a doctor to treat a woman with a serious illness because she is pregnant would be grounds for complaint and could be considered to be professional misconduct.

Again, this gives the impression that the Medical Council will only tolerate termination of pregnancy by way of the doctrine of double effect. However, in a frank article in *The Irish Times*,[8] the Master of the Rotunda, Professor Peter McKenna, admitted that this use of the doctrine of double effect causes difficulties. He referred to a case where a pregnant woman was suffering from a life-threatening case of hypertension where the pregnancy was terminated. He stated:

> Nobody that I know feels that this [was] the incorrect thing to do. What the argument is over is whether this is 'treatment' or a termination. The reason why people argue over it is that if you call it 'treatment' you can say there is never a case to justify termination in Ireland and get that written into our Constitution. If you call it

---

[8] *The Irish Times,* 10 February 2000.

> 'termination' you acknowledge there are sometimes cases that defy a blanket ban – that is the nub as to why people argue over this.

The *Guide to Ethical Conduct and Behaviour* (2004) sets out the current position of the Medical Council, that is that termination of pregnancy can occur when there is real and substantial risk to the life of the mother. It also includes the submission of the Institute of Obstetricians and Gynaecologists to the All-Party Oireachtas Committee on the Constitution in its interpretation of the ethical responsibilities to the child *in utero*. The relevant element to this submission states:

> In current obstetrical practice rare complications can arise where therapeutic intervention is required at a stage in pregnancy when there will be little or no prospect for the survival of the baby, due to extreme immaturity. In these exceptional situations failure to intervene may result in the death of both mother and baby. We consider that there is a fundamental difference between abortion carried out with the intention of taking the life of the baby, for example for social reasons, and the unavoidable death of the baby resulting from essential treatment to protect the life of the mother (2004: 44).

From the Guidelines, it would appear that neither Miss D nor the woman at the centre of the *D v Ireland* case fall into that category of woman who could procure a termination of pregnancy in this jurisdiction: while their unborn child was physically immature and had little prospect of survival outside the womb, thus satisfying the first limb, the life of the woman was never in danger, so the second limb of the test was not satisfied.

In interpreting the guidelines of the Medical Council, the Constitutional Amendment and the *X* case in tandem, it would seem that a doctor in Ireland has the capacity to terminate a pregnancy where she is of the opinion that there is a real and substantial risk to the life of the mother, which includes a risk of suicide. Kingston and Whelan go so far to say that if the doctor did not terminate an *X*-case type pregnancy, he or she could face a civil suit (1997: 24). This, however, is unlikely given the marked reluctance of the courts to impose positive obligations on doctors to treat patients. However, it is also true to say that such a doctor could face disciplinary procedures under the Medical Council guidelines if it were established that there was no real threat to her life, and criminal prosecution under the Offences Against the Person Act 1861.

In the aftermath of the *Miss D* case, it was reported that Dr Declan Keane, master of the National Maternity Hospital in Holles Street, stated that there was "a strong cohort" of obstetricians who believed that terminations should be carried out in this country if the baby had absolutely no chance of life outside the womb. However, Miss D would not necessarily qualify here: when born, her child would have survived for a short period of time – it did in fact have a chance of life, however, brief, outside the womb.

Miss D in the High Courts: A New Departure

Just one year after the European Court of Human Rights decision in the *D v Ireland* case, the HSE, an arm of the Government, tried to prevent Miss D from travelling to terminate her pregnancy. The HSE was roundly criticised for refusing to facilitate Miss D in her wish to travel to the United Kingdom for an abortion. One could argue, however, that HSE was simply applying legal precedent, and obeying what they correctly thought was the legal position concerning young people travelling for an abortion. Geoghegan J had explicitly stated, albeit in an *obiter* statement, that no court could sanction the travel of a woman where she was seeking to obtain an unconstitutional termination of her pregnancy.

McKechnie J in the High Court had to consider two questions: first, whether Miss D was entitled to an order restraining the HSE from preventing her travelling abroad for an abortion; second, an appeal from the decision of Justice Brennan refusing to grant the HSE an order allowing the girl to travel to the United Kingdom.

McKechnie J in delivering his *ex tempore* decision stated that he "firmly and unequivocally held the view that there was no law or constitutional impediment preventing Miss D travelling for the purpose of terminating her pregnancy", and that the right to life of the unborn cannot interfere with the right to travel for an abortion (*The Irish Times*, 2007n). On this basis, it was unnecessary, he held, to decide whether the foetus was an "unborn child" within the meaning of the Constitution. The case was "about the right to travel", not about abortion or a decision to terminate the existence of a healthy foetus or a disabled child (*The Irish Times*, 2007n).

Considering the question of whether the HSE were correct in seeking District Court approval for Miss D to travel to the UK to termination her pregnancy, he stated:

> ... there was no law or provision of the Child Care Act which restrained a child in care from travelling for an abortion or which would support the HSE's claim that District Court permission was required for travel. Miss D's right to travel for an abortion was unaffected by Article 40.3.3 of the Constitution (*The Irish Times*, 2007n).

Thus, McKechnie J held that Miss D's right to travel took precedence over her unborn child's right to life in Article 40.3.3°. There was a shift from Geoghegan J's position, where he believed that State, and the Courts, were under an obligation to protect the right to life of the unborn to the point that the Court could not positively sanction travel for an unconstitutional abortion to McKechnie J's decision, where the right to travel was paramount, trumping the right to life of the unborn child. It appears, then, that the Courts will under no circumstances grant an application preventing a woman from travelling for an abortion.

A "Constitutionally Permissible" Abortion?

In terms of what is a "constitutionally permissible" abortion, the situation is as unclear as ever. It is established that in circumstances where the life of a woman is at risk, including a risk of suicide, it is constitutional for her to terminate her pregnancy. Nonetheless, the medical profession refuse to carry out terminations in these circumstances. The reason for this seems to be that, while the law will allow terminations in these circumstances, a doctor who proceeded to carry out the procedure could face disciplinary action and face being struck off the registrar. This decision could be appealed by the doctor, in a *R v Bourne*[9] (1939) type of case, but this is a risk few, if any, practitioners would take.

---

[9] Here, a fourteen-year-old girl became pregnant as a result of rape. Bourne performed an abortion on her, as her parents feared that the continuation of her pregnancy would have

Consent to Medical Treatment by Young People

It is presumed that the reason McKechnie J held Miss D was capable of making a decision to travel to the United Kingdom to terminate her pregnancy when Miss C was not, is due to section 23 of the Non-Fatal Offences Against the Person Act 1997 which governs the law concerning the medical treatment of young people. This section is a replica of section 8 of the English Family Law Reform Act 1969[10] and provides:

> (1) The consent of a minor who has attained the age of 16 years to any surgical, medical or dental treatment which, in the absence of consent, would constitute a trespass to his or her person, shall be as effective as it would be if he or she were of full age; and where a minor has by virtue of this section given an effective consent to any treatment it shall not be necessary to obtain any consent for it from his or her parent or guardian.
>
> (2) Nothing in this section shall be construed as making ineffective any consent which would have been effective if this section had not been enacted.

While there has been a large amount of academic scrutiny of the provision, where it has been argued that the right to consent to medical treat-

---

an adverse affect on her mental state. Bourne, having performed the abortion, then contacted the police to obtain clarification on the law. He was prosecuted under the 1861 Act, and the Court in directing the jury held that in the case of abortion under the Act, there may be justification for the Act when "it is reasonably certain that a pregnant woman will not be able to deliver the child which is in her womb and survive". See further Kingston, Whelan and Bacik (1997: 62-65).

[10] Section 8 of the Family Law Reform Act 1969 states:

> (1) The consent of a minor who has attained the age of 16 years to any surgical, medical or dental treatment which, in the absence of consent would constitute a trespass to his person, shall be as effective as it would be if he were of full age: and where a minor has by virtue of this section given an effective consent to any treatment it shall not be necessary to obtain any consent for it from his parent or guardian.
>
> (2) In this section 'surgical, medical or dental treatment' includes any procedure undertaken for the purposes of diagnosis, and this section applies to any procedure (including, in particular, the administration of an anaesthetic), which is ancillary to any treatment as it applies to that treatment.
>
> (3) Nothing in this section shall be construed as making ineffective any consent which would have been effective if this section had not been enacted.

ment is limited by, for example, Article 41 and 42 rights of parents.[11] Following the enactment of section 23, they state that there are two possible interpretations of the legal position. McMahon and Binchy consider the impact of the section and argue that, on the one hand, they state, it could mean that the parents or guardians are disentitled in any case to take any legal steps in respect of the treatment (2000: 641). This would mean that section 23 endows 16- and 17-year-old young people with an absolute right to consent to medical treatment in the absence of parental consent. However, they note that there is another perspective:

> On the other view, what s 23 does is to render the consent lawful to the extent that it can not be regarded as unlawful by reason merely of the failure to obtain the consent of the parents or guardians. On this latter view, the trusteeship function is not disturbed and parents or guardians remain entitled (to the uncertain extent that they have such an entitlement) to take proceedings with respect to the treatment in the same way as they can with respect to any other lawful activity – an employment contract, for example – in which their minor child engages (2000: 641).

Quill argues that the position is even muddier – section 23, he observes, certainly provides that the consent of a minor aged sixteen or over to medical or dental treatment will provide a defence against a *criminal* assault charge, but it is not clear whether the Act also applies to a civil claim; though he admits that one would expect the courts to take some guidance from this in respect of such a claim (2004: 196). Thus, it could be argued that section 23 is not in fact a facilitative section at all; rather it simply provides a defence for a doctor to a criminal action post-treatment.

Whatever about the *general* position in relation to consent to medical treatment, other commentators question the application of section 23 when it applies to consenting to contraceptive treatment. The question as

---

[11] As it could be argued that the position in relation to section 23 and 16- and 17-year-olds has now been resolved by the *Miss D* case, it is the opinion of this author that an avenue has been opened for the acceptance of Gillick Competence in Ireland. However, this issue is beyond the scope of this essay. Thus, for the present purposes, the term "young person" refers to those aged between 16-17.

to whether there is any constitutional barrier to medical treatment is further complicated by the case of Re Article 26 and the Regulation of Information (Services Outside the State for the Termination of Pregnancies) Bill 1995. Here, it was argued that because the term "woman" was not defined in the Act, a young person could seek abortion information without the knowledge or consent of her parents, thus rendering the Act unconstitutional as a violation of Articles 41 and 42. Hamilton CJ stated in response to this argument that

> it must be presumed that in the giving of such information, counselling and advice, the person giving same will have regard to and give advice in accordance with the principles of Constitutional justice and if there is any departure from these principles, such departure would be restrained and corrected by the Courts (1995: 115).

In terms of other legislation on the issue, section 4(1)(a) of the Health (Family Planning) (Amendment) Act, 1992 further provides that contraceptives may only lawfully be sold to persons over the age of 17 or someone under the age of 17 who has a prescription for contraceptives. Thus, it would appear that a minor over the age of sixteen can receive contraceptives without the need for involvement of their parents.[12] Donnelly, however, argues that it would be contrary to the authority of the family under the Constitution to provide contraceptive treatment to a child aged under 17 without the consent of her parents (1995: 21). On this line of reasoning, there should be no distinction between 16 and 17 year olds: though Mills makes the point that it is questionable whether the provision of contraceptives amounts to "medical treatment" under the 1997 Act, "not being a treatment or procedure in the commonly understood sense of the word" (2007: 81).

As regards the provision of contraceptive treatment and particularly abortion information, Donnelly (2002) notes that it is "at least arguable" that Article 42 of the Constitution would prevent an interpretation of the

---

[12] This position may not be an absolute one. In England and Wales, under a similar provision, courts have found that the consent or refusal of a minor can be overridden where the court deems it to be in the minor's best interests. See, for example, *In Re W (A Minor) (Medical Treatment: Court's Jurisdiction)* (1992); *Re C* (1997).

1997 Act that would interfere with a parental right to control their children's right to contraceptive treatment. This is an issue which must face doctors on a regular basis, and Donnelly observes that, while each doctor's decision will be based on the individual circumstances of the case, "he is hampered in reaching this decision by the absence of clarity in relation to the legal framework that binds him" (2002: 50). The only guidance given to doctors is equally lacking in clarity: the Medical Council's *Guide to Ethical Conduct and Behaviour* (2004) states:

> If the doctor feels that a child will understand a proposed medical procedure, information or advice, this should be explained fully to the child. Where the consent of parents or guardians is normally required in respect of a child for whom they are responsible, due regard must be had to the wishes of the child. The doctor must never assume that it is safe to ignore the parental/guardian interest.

Where a young person is in the care of her parents, it would appear that a doctor would at least have to consider asking the young person to involve her parents in the decision. Without this, it would be possible that the parents could take a civil action against the doctor (Quill, 2004).

Young People in the Care of the HSE

There are seven types of order which can be made under the Child Care Act 1991, and the HSE and the court have varying powers in relation to the medical treatment of those children when the order is made. There are three essential ways in which "medical or psychiatric examination, treatment or assessment" can be consented to on behalf of a child.

1. Application to District Court by HSE

This applies only to supervision orders. Under section 18(5) of the Act, if the court decides that it is not necessary for a care order to be made, but that it is desirable that the child be visited periodically in his home by or on behalf of the health board, it may make a supervision order. Where the court makes such an order, it may, under section 19(4) of the 1991 Act, on the application of the health board, give such directions as it sees fit "as to the care of the child, which may require the parents of the child or a person acting *in loco parentis* to cause him to attend for medical or psychiatric examination, treatment or assessment."

2. Decision made by District Court on application of HSE or other interested party

This is provided for under section 13(7) of the Act, and applies to emergency care orders, interim care orders and interim special care orders. Section 13(7) authorises the District Judge, rather than the HSE to give directions as to any medical or psychiatric examination, treatment or assessment of the child. The decision to order such examination, treatment or assessment can come be made on foot of the motion of the District Justice, or on the application of any other person, including the HSE. In the *C* case (1998) this section was used to order the termination of C's pregnancy on foot of an application by the HSE. The case is important in a number of respects. First, it was made clear in the case that the HSE and the District Court could override the decision of the parents where the best interests of the child demanded so. Second, it is also clear from the case that while the wishes of the child were made clear, ultimately the decision-making power rested with the District Court Judge.

3. Decision made by HSE, with District Court exercising a supervisory jurisdiction

This relates to care orders and special care orders. Section 18(3)(b)(ii) provides that the HSE can give consent to any necessary medical or psychiatric examination, treatment or assessment with respect to the child; and give consent to the issue of a passport to the child. Sub-section 4 of section 18 confirms that any consent given by the health board in accordance with the section shall be sufficient authority. A seemingly similar situation arises in relation to Voluntary Care Orders made under section 4(1) of the Act. When maintaining care over the child, the HSE has the duty to "have regard to the wishes of a parent having custody of him or of any person acting *in loco parentis* in the provisions of such care" though ultimately, it would appear that the decision making power rests with the HSE. There is no specific provision in section 4 dealing with the medical treatment of the child. Presumably, decisions are made by the

HSE, with due regard being given to the wishes of a particularly mature young person.

It would appear from the decision in the *Miss D* case that when a young person in the care of the HSE reaches the age of 17 – and perhaps 16 – they can make decisions as to their medical treatment and lifestyle generally. It is expected that McKechnie J based his decision on sections 3 and 24 of the Act, which provide that where the Court or the HSE are concerned with the care of a child, they must give "give due consideration, having regard to his age and understanding, to the wishes of the child." Miss D was deemed capable by McKechnie J of making decisions as to her welfare and care, and thus, her decision was determinative of the issue. Whether the case was decided on the basis of Miss D's stated maturity, or on the basis of section 23 of the 1997 Act remains unclear. Because of this, it has left the HSE in the unusual position of not knowing whether they need to apply to the District Court under sections 13 or18 to make orders relating to the care of a young person where that young person is deemed particularly mature. It remains to be seen if the HSE will appeal that part of the order to seek clarification on the issue.

Further, if the case was in fact decided on the basis of the right to travel, it would appear that this right is bordering on absolute where a pregnant teenager is concerned. It would appear that McKechnie J was of the opinion that nothing in either the Child Care Act 1991 nor Article 40.3.3° could be used to prevent Miss D from travelling: in this case, were a 16 year old to travel to the UK in order to prevent her unborn child being taken into care, or a 17-year-old girl to travel to Amsterdam to start a career as a prostitute, or a 17-year-old boy to go to the UK to start a business, there would appear to be nothing the Health Service Executive can do about it. Serious questions must be asked, then, about the capacity of the HSE to fulfil its obligations under the 1991 Act to care for children in its area on foot of the judgment.

Conclusion

Twenty-five years after the introduction of Article 40.3.3°, the legal position in relation to termination of pregnancy and the right to life of the unborn has never been so unclear. What can be said for certainty is that, first, were a future Miss X or Miss C situation to arise, while it would be constitutionally permissible for her to have an abortion in this jurisdiction, she would be obliged to travel due to the seeming refusal of the medical profession to carry out such a termination.

Regarding children in the care of the HSE, first, it would appear that they have the right to consent to medical treatment. Whether this applies to children in the care of their parents seems unclear, but McKechnie J did seem to put weight on the growing autonomy of young people, which can hardly only apply to young people in care. Second, it would appear that where a child is in care, they are entitled to travel without the consent or approval of the HSE or the District Court. Again, it would appear illogical for this to apply to children in the care of the HSE and not their parents. While it is argued that such a position is compatible with Article 12 of the UN Convention on the Rights of the Child, and promotes the autonomy of young people, it is unlikely that Irish parents would be happy about their 16-year-old daughter going to the UK to terminate her pregnancy without their permission.

Finally, once again, the incoherency and inconsistency in the approach of the State, particularly the HSE is confusing at best. The State, through the HSE, refuses permission to travel, then does not oppose court applications by pregnant women who wish to leave the State; it argues in the European Court of Human Rights that, in certain circumstances, termination of pregnancy can be carried out in the State then refuses permission to travel for exactly that type of termination. At the very least, Guidelines should be issued immediately to the HSE and the medical profession clarifying the legal position in cases like these.

Twenty-five years after the introduction of Article 40.3.3° it is time for the legislature to stop expecting the courts to clarify the scope, depth and breadth of the constitutional provision and either legislate comprehensively for how right to life of the unborn is to be protected and vindicated, or to propose a removal of a provision which has caused nothing but confusion, turmoil and upheaval in this State.

Bibliography

Donnelly, M. (1995) "Capacity of Minors to Consent to Medical and Contraceptive Treatment" *Medico-Legal Journal of Ireland* 1: 18-21.

Donnelly, M. (2002) *Consent: Bridging the Gap between Doctor and Patient* Cork: Cork University Press.

Duncan, W. (1987) "The Child, the Parent and the State: the Balance of Power" in Duncan, W. (ed) *Law and Social Policy: Some Current Problems in Irish Law* Dublin University Law Journal: 23. .

Irish Medical Council (2004) *Guide to Ethical Conduct and Behaviour* (6th edition), Dublin: Irish Medical Council.

Kaplan (2002) "The Right of a Minor in Israel to Participate in the Decision-Making Process Concerning His or Her Medical Treatment" *Fordham International Law Journal* 25(5): 1085.

Kingston, J. and Whelan, A., with Ivana Bacik (1997) *Abortion and the Law,* Dublin: Round Hall Sweet & Maxwell.

Madden, D. (2002) *Medicine Ethics and the Law* Dublin: Butterworths.

McMahon and Binchy (2000) *Law of Torts*, Dublin: Butterworths.

Mills, S. (2007) *Clinical Practice and the Law* Dublin: Butterworths.

Rooney, S. (1998), "The Medico-Legal Impact of Consent to Treatment of Under-aged Drug Users" *Medico-Legal Journal of Ireland* 4: 74.

Skegg, P.D.G. (1973) "Consent to Medical Procedures on Minors" *Modern Law Review* 36(4): 370-381.

Tomkin, D. and Hanafin, P. (1995) *Irish Medical Law*, Dublin: Round Hall.

Ward, P. (2005) *The Child Care Acts Annotated and Consolidated* (2nd edition) Dublin: Round Hall.

Cases

Attorney General v X [1992] 1 IR 1.

A and B v Eastern Health Board and C [1998] 1 ILRM 464.

D v Ireland Application No 26499/02 28 June 2006.

Eastern Health Board v McDonnell [1999] 2 ILRM 382.

G v An Bord Uchtala [1980] IR 32.

Gillick v West Norfolk and Wisbech Area Health Authority [1986] 1 AC 112.

In Re W (A Minor) (Medical Treatment: Court's Jurisdiction) [1992] 3 WLR 758.

L v L [1992] 2 IR 77.

Re Article 26 and the Regulation of Information (Services Outside the State for the Termination of Pregnancies) Bill 1995 [1995] IR 1.

Re C [1997] 2 FLR 180.

Society for the Protection of the Unborn Child (SPUC) v Grogan (No. 5) [1998] 4 IR 343.

Newspaper Reports

The Irish Times (2007a) "Court must rule again on abortion dilemma" 1 May.

The Irish Times (2007b) "Girl seeking abortion challenges HSE" 1 May.

The Irish Times (2007c) "The case of 'Miss D' was stranger than fiction" 12 May.

The Irish Times (2007d) "HSE may appeal part of Miss D ruling" 11 May.

The Irish Times (2007e) "State has no power to stop teen going to UK, court told" 1 May.

The Irish Times (2007f) "State says HSE has no power to stop girl leaving" 2 May.

The Irish Times (2007g) "Forcing teen to have baby 'inhumane', court told" 3 May.

The Irish Times (2007i) "HSE worker asked gardaí to restrain girl" 4 May.

The Irish Times (2007j) "HSE sought to deny pregnant girl a passport" 5 May.

The Irish Times (2007k) "District Court refuses girl permission to travel for abortion" 7 May.

The Irish Times (2007l) "State lawyers insist Miss D does not require HSE permission or court order to travel" 8 May.

The Irish Times (2007m) "Right to life 'continues until death'" 8 May.

The Irish Times (2007n) "High Court rules that girl can travel for abortion" 10 May.

The Sunday Business Post (2008) "New legal challenge to abortion laws looms" 30 March.

15

Psychological Effects of Abortion and Informed Consent

Prof Patricia Casey

Abortion is one of the most contentious issues in international socio-political discourse at present. Not only are the discussions driven by philosophical, ethical and religious considerations but also by medical, political and social ones. The medical discussions focus on the impact that continuing pregnancy might have on the woman's physical health or life. In recent years debate has emerged about the psychological impact of abortion or of continuing an unwanted pregnancy.

For any procedure/intervention or treatment in medicine it is assumed that fully informed consent will be obtained. This has two elements – the capacity of the person to make that decision and the amount of information that is available to them. This chapter will specifically focus on the latter with specific reference to the psychological aspects of abortion. In particular, the question concerning whether abortion has adverse psychological consequences and whether there are psychological indications for abortion will be examined. The incorporation of these into informed consent procedures will also be considered.

Some of those engaged in the debate on the psychological consequences of abortion argue that there is a specific syndrome that women experience following abortion, called post-abortion syndrome (PAS). It is believed that this name is justified since the focus of symptoms is on the abortion and the pregnancy loss. However, this is not a recognised psychiatric term at this point and will not be used in this chapter. Instead the focus will be on a variety of psychiatric conditions that can be precipitated by life events such as depression, substance misuse, etc. and behaviours such as self-harm and suicide and the emphasis will be on long-term consequences as distinct from short-term distress.

Background

For many years it was stated that the long-term psychological impact of abortion on women was negligible and that any problems arising represented the continuation of previous symptoms (Royal College of Obstetrics and Gynaecology, 2004).

This view was articulated by the Royal College of Psychiatrists when in 1994 it issued a statement as follows:

> [T]he risks to psychological health from the termination of pregnancy in the first trimester are much less that the risks associated with proceeding with a pregnancy which is clearly harming the mother's mental health. There is no evidence in such cases of an increased risk of major psychiatric disorder or of long-lasting psychological distress. For the minority who do develop psychiatric disorder, there are predictable risk factors… (Royal College of Psychiatrists 1994).

Referring to second trimester abortions that statement continued:

> There is evidence of an increased risk of both distress and depressive illness in the medium term which does not appear to persist beyond the first year. This small number of women in great distress will include those who have had diagnosed a foetal abnormality, as well as women who have failed to realise that they are pregnant – menopausal women, the very young, patients with severe psychiatric disability, and the severely handicapped. Despite the increased risk of psychiatric disorder, this is still likely to be less than the risk of continuing with the pregnancy, and for these women in the least detrimental alternative (Royal College of Psychiatrists, 1994).

However, following hearings by the United Kingdom Science and Technology Committee in late 2007, in relation to the proposed Human Fertilisation and Embryology Bill, that committee recommended that the Royal College of Psychiatrists should update its guidelines. This it did and the following position statement issued on 14 March 2008:

> In the Government Response to the Report from the House of Commons Science and Technology Committee on the Scientific Developments Relating to the Abortion Act 1967, the following request was made:
>
> > In view of the controversy on the risk to mental health of induced abortion we recommend that the Royal College of Psychiatrists update their 1994 report on this issue
> >
> > The College has undertaken a literature review to inform the following position statement, which includes the recommendation that a full systematic review around abortion and mental health is required.
> >
> > The Royal College of Psychiatrists is concerned to ensure that women's mental health is protected whether they seek abortion or continue with a pregnancy.
> >
> > Mental disorders can occur for some women during pregnancy and after birth.
> >
> > The specific issue of whether or not induced abortion has harmful effects on women's mental health remains to be fully resolved. The current research evidence base is inconclusive – some studies indicate no evidence of harm, whilst other studies identify a range of mental disorders following abortion.
> >
> > Women with pre-existing psychiatric disorders who continue with their pregnancy, as well as those with psychiatric disorders who undergo abortion, will need appropriate support and care. Liaison between services, and, where relevant, with carers and advocates, is advisable.
> >
> > Healthcare professionals who assess or refer women who are requesting an abortion should assess for mental disorder and for risk factors that may be associated with its subsequent development. If a mental disorder or risk factors are identified, there should be a clearly identified care pathway whereby the mental health needs of the woman and her significant others may be met.

> The Royal College of Psychiatrists recognizes that good practice in relation to abortion will include informed consent. Consent cannot be informed without the provision of adequate and appropriate information regarding the possible risks and benefits to physical and mental health. This may require the updating of patient information leaflets approved by the relevant Royal Colleges, and education and training to relevant health care professionals, in order to develop a good practice pathway.
>
> These difficult and complex issues should be addressed through additional systematic reviews led by the Royal College of Psychiatrists into the relationship between abortion and mental health. These reviews should consider whether there is evidence for psychiatric indications for abortion (Royal College of Psychiatrists, 2008: 2).

What had led to the change between 1994 and 2008? Commenting on this in an editorial in the *Psychiatric Bulletin* (Fergusson, 2008) the writer observes:

> The contrast between the recent statement and the 1994 statement arises from a growing body of evidence that has suggested that women may be at increased risks of mental disorders (and notably major depression, substance use and suicidality) following abortion. At the same time not all studies have found this with the result that there have been ongoing debates about the extent to which linkages between abortion and mental health may be explained by methodological artefacts relating to: the ascertainment of exposure, the ascertainment of outcome and control of confounding factors (2008).

This chapter will examine some of these studies and will focus generally on studies published since 2000, since these are more methodologically robust when compared to the older studies, although in a few specific areas, where there is little recent data, e.g. refused abortion, older studies will be cited.

Debate

As outlined above, there is continuing debate about the relationship between abortion and subsequent mental health problems. Not surprisingly, two broad divides are seen with each identifying specific flaws in the other's approach to studying this question.

Those who argue that psychiatric disorders do occur post-abortion point to a number of flaws in the studies that have failed to demonstrate this. These include:

- the absence of long-term data spanning years/decades;
- high attrition rates in follow-up studies reducing the potential for identifying psychological problems (those with psychological problems probably being most likely to default);
- small sample sizes reducing the statistical power of the study to identify mental health problems;
- unreliable ascertainment of those having abortion;
- inadequate assessment of outcome, e.g. self-report, failure to use structured interviews.

On the other hand criticisms directed at studies demonstrating adverse effects are:

- the failure to control for confounders such as previous psychiatric history;
- using inappropriate comparison groups, e.g. comparing women having abortions with those from the general population;
- limited outcome measures, e.g. psychiatric hospitalisation, receiving out-patient treatment;
- the use convenience rather than random samples, e.g. women seeking treatment;
- the use of anecdotal evidence.

Gradually, however, the quality of studies has improved in recent years and the imperative of controlling for these background factors has been taken on board, to a very significant degree. In addition, the follow-up periods have become much longer than previously.

Nevertheless, the exact nature of the relationship is still a matter of debate with some arguing that this link is not a causal one, i.e. that there are factors other than the abortion that have caused the mental health problem (the view of the 1994 statement above) while the contrary view is that abortion was the trigger and without it the emotional problem would not have arisen.

The only study design that would allow for a certain evaluation of the impact of abortion on women's mental health would be to randomly assign women to abortion or to continuing pregnancy. Clearly this would be an impossibility and deeply unethical. In the absence of this definitive approach a variety of study designs are necessary to examine the issue of the nature of the link between abortion and mental health.

One such method is to examine the effects of denied versus allowed abortion on women's mental health. Of course studies of this type are not possible now with abortion rarely if ever denied except, in rare situations where the upper time limit has passed. Studies of refused abortion are therefore old and have significant limitations. Study designs that are required to assist in unravelling the question of the nature of the association between abortion and adverse psychological outcomes, in the obvious absence of denied abortion studies, are listed below (Fergusson, 2008).

Table 15.1: Studies to Determine the Nature of the Abortion-Mental Illness Health Link

Longitudinal studies of women's mental health
Case-control studies examining abortion as a risk factor for mental health problems using as controls women giving birth, women experiencing miscarriages, women with unintended pregnancies carried to term
Sibling and twin studies to control for hidden confounders
Intervention studies to reduce risk of mental health problems following abortion
Studies of specific groups, i.e. those having abortion for foetal anomaly, young women experiencing abortion etc.
Studies of specific disorders post-abortion, e.g. depressive illness, substance misuse, self-harm
Qualitative studies examining women's reaction to abortion

Many recent studies have overcome the flaws of the earlier studies but further investigations are required so as to definitively answer questions relating to the relationship between abortion and adverse mental health outcomes.

Denied Abortion, Unwanted and Mistimed Pregnancy

One of the arguments in favour of allowing abortion for unwanted pregnancies is that the outcomes for such children where the abortion is denied are psychologically adverse. The seminal study that examined denied abortion was called "Born Unwanted". This study (Kubicka et al., 1995), initially and later analysed by David (2006), examined a group of women in Prague who had unwanted pregnancies and were refused abortion twice (although the second refusal was the ratification of a prior administrative decision). Using a dataset of 220 children born in 1961-63 in Prague, their development and mental well-being were evaluated at five time points up to age 35. They were matched at age 9 with 220 children from accepted pregnancies. Because of problems interpreting the data, comparisons with siblings were made at the last two time points only. The study found that psychosocial differences between those from the denied abortion group and the wanted pregnancies widened up to the age of thirty and then decreased. These related largely to psychosocial adaptation and mental health. At the final analysis, when the "unwanted" children were compared with their "wanted" siblings the differences for men were no longer significant while for women the differences persisted. This suggests that for men the differences were related to familial background rather than to the wantedness of the pregnancy *per se*.

A more recent study of denied abortion that is still cited (Gilchrist, 1995) examined the psychological outcome of over 13,000 women with an unplanned pregnancy in Britain. It is thus worth describing at length. The women were classified into four groups: those who had a termination of pregnancy (TOP) (n = 6,410), those who did not request a TOP (n = 6,151), those refused TOP (n = 378) and those who changed their minds before the termination was performed (n = 321). Psychiatric disorder was diagnosed by the general practitioner. This study reported that at follow-up psychiatric illness was similar in the pregnancy and TOP group and that those with a previous history of psychiatric disorder were most at risk of recurrence. However, deliberate self-harm (DSH) was more common in those undergoing TOP or refused TOP than giving birth, even after controlling for age, marital status, educational attainments etc. Those with no prior history of psychosis had a lower risk of developing same post-abortion than those giving birth, but psychosis requiring admission was the same in the two groups. However numbers for psychosis were small, making generalisation problematic. The general practitioner had responsibility for making the psychiatric diagnosis. Psychiatric disorder was equally common in the pregnancy and TOP groups and those with a prior psychiatric history were at highest risk. Self-harm was more common in those having or being refused a TOP than those giving birth, even when various age, marital status, educational attainments etc. were controlled.

This study also has a number of major flaws among which the most important is that diagnosis was made by over 1,500 volunteer general practitioners in England and Scotland between 1976 and 1979. No quality controls were in place to ensure consistency in applying diagnostic criteria between all the practices and over time. Data collection concluded in 1987. Since this study was taking place at a time when general practitioners had much less training in psychiatry than is currently the case, failure of detection cannot be ruled out. Even more fundamentally, this study required that diagnosis be made on the basis of consultation with a general practitioner. However, many women with psychological problems do not consult their doctors, even now, and the additional barrier of the stigma of abortion may have further deterred women from attending their general practitioners. In addition, women who develop post-abortion problems do not generally consult with either the referral agent or the abortion provider, introducing a further source of bias at least for those who were referred for abortion by the general practitioner. Since the participating doctors were volunteers their own bias may have influenced diagnosis. So, bias from these sources (failure to consult, failure to diagnose and selection bias in the general practitioners) is a real possibility. While self-harm was higher in the received and denied abortion groups than in the other two groups, the authors speculate that this may have been due to unexamined confounders such as poor social circumstances associated with seeking an abortion in the first instance.

However, this dataset was not examined further to establish this or to elucidate what these confounders might be. In addition, the number engaging in self-harm in the refused group was too small (1) to draw any meaningful conclusion.

A recent approach to dealing with the consequences of unwanted pregnancy on children, in the absence of refused abortion as used in the Kubicka study, was that undertaken in the US. Using the dataset from the National Longitudinal Survey of Youth, Joyce (2000) examined data on over 9,000 children up to the age of 13 born of pregnancies identified by their parents as wanted, mistimed or unwanted. The study measured child cognitive and social development as well as maternal behaviours related to child health. The results show that while those experiencing unwanted pregnancies present late for pre-natal care, smoked more during pregnancy and were less likely to breast feed, these findings were not regarded as robust due to the varying results according to the statistical model used. The children of unwanted pregnancies did exhibit lower scores on some cognitive and behavioural measures, but when environmental factors were controlled the differences between the "unwanted" children and the children of mistimed or wanted pregnancies disappeared. The study concluded:

> Policies that reduce births resulting from unintended pregnancies may only have a limited effect on the health and development of a particular women's children. In contrast, policies that reduce the social and environmental deficits into which unwanted children are born, or directly target adverse infant health and child development, hold greater promise for improving these outcomes (Joyce, 2000: 93).

A more recent study (Miller, 2007), examining the relationship between pregnancy wantedness and child development among a cohort of 78 low income Black primiparous women who had applied for an early parenting programme, found that pregnancy wantedness, as measured by questionnaire, was not associated with the attachment security of the children at age 14 months.

While early studies suggest an adverse effect of pregnancy unwantedness on child development and mental health, recent studies have found no association, when confounders are controlled. Studies in this field are scarce. Studies on denied abortion are no longer feasible and the focus instead has shifted to examining unwanted, mistimed and planned pregnancies.

Adverse Psychological Reactions – Longitudinal and Case-control Studies

One of the best designed longitudinal studies to examine the question of the link between abortion and post-abortion psychiatric disorder emerged recently (Fergusson, 2006) using a dataset derived from the general population. The author, himself a pro-choice advocate, set out to test the hypothesis that those who developed mental health problems post-abortion did so because of prior vulnerability. The methods adopted addressed the criticisms of earlier studies that used inadequate diagnostic tools, that had short-term follow-up and high attrition rates, and that inadequately controlled for confounders,

Using impeccable methodology, the investigator examined data from the 25-year longitudinal birth cohort study of 1,265 children from Christchurch, New Zealand. Over 500 women with a history of pregnancy/abortion/no pregnancy from birth to the age of 25 were identified and face-to-face interviews conducted at four time points. The attrition rate was very low at 17- 20 per cent and inaccurate disclosure of abortion was calculated at 19 per cent, a figure much less than in other studies. Psychiatric diagnosis was made using structured interviews in preference to clinical interviews, and extensive data on childhood and family adversity, behavioural problems as well as psychiatric history were controlled for in the analysis.

The results showed that among those who had abortions compared with those who had not been pregnant, or who had delivered, there was a significantly higher risk of major depression (41.9–78.7 per cent depending on age group), anxiety disorder (39.2–64.3 per cent), suicidal ideation (27–50 per cent) and illicit drug dependence (0–12.2 per cent) and that when confounders were controlled, all of these, with the exception of anxiety disorders, continued to show significantly higher risk ratios in the abortion group.

A further prospective analysis was carried out to determine the likely direction of the association between psychiatric disorder and abortion, i.e. whether psychiatric disorder caused the person to seek the abortion or whether abortion led to the disorder. The investigator examined whether the person's pregnancy/abortion history prior to age 21 predicted subsequent mental health history when confounders were controlled. The results are as follows:

Rate ratio:

- No pregnancy, 0.6
- Pregnant no abortion, 0.67
- Abortion group, 1

The author's conclusions are as follows:

> The present research raises the possibility that for some young women, exposure to abortion is a traumatic life event which increases longer-term susceptibility to common mental disorders. These findings are inconsistent with the current consensus on the psychological effects of abortion. In particular, in its 2005 statement on abortion, the American Psychological Association concluded that well designed studies of psychological responses following abortion have consistently shown that the risk of psychological harm is low … the percentage of women who experience clinically relevant distress is small and appears to be not greater than in general samples of women of reproductive age.
>
> This relatively strong conclusion about the absence of harm from abortion was based on a relatively small number of studies which had one or more of the following limitations … the statement appears to disregard the findings of a number of studies that had claimed to show negative effects for abortion…. While it is possible to dismiss these findings as reflecting shortcomings in the assessment of exposure to abortion or control for confounders it is difficult to disregard the real possibility that abortion amongst young women is associated with increased risks of mental health problems (Fergusson, 2006: 19).

Not surprisingly, this study has been criticised by some who say that not all confounders were controlled for. While childhood adversity and prior psychiatric history were, other less obvious ones might not have been. Issues relating to the decision-making process such as coercion or violence are among the likely candidates that have been suggested.

The above study is one of a number (Reardon and Cougle, 2002; Reardon and Cougle, 2003; Rue et al., 2004; Cougle, Reardon and Coleman, 2005; Cougle, Reardon and Coleman, 2003) that have suggested a causal role for abortion in the genesis of subsequent psychiatric disorder.

Yet not all studies agree with the findings of the Fergusson study and other studies above. One that generally failed to identify significant adverse effects from abortion was carried out in the US (Major et al., 2000). Women arriving at abortion clinics in three sites were evaluated one hour before the abortion and one hour, one month and two years after the procedure. Measures of depression, post-traumatic stress disorder, self-esteem and satisfaction were evaluated. Prior mental health was examined as a possible predictor of psychological response. A total of 1,043 women were eligible; 882 were initially interviewed and 442 were interviewed at follow-up. Using a combination of face-to-face interviews and mail contact the author found that depression scores decreased, self-esteem increased, while negative emotions also increased and decision satisfaction decreased. Interestingly, PTSD was identified in 1 per cent of the population while depression was identified in 22 per cent at two year follow-up, a figure the author says is similar to that in the general population. However, this figure for the general population is the lifetime national rate for depression in that specific age group (Blazer et al., 1994) and not the two year local rate for Buffalo, as measured in the current study, so like is not being compared with like. A history of pre-pregnancy depression was shown to be a risk factor for adverse reactions, as was younger age and having other children pre-abortion.

Other studies have recently been published that also have failed to identify any association between abortion and mental disorder (Rees and Sabia, 2007; Schmiege and Russo, 2005; Zabin, Hirsch and Emerson, 2005), and one (Taft and Watson, 2008) suggested that the apparent association was mediated by partner violence. However, a recent study of inner city, low income women, the Fragile Families Study, examined whether depressive symptoms before the abortion determined subsequent depression (Rees and Sabia, 2007). It found that the prevalence of depression was 15.5 per cent among those not experiencing a pregnancy, 21 per cent in the delivery group and 33.5 per cent in the abortion group. When variables such as race, age, ethnicity, age, income, marital status and number of children were controlled, the abortion group had more than double the risk of depression as compared to the non-pregnant group, while those giving birth were one and a half times as likely to develop depression.

Case-control studies are those that compare cases, in this instance, women having an abortion, with controls. A crucial facet of these studies is choosing the correct control group as this will depend on the question being asked. In some instances this might be women giving birth, in others it might be women experiencing other pregnancy loss events such as comparing women experiencing miscarriage with those undergoing abortion.

It might be expected that women experiencing a miscarriage would experience greater emotional trauma than women having abortion, as the former are mostly experiencing a loss that was not desired while the loss associated with induced abortion is generally intended (except when the abortion is carried out for foetal anomaly).

A series of Norwegian studies (Broen et al., 2005, 2006) arrived at findings that were unexpected. Moreover, the sample size was small so differences would not necessarily be expected. This study examined 40 women who experienced miscarriages and 80 women who underwent abortions using psychological interviews at 10 days (T1), six months (T2), two years (T3), and five years (T4) after the pregnancy termination using valid interview schedules. Prior psychiatric history was controlled for. The results were surprising in that women who had had a miscarriage exhibited significantly more rapid improvement in scores of depression and distress throughout the observation period. Those who experienced induced abortion exhibited a different pattern and had significantly higher scores than the miscarriage group at two and five years after the pregnancy termination, and at five years 20 per cent had scores that indicated psychiatric caseness, i.e. the person would ordinarily be diagnosed by a psychiatrist as having a recognisable psychiatric condition. The authors of this study concluded that women experiencing an induced abortion have higher and more persistent mental health problems than those experiencing a miscarriage.

Adverse Psychological Reactions – Ecological Studies

While the above studies have involved face-to-face interviews, others have been ecological in nature, i.e. examining data from national registers. Using this approach, diverse datasets can be linked, e.g. abortion and psychiatric admission.

A record linkage study (Reardon et al., 2003) of the California Medicaid records of women aged 13–49 at time of childbirth/abortion in 1989 followed them for up to four years. The aim was to examine the frequency of psychiatric hospitalisation following childbirth or abortion. The dataset comprised women whose pregnancy ended in abortion (15,299) or in delivery (41,442), but those with prior admissions were excluded. As this used Medicaid data, all were low income women.

Significant differences in admission rates for women who had abortion compared to those giving birth were found. The odds ratios for different diagnostic groups were all higher in the abortion group as compared to the pregnancy groups as seen below:

- Adjustment reactions (odds ratio 2.1)
- Depressive episode (odds ratio 1.9)
- Recurrent depressive disorder (odds ratio 2.1)
- Bipolar disorder (odds ratio 3).

Overall, the post-delivery admission rate was 634.8/100,000 and for those having an abortion the post-abortion admission rate was 1117.1/100,000, representing an odds ratio of 1.7. Thus, psychiatric admission rates were higher in women post-abortion than post-partum.

This study replicates the findings of one of the earliest studies (David et al., 1981), addressing the possible psychiatric effects of abortion, which found that women post-abortion had higher rates of psychosis (18.4/10,000) compared to those who has psychosis post-partum (12/10,000).

Using that same dataset as Readron et al. (2003) outlined above, Coleman et al. (2002) examined new out-patient contact following abortion. The objective was to ascertain the rate of first-time psychiatric out-patient contact up to four years post-abortion while controlling for pre-existing psychological problems, age, number of pregnancies and months of eligibility. The dataset involved 14,297 in the abortion group and 40,122 in the birth group.

The results indicated that Medicaid claims were higher throughout the follow-up period in the abortion group, being highest in the first 90 days post-abortion (63 per cent more claims), reducing at each time point thereafter with 42 per cent more claims at day 180, 30 per cent more claims at one year and 16 per cent more claims at the end of the follow-up period.

Taken together these longitudinal and ecological studies show that psychiatric complications after abortion may occur and there is evidence that they are present even when vulnerabilities factors are taken into account. However, not all studies have demonstrated this while others have identified prior psychiatric history as an explicator of the adverse reactions. In addition, several studies have shown that psychiatric contact is higher in women following abortion but these studies do not provide an explanatory model. Further longitudinal and case control investigations are required with control for confounders additional to those already included to answer these questions.

Substance Misuse

While most work has examined psychiatric disorder in general, especially depressive disorders, some have focussed on other specific conditions and the association between abortion and substance misuse has been the subject of some recent studies (Reardon and Ney, 2000).

The most recent investigation used data garnered from the Young in Norway Longitudinal study (Pedersen, 2007). In this study, 768 females who were 12-15 years old at the time the study began were followed and interviewed over four time points until they were 26 years old. The aim was to examine levels of nicotine dependence, alcohol problems, cannabis use and other illicit substance use in those who by the age of 27 i), had never been pregnant, ii), had been pregnant and given birth, and iii), had been pregnant and had an abortion. Pre-pregnancy confounders such as social background, family history, pre-pregnancy substance use, conduct problems, depression, schooling and sexual history were controlled for in the statistical analysis. The results indicated that those who had abortions were at increased risk of all categories of substance misuse when possible confounders were controlled (odds ratios 2–4.7) while risk was lowest for those who delivered (odds ratios 0.1–0.8), even when compared to the never pregnant group. A subgroup analysis of those who had abortions later in the follow-up period (thus eliminating those who had abortions at a young age and might be considered vulnerable because of age) found that with the exception of those who still lived with the father of the aborted baby, all others obtaining abortions had 2–4.7 times the odds of experiencing substance use difficulties when more recent confounders were controlled. The authors concluded that "the study indicates that, for some women, exposure to an abortion may be a traumatic life event that increases the susceptibility to substance dependence and problems" (Pedersen, 2007: 1976). In this regard the findings of Fergusson et al. (2006) are replicated although with similar caveats concerning the possibility of confounding from non-observed variables.

So while substance abuse is higher in those having abortions, and this may be a causal link, further studies are required to clarify this.

Self-harm, Suicide and Abortion

Using an ecological approach using record linkage methods has made it possible to identify women with perinatal hospitalisation associated with abortion, childbirth, miscarriage and cross-tabulate them against suicide records. Using this method in Finland (Gissler, Hemminki and Lonnqvist, 1996), one study found that 5.4 per cent of all suicides in women were pregnancy-related. The suicide rates in different groups were as follows:

Table 15.2: Suicide Rates in Different Female Groups in Finland

Mean suicide rate among women in Finland – 11.3/100,000
Suicide rate associated with birth – 5.9/100,000
Suicide rate associated with abortion – 34.7/100,000

There are several interpretations for these findings, the first being that abortion causes women to take their lives. An alternative explanation is that abortion may be a marker for behaviours that are linked to abortion seeking and suicide and impulsivity or mental illness are possible candidates. In other words, these personality and illness variables might be confounders. However, it is not possible to answer this question using this dataset.

A more recent study (Gissler, 2004), also using the Finnish database, found that all cause mortality (natural and pregnancy-related) was higher in the induced abortion group that in all others (Table 15.3).

Table 15.3: Mortality Rate for Women in Different Pregnancy States

	Non-pregnant	**After Birth**	**Spontaneous Abortion**	**Induced Abortion**
Total	57/100,000	25.9	55.7	82.3
Natural causes	32/100,000	16.3	21.1	22.3
Pregnancy-related	N/A	3.9	3.4	1.3

A further study (Gissler, 2005) examining external causes of death (unintentional injuries, homicide and suicide) covering the years 1987-2000 led the author to conclude "the low rate of deaths from external causes suggests the protective effect of childbirth, but the elevated risk after a terminated pregnancy needs to be recognised in the provision of health care and social services" (Gissler, 2005) Furthermore, referring to practice in Finland, the investigator commented "The new recommendation for post-induced abortion care, however, includes the statement that a check-up visit is necessary in order to detect signs of depression and to identify the rare cases of psychosis after an induced abortion" (Gissler 2005).

Using a similar methodology, a US study (Reardon et al., 2002) examined the Medicaid records of over 173,000 women between 1989 to 1997) and found that compared with women who delivered, those who had an induced abortion had a 1.62 increased mortality from all causes, a 2.54 increased mortality from suicide and accidents (1.82) and that higher death rates associated with abortion appear to persist across time and across socio-economic boundaries. As in the Gissler study the direction of the link between abortion and suicide cannot be demonstrated using this methodology.

A study mentioned above (Gilchrist et al., 1995) provided early evidence of an association between abortion and deliberate self-harm, with a 1.7 relative risk of self-harm among those who had an abortion compared to those whose pregnancy ended in birth. They also found that among those refused abortion there was an increased risk of self-harm, with a relative risk of 2.8 but the number (9) was too small in the latter to draw definitive conclusions.

Fergusson et al. (2006) also found an increased risk of self-harm in those having an abortion as compared to those whose pregnancy ended in delivery or those who were never pregnant, even after controlling for confounders.

In summary, while there is an increased risk of suicide in those having abortions as compared to other groups, it cannot definitively be stated that abortion causes suicide although this is clearly one possibility. With regard to self-harm, there are indicators that even when confounders are controlled there is an association that may be a causal one but further studies are required controlling for other possible confounders.

Abortion for Foetal Anomaly

While controversy exists with regard to the psychological complications of abortion generally, there is agreement that among women having abortion for foetal anomaly the psychological effects are indeed significant and appropriate intervention needs to be provided in the aftermath. There have been a number of recent studies providing further evidence of this. Most of the recent studies find high levels of distress, which seems to persist and be of such severity as to constitute recognised psychiatric disorder such as major depression or post traumatic stress disorder.

A pilot study (Davies et al., 2005) of women age 20-40 years, 14 having first trimester abortion for ultrasound diagnosed foetal abnormality and 16 having second trimester abortion for the same reason, were examined six weeks, six months and 12 months after the abortion using a number of psychological measures of distress, depression and grief. Both groups had high levels of symptomatology throughout. For depression,

36 per cent, 39 per cent and 32 per cent were above the cut-off score for diagnosing this condition at the three time points. For post-traumatic stress disorder the percentage above the cut-off at the three time points we 67 per cent, 50 per cent and 41 per cent. The authors concluded that "psychological morbidity following termination for foetal anomaly is prevalent and persistent" (Davies, 2005).

Using a larger sample another study (Kersting et al., 2007) compared 62 women having abortions for foetal anomaly between the fifteenth and thirty-second week with 65 who gave birth to a healthy child. Using a variety of measures of grief, depression, etc. the sample was followed for 14 months. By 14 months 16.7 per cent met criteria for a manifest psychiatric disorder while 25 per cent were "critically affected" by the loss, for up to six months after the event.

The study with the longest follow-up period (Korenromp et al., 2005) examined 254 women for two to seven years post-abortion. Using validated measures of grief and post traumatic stress disorder, 17.3 per cent had scores in the pathological ranges and poorer prognosis was associated with gestational age, compatibility with life and perceived partner support. Abnormal scores were distributed equally across the whole time period. These findings led to the authors concluding that "termination of pregnancy for foetal anomaly is associated with long-lasting consequences for a substantial number of women".

In conclusion, a body of recent research demonstrates the serious and persistent nature of the response to abortion carried out for foetal anomaly.

Qualitative Studies

Qualitative analysis is a technique of in-depth interviewing and transcript analysis to identify themes that emerge in relation to particular areas of psychological (or other) interest. Sample sizes are small and the analysis eschews numbers in favour of statement content. This method is useful when there is little knowledge, doubt or uncertainty in a sphere of interest. For that reason this is an area that could be exploited to inform our understanding of the various reactions of women to abortion.

Typically those commenting on the psychological reaction to abortion (Adler et al., 1992) describe distress before the abortion followed by relief afterwards. An exception to this was the finding (Major et al., 2000) that dissatisfaction with the decision increased notwithstanding the finding that 72 per cent were still satisfied with their decision at two years follow-up while another study (Kumar and Robson, 1987) found that adverse emotional reactions may occur during subsequent pregnancies, termed "reactivated mourning" by the authors.

In a recent qualitative study (Goodwin and Ogden, 2007), Interpretative Phenomenological Analysis was used to analyse the transcripts of 10 women who had an abortion one to nine years earlier. The results found that while some described the linear pattern mentioned above, some also experienced upset that persisted, others had a positive experience initially only to negatively reappraise subsequently, while others experienced no negative emotion at any point. These appraisals were linked to views of the foetus as human, or not, an ability to defend against the belief that society is judgemental, a belief that society is critical of those seeking abortion, or alternatively that it negates the emotional impact of abortion and the availability social support. The authors conclude that responses to abortion do not follow the suggested linear patterns but "are located within both the personal and personal context". At the time of writing this was the only qualitative study that this writer could find examining the long-term patterns of responses to induced abortion.

Is Abortion Helpful to Women's Mental Health?

This chapter so far has focussed on whether abortion causes harm to the mental health of women and, if so, on the possible underpinnings of this. Yet the law in Britain and in some other jurisdictions requires that continuing the pregnancy should pose a greater threat to the woman than does terminating it. Indeed, 94 per cent of abortions in Britain invoke this ground. Such a justification requires strong evidence that the mental health benefits of abortion outweigh the mental health risks associated with unwanted childbirth; in other words, that the termination would benefit the woman. Commenting on this, Fergusson (2008) states:

> Although decisions on whether to proceed with induced abortion are made on the basis of clinical assessments of the extent to which abortion poses a risk to maternal mental health, these clini-

cal assessments are not currently supported by population level evidence showing the provision of abortion reduces mental health risks for women having an unwanted pregnancy.

As well as the lacuna in studies demonstrating mental health benefits from abortion, there is also a hiatus in those examining the criteria applied when doctors refer a woman for abortion. Is this based on her distress level? How is distress measured? What are the quality assurances that distress, which is not a mental health problem but a problem of living, is not conflated with mental illness? How do doctors balance considerations of short-term distress with possible long-term outcomes?

Areas of Agreement

In an emotive topic such as induced abortion there is likely to be little agreement between proponents on both sides of this divide. And the issue of whether abortion per se or some other aspect of the decision making process that culminates in abortion is responsible for the trauma reported in some of these studies is a matter for debate. However, there are some areas of commonality and these are shown in Table 15.4.

Table 15.4: Risk Factors for Post-abortion Mental Health Problems

Previous psychiatric history
Poor social support
Late abortion
Abortion for foetal anomaly
Those who are ideologically/religiously opposed to abortion
Ambivalence about abortion
Qualitative studies examining women's reaction to abortion
Coerced abortion
Strong maternal instincts
Abortion in the very young

Implications

While there is disagreement about aspects of the association between abortion and adverse mental health outcomes, there is also agreement about some. For example, those with a prior psychiatric history of mental illness, women who have religious objections or are ambivalent etc. as summarised in Table 15.4 are at increased risk of adverse emotional consequences. Women meeting these criteria should be informed of this when they present requesting an abortion.

The fact that there is dispute as to whether abortion is a direct cause of mental health problems post-abortion or whether the link is through some mediator, such as poor social support or the result of failure to identify confounders, should lead to caution in the information that is given to those seeking information on abortion. Arguably, it cannot be definitively claimed any longer that abortion is psychologically benign since a number of recent studies have arrived at contradictory results, a finding recognised in the Royal College of Psychiatrists' recent statement and acknowledged by others (Fergusson et al., 2006; Fergusson, 2008; Pedersen et al., 2007). At the very least, the fact that uncertainty exists needs to be highlighted so that informed choices can be made, a requirement also emphasised in the Royal College of Psychiatrists 2008 statement.

In order to make decisions about any medical or surgical matter fully informed consent must be obtained. This involves providing information on the risks and benefits, and when there is genuine uncertainty stemming from a significant body of conflicting studies this must be conveyed to the patient. To withhold this information is for the doctor to assume the decision-making role and to place the patient at a disadvantage in making her choices. Failure to inform could ultimately lead to legal action by those who felt incompletely appraised of possible consequences.

There is then the further question of how this information should be given. Those who are in crisis, whether receiving bad news about a serious illness or faced with an unintended pregnancy, are less able to assimilate and process information than those routinely receiving it. In order to facilitate satisfactory processing and understanding, the provision of written material is recommended.

A Final Thought

Considering the issue of whether abortion causes later mental health problems, and the debate about the nature of the association between these, several broader issues arise. In this regard it is worth examining the nature of the relationship between other major life events and mental health problems. For example, it is known that there are a number of social risk factors for many psychiatric disorders, such as major depression, post-natal depression, post-traumatic stress disorder, eating disorders etc. yet there is no suggestion that these conditions do not exist simply because they occur in those with particular vulnerabilities and risk factors. The same argument could be applied to mental health problems following abortion – the fact of risks and vulnerabilities should not invalidate the emotions described by some women after abortion. Indeed, the decision to terminate a pregnancy is a complex one that draws on many influences – personal, interpersonal and social – culminating in the abortion. While it is vital to understand the mechanisms driving this decision and the path by which abortion may lead to mental health problems, this should not cloud our appreciation that for some women there are negative emotional consequences, irrespective of the mechanism by which they are generated. Whatever the mechanism, the importance of providing sensitive and supportive services, and interventions that acknowledge the needs of this group of women, cannot be overlooked (Gissler, 2005; Royal College of Psychiatrists, 2008).

Bibliography

Adler N.E., David, H.P., Major, B.N. et al. (1992), "Psychological Factors in Abortion: A Review", *American Psychologist* 47: 1194-1204.

Blazer, K.G., Kessler, R.C., McGonagle, K.A. and Swartz, M.S. (1994), "The Prevalence and Distribution of Major Depression in a National Community Sample: The National Co-morbidity Survey", *American Journal of Psychiatry.* 151: 979-986.

Broen et al. (2005), "The Course of Mental Health after Miscarriage and Induced Abortion: A Longitudinal, Five-Year Follow-Up Study", *BMC,* 12(3): 18.

Broen, A.N., Moum, T., Bodtker, A.S. and Ekeberg, O. (2006), "Predictors of Anxiety and Depression Following Pregnancy Termination: A Longitudinal Five-Year Follow-Up Study," *Acta Obstet Gynecol Scand*, 85(3): 317-23.

Coleman et al. (2002), "State-Funded Abortions Versus Deliveries: A Comparison of Out-Patient Mental Health Claims over Four Years," *American Journal of Orthopsychiatry*, 72(1): 141-152.

Cougle, J.R., Reardon, D.C. and Coleman, P.K. (2003), "Depression Associated with Abortion and Childbirth: A Long-Term Analysis of the NLSY Cohort," *Medical Science Monitor*, 9(4): 105-112.

Cougle, J.R., Reardon, D.C. and Coleman, P.K. (2005), "Generalized Anxiety Following Unintended Pregnancies Resolved Through Childbirth and Abortion: A Cohort Study of the 1995 National Survey of Family Growth," *Journal of Anxiety Disorders*, 19(1): 137-142.

David, H.P. (1981), *Family Planning Perspectives*, 13(1): 32-34.

David, H.P. (2006), "Born Unwanted, 35 Years Later: The Prague Study," *Reproductive Health Matters*, 14(27): 181-190.

Davies, V., Gledhill, J., McFayden, A. et al. (2005), "Psychological Outcome in Women Undergoing Termination of Pregnancy for Ultra-Sound Detected Fetal Anomaly in the First and Second Trimesters: a Pilot Study. *Ultrasound Obstet Gynaecol*, 25(4): 389-392.

Fergusson, D. (2008), "Abortion and Mental Health," *Psychiatric Bulletin*, 32 321-324.

Fergusson, D. et al. (2006), "Abortion in Young Women and Subsequent Mental Health," *Journal of Child Psychology and Psychiatry,* 47(1): 16-24.

Gilchrist, A.C. et al (1995), "Termination of Pregnancy and Psychiatric Morbidity," *British Journal of Psychiatry*, 167: 243-248.

Gissler, M. (2004), "Pregnancy-Associated Mortality after Birth, Spontaneous Abortion, or Induced Abortion in Finland, 1987-2000," *American Journal of Obstetrics and Gynaecology*, 190(2): 422-427.

Gissler, M. (2005), "Injury Deaths, Suicides and Homicides Associated with Pregnancy, Finland 1987–2000." *European Journal of Public Health*, 15(5): 459-463.

Gissler, M., Hemminki, E. and Lonnqvist, J. (1996), "Suicides after Pregnancy in Finland, 1987-94: Register Linkage Study," *BMJ* 313: 1431-1434.

Goodwin, P. and Ogden, J. (2007), "Women's Reflections Upon Their Past Abortions: An Exploration of How and Why Emotional Reactions Change over Time." *Psychology and Health*, 22(2): 231-248.

Joyce, T.J., Kaestner, R. and Korenman, S. (2000), "The Effect of Pregnancy Intention on Child Development." *Demography*, 37(1): 83-94.

Kersting, A., Kroker, K., Steinhard, J. et al. (2007), "Complicated Grief after Traumatic Loss: A 14-Month Follow-Up Study," *European Archives Psychiatry and Clinical Neuroscience*, 257(8): 437-434.

Korenromp, M.J., Christiaens, G.C., van den Bout, J. et al. (2005), "Long-term Psychological Consequences of Pregnancy Termination for Fetal Abnormality: A Cross-Sectional Study," *Prenatal Diagnosis*, 25(3): 253-260.

Kubicka, L., Matejcek, Z., David, H.P. et al. (1995), "Children from Unwanted Pregnancies in Prague, Czech Republic Revisited at Age 30," *Acta Psychiatrica Scandinavica*, 91: 361-369.

Kumar, R. and Robson, K. (1987), "Psychological Medicine: Previous Induced Abortion and Ante-Natal Diagnosis" in *Primiparae: Preliminary Report of a Survey of Mental Health in Pregnancy*, 8: 711-715.

Major B., Cozzarelli, C., Cooper M. L., Zubek, J., Richards, C., Wilhite, M. et al. (2000), "Psychological Responses of Women after First-Trimester Abortion," *Archives of General Psychiatry*, 57(8): 777-784.

Miller, W.B., Sable, M.R. and Csizmadia, A. (2007), "Pregnancy Wantedness and Child Security. Is There a Relationship?" *Maternal and Child Health Journal,* 12(4): 478-484

Pedersen, W. (2007), "Childbirth, Abortion and Subsequent Substance Use in Young Women: A Population-Based Longitudinal Study," *Addiction*, 102(12): 1971-1978.

Reardon, D.C. and Cougle, J.R. (2002), "Depression and Unintended Pregnancy in the National Longitudinal Survey of Youth: A Cohort Study" *British Medical Journal*, 324: 151-152.

Reardon, D.C., Ney, P.G., Scheuren, F. et al. (2002). "Deaths associated with Pregnancy Outcome: A Record Likage Study of Low Income Women". *Southern Medical Journal*, 95(8): 834-841.

Reardon D.C. and Ney, P.G. (2000), "Abortion and Subsequent Substance Abuse," *American Journal of Drug & Alcohol Abuse*, 26(1): 61-75.

Reardon et al. (2003), "Psychiatric Admissions of Low-Income Women Following Abortion and Childbirth," *Canadian Medical Association Journal*, 168(10): 1253-1256.

Rees, D.I. and Sabia, J.J. (2007), "The Relationship Between Abortion and Depression: New Evidence from the Fragile Families and Child Wellbeing Study," *Medical Science Monitor*, 13(10): 430-6.

Royal College of Obstetricians and Gynaecologists (2004), *The Care of Women Requesting Induced Abortion. Evidence-based Clinical Guideline Number 7.* Royal College of Obstetricians and Gynaecologists.

Royal College of Psychiatrists (1994). *The physical and psycho-social effects of abortion on women.* London: The Royal College of Psychiatrists.

Royal College of Psychiatrists (2008). *Position statement on women's mental health in relation to induced abortion.* [cited 7 April 2008]; Available from: http://www.rcpsych.ac.uk/members/currentissues/mentalhealthandabortion.aspx

Rue, V.M., Coleman, P.K., Rue, J.J. and Reardon, D.C. (2004), "Induced Abortion and Traumatic Stress: A Preliminary Comparison of American and Russian women," *Medical Science Monitor*, 10(10) [cited 1 December 2004]; sr5-sr16]. Available from: http://www.medscimonit.com/pub/vol_10/no_10/4923.pdf.

Schmiege, S. and Russo, N.F. (2005), "Depression and Unwanted First Pregnancy: A Longitudinal Cohort Study," *British Medical Journal*, 331: 1303.

Taft, A.J. and Watson, L.F. (2008), "Depression and Termination of Pregnancy (Induced Abortion) in a National Cohort of Young Australian Women: the Confounding Effect of Women's Experience of Violence," *BMC Public Health*, 8(1): 75.

Thorpe, J.M., Hartmann, K.E. and Shadigian, E. (2003), "Long Term Physical and Psychological Health Consequences of Induced Abortion: Review of the Evidence," *Obstetrical and Gynecological Survey*, 58(1): 67-79.

Zabin, L.S., Hirsch, M.B. and Emerson, M.R. (1989), "When Urban Adolescents Choose Abortion: Effects on Education, Psychological Status and Subsequent Pregnancy," *Family Planning Perspectives*, 21(6): 248-55.

Index